Don't Cry for Me

An Autobiography

Arthur Leggett

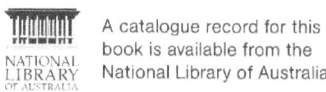
A catalogue record for this book is available from the National Library of Australia

All rights reserved.
Copyright © 2006 Arthur Leggett.
First published 2006 Paperback edition.
2nd Edition published 2019
ISBN 9781876922658

Linellen Press
265 Boomerang Road,
Oldbury, Western Australia
www.linellenpress.com.au

Foreword

If a man is born at the end of a turbulent period in the world's history, and manages to live beyond the stated three score years and ten, then he is bound to be caught up in events beyond his control yet his existence is influenced by their outcome.

He is also entitled to battle through Life to the best of his ability and, nearing its end, look back and say, "Phew!!"

These are the facets I have endeavoured to portray in this autobiography.

I am an ordinary sort of fellow and if you can see Life at this level then we should share a few pleasant moments through these pages.

*****

Contents

Foreword	iii
Contents	v
Acknowledgments	vii
Chapter One	1
Chapter Two	6
Chapter Three	19
Chapter Four	29
Chapter Five	36
Chapter Six	50
Chapter Seven	72
Chapter Eight	78
Chapter Nine	91
Chapter Ten	106
Chapter Eleven	121
Chapter Twelve	126
Chapter Thirteen	138
Chapter Fourteen	161
Chapter Fifteen	176
Chapter Sixteen	191
Chapter Seventeen	205

Chapter Eighteen	240
Chapter Nineteen	258
Chapter Twenty	269
Chapter Twenty-One	286
Chapter Twenty-Two	308
Chapter Twenty-Three	333
Chapter Twenty-Four	357
Chapter Twenty-Five	369
Chapter Twenty-Six	384
Chapter Twenty-Seven	392
Chapter Twenty-Eight	403
Chapter Twenty-Nine	423
Chapter Thirty	434
Chapter Thirty-One	466
Chapter Thirty-Two	485
About the Author	489

Acknowledgments

The outline of the Western Desert, Greece and Crete Campaigns, as well as comments of Senior Officers, are extracted from The History of The 2/11(City of Perth) Australian Infantry Battalion with permission of its compiler Colonel K. T. Johnson M.B.E.. E.D. (Ret'd)

Chapter One

There is nothing really romantic in looking at the rear end of a horse as it trots along between the shafts of a milk cart heading back to the dairy after completing the morning's run; but The Boss chatted away in the manner of 'Old Blokes' who had lived a rather rugged life, and his yarning lifted my imagination away beyond the scrub country and red soil stretching thousands of miles north and east of Laverton.

I don't suppose he was really an 'Old Bloke'. At that point in Time, around 1935, I was a 'Young Bloke' and Mr Hilliard, who was probably about the same age as my Dad, was telling me about things which my Dad never mentioned.

"We crept out in front of the trenches one night to see what the Germans were up to and we run into a German patrol," he explained. "We all started shooting and we killed some of them but they shot a couple of our mates as well. Then all hell broke loose. Flares went up from both sides and the Germans started throwing hand-grenades from their trenches. One of them went off right beside me and knocked me into a shell-hole. It was a stinking hole with a pool of water and a dead German in it. I reckon he had been there a couple of days. I stayed there all day until I could creep back to our lines in the dark. My arm was full of shrapnel but it is O.K. I can still use it but bits of metal keep wandering through my body and eventually come out anywhere. A bit came out through the end of my big toe last month. 'Ere, look at this!"

He rolled up his sleeve to show me an upper arm peppered with tiny black spots of metal.

"Gee!" I exclaimed. "You were lucky!"

"I reckon anyone who came home from the war was lucky. A war's a bloody stupid thing and a man is never the same again. Look at your old man. He's buggered."

"My Dad?"

"Yair, your Dad. Don't you know he was caught in a gas attack in France and his lungs are stuffed?"

I didn't know simply because my Dad never spoke about the war.

"Mr Hilliard, how do you know?"

"We were having a few beers in the pub before you came up here. We started to talk about the war and he told me he came up here because the air was dry and it helps a bit. Your old man is a tough old bastard."

My old man was a tough old bastard – his lungs are stuffed – didn't you know?

I looked across the scrub-covered country stretching to the distant horizon.

Slowly – ever so slowly – during the next few weeks, the jumbled, seemingly unrelated pieces of my short seventeen years of Life began to take shape and form a pattern.

The first ten years had been spent living in hot, dry country and my earliest recollections relate to a little town named Bingara in northern New South Wales.

My Dad was a skilled shoe and boot maker, having served his apprenticeship with a firm named Rabbits in London prior to emigrating to Australia around 1912. He opened up a shop in a timber-framed, galvanised iron structure in the main street. Our house was behind the shop and attached to it was a tank-stand under which black snakes gathered to keep cool.

A few other buildings made up the business centre stretching along the town's 200 metres of unsealed main street. Each building had its own character even as each of the town's male inhabitants had his own characteristics.

Mr Moll was a wool-buyer who owned the large, galvanised-iron shed. Bales of wool were stacked to the roof in this shed and the merchandise was protected from rat, mice and small boy infestation by a tame 12ft long python. Mr Moll was a really big man and his proportionately large moustache was a constant source of wonder to us kids viewing it from our point of observation.

Mark Bridges, the local carpenter, was a bit of an entertainer and I recollect him on a stage during a concert, his face painted red, shouting some monologue in a manner frightening me immensely because I had never seen anyone carry on like that before. As a carpenter he made coffins as required. Obviously, with these qualifications, he officiated as the town's undertaker. Besides, he owned the hearse and horses.

Ikey Fader had built a store next to Mr Moll's shed. It was an imposing two-storied structure with living quarters on the top floor and emblazoned across its ornamental facade, was the announcement:

FADERS EMPORIUM

1923.

Mr Fader had no family. He lived on the premises with a young man he was 'training for the business'. Although I was only four, maybe five, Mr Fader invited me for tea every Friday. The meal would always consist of rissoles and Mr Fader would invariably interrupt my childhood prattle with the stern command, "Artur! Eat up your rissoles!" This edict, when related at home, became a jocular domestic saying which grew into a family verbal heirloom still used by my sister and I seventy years later.

Fred Carlos, the town's barber, had died. There were comments going around concerning his demise. He had been a very sick man for a long time and, upon admittance into hospital, he was given a bath. Rumour had it that the bath had killed him.

Dad had gone missing on the Saturday morning of Fred Carlos' funeral.

90% of Bingara's male population, at that time, were returned servicemen. The war hadn't been long over and the sense of comradeship developed during those years still influenced their attitude towards Life.

It appears – according to my Mum – Dad, Mr Moll, Mark Bridges and a few mates were holding a wake in Mark's back shed using the coffin, complete with Fred in it, as a bar.

Around mid-day Mr Moll brought Dad home in a wheelbarrow commenting: "The funeral's about to get under way and we don't want him getting mixed up in the coffins."

The hearse, pulled by two black horses, made its slow way down the main street later in the afternoon. Mark Bridges, wearing the appropriate attire, which included a black top hat, sat in the driver's seat with the reins in his hands.

Fortunately the horses knew their way to the cemetery because the only conscious movement made by Mark Bridges was when he solemnly doffed his top hat to my Mum standing on the front verandah as the procession passed our house where Dad was deeply asleep in the front room.

Ted Lynch, the barman at the pub, was my friend. I would toddle down there when things were quiet in the afternoon, and enter the bar looking for Ted. He would sit me on a stool, pour a lemonade and offer it to me with great aplomb. If any casual drinker dropped in for a 'Jimmy Woodser' I was introduced as 'Master Leggett' and briefly involved in any ensuing conversation before I was diplomatically bade 'Good afternoon'.

Mum and Dad, after a few years in Bingara, decided to move to Moree. There were probably several reasons for this decision; possibly because Moree was a much larger town with a school more suitable for my sister, Joyce, and I who were approaching school age; the population was greater and, logically, it would increase Dad's income. Besides, I think Mum was expecting a baby.

My last recollection of Bingara was the sudden realisation that we were going and clinging desperately to Ted Lynch as I sobbed uncontrollably before being pulled away and deposited on Mum's lap in someone's car.

Chapter Two

Chester Street was a good street to live in but I have since been told Moree was a good town to live in during that period of the gathering world depression.

Dad opened a boot maker and repairers shop in Balo Street and soon had three men working for him.

My elder brother, Syd, attended Moree Primary School where, in due course, Joyce and I also commenced our scholastic career.

Meanwhile our family had increased with the arrival of our sister, Patricia Ivy. She had been named after two of Dad's sisters who were mysterious women known as 'aunties' and lived in some unknown country called England. We knew there was an 'England' somewhere because pictures of St Paul's Cathedral, Westminster Abbey, The Houses of Parliament, King George the Fifth and Queen Mary were hung on the walls of our lounge room.

The hazards of school life extended beyond the routine of learning whilst under the constant threat of punishment. Rain rarely fell and when it did the dusty soil was turned into mud. Not just ordinary mud, but a thick, cloyey, gooey substance for which the red plains around Moree are noted. Playtimes and lunch times were times for mud rings when 20 to 30 bare-footed urchins ran around in a circle roughly 50 feet in diameter. The longer we ran the more sloppy the mud became and, obviously, the mud ring was going to start winning.

A loud 'Hooray!' rose upon the air as youngsters lost their footing and slid into the ooze. Falling over was bad enough but the ring of runners couldn't stop and the boy behind took great delight in jumping over you and seizing the opportunity to splash more mud on your clothes.

All this took place at the far end of the school-ground away from the attention of the duty teacher and there was no alternative but to send the mud-bespattered child home. This usually meant the cane at school, a hiding at home and jeers from your classmates.

But, Gee! It didn't rain very often and we had to make the best of it. The town's water supply came from one of the mud holes in the Mehi River and was usually cut off from 10am until 4pm. The school had one water tank, its contents supplied from the roof of the adjacent, two-storied building. A common sight was a queue of children leading to this tank where the headmaster stood, watch in hand, allowing each child ten seconds to gulp water. I have often wondered how many mosquito larvae and frogs eggs were swallowed in those ten seconds.

Moree's temperature was always around 100 degrees Fahrenheit in the summertime and, on Friday afternoons, we were marched along the dusty, shimmering road and across the high, wooden traffic bridge spanning the river, to the Bore Baths to learn to swim in water that gave off steam and a subterranean odour. The skin on our hands and feet went white and became wrinkled as we slowly cooked whilst mastering the intricacies of breast stroke.

Sgt. Singleton was in charge of the police station.

His youngest daughter was in my class; so were two Aboriginal lads named Barlow and Duke respectively. Barlow's father was a black-tracker with the Police Force but that didn't stop Barlow Jnr. and his colleague from rubbishing the police sergeant's daughter. I had a bit of a crush on this girl; consequently, and on numerous occasions, I issued a challenge to Messrs. Barlow and/or Duke to put their fists up after school.

Many a time I would arrive home with a black eye or my nose running blood all down my shirt front. Mum was horrified at these unexpected and alarming appearances but Dad regarded it as part of the process of growing up and advised me to go at them harder next time.

I followed his advice without any apparent change in the eventual outcome but, to the Police Sergeant's daughter, I was a knight in shining armour.

By the time I was eight or nine years old I had made quite a few friends, most of whom lived in Chester Street. Tommy Highton lived diagonally opposite, Lance Taylor lived next door, Wally Conroy lived further up the street and, beyond his house, Harry Lennan lived in a house buried underneath pepper trees.

'Stumpy' Brush lived in Chester Street, too. Stumpy was the town's taxi driver and owned an Hupmobile soft-top tourer with wooden-spoked wheels. He was a short, plump man who had been in the war with my Dad. He was also a very sick man and, when going to Sydney for a check up with The Department of Repatriation, he was killed in a train accident.

Stumpy was a sick man?

I didn't know it but my Dad was a sick man and most of his mates were sick men. When I think back on that period of my life, and right up through my teenage years, I become conscious of the sinister overtones of decaying health brought back by that generation from The 1914-18 War.

Noel Humphries lived nearly opposite our house. His place was different. Down the far end of their yard was a cattle yard made of old dried-out gimlet gums rotting away at the ends where the bolts held them together; but they served as mountains, ships, trains, castles or any other figment of our boyhood imagination until, after a couple of nasty falls amidst wreckage, they were declared 'Out Of Bounds' by parents who had tired of carrying bawling, injured children home.

Another peculiar thing about the Humphries was that Mr Humphries was always away. Noel claimed to have an older brother named Carl but he, too, was away with his father. Us kids often queried Noel about their absence but invariably received the same answer: "Aw' they'll be back one day."

That day eventually came around. Noel, his eyes aglow and happiness written all over his face, caught up with us on the way to school.

"My Dad's coming home today," he announced.

"How do you know?"

"Me Mum told me he'll be home when I get out of school this arvo."

We went home with Noel just to have a look at him.

He was a big man! He towered above us; he was ever so broad across the shoulders and his arms were so strong that he picked one of us up in each hand and held us above his head to nearly touch the kitchen rafters.

"Are these your mates?" he bellowed in a deep, powerful voice.

Fortunately Noel acknowledged we were his mates otherwise, I fear, we would have remained up there looking down at that sandy moustache and laughing grey eyes forever.

"Have you still got Baldy?" asked Noel.

"My flamin' oath," roared Big Brother. "He's down there with the rest of them."

"C'mon!" shouted Noel.

We raced down the gravelled street and there, on the lush, green grass growing on the flat area beyond the dip at the end of Chester Street, were twenty-five to thirty massive bullocks grazing around an immense bullock-wagon piled high with bales of wool from some sheep station away out back.

Noel's big brother arrived.

"Here, Baldy!" he roared. "B-a-l-d-y! Come 'ere, you old bastard, come 'ere!"

We looked at each other. He swore! Miss Faulkner, our schoolteacher, wouldn't like that.

A bullock, twice my height, detached itself from the mob, ambled over to us and continued to munch grass.

Big Brother lifted Noel and placed him on the creature's back.

"You jokers want a ride?" he asked.

It didn't matter whether we wanted a ride or not; three more of us were picked up and placed upon the prickly spine of Baldy The Bullock.

Big Brother grabbed hold of one of Baldy's horns and proceeded to lead us through that sea of waving destruction which miraculously parted at his command of, "Get out of the way, you lazy bastards, or I'll kick your guts in!"

I was horrified! The bullock's backbone moved as it walked, the skin loosely moved on the backbone and I slid forwards and backwards causing the bristles to stick into my legs and penetrate my pants. I expected, at any moment, to slide off from this agony to where, no doubt, I would be trampled to death or impaled on one of those soul-chilling horns and tossed high into the air like the Spanish bullfighter in one of my picture books.

Arriving back at the starting point we immediately slid off and dropped to the ground. I noticed the only one to stand and pat the grass-munching animal was Big Brother's brother – Noel!

It was his proudest moment!

The rest of us stood back recovering from the shock.

Next day I was sitting in the kitchen of Mrs Nell, our Sunday School Teacher, and boasting of our bullock ride.

"I don't think you should go near them again," she admonished, "I saw them drinking and swearing in the hotel, today. (she obviously meant Mr Humphries and Big Brother; not the bullocks) I'm afraid they are rather common people."

Common people? They were giants! They were kings! They were bullock drivers!

We lived in a semi-detached, plaster-walled, galvanised iron roofed house with an enormous back yard with the lavatory down at the far end. A night-time journey to the dunny's seclusion required considerable courage; especially at night when the hot breeze scraped the pepper tree's overhanging boughs across the tin roof.

Just about every house in the town had pepper trees growing in the backyard, probably because they were drought-resistant and provided good shade for the chooks during the heat of the day.

Mrs Nell's chooks roosted in her pepper trees. She also had two dogs, a pet kangaroo and numerous domestic cats that multiplied with persistent regularity. One day, during her absence, the dogs took to the kangaroo and killed it. The dogs were then banished leaving the cats in full possession.

Even as a child I sensed Mrs Nell was different. Her skin was not the same colour as my Mum's skin and it was scarred in many places. She was widow battling to bring up two sons and two daughters as well as to educate them above the average standard. She also kept boarders yet found time to clean the brown, weatherboard Church of England in the next street.

I liked to help her with this task but my idea of polishing pews was to place a cloth upon the seat, take a run, thump my stern onto the cloth and slide along the pew's length; an exercise she would halt by saying:- "Arthur, enough! Remember you are in The Lord's House."

Life is tough on some people and it was damn tough on her. Mum told me her story many years later. Mr Nell was a German engineer who worked for many years in India where he married Mrs Nell, an Anglo-Indian. They came to Australia where, settling in Moree, he established a garage in a two-storied building with a residence above and a workshop below. A patriotic mob, during the period of the 1914-18 War, set fire to the garage and burned it to the ground. The family escaped but Mr Nell dashed back into the office to save the books. He perished in the fire.

Dad negotiated with Mr Brown, the town's barber, to purchase the neat, weather-board house on the other side of Mr Taylor's place.

One of Dad's first projects in the new house, was to run a three-inch diameter pipe from the bath tub outlet to an area of the backyard where he was endeavouring to grow vegetables. He blocked one end of the pipe then spent hours daily, with a hand drill, drilling 1/8th inch diameter holes along its length.

The theory was, when the plug was pulled out of the bath tub, water would flow into the pipe and squirt all over the garden; thereby making use of the precious wastewater.

Unfortunately the bottom of the tub was only two feet above ground level and, instead of squirting copiously all over the garden the water sort of crawled out of the pipe in a disinterested manner before collapsing about two inches away from the exit point.

Dandelions grew in abundance along the length of that pipe and provided refuge for a horde of marauding snails that meandered through the garden at night devouring everything in its path.

We had the first wireless in the town.

It was a massive thing measuring three feet long, a foot high and a foot deep with knobs and dials all over the front panel. A two feet high speaker, curving gracefully upwards like a cobra and belling outwards like a flower in full bloom, stood on top of this impressive apparatus.

Such a magnificent instrument required an equally magnificent outdoor aerial and ground-pin. A long, wooden pole was affixed to the dunny at the far end of the backyard, another was attached to the brick chimney of the lounge-room fireplace and another was set off at right-angles and wired to the fence. A wire was strung from the outer poles back to the house thus ensuring broadcast waves would hit a full length of wire. The earth-wire went down through the lounge-room floor to one of Dad's 12 inch files buried in the ground to act as an earth-pin.

I was allocated the task of daily pouring a jam-tin full of water on it to assist in good earth conduction.

Dad would sit in front of this thing at night, twisting dials and twirling knobs, endeavouring to refine its squeaks and squawks into some form of wireless entertainment

There was one day I shall never forget. Mum and I were listening to it around 11am when the Queensland commentator's voice came over clear from Eagle Farm: "– the giant plane is now circling low over this great crowd as it comes in to land –" Kingsford-Smith had completed the first flight over the Pacific and from that moment he became my boyhood hero.

Mr Burns was a big, heavy man so it seemed logical to us kids that he should be known as 'Fat Burns'.

Fat had a four-wheeled, flat-topped dray pulled by a light draught horse which knew its way around the town with a knowledge equal to its master. With this conveyance Fat conducted a delivery service from the railway station in East Moree to shops around the town.

He sat on the right-hand, front corner of the cart causing it to sag far more than the weight of any merchandise placed elsewhere on the wagon. He also had long, powerful arms and, in his right hand, carried a six foot long whip with a thong of equal length.

Whenever Fat planned a right-hand turn he would extend his arm straight out from his shoulder and it seemed this muscular limb, plus the whip-handle, plus the plaited thong, blocked out the street to any other traffic and, printed in my youthful mind, was the impression of a Spanish galleon under full sail, hotly pursuing a protesting horse.

The arrival of this combination at the end of the street, when the day was done, was the signal for a waiting group of children to rush out from the dusty footpath at his loud bellow of, "Whoa!"

We reached up to the tray's level and laboriously climbed aboard. Then began a wondrous, noisy, breath-taking dash down the street to Fat's place. The wooden-spoked, steel-rimmed wheels clattered along the gravel road, the horse's hooves clip-clopped at a trotting pace, the harness jingled, the kids shouted and Fat added to the noise by bellowing: "I can't hold her! I can't hold her! I think she's bolted! Hang on for your lives!"

Fortunately he always seemed to regain control just as the horse turned into the driveway that ran down beside his house to the tin shed that served as stable for this fiery beast where it placidly stood waiting to be unharnessed.

A small hole in the tin fence enabled me to slip into the back lane and climb over our gate opposite.

The back lane was thoroughfare of drama and excitement. It was always referred to as 'the back lane' because it was at the back end of the yard and separated our property from the backs of the properties in the next street. Its narrowness, bounded by six feet high fences, imparted an alert sense of awareness in a small boy. Once I entered the lane I was 'in it'. There was no way of escape until I emerged at the other end or by scrambling back over our own gate. All kinds of horrors and threats to existence lurked within its length.

Along the back lane would come the 'dunny cart', 'the rubbish cart', 'the clothes prop man' as well as 'the woodman'. Their horses and carts seemed to almost block the laneway from fence to fence. Getting past these obstructions was fraught with danger. The horses were so big! They always looked down from their superior height, blew their noses as I drew near, lifted and stamped their hind legs as I passed then flicked their tails to sting my face; in addition to these trials, the rubbish man pretended to stumble and drop a dustbin on me or the dunny man vowed to put me in one of his dunny-pans and clamp the lid on.

Most families owned big black dogs with strong territorial rights extending beyond the fence-line and into the laneway. They would race along the length of the paling fence at a ferocious rate, stirring up a cloud of dust, barking and threatening to destroy the fence before commencing to tear pedestrians to shreds.

Mr Wilson's back yard was immediately opposite ours and he had a new, six feet high, galvanised-iron fence erected across its width. With sticks in our hands we would rattle our way along its length making a most satisfying din. Mr Wilson shouted from his back verandah, "Get out of there, you kids!" but we couldn't see him and he couldn't see us so we replied, "Old Clarrie Wilson! Old Clarrie

Wilson!" This enjoyable past-time was carried out at frequent intervals until my Dad said Mr Wilson had been into his shop and I had better stop being rude to him and leave his back fence alone.

I might defy Mr Wilson but my Dad was a different matter.

Problems began to emerge in our family.

Dad began to drink and occasionally came home the worse for wear. He wasn't a drunkard and I suspect his ill-health used to get the better of him. A big percentage of the town's male population were ex-servicemen and a casual drink at the end of a day could build up into quite a session.

Mum and Dad, no doubt, had arguments which never erupted in the presence of us children but the outcome of one resulted in Mum taking my brother, our two sisters and me to Newcastle for a holiday. The preparation for the journey was a period of feverish activity.

Syd made wind-driven propellers out of pine. These had a pin driven through the boss and into the end of a clothes peg. When held out through the window of a train travelling at 40 miles an hour they whirred around at a terrific rate.

It was a long train journey. We travelled all night sitting up in the box-like compartment; changing trains in the darkness at Waratah and arriving at Newcastle early next day.

We occupied the top floor of an apartment house run by Mrs Thorpe at No.7 Parnell Place.

Parnell Place; a magical street with a garden of flourishing, colourful flowers growing right down the centre of it! A garden in the middle of the street!

Furthermore, at the end of the street was the tram depot; big sheds which disgorged massive, exciting machines to take people anywhere. Dozens and dozens of them constantly coming and going. I sat on the edge of the gutter for hours at a time just to watch them until the drivers eventually became aware of my daily presence and gave me a hand-wave as they left the depot. Oft times Mum would be embarrassed when travelling into the city centre as a driver or conductor greeted me and chatted during the journey.

At the other end of Parnell Place was the exhilarating grandeur of the Pacific Ocean!

I had never seen anything like it!

The water stretched for miles and miles up and down the coast and out to the horizon as far as the eye could see; the wind blowing off it wasn't hot, dry and dusty. It was cool!

Some days the ocean gently lapped around the rocks and allowed us to explore the still, clear pools of salt water; other days it would curl angrily, roll with a roaring rush and smash itself against the rocks to hurl masses of foaming, hissing spray high into the air.

So much water! Always alive and breathing!

Mr Thorpe worked for The Harbour Authority. His job was handling the launch taking the pilots out to ships as they entered the harbour. He invited me to spend a day with him and great was my excitement as I clambered aboard a smart launch which immediately commenced to plow over to a ship making its way around Nobbies Head and into the river. The ship grew bigger and bigger as we drew nearer until it seemed to block out the harbour's entrance and the sky. Its side towered above us and moved in a manner that threatened to topple and engulf us at any moment. The pilot, complete with attaché case, jumped on to the lowered gangway and ran up the steps. We pulled away and headed back to tie up at the wharf.

Mr Thorpe adjourned to the office leaving me in the craft to bob up and down on the river's wavelets.

I was horribly seasick and vomiting over the side within half an hour. I couldn't get off the boat because the space between the wharf and the launch was too big for a small boy to jump and, anyway, I didn't care if I died.

An hour passed before Mr Thorpe came to check on me. He jumped into the craft, picked me up without any effort, and carried me into the office where I was laid on a sofa to sleep for the rest of the day.

Not exactly a pleasant outing.

Dad regularly came to visit. He left Moree on a Friday night, spent the week-end with us and, wrapped in a massive overcoat, returned to Moree on the Sunday night. This went on for three months and, during this period, we didn't attend any school.

Consequently, when we returned to Moree, our standard of education was so poor that Joyce and I were placed in grades below our age group and we were the despair of our teachers.

Catching up on education, in our household, was quite a problem because Dad had fixed ideas on this topic.

"It's the teacher's job to teach you at school," he asserted, "So you're not to bring homework into this house. Let them do their job where it's supposed to be done."

This attitude was incomprehensible to the teachers, especially where Syd was concerned. He was quite a brilliant student. The headmaster even went to Dad's shop to discuss the situation and pointing out that Syd had the capability to qualify for entrance to a university in Sydney.

Dad countered with the philosophy that Syd would one day have to commence working for a living and he would be employed behind the counter in the shop. This came to pass as soon as Syd was old enough to leave school and, at 14 years of age, he controlled the flow of work necessary to make the business pay.

Nevertheless, this edict prohibiting homework plagued the education of my sisters and I even after we qualified out of primary school.

Dad firmly believed a man must work with his hands and produce. A man who worked with his brain was a loafer and any man who worked for the government was a parasite on the community.

Unfortunately, children are very impressionable. He was my Dad.

He must be right. So I carried this philosophy with me into my adulthood, and my life (as well as the life of my family) has been retarded by its influence.

Oh; I don't condemn him. He was born within the working class in London and apprenticed in a trade demanding concentrated, physical effort directed at the job on the workbench. He migrated to Australia where, within a few years, he was caught in the soul-bruising disillusionment of The Great War To End All Wars before being returned to Australia with lungs causing physical and emotional distress to a life that was being prematurely shortened.

I reckon I would be a bit crooked on the world, too.

I was ten years old when we moved to Sydney to reside in the suburb of Manly. I don't know the reason for this move. Mum always maintained that the heat of Moree's long, hot, dry summers was too much for all of us but I had a feeling that Dad's health required better medical treatment and the doctor advised him to move to Sydney where he could get it.

Mum and us children made the long train journey to Sydney and the short ferry ride to Manly where we stayed in a guest-house until our furniture arrived. We then moved into a semi-detached house at the top of the hill in Fairlight Street. Mum equipped the house with second-hand furniture and filled it with boarders.

Dad stayed in Moree to carry on the business until it, and the house, were sold. He came to Manly and assisted Mum in the boarding house for quite some time before opening a small boot and shoe repair shop down in the town.

Meanwhile, The Great Fire of Moree razed Balo Street to the ground.

Chapter Three

Manly was Shangri-la to a ten year old boy who had spent his life in the hot, dry country.

Our house, high on the hill at the top of Fairlight Street, looked over North Harbour and the thickly wooded slopes of Dobroyd Point and the view extended right up the harbour, past The Heads, and as far as Bradley's Head.

Southerly busters in the winter stomped aggressively up the harbour to blanket out the view with massive dark clouds and wind then noisily hurl rain against the window panes stretching across the back of the house. Oft times we were caught hiking on Dobroyd Point during a squall and, when the rain ceased, the world became beautiful as raindrops, clinging to the gum leaves, glistened with a myriad of colours in the sunlight of a newly-washed world.

Summertime was beach time. Swimming in the calm of the harbour beach at one end of the main street and challenging the waves of the boisterous ocean at the other end.

I had made new friends at school and this wondrous period of our youth was spent swimming, surfing, hiking and camping on Dobroyd Point or in Frenchs Forrest.

We also went to school but that didn't seem to be very important at the time.

The Manly Ferries fascinated me. They appeared so big and, in peak periods, carried 400 people. I enjoyed being on the wharf when they arrived every 15 minutes at the end of the day carrying humanity that ran down the gangway, poured itself along the wharf and flowed away in all directions.

A big percentage of the male element disappeared into the bar of The Hotel Manly which closed at 6pm. To stand between the ferry and the hotel when this wave surged across the roadway was a very dangerous experience.

Southerly winter gales blew strongly up the coast pushing large swells through The Heads and across the harbour to Middle Head or Dobroyd Point where they smashed themselves against the rocks and hurled masses of spray high, like giant fists shaking in anger at the headlands towering overhead.

The ferries, on such days, moved over towards Dobroyd Point then turned towards The Heads to buffet their way into the swell before swinging around to ride the following sea until they disappeared around Bradley's Head.

The call of such an exciting ride presented a challenge.

The return fare to Circular Quay was two pence. Getting tuppence from my hard-working Mum wasn't easy until I convinced her I only wanted it for a loan and guaranteed repayment.

The turnstiles were at the Circular Quay end of the journey. I boarded the ferry at Manly, stood at the front of the upper deck and thrilled to the rise and fall of the boat as the bow flung spray all over the foredeck. I hid myself in the 'No Children Allowed' smoking compartment when the craft docked at Circular Quay, then went through the same exhilarating ride back to Manly where I returned the tuppence to my intrigued Mother who wondered why I wanted it in the first place.

We had a tin canoe gang. It wasn't actually organised – it kind of just happened.

The landlord, who lived next door, had the house re-roofed and placed the old sheets of galvanised iron under the foundations of our house. After they had lain there for several months we reckoned he had no further use for them.

Canoes! That's what we wanted and my mate, Harry, knew just how to make them!

Six sheets of the landlord's galvanised iron were dragged out from under the house and on to the cement floor of the back verandah. We bashed them flat with hammers, the backs of tomahawks or bricks but, my word, we got them fairly flat then chopped the rusty ends off with the tomahawk. The ends were then bent up and nailed to a piece of pine from Texaco kerosene cases.

This didn't make the ends watertight and several nail holes needed plugging.

Condamine Street was rather steep, especially up near the dairy end so, on Sunday, we went there and dug a bit of a hole in the gutter. The summertime heat melted the adjacent tar, causing it to run into the hole. The next afternoon we levered the tar out of the hole then carried it home to melt it in a jam tin over a stick fire and pour it along the timber at each end of the canoe. This process was not without an element of danger. If a globule of molten tar landed on bare skin it burnt a hole and if it landed on clothing there was the possibility of a whacking from irate parents.

We made paddles by shaping bits of pine case and nailing them to broom handles. I still have a twinge of conscience when I recall the number of brooms knocked off in the neighbourhood during this engineering project.

Came the big day!

Six of us kids carried six canoes down to the water and set out for Dobroyd Point. Of course we paddled in formation just like the fighter pilots in 'The Dawn Patrol'. Gee! That was a beaut picture. 100% All Talkie with Colour and Richard Barthelmess as The Squadron Leader!

There were times when, as a kid, I reckoned the whole world was crooked on me.

This was the very day when the landlord was sitting on his back verandah gazing out over the harbour through his field glasses.

He goes pounding into our place!

"Your boy!" he hollers at Mum, "He'll die! Look at him out there with his mates in the middle of the harbour! It's lousy with sharks out there! They've pinched my bloody galvanised iron and made canoes out of it! I wondered what the hell all that noise was going on under the house. They'll die out there! And what about my galvanised iron?"

Well – we didn't die. We paddled all the way across to Dobroyd Point, had a sunbake on the beach and paddled back again. Those canoes were as safe as houses. Gosh! They were nearly six feet long and had a good six inches of freeboard.

My big brother, Syd, was waiting on the beach. I was always suspicious if he turned up when me and my mates were having a good time. He always seemed to louse things up, somehow.

But, this time, he was wildly excited about this beaut canoe I had made and wanted to know if I would let him have a ride in it.

How could I refuse? He usually belted me over the ear-hole and took things off me.

The clumsy cow! He had hardly gone 150 yards when he lost his balance, tipped her over, and weeks of hard work, the pride of my eye, disappeared into 30 feet of water never to be seen again. He never even brought the paddle back.

It was bad enough having Mum going crook at me for paddling around in a canoe that wasn't safe for my brother to ride in but the landlord was in a lousy mood, too.

"Who's going to pay for my galvanise iron?" he yelled as he danced around, "I'll tell you who! You're going to pay me, young fellow, that's who! For the six sheets of it. The day you start work you're going to start paying me or I'll have the police on to you for thieving!"

He stomped off leaving behind an eleven year old boy who, for months afterwards, lay awake at nights wondering how he could get a job and expecting to hear the police pounding on his door at any moment.

Fortunately, three months later, we moved to another part of the town and I never saw the landlord again; so the problem was eliminated.

Thirty years later, with my foot on the brass rail and a glass in my hand, I said to Syd, "Jeez! I was so hopping mad I wouldn't have cared if you had gone down with it. I could never understand how you managed to capsize the bloody thing!"

"Aw; it was easy. Mum gave me two bob to tip it over."

Like I said, there were times, as a kid, when I reckoned the whole world was crooked on me.

The Saturday afternoon matinees at The Olympic Theatre in Sydney Road or The Rialto Theatre in The Corso were the social highlights of the week. During the week days we were segregated children; boys were separate from girls and were in graduated classes; all were supervised by discipline-orientated teachers but, in the Saturday afternoon matinees, we were a herd of unbridled animals turned loose to frolic on the green pastures of our stimulated imaginations.

We cheered, yelled, stamped or boo-ed as the action on the screen dictated. Pandemonium broke loose as Tom Mix slowly realised the heroine was in the hands of 'The Baddies' and about to suffer a fate worse than death. The excitement of his leap into the saddle and his dust-stirring disappearance into the distance was further heightened by the three-piece orchestra playing an excerpt from "The William Tell Overture"; a contribution to the arts lost in the bedlam of stamping feet and screaming, immature voices.

Wonderful things were happening to movie pictures in the late 1929s and 1930s.

The advertising billboards began to carry the phrase: "100% All Talkie".

Talking pictures! When the actors came on the screen and said something, instead of disappearing while the captions were flashed on, you could hear them speaking! When they looked at you and spoke you felt as though you should answer them and be polite like your parents taught you to do when adults spoke to you.

This technique was utilised to the utmost by film-makers.

The first half of the programme was usually made up of unrelated 'shorts' and the advent of sound brought in another aspect – Music!

One evening, when I went to the pictures with my parents, a caption simply read, "The Waltz Of The Flowers" played by some orchestra then, on the screen, appeared a symphony orchestra. I had never seen so many musicians together!

There were violins, oboes, flutes, slide trombones, big drums – everything!

The conductor came on, bowed, lifted his arms – and they all played!

I could visualise the acres and acres of flowers they were trying to tell me about and a whole new emotional garden suddenly blossomed within me.

The billboards, within a short space of time, also advertised "100% All Colour!"

Colour! The wonder of the opening scene in "The Trail Of The Lonesome Pine" when Henry Fonda, walking along a lakeside track surrounded by pine trees with mountains in the background, picked up a stone and hurled it into the water.

The sound of the stone landing in the water, the splash of white spray against the blue, the ripples spreading to disturb the reflection of the mountains in the lake – oh; such joy and beauty!

I was growing during a period of time when movie pictures were also maturing and developing. They provided many enchanting, emotionally-stimulating moments for which I am, to this day, very grateful.

Gordon Haygarth was my best mate around this time. His eldest brother, Roy, owned a 4 cylinder Chevrolet 'Peacock' Panel Van with which he conducted an ice round during the summertime. All his clients required ice for the week-ends so he gave Gordon and I a Saturday morning job on his ice cart.

I slept at their place where we arose at 4am, grabbed some breakfast, dived into the van and drove across The Spit Bridge to Mosman Ice Works where we loaded it with blocks of ice. It was not a very big van; I estimate its floor space to be about 6 feet by 5 feet with a height of 5 feet. We packed it chock-a-block full!

This mass of frozen liquid was transported down the long hill to The Spit Bridge and up the other side of the steep incline to Manly in a vehicle equipped with wooden-spoked wheels, 4 ply tyres and mechanical brakes!

The ice round was hard work for a boy. Basically, it meant getting hold of a block of ice, wrapping it in a Hessian bag, putting your arm around it, carrying it into a house, placing it in an ice chest and leaving the house without wakening the occupants.

It didn't always work out that way.

A nine-penny block of ice weighed ten pounds and climbing up the steep pathways of Manly was no small task; especially in the period of darkness before dawn.

Children left bikes and toys in the pathways, flywire doors shut quickly before I was through them, entering a strange house whose occupants were unknown to me was awesome and the lid was usually on top of an ice chest as high as my shoulders. Lifting a block of ice that high was a maximum effort. Oft times it would slip and land with a crash which, I am sure, not only woke the residence but the neighbours as well.

The distribution of the van-load was followed by a dash back to Mosman to reload and return to Manly.

Gradually, during the course of the morning, we worked our way through the area between Manly and Balgowlah to finish around mid-day.

We weren't the only people engaged in this activity. Manly Fresh Food and Ice Company had a big, yellow cart, drawn by two horses delivering ice around The Village. My brother, Syd, worked on that one.

I received the sum of two shillings for this eight hours work; an exciting amount of money allowing me to take Mary Banner or Joan Mildwater into the nine-penny seats at the matinee that arvo and buy us a threepenny ice cream as well.

Aunty May came to visit us from Perth. She was a real aunty. A genuine relative. Dad had spoken of her many times over the years but, to us, all our relatives were mystical creatures living somewhere else so her holiday with us was quite an event.

In fact, it was quite a whirlwind.

She was most surprised to learn we did not have a radio.

"Can't afford one," said Mum.

"Nonsense. We must have music in the house. I'll fix it."

A radio salesman appeared next day and installed the latest Philips Radio in our lounge room.

"May!" admonished Mum, "You shouldn't have done that. It must have cost at least twenty pounds."

"Oh; I haven't bought it," replied our genuine relative, "I've only got it on approval for fourteen days. We'll send it back then."

She did. And promptly had another installed from a different shop. She returned this one at the end of a fortnight before catching the boat back to Perth and leaving behind a nephew and a niece with a thousand questions to ask.

Mum said, "She's always been like that."

Dad said, "That's my sister."

Neither answer seemed satisfactory but, within a few short years, we came to realise they were the only answers to fit any situation involving Aunty May.

Syd commenced work with a radio manufacturing firm named Stromberg Carlson whose premises were on the other side of the city. Syd had to be woken at 6am; a difficult task because Syd was very fond of sleep. He would daily disappear down the hill at a fast pace to catch the ferry by the skin of his teeth. He promptly stretched out on a seat to sleep all the way to Circular Quay where the clanging of the engine-room bell awoke him. He also slept all the way home at the end of a day. The impressive beauty of Port Jackson, in fair weather or foul, was lost to him.

I don't know what he did at Stromberg Carlsons but the knowledge gained stayed with him and he was engaged in the radio-electrical trade for the remainder of his life.

I was around twelve years of age when Dad vanished! He simply disappeared!

Mum informed the police who found him up in Brisbane.

He returned home and carried on repairing boots and shoes.

I can only conjecture as to the reason for this episode. Perhaps it was the emotional after-effects of the war years; he was so damned independent in his attitudes, belligerently rejecting the assistance made available to ex-servicemen by The Department of Repatriation. Perhaps it was his health or perchance it was an alcoholic problem of which I was not aware but tensions built up inside him; he would withdraw into himself and vanish.

Mum took him to a doctor who immediately recognised Dad's war-illness symptoms and informed him he was going to get a pension whether liked or not because he owed it to his wife and children.

Dad disappeared again two years later.

This time he wrote from Griffiths where he had taken over a boot and shoe repair shop. There must have been a domestic upheaval over this event. We still had the shop in Manly and Mum was under a lot strain in closing it down and arranging the disposal of the few pieces of equipment and machinery. Syd quit his job and went to Griffiths where he secured employment in a radio electrical shop but his main reason for going there was to be company for Dad. The family couldn't move to Griffiths because there wasn't a vacant house in the town.

Syd and I matured rather rapidly during this stage of our family history and became aware of the commitments we had inherited in keeping the family together but, right then, we were a family divided with him and Dad in Griffiths while Mum, my two sisters and I reluctantly remained in Manly.

I'm sure it was Mum's influence that brought about the decision to move to Perth where Dad would be with his three sisters and, perhaps, more relaxed within himself.

Poor Mum was left with the distressing task of arranging our passage west; this also meant selling all our household effects and confining our worldly possessions to a wooden crate for transport to Perth.

The fifty pounds she received for a houseful of furniture covered our fares; twenty five pounds for Mum, ten pounds each for Joyce and I whilst our sister Patricia, being under five, travelled free.

The *M.V. Westralia* sailed through Sydney Heads carrying a family existing at its lowest ebb.

Chapter Four

The *S.S. Westralia* displaced 12,000 tons and was an acceptable alternative to a seven-day trans-continental train journey. Although she was a comparatively small ship her owners managed to segregate her human cargo into 1st and 3rd Class; consequently, the demarcation between passengers was quite distinct. Glossy phraseology such as 'Tourist Class' had not yet been dreamed up by sales organisations. You were either 1st, 2nd, or 3rd Class in everything and this designated the social strata in which you circulated.

3rd Class provided a 4 berth cubby-hole forrard in the bow of the ship. Air-conditioning was unknown and the quarters were ventilated by a canvas chute slung from the mast plus a couple of wind-catching vents. The bow would rise and fall some twenty to twenty five feet when she was running into a slight swell and we were sea-sick most of the time at sea; particularly between Melbourne and Adelaide.

Our Mum, despite her strength of character, oft times doubted the wisdom of her decisions and, on numerous occasions, consulted me to seek support. I had no knowledge of worldly affairs but I was conscious of the fact that she was a woman with problems so I supported her with affection and courtesy as well as encouraged my sisters to do the same. I think we managed to impart a sense of family unity which, to a mother, is important at any time.

Our first few months in Perth were months of considerable hardship and physical discomfort

We stayed with Aunty May and Uncle Jack who lived opposite Hyde Park in William Street. The house was rather crowded with two cousins and a couple of boarders as well as our family. Aunty May was a battler. Apparently she had always been a battler reaching out for dreams beyond her attainment or, perhaps she was simply facing up to the economics of the times and ensuring she would never again be 'short of a few bob' like they were when they walked off the farm during the depression which was still exerting its influence. The exodus from the farm must have been a fairly recent event but, to a fifteen-year-old boy, four years is a quarter of a lifetime. It was only later, in my more mature years, that I comprehended the stresses and disillusionment associated with such an event. I wish I could have appreciated these aspects of Life at the time then, perhaps, I would have been more conscious of Aunty May's kindnesses and less aware of her 'straight-up-and-down' attitudes so necessary in those days of hardship.

I slept on a stretcher on the back verandah. I slept cold. I had never slept cold before and it sticks so vividly in my mind. Joyce told me that she slept cold also.

It was a difficult period for Joyce and me. Neither of us wanted to go back to school again; Mum wasn't sure what to do with us and deferred making decisions until we were more settled.

These decisions were brought to a head somewhat unexpectedly by Aunty May. Our migration to Perth was partly the outcome of the strong influence and advice she exerted on us during her visit to Manly and, except for the small amount of money Dad managed to send us, we were broke.

Nevertheless, within three weeks of our arrival she found us an unfurnished, semi-detached house in Glendower Street 'just around the corner'.

I never worked out the advantage of being just around the corner, but there we were.

Our landlord was a Mr Morris. Jewish people are reputed to be shrewd and he promptly surmised that we were in rather poor and distressed circumstances. He owned a multi-storied clothing factory in

Pier Street and promptly gave Joyce a job at twelve shillings and sixpence a week to help with our family finances.

A considerable number of women were employed in the factory and I often wondered what sort of an education Joyce was receiving amongst these more mature women. She was fifteen months younger than me and for as long as I could remember I had always had a protective attitude towards her. Indeed, as we grew older, I preferred her company to other girls at dances and outings. This was a rather negative attitude and I should have been looking for girlfriends of my own. Obviously boys would, in due course, be attracted to her and I would be left out in the cold but, at this period in our lives, we probably needed each other's company and we were good cobbers.

I got a job as a messenger boy, under rather dubious circumstances, with Hugo Fischer Pty. Ltd. I was just over 15 years of age so, in my application, I understated my age by six months.

Me; a messenger boy in Perth?

I had been in Western Australia only a few weeks and the names of the city's streets were unknown to me. I had no idea where they were nor the situation of any of the business houses within the city block.

The firm occupied, and probably owned, a three-storied building in Wellington Street. There was a tannery somewhere down the coast around South Fremantle but the second floor of the Perth building was the factory.

The whole floor was covered with a conglomeration of iron machinery which, at the sound of the 8am bell, burst forth into a mighty whirring roar as it cut, twisted, pulled, stamped, polished, punched or sewed leather into merchandise ranging from suit-cases through to travelling bags, industrial belting, handbags, pump buckets, harness reins, sulky harness, leather soles and raw-hide buckets as well as numerous other leather goods.

This productivity and noise promptly ceased at 12 noon only to recommence at 1pm and carry through until 5pm five days a week and four hours on Saturday morning. Air-conditioning was unknown and when the temperature in Wellington Street reached 100 degrees Fahrenheit the atmosphere in the factory was heavy with the aroma of leather, human bodies and hot machinery

The top floor was different. Straddling the building from wall to wall were the timber roof-trusses supporting a galvanised iron roof and within this summer-time hot-house, sitting on a small stool and surrounded by straw, was a small industrious man who made horse collars. Not just pretty-looking collars for sulky-pulling show ponies but great big collars designed to fit Clydesdales, Suffolk Punches or any other massive, cross-bred, plough-pulling horse throughout the state. He worked up there all day on his own. No machinery – just an awl, a needle and thread, a mallet and years of experience.

He turned out the best horse collars in Western Australia.

This level, with its straw-covered floor and wooden beams, was a fire hazard of the first order so the little collar-maker didn't smoke during working hours. He chewed tobacco instead; a repulsive habit producing copious quantities of juice which had to be dispensed with. This gnomish-looking character could expectorate, in quantity, and hit a spot on the wall twelve feet away where it would slide downwards towards the floor. This dark stain, supported by years of liquid reinforcement, covered a strip of wall three feet wide and stretching all the way down to the ground floor where, presumably, it seeped beyond to eventually discolour the building's foundations.

Fortunately he worked at the rear of the building and this phenomenon was not visible from the showrooms.

I was kept busy. I would be loaded with parcels for delivery all around the city block and, upon my return, be loaded up again and repeat the same circuit. All this was done on foot and it became a very physically demanding job.

4pm was designated as 'Rail Time!' It was also the time when I commenced my daily struggle with the firm's hand-trolley. It was a solid, antagonistic creation similar to the type used by railway porters at the time. Two arms, made of three-inch square jarrah, rose from a steel step at ground level to end in curved handles in line with my shoulders. A steel wear-plate protected these arms and the wheels were of solid steel about eight inches in diameter and three inches wide.

On to this crude conveyance were loaded four or five of these great, big collars designed to fit Clydesdales, Suffolk Punches or any other cross-bred, plough-pulling horse throughout the state.

"There's no need to tie them on! They won't fall off! Just get going! You're late for rail already!" (I was always late for rail.)

The first time I approached the ramp leading to the rear exit of the warehouse the front edge of the steel base dug in and the whole lot was flung off! I lay along the back of the overturned trolley with my head resting hard against the top bar and my shins slammed against the axle as the men rushed past to inspect the merchandize for possible damage.

The trolley component of the firm's transport system was reloaded and the human component was told to "Pull the bloody thing up the ramp – don't push it!"

February, in Perth, can be very hot and often the sun-heated tar stuck to the wheels of the trolley as I pushed my load along Wellington Street and up over The Horseshoe Bridge to the Railway Goods Receiving Shed in Roe Street.

This depot has long since been demolished and the garden opposite the Art Gallery was once an area of tin sheds, platforms, steam locomotives shunting goods wagons and four-wheeled, steel-rimmed carriers' carts pulled by massive horses whilst dust and dirt hung overall.

My horse collars were individually lugged from the street into the building under the bridge where, with a mighty effort, they were swung up on to the great, wooden counter built between the bridge's supporting buttresses there to be taken by an old, cranky, railway employee who invariably directed the attention of his workmates to my inability to lift a horse collar on to the counter.

After ridding myself of this load I'd hurry back to the warehouse to make another delivery within the city before 5 o'clock.

The accountant was becoming more insistent with his request to see my Birth Certificate. I had been stalling him off by saying it had to come from The Registry Office in Manly but, as ten months had now passed, I couldn't keep stalling any longer so I submitted the document to him. He summoned me into his inner sanctum to inform me that, as I was over 15 years of age, they would be obliged to pay me an extra two shillings and sixpence; this would bring my wages up to fifteen shillings a week and this they were not willing to do. Besides, I had told a falsehood about my age in the first place and they felt they couldn't trust me; a statement conveniently overlooking the dozens of C.O.D. deliveries I had made around the town.

However, they did buy me a new tyre for the rear wheel of my bicycle to replace the one I had worn out in their service so I felt they weren't such a bad mob after all.

The situation was rather grim.

I was living in a strange city without friends or contacts, approaching sixteen years of age and becoming too old to be employed and unable to contribute to the family finances.

My Dad had sold, or abandoned, the business in Griffiths and had joined us a few months earlier. Ever industrious, he opened a boot and shoe repair shop in William Street near the northern end of The Horseshoe Bridge but it wasn't producing an income either.

Months passed before my cousin managed to get me a job at the modelling works where he worked as a moulder making sheets of ceiling plasterboard. Baled hemp, imported from India, had to be teased out prior to being mixed with plaster on the forming tables. The hemp was cut into short lengths by grabbing a piece with both hands, held about six inches apart, and running it up and down a long, sharp, slanting blade then teased by feeding it through two rapidly spinning spiked drums rotating in the same direction at different speeds.

The teased hemp was gathered by the armful, carried along a

catwalk and dropped down chutes adjacent to the workbenches below. All of this action had to be carried out at a fast tempo in order to meet the demands of the tradesmen on piecework.

Consequently, during the course of the next few weeks, I cut my hands rather badly on several occasions and, because the hemp-teasing was done in a dust-filled, enclosed space, I developed a cough which persisted all night during my sleep.

This circumstance greatly worried my father who persuaded me to give the job away and go canvassing for him. The plan was for me to be on a commission basis and go door-knocking for shoe repairs which would be delivered back to the client the next day.

I honestly feel my father was genuine in his desire to get me away from hemp-teasing and provide me with a bit of pocket money but after weeks of knocking on doors where I was not always politely received, and only picking up one pair of shoes, I was becoming quite depressed.

I'm sure Mum pointed out this condition to Dad and the project was abandoned.

I answered an advertisement in *The West Australian*, stating: Wanted. Boy for general farm work. Apply Box No…… this office.

A few days later I received a letter asking me to be at an address in the city at 10am next Saturday morning.

Chapter Five

A group of six boys around my age was standing on the footpath outside the address in William Street waiting to be interviewed by Mr Collins, a farmer looking for a lad to work as a general farm hand, (commonly known as a 'rouse about') on his property somewhere in the country.

He did his interviewing just off the street in the lobby of an accountant's office by writing down the details of each boy in a notebook then asking him to wait outside while he dealt with the next lad. This procedure lasted about half an hour before he came out to tell me that I had got the job and thanked the rest for attending.

He told me the farm was at Mandiga and he was in Perth on holidays. I was to be at a suburban address the following Monday week to go to the farm in the car with him and his wife.

'Where's Mandiga?" asked Dad when I arrived home.

"I don't know."

We pawed over an atlas and, after much scrutiny, discovered that Mandiga was a small siding about 180 miles from Perth on the Mukinbudin line. Towns were never on highways. They were always on a railway line denominated by the town at its terminal.

Dad came to see me off. I suspect he wanted to meet this man who was taking his boy out into the vast spaces beyond the end of the tramlines.

Mr Collins turned out to be a fine type of man who looked after me to the best of his ability. He owned a Dodge four cylinder, open tourer car complete with canvas roof and wooden-spoked wheels. The rear seat and the floor space were already packed high with groceries, tinned food and vegetables leaving just enough space for me to squeeze in beside the merchandise. My case was roped to two other cases on the luggage rack at the rear of the vehicle.

It was a long haul to the farm situated some seven miles from Mandiga. We had lunch at Northam where the bitumen cut out and, speeding onwards through Dowerin and beyond at a steady 40 miles per hour, we arrived at the property late in the afternoon just as the setting sun was painting the sky a magnificent, deep red which meant there 'was a bloody dust storm over there somewhere'.

There was a son named Dick, aged twenty-one, and a daughter, Pat, aged around eighteen. She and Mrs Collins cooked terrific meals. I was well fed, shared a room in the house with Dick, my bed was comfortable and clean, my washing was done for me and, generally, I was treated as one of the family.

Mr Collins story was interesting. He and his brother, Charlie, were blacksmiths who had a coach building business at Midland Junction. The advent of The 1914-18 War caused them to shut down so, having purchased 3,000 acres of land near Mandiga, they split it in half and took up farming.

It was not a very big farm but they made a living out of it during a period in our history when no farmer was prosperous.

Next day, at dawn, I was introduced to some of my future duties. Dick and I, carting two buckets, made our way through the gloom to the cowshed where I was shown how to coax a cow to stick her head through the bail by offering her food, how to tie her nearside leg back so she couldn't kick the bucket, how to squat on a three-legged stool and hold the bucket between my knees and how to grasp the cow's tits in order to extract the milk.

This was a most embarrassing thing to do; after all, they were her tits!

Amidst loud guffaws from Dick, I coaxed two buckets of milk from two cows. During the ensuing week I mastered the knack of milking and found myself carrying two buckets and a hurricane lamp through the pre-dawn gloom to the milking shed on my own because Dick had boarded the train for a week's holiday in Perth.

Egg gathering was another challenge in which I had to pit my wits against the chooks. The fowl house was a structure of gimlet gum uprights and cross-members with a roof of straw which had been pitched up there and more gimlet gums laid across the top to prevent the straw being blown away in a high wind. Perches and laying boxes were set around under this shelter but the enclosing wire-mesh fence was in such a poor state of repair that the fowls ranged around all through the adjacent scrub.

They are very cunning creatures – chooks.

Beyond the chook yard was the smithy; another bush timber shed with a galvanised iron roof and containing all the mystifying and exciting tools of a professional blacksmith's forge.

The railway line through Mandiga was being reconditioned and old jarrah sleepers were available to the surrounding agricultural community at the cost of sixpence each. Mr Collins purchased a considerable number of these in order to build a bull pen and, once we had transported them to the farm on the Morris truck, we commenced a job which introduced me to hard earth, crowbars, shovels, sweat and blisters.

The bull was a big Jersey with pointed horns and it would fight at the drop of a hat. He had several cows already in calf and a group of young heifers, too young for breeding, who were being persistently propositioned by him. Obviously he had no morals and the impressive formidable-looking pen had become a necessary structure which we completed upon Dick's return.

Separating the bull from the herd wasn't an easy process as he aggressively refused to follow the trail of oat sheafs laid across the open ground leading to his newly constructed domain. We eventually reached a compromise by allowing one of the cows to accompany him along the trail of no return while we watched from a safe distance like

Red Indians stalking a wagon train. As the bull suspiciously snorted his way into the pen Dick raced over and slid the sliprail sleepers into place; thus separating the two animals. The cow was shoo-ed back to the herd.

I thought this rather cruel because, obviously, they were friends.

I was entering a phase in Life where my sensitive and inexperienced nature was to be shocked time and time again. This characteristic was obvious to Mr Collins and Dick. The latter's guffawing laughter would at times swamp me with humiliation as farm life gradually revealed my worldly innocence. Months passed before I learned to accept his unintentional scoffing with tolerance but, even today, I wonder what psychological scars I carried long after I returned to Perth.

I wasn't even aggressive enough to smack Old Nell on the rump when I told her (nay; asked her) to "Giddup." Old Nell was a big, docile draught-horse who tolerated my inexperience as I learned to harness her and back her into the dray with head-bobbing and nose-blowing – a routine that oft times caused Mr Collins to smile as my face was usually in line with her nose.

We poisoned hundreds of rabbits. The long summer months had dried out the dam. Water was in the trough within the sheep yard. The sheep, having had their evening drink, wandered out into the stubble-covered paddocks and the trough was covered with boards. Motor tyres, cut around the outside perimeter to form a trough, were spread through the sheep yard and filled with a mixture of water and cyanide. Every morning for weeks I tipped the tyres over and picked up a dray-load of dead rabbits to be carted away to a distant paddock and dropped down an old well.

Rabbits were a real pest and keeping their numbers down was a constant problem. They were not all exterminated. There are always survivors in any catastrophe and, next year, they would be just as plentiful as ever.

My wages were ten shillings a week and keep. Mr Collins paid me every month with a 'crossed cheque' which meant the money had to go into a bank account. He had had young chaps working for him who diligently mailed their cheques to parents in Perth only to find the money had been spent when they required it at a later date.

Consequently, along with the cheque had to go a withdrawal form and instructions detailing what to buy with the money. The first cheque purchased work boots, the next purchased dungaree work pants, then warm socks and a shirt. Gradually I was beginning to look and feel like a farmhand.

We had our first good rain and commenced preparations for ploughing.

The first commitment was chaff-cutting. A cranky, single-cylinder Sunshine Engine was coaxed into life by spinning the flywheel until the engine fired into a bad-tempered dance performed upon two logs serving as a base. A long leather belt transmitted power from this dancing bomb to a machine designed by the devil. Sheaves of oats were pulled from the haystack and fed into this machine which reduced them to chaff and conveyed the end product, via bucket elevator, into a shed at the end of the stables.

The engine banged and thumped all day, the cutter's knife blades swooshed and chopped, the bucket elevator clattered and rattled, a fine insidious dust hung overall and chaff itch could be felt all over the body within a short space of time.

Chaff cutting was a lousy job and I feel itchy just writing about it.

The stables were made of bush timber. The uprights, the roof timbers, the stalls, the mangers and the rail fence around the stables were all gimlet gum or eucalypt. There were two rows of horse stalls facing each other and forming a corridor with one end leading to the chaff room. Harness hung on pegs driven into the uprights flanking the corridor. Hames, bits, bridles and draught-horse collars gave off an aroma of leather and horse sweat.

The horses were brought in from a paddock where they had been grazing since the end of last year's harvest. Boisterous mountains of horseflesh came pounding into their own specific stall to snuffle their noses in a manger where a feed of chaff, oats and molasses had already been placed.

They were fed molasses for a few weeks to 'sand them', I was told.

Whilst the two rows of horses were munching noisily, aiming sly kicks at each other, squealing, backing out rapidly to return to feeding again, I was escorted along the corridor between the feed boxes and introduced to them. The horses were supremely indifferent but I was awestruck at the immediate proximity of so much animal life. Each one, when it lifted its head, was twice as high as me, their necks and shoulders were so big, their legs were as thick as my waist and to each leg was attached a hoof that was lifted and thumped down again in a most alarming manner.

"Now I'll show you how to curry comb and brush them."

Oh no! Go into one of those stalls where a monster swayed and thumped about! Supposing it lifted one of those hoofs and dropped it on my foot! Supposing it kicked me! Supposing it just didn't like me!

I had always maintained I was fond of horses but these were real!

An hour later the horses and I had something in common. We had all been through an ordeal.

They were kept in the stables for a few days 'to feed up and quieten down a bit'. "They're a bit frisky after being out in the paddock."

Dawned the day when ploughing was to commence.

Dick and I, each carrying a hurricane lamp, left the house in pre-dawn darkness. He went to the stables to rouse up and feed the horses and I went to the cowshed to do the milking. We met again at breakfast and headed for the stables as the eastern sky heralded the arrival of the morning sun.

"I'll show you how to put the collars on and be sure you put the right collar on the horse."

This was no problem as the correct collar, suited to the shape of the horse's shoulders, hung on a post at the feed-box end of the stall. Dick lifted a collar off a peg, undid the strap at the top, stepped into a stall, spread the collar into a U shape, slipped it past the shoulders until it fitted snugly around the horse's neck, buckled up the strap at the top, stepped out of the stall and said, "Go on. 'ave a go."

I lifted a collar off a peg and it went straight to the ground.

I was angry! Damn the bloody thing! It was bad enough to have been sweating and struggling to push a trolley-load over The Horseshoe Bridge in the mid-summer heat without making a fool of myself with one right now!

I undid the buckle, stepped inside the stall and with a tremendous effort pulled apart far enough to get it over the horse's neck. I had my arm around the horse, doing up the buckle, when it decided to have another mouthful of chaff.

It moved forward pinning me between the collar and the feed box.

"Guffaw! Guffaw! Back up, Mollie, back up!"

Mollie backed up and I escaped.

"Next time tell her to back up. It's always like this at first. You'll get the hang of it after a while."

Fitting bridles over gigantic heads and coaxing cold bits into warm mouths equipped with enormous teeth was yet another harrowing experience.

Strange to relate, in time, I did get the hang of it.

Eight horses were lined up side by side and attached to each other by a short strap clipped to the bits. A long, leather rein was clipped to the bits of the two outside horses.

Dick hung on to the rein, "O.K., boy, let the rails down!"

Eight horses, in line abreast, charged at the opening with Dick hanging back on the rein and shouting, "Steady, you bastards, steady!"

They were pointed in the direction of the paddock where the plough had been left at the end of the previous season and whither they made their way nudging, kicking and tail-swishing to express their annoyance at the prospect of commencing another season's work.

Arriving at the plough, Dick skilfully swung them across the front so each horse was standing between two chains lying on the ground.

"Righto, boy, hook 'em up!"

"Eh?"

"Pick the chains up and hook 'em on to the collars."

It was a fact! He wanted me to walk in front of that row of snorting, steam-blowing, side-kicking, stamping horseflesh, pick up ice-cold chains with frozen fingers and slip them on to metal hames attached to collars wrapped around necks away above my head!

"C'mon! I can't hold them all day!"

I was committed.

Ten agonising, fear-filled minutes later Dick softly said, "Giddup."

The horse threw themselves into the collars, the chains tightened and The Sundercut, 10 disc, stump-jump plough moved off down the paddock leaving behind a badly-shaken, homesick, city boy standing in the middle of bare fields that stretch to the horizon.

While Dick was ploughing I worked with Mr Collins in the blacksmith shop making cultivator points. Plough discs were brought to a cherry-red heat, pulled out of the fire with firmly gripped tongs, thumped on to the anvil and, with a long-handled cold chisel, he traced out a point as I hit the chisel with a sledgehammer – a new skill which had not been acquired without considerable fear of injury to both instructor and pupil.

Winter was fast approaching, rain fell periodically, the wind was becoming colder and I reckoned the smithy's shop was a good place to be in.

This happy state of affairs, alas, was soon to come to an end.

"There's a lot of mallee roots coming up in that top paddock," announced Dick one night at tea.

Next day I was introduced to mallee root picking. It seemed there were still many roots below the surface and as the plough came along it dug under and lifted them out. They had to be removed from the paddock.

The process was quite simple. 'The Boy' was to walk up and down the paddock throwing them into heaps to be picked up with a horse and dray later.

After the team, the plough and Dick had commenced their scar-creating plod across the face of the earth I began a week of daily misery.

There were 500 acres in that paddock.

Some of the partially lifted roots were prised out of the soil with considerable effort. I would decide on a central point then walk around it in a radius of 20 feet tossing roots into the centre until I had heaps lined in rows. The earth was damp and uneven, my hands were still far from work-hardened, the wind blew cold across the countryside, the sky was overcast with dark, heavy clouds and I could see the rain coming for miles across the neighbour's paddocks and there was no place to go for shelter.

The ploughing of that paddock was eventually finished and Old Nell was harnessed into the dray to be driven to the rows of mallee roots which were loaded, carted off and thrown on to the stack behind the house.

The stack was 12 to 15 feet high and formed a horseshoe right around the rear of the house; the only break was a gap in the centre allowing a pathway from the house to the dunny.

Mallee roots are valued as fuel for both cooking and warming. They give off an abundance of heat, glow for long periods and burn to a white, powdery ash.

When I re-visited the farm, over 30 years later, this stack had only been a third consumed so, in theory, it should provide the descendants of Mr Collins with fuel and warmth right past the turn of the century.

There were numerous occasions when the callousness of farming made me feel quite ill; another weakness in my character giving rise to more humour than understanding.

The first was the crutching of the sheep after they had been on green feed for a few weeks. The insidious eating away of flesh by blowfly maggots, the cutting away of slimy, putrid wool with hand shears, the stench of it all and the helplessness of sheep was hard to emotionally accept.

The handling of lambs, too, was another aspect of emotional hardening. The manner in which they ran, bleating, to their mothers after being tailed and castrated; seeing the flock trail off into the paddocks after the evening drink leaving behind a bewildered lamb running up and down on the wrong side of the wire-mesh fence; lifting the lamb over the fence only to find it dead in the morning, its tongue bitten out by a fox because the ewe's flock instinct was greater than its mother instinct.

Dick, of course, gave me many a shock. He didn't always mean to shock me but, as he had been born and bred on the farm, routine things to him appalled me.

We wanted a sheep for meat. He simply selected one out of the flock, carried it into the shed, threw it on its back in a cradle, slit its throat and watched it gurgle its life away without batting an eyelid.

After the carcase was skinned, gutted and washed it was promptly placed in a calico bag, raced over to the house and placed in an elongated meat-safe on the verandah. The trick was to place the sheep in the safe, pull off the calico bag and shut the door before the blowflies could get to it. Frequent checks were made to ensure the blowflies hadn't had a win.

Another time the horses were harnessed and standing waiting to move off to the plough when Dick moved them up a few yards, gave me the reins to hold, then walked back to minutely examine a freshly dropped heap of horse manure with a stick.

"Watcha doin'?"

"Looking for sand. We might have to give them some more molasses and bran."

"Oh. Is that how you do it?"

"Do you know any other way?"

I didn't so I didn't pursue the topic further.

Toby was a good looking, bad tempered saddle horse and getting the bit into his mouth without being bitten was quite an accomplishment. Holding his head at arm's length in order to protect my ribs from a bite, I'd lead him into a stall where his head was securely fastened to a rail for safety. He was still capable of administering a 'cow-kick' while the saddle girth was being tightened and, when preparing to mount, his head had to be pulled right around to the offside and held there; otherwise a bite on the arse would result. Then, having thrown my leg over the saddle, his head had to be pulled straight to avoid a bite on my foot as it was placed in the stirrup.

Except for these little quirks of character he was quite an obedient horse. He just didn't like people, that's all.

I learned to ride on that horse. True, it was not accomplished without a couple of nasty bites and a few kicks but I had become determined to attain some farm-type capabilities in order to rise above 'The Boy' stigma. Toby would be ridden around the farm paddocks on Sundays or, as my skill improved, taken for a few miles along the roads bordering the farm. My proudest moment was to return from one of these outings and report some problem with the sheep requiring Dick's attention.

Mr Collins had a bachelor nephew gradually establishing a farm, assisted by a colleague, a few miles along the road.

These chaps, besides being good types, had a wireless!

The radio programmes were published in 'The West Australian' and, when Sunday night's programme announced a musical radio play, I oft times rode Toby to their shack after tea, listened to a musical play coming over the crackling air-waves then, around 9:30pm, rode Toby back to our stables through the pitch black night.

Nowadays I realise what a bloody headache I must have been to everyone. These chaps must have been up at daylight, fed their horses and probably milked a couple of cows, gone into Bencubbin to play cricket all day, come back home to milk and feed animals then, just as they were contemplating sleep before a hard day's work tomorrow, this roustabout from Uncle Dick's would arrive to listen to the radio!

Mr Collins, too, must have had his sleepless periods waiting for the sounds of me putting Toby into the stable.

But none of them could have realised how spiritually uplifting it was for me to hear Gladys Moncrieff singing in 'The Maid Of The Mountains' after so many months without hearing one note of music.

The family purchased a radio that year. It was truly a family effort; each member contributed five pounds to make up the purchase price. It was switched on to hear the evening news then switched off to conserve the batteries – a necessary procedure as the price of dry cell batteries was quite an expense when viewed in the economic light of the day.

After I had helped Pat with the tea-time dishwashing we all sat in the large drawing room. where the open mallee fire gave off its warmth, the mantle of the Aladdin kerosene lamp glowed brightly, Mr Collins read the paper, Mrs Collins did tapestry work or knitted. The rest of us read books. Nobody spoke.

It was there that I learned the value of silence and a good book.

A lot of moulding was done on that farm – most of it for the good.

Seeding time arrived.

The 1928 model four-cylinder truck was loaded with a ton of wheat and super. The horses, having been fed, were harnessed as a team with the long, leather rein attached to the two outside horses.

Dick, before scrambling into the vehicle, tossed me the reins, "Here you are, boy, now don't let them play up on you and I'll see you at the drill."

Me?

Eight horses?

I politely requested them to "Giddup".

They moved off so I followed them with my hands tightly grasping the rein; I swung them through the top gate, drove them to the drill where Dick was pouring seed wheat into the box, pulled hard on the offside rein to swing them across the front of the machine then hard on the nearside to line them up, shouted "Whoa back, you bastards!" and backed them into position between the chains laying on the wet earth.

"Not bad," said Dick.

I felt magnificent!

The 'follow up' rains never came and, during the next few months, it became clear "she was going to be a crook year."

The crop sprouted and grew about six inches but no taller. The fallowing being finished and the crop an obvious failure, the horses were turned out on to it and Mr Collins explained he could no longer afford to employ me.

My suitcase was placed on the back seat of the Dodge Tourer and I was driven to Mandiga siding to await the train from Mukinbudin.

The rumbling of the train and the choofing of the engine penetrated the stillness of the black night long before the headlight's beams could be seen cutting a swathe through the gimlet gums as the train groped its way along the rails to the siding.

There was no platform and the train came to a noisy halt as the buffer of each carriage slammed into the one ahead. The train was a 'mixed' train carrying goods as well as passengers. The two passenger carriages at the rear were of the 'dog box' design having two seats facing each other across the carriage with a toilet in one corner. The trouble was to find a seat in the dark. By climbing up the side of the train, pulling the door open and peering inside, one could determine if the unlit compartment was full. The word 'full' meant if someone was laying full length along each seat. The door would be pushed shut and the process repeated until I eventually found a vacancy.

I clambered in, my suitcase was slid along the floor, a quick handshake, the door slammed and the train continued on its jolting, jarring journey into the blackness. I unstrapped the blanket from the side of my suitcase, stretched out along the seat and, with my arm as a pillow, was soon lulled to sleep by the rhythmic rumble of steel wheels on steel rails.

We arrived at Dowerin five hours later, having covered fifty miles in that time.

The train's arrival at Northam Station, on the western side of the town, was greeted by a man standing on the platform, ringing a bell and shouting: "Northam! Northam!"

Breakfast!

Doors were flung open all along the lengths of the carriages to disgorge passengers who hurried along the platform like sheep in a race to disappear into the dining room.

The available food was a pie or a pastie with tea or coffee served in thick, heavy, standard issue 'Railway' crockery bearing the motif 'W.A.G.R.' in a purpley-bluish colour which I have never since seen duplicated.

The food was served piping hot; the pies and pasties having been stewing for several hours, whilst the tea or coffee had been made, more or less, for a train now running two hours late.

The trick was to consume this lip-and-tongue-scalding nourishment before the engine-driver began blowing impatient blasts on his whistle; a noisy announcement that echoed throughout the surrounding countryside causing passengers to gulp down hot coffee, pick up overheated pies and run back to their compartments whilst boiling meat and gravy escaped from soggy pastry to trickle a scalding pathway across their hands.

Doors were slammed shut, the engine belched out clouds of smoke and steam, the slack was taken up on the buffers, carriages jolted into motion and the train continued on its way to Perth.

Chapter Six

There was strong affection within our family, probably because of the past few year's tribulations, and I felt good to be home once again; but I was so ignorant of the ways of the world and so lacking in perception that I failed to see our family's situation even though it was right under my nose.

Mum was facing the circumstances and had moved to a larger house in Francis Street where she was taking in boarders. One daughter was still going to school, one daughter was bringing in twelve shillings and sixpence a week, one son was still in New South Wales and contributed nothing, one son was unemployed and had to be fed and Dad was away again.

Dad had ceased boot and shoe repairing. That type of work had become too much for his physical capabilities so he had decided to give it away for a while until his health 'picked up a bit'.

He had taken a job as the orderly at Laverton Hospital.

Personally, I think he was trying to run away from the emotional bewilderment into which he was being plunged by the passage of time. He had an independent spirit and was immensely proud of his ability to 'earn a crust.' Now he was faced with a situation where the physical demands of the job were beyond him.

Many, many years later I began to understand him but, by that time, it was too late. All through those wonderful green years, while I was growing into manhood, my Dad was slowly dying.

Surely, a teen-aged youth, growing up in the beautiful, sun-drenched city of Perth, is not expected to understand or visualise the muck, the stench, the acceptance of temporary life or the horror of existence in the trenches of France.

Surely, such a lad awakening in the morning to breathe in the air of a new day is not expected to compare this blessing with the insidious creeping of mustard gas across No Man's Land.

Some men died an agonizing death right there and then. Others 'escaped' to die a slow death over the next twenty-five years or so. And while they were dying they were trying to build – trying to build a family, trying to build a business to provide security for that family but The Cause was lost before it even started.

"Joyce, where is Laverton?"

"I don't know exactly. Somewhere on the goldfields."

"Gee! That's a long way away."

"I know, but Mum says it is only for a little while until things get better."

I was back on the morale-destroying routine of looking for a job – any job!

'The West Australian' was delivered by 6am. I grabbed it, turned to 'Situations Vacant' ran my fingers down the column until I came to:

Boy Wanted..

Boy Wanted..

Boy Wanted..

Selecting two or three I considered 'most likely', I dressed, had some breakfast, jumped on my bike and pedalled into the city where I stood in a short queue which grew longer every minute while we waited for the doors to open.

Nine times out of ten, when the doors opened, we were told the situation had been filled. Obviously somebody who knew someone in the firm had secured a job for a relative's boy by pulling a few strings over the telephone.

I pedalled like blazes to the next likely position but, by then, it was after 9 o'clock and that job was also gone.

When I received a letter from Dad saying the local dairyman was looking for a boy I promptly decided to take it.

Finding two pounds ten shillings for the fare was a bit of a problem as I had used all my bank account or given it to Mum. Fortunately, the government had a scheme whereby, if you had secured a job in the country, it advanced the fare and you repaid it over the next six weeks. This would be no problem as the job paid three pounds a week and keep.

The train left Perth at 8pm and arrived in Kalgoorlie around 10am the next day.

The journey had been a nightmare!

The 'dog box' type carriages were full and I was in a compartment with six men returning to the goldfields after their annual holidays. They were big, rough, uncouth and different to any I had hitherto met and they drank in a boisterous manner from a large stock of bottled beer kept in brown paper bags stacked under the seat.

The noisy session grew louder as the night stretched into the hours beyond midnight. By the time the train had reached Merredin all the compartment's occupants, except me, were lolling around in a variety of grotesque postures associated with drunken sleep.

I was sitting near the toilet door. Vomit was on the floor beside me where one of the drunks had failed to get to the toilet door in time and stench wafted around the brightly-lit compartment.

I felt ill, frightened and tense with anxiety. Ill with the stink of this smoke-filled compartment from which I was unable to escape; frightened of these muscular men and their potential to do physical harm in a mood of drunken anger; tense with anxiety because the one who had been sick had said he was only going as far as Merredin where the engine was now slowly panting as it took on water from the overhead tank while the train guards and porters were unloading merchandise from the goods wagons; their noisy activity and shouting voices creating a racket shattering the quietness of the slumbering town.

Obviously I was going to have to awaken this sleeping character.

I tapped him politely on the knee.

"Hey, mister. We're at Merredin."

No response. I gently shook his shoulder.

"Hey, mister. We're at Merredin."

No response. I held on to his shoulder and shook him so vigorously he bumped the man on the other side of him.

"What the f.... hell's going on here?"

"This bloke wants to get off at Merredin and I can't wake him up."

"Where the f..... hell are we now?"

"Merredin."

"Christ!"

He rose to his feet, slung the drunk over his shoulder, opened the carriage door, walked out on the platform and gently laid his burden on a seat.

He returned to the carriage. "Which is his case?"

"That one," I said, indicating a battered suitcase on the overhead luggage rack.

He lifted it down and placed it by the seat where his former drinking companion was snoring lustily.

Re-entering the train he swayed unsteadily until he lifted an enormous paw to grip the luggage rack. He stood there stupidly blinking his eyes and looking like King Kong surveying a scene of carnage.

Several moments passed.

"You poor, little bugger," he said, "S'posin' you sit up here by the window. Here, I'll open it for you. Then I can lie down on the rest of the seat. Turn the bloody light off, too."

He made me as comfortable as the situation permitted, switched off the light, stretched out on the seat with his feet nudging my leg and, with his head resting on the wooden armrest by the toilet door, promptly fell asleep.

This was my first encounter with the 'goldfields type' of person and I was emotionally shocked and disturbed by the experience.

Years later, in situations never visualised then, I was to value their peculiar code of mateship and conclude they were a good type of bloke to have around when there was a fight on; especially if they were on your side.

But, just now, I was sixteen years of age, my Mum and two sisters were in Perth, Mr Collins and his family were in Mandiga, my Dad was in Laverton and I was curled up by the corner window of a compartment full of drunks as the train clattered and swayed through a moonless night towards an uncertain future.

Coolgardie!

Kalgoorlie!

Magical names which had stimulated my imagination ever since I had first heard the history of the W.A. goldfields from Mr Quinliven, our geography teacher at Mosman Junior Tech.

The discovery of gold had caused a great influx of people from all over the world and men had perished wandering over these waterless wastes but the two cities had blossomed like flowers in the desert. And I was surprised to find the 'wasteland' was covered in salmon gums with wildflowers growing in abundance.

I stepped out of the train filled with a sense of excitement.

Many a time, as a messenger boy, I had stood on The Horseshoe Bridge to watch The Kalgoorlie Express, dust-covered and grimy from its long journey, steam into Perth Station and thrilled to the sight and sound of doors opening, people greeting people, doors slamming with that sound peculiar to carriage doors being slammed whilst the massive locomotive nonchalantly puffed with a resonant noise as it tossed clouds of steam high into the air to waft out through the louvres in the station roof.

Now I was standing on the platform where those journeys commenced!

Thus was established a romantic attitude towards the goldfields which is still with me but, on this day, my first impression was …. tin!

The roofs were corrugated iron, the fences were corrugated iron, the internal ceilings of the cafes were pressed tin, the internal walls were finely corrugated tin and, in many cases, the external walls were also tin.

I realise, now, that tin was a readily transportable building material and if a building became derelict, as they frequently did on the goldfields, it could be knocked down and the material transported elsewhere.

The train journey to Laverton was a tedious, boring episode at a speed conveying the impression that the train didn't really want to be meandering along the rails disappearing into the shimmering, monotonous distance.

Dad was there to meet me. We wandered over to The Laverton Hotel, dumped my suitcase on the footpath and went inside to meet my new boss.

Mr Hilliard didn't own the pub. He was having a few beers while he waited for the train; a risky procedure as the train was often several hours late. He bought me a ginger beer before deciding to set off for the dairy about five miles out on the other side of The Lancefield Gold Mine at Beria.

His vehicle was an Oldsmobile tourer of doubtful vintage. It was without the canvas hood which had "blown off in a willy-willy some time ago." It had wooden wheel-spokes as well as running boards where the battery was held firmly in place by a length of twisted fencing wire. Two large headlights sat on a tubing fixed between the mudguards and the radiator surrounds.

"Aw; she's good enough for around here," my new employer

assured me.

The road wasn't sealed and the old tourer picked up speed until it was dancing along the top of four inch deep corrugations and leaving a long, billowing cloud of red dust trailing behind.

We turned off the road at Beria and wound our way past numerous humpies to the dairy. The house was a timber-framed structure with a galvanised iron roof but the internal and external walls were made of Hessian liberally coated with whitewash. I had never seen a house built like this before but I soon learned galvanised iron and Hessian were common materials in this part of the world.

"Besides," said The Boss, "it never rains out here, anyway."

My quarters were about 150 feet from the house. It was a humpy made of bush materials and scrap materials. Eight gimlet gum posts were stuck in the ground about six feet apart and, to these, was nailed a motley collection of iron sheeting and Hessian to form a room with a door on one side and a window hole in the other. A four inch gap between the top of the wall and the roof allowed ventilation.

An additional lean-to had been added by running wire-mesh out to two more posts and throwing mulga-bush foliage on top to provide shade.

A dressing table, consisting of two stacked kerosene cases, was supplemented by a mirror leaning against the wall. An enamel bowl and pitcher completed the accessories.

The bed was a wooden-framed stretcher with clean sheets and pillowcases; a gesture zealously maintained by Mrs Hilliard in the months that followed.

I never felt annoyed or dismayed at these surroundings. I was standing on my own two feet! This was the goldfields! This Life was adventure!

Milking began at 3am the next morning.

The herd was a motley mob. It included a couple of good Friesians, 5 Guernseys and the rest were not much better than scrub cattle; about

30 in all and they were milked by hand. The milk was strained into churns then hoisted into the cart with the taps protruding through the rear wall.

A quick cup of tea followed the milking. The horse was harnessed into the cart and the delivery round commenced in the pre-dawn darkness.

The clientele was mostly Jugo-Slav and Italian workers living in humpies spread around the countryside surrounding the mine. There were no roads or laid out streets; only tracks made by the steel rims of the cart's wheels.

Here was a problem. The names were not 'British'. They were funny, foreign names ending with 'I', 'O' or 'itches', the likes of which I had never heard before, let alone pronounced.

I set about learning the milk run the same way I had learned poetry at school. The horse pulled up outside a humpy and Mr Hillier told me the owner's name. I repeated to myself, over and over, until I had got it fixed in my mind. Then I added the quantity of milk. The horse moved on to the next humpy and the mental process was repeated. Then I added the first name and kept repeating them.

So it went on around the whitewashed humpies scattered willy-nilly like snowflakes across the scrub-covered countryside.

The horse then trotted along the flat, featureless track to Laverton. where, happily, there were streets and people with 'English' names.

We made our way uphill from the dry creek bed at the edge of the town to the hospital and the doctor's house then meandered down through the houses; finally leaving the town through the main street.

Well, we nearly made straight out of town. As we passed the hotel the horse swung off the road and stopped beside the brick wall of the two-storied building. Mr Hilliard invited me inside for a ginger beer while he had a drink.

What would my Mum think of me going into a crowded hotel bar at nine o'clock in the morning?

The drives back to the dairy were spent in getting to know each other in the manner peculiar to men whose paths have crossed on the Roadway of Life and must continue together for a while.

It was during one of these drives, as we drove along the two-wheeled track beside the road to Beria with sun warming our backs and the horse trotting tirelessly along, that I learned my Dad was 'buggered'.

I also learned Mr Hilliard hadn't really settled down since the war and he freely admitted the life he was living wasn't doing the right thing by his wife and kids. His young daughter was going to the school in Beria and his son, nicknamed Waddie, would be starting school next year. This meant he was beginning to grow and Mrs Hilliard didn't want him to grow in a place like Beria. So, he reckoned he would have to get out of the place before long.

"What will you do with the dairy? Sell it?"

"Oh; I don't own the dairy. I'm only leasing it from Mr Harris who lives in Laverton. He owns all the station property around here. Laverton is built on his property. So is the Lancefield Mine and all the other little shows around the place."

I had trouble mentally assimilating this situation. A man owned a quarter acre block in the city. It was his. Nobody could come on to it without his permission. Certainly no one else could build on it. But here was a railway line, a railway station, goods shed, the town of Laverton, the Lancefield Mine and the humpies scattered around it – all built on land owned by Mr Harris.

It all took a lot of understanding.

Once the milk churns were scalded and the horse fed the rest of the day was my own until 3pm when we milked again.

As soon as I was alone I wrote down the names of the customers and the milk quantities in order of delivery then learned the list off by heart. I didn't get it right the first day but by the end of the third day I could recite it through to myself.

Whilst having lunch on the fourth day I told The Boss I reckoned I could handle the run by myself.

"Aw; I think it will take another week or so," he said. "There's over fifty customers to call on, you know."

I recited the list of customers and quantities.

"Gawd Struth!" he exploded, "Awright! You're on! Tomorrow you can have a go on your own!"

The next day I did the round on my own to be greeted, upon my return, with this question: "Eh, I've been thinking. You might know the names of everybody but how do you know where they live? They're scattered all over the place."

"That was easy. I smacked the horse on the arse and when he stopped outside a place I'd go in and put some milk in the billy."

"You'll do," he said. "And you didn't have any trouble with the horse?"

"Only when I was leaving the town. He swung up against the pub wall and I had a bit of trouble getting him to start again."

"Yair; well, tomorrow, try getting out of the cart, walk around the pub and get back in again. I think he'll be all right."

The passage of time brought several highlights.

One day, during lunch break, about fifty cows came out of the scrub at a fast trot. Fortunately the gate to the paddock containing the water trough was open because they charged straight in to surround the trough and drank all it contained.

They also guzzled off half the water in the holding tank.

"Where the hell have they come from?" I asked.

"That's the rest of the herd. They're all dry so I turned them out to graze on the scrub in a paddock a couple of miles from here. It looks as if the mill's broken down and they've run out of water. We'll leave them here tonight and have a look in the morning."

The Boss and I drove out to the mill next day and found the trough dry. He replaced the pump buckets with new ones made by Hugo Fischer Ltd., got the water slurping into the holding tank in unison with the windmill's sighing rhythm and reckoned "She'll be right, mate."

Nevertheless, he expressed concern over the incident and intimated 'someone' should come out and check the windmill once a week. I asked if I could do it because it would give me a chance to do some riding as well as give the saddle horse some work.

He seemed reluctant to agree and asked, "Don't think you'll get lost out here in the scrub?"

"No. There's a definite track running past this turn off to the mill. You can't go wrong?"

"Yair, I suppose so. The main track goes on to a gate in the top boundary fence of this paddock. We might as well make sure it is closed while we are out here so's the cattle won't get into the next paddock where they're baiting for wild dogs."

We drove to the top gate, checked it out and returned to the dairy.

A week later I saddled the horse and went off to check the mill.

"By the way," said The Boss, "you might as well check that top gate while you are out there."

I rode straight out to the gate, planning to check the mill on the way back.

The horse was a cunning mare that no amount of rib kicking would make go faster than a trot. She had been idle for a month and was sadly out of condition so I didn't really blame her for not unduly exerting herself in the heat.

Trotting is a tiring gait for the rider and, after a few miles, my posterior and legs were beginning to feel the effect of continuous lifting and lowering. The top gate was O.K. so I followed back along the track to the mill turn off where I had a bit of trouble convincing the mare we were going to check the mill but the application of a switch, broken off from a bush, helped to change her mind.

The mill was functioning efficiently and I set off back to the dairy.

The horse played up again at the track junction and things got a bit exciting for a while but I eventually had her trotting in the direction I wished to go.

Imagine my misery when we arrived back at the top gate!

With aching limbs and sore bum I turned the horse for home.

The damned thing, as though to say, "I told you so", immediately broke into an effortless canter. I was doubting my sense of direction so I held the reins loose and let the mare pick her own course. We arrived back at the dairy in a seemingly short space of time.

I didn't say anything to The Boss about this incident but I had learned a very frightening and invaluable lesson; it would be so easy to get lost in the endless miles of featureless bush surrounding the dairy in all directions.

The following week I set out for the mill again, this time taking the dog with me. I had seen pictures of stockmen travelling with their dog trotting obediently behind but this dog obviously hadn't read the same books. He took off into the scrub on one side of the track then re-appeared to vanish into the bush on the other side. Half a mile on I'd find him sitting beside the track, grinning from ear to ear and clearly saying, "Aha! You thought you had lost me, didn't you?"

I had checked the mill, closed the last gate on the way back and remounted when a four feet long goanna came crashing through the scrub hotly pursued by that crazy dog. The lizard ran straight up the horse's hind legs and hung on to her rump. The horse promptly snorted, plunged and bucked as it endeavoured to get rid of its unwanted passenger. The bungarra stayed but I left to land on my arse in the dust. The reptile hung on, the horse reared and bucked, stirring up a cloud of dust in its antics. I hung on to the reins expecting to be killed at any moment while the dog ran around the outside of this miniature tornado barking and adding to the turmoil.

The drama probably lasted less than thirty seconds but it seemed like a thousand years before the bungarra was chucked off to race across the scrub and scale to the top of the gate's straining post from which height it looked disdainfully down at the dog barking and stirring up more dust.

I led the horse away from the scene, calmed her down, remounted and continued on my way, leaving the dog to carry on his argument with the pole-sitting lizard.

"Cripes! What happened to you?" asked The Boss as he surveyed the sweating horse and the layer of dust covering us.

I told him the blood-chilling tale.

"Jeez!" he laughed, "You were lucky. They usually run right up your back and sit on your head!"

The dog arrived half an hour later wearing a big grin. He hadn't had so much fun for ages but I ignored the suggestion I take him with me next time.

After I had been working about two months on this job Mrs Hilliard took herself and the two children off to Kalgoorlie for a fortnight in order to visit some relatives. The separation of my quarters from their dwelling isolated me from the unwanted but understandable domestic tension. Mrs Hilliard hated the place and everything associated with it and she was taking herself off to Kalgoorlie to get away for a while.

A few days later, upon returning from the deliveries, I was surprised to see a ladder leaning against the white wall of the house and high upon it was a coal-black Aboriginal with a paint brush in one hand, a bucket in the other and spreading whitewash all over the Hessian with considerable enthusiasm but not a great deal of skill.

"What's going on?" I enquired as we unloaded the cart.

"Aw; I thought I'd give the place a bit of a facelift while the missus is away. It's getting a bit draughty inside, anyway."

"What's the Abo's name?"

"Jimmy. He's quite a good bloke. Used to be a police boy. I told him I could give him a fortnight's work but he'll have to go before the missus gets back. She can't stand them around the place."

Next day The Boss informed me that Jimmy's lubra had turned up and they were camping in a couple of old water tanks about 100 yards across the flat and dead in line with the front door. It was against the law to pay them money so The Boss arranged to supply them with tea, sugar and bread.

The following day he told me Jimmy's mother-in-law had arrived and the day after I was advised that Jimmy's mate had moved in.

"I don't like this," said The Boss. "There's too many of them over there and they're bound to start fighting amongst themselves."

"Fighting? What will they want to start fighting over?"

He pondered over this then apparently decided it was time I had a lesson in Life.

"Aw, well; there's a lot of Italians and Slavs who haven't got any women of their own in this country. So, on pay days, these bucks take their lubras around the different humpies and while the blokes are inside with the lubras the bucks pinch whatever grog they can find around the place. They take it back to their camp, get full, and start fighting."

"Can't they get full without fighting?"

"Not these blokes. Besides, if they don't look like fighting, the lubras egg them on and things get a bit rough. They go mad with grog and could kill each other."

The mental pictures this conversation painted in my prudish mind were horrendous!

We were milking in the darkness about half way through the second week when a fire flared up over in the black's camp. Loud shrill voices were heard and a rifle shot rang out.

The Boss jumped up and ran towards the fire, shouting, "Arthur! Rip down to the house and bring my rifle and some bullets!"

I raced down to the house to find the rifle and several boxes of ammunition. My mind had already created a scene from the American Wild West.

Hurrying to the fire I found the spot deserted. I stood there not knowing what to do and holding the rifle close to my side.

A noise behind made me swing around. Jimmy's mate stood less than three feet away, his eyes bleary with drunkenness, his breath smelling like a vine vat, and carrying four wicked-looking spears upright in his hand.

"Jimmy kill 'em. Jimmy kill 'em," he muttered, his words drifting across the intervening space on a wave of anti-social atmosphere.

I stepped back in order to avoid his foul breath and, in doing so, disclosed the rifle.

Jimmy's mate lowered his spears to a horizontal position.

"God!" I thought, "Speared to death by a drunken native in the bush beyond Laverton!"

I swung a right hook from the waist and felt my fist land on his chin. It hurt! Jimmy's mate dropped to the ground. The Boss appeared and kicked the spears out of reach.

"What the blazes are you doing?"

"He was going to spear me so I dropped him."

The Boss gave me a long hard look. Jimmy's mate came around and staggered to his feet. The Boss grabbed him by the shoulder and pointed to the curb.

"Git!" he commanded. "That way and don't come back. No more back here! Understand?"

He didn't receive an answer but Jimmy's mate disappeared into the darkness.

"C'mon," he said to me. "Let's get on with the milking."

We tramped back to the milking shed surrounded by a silence which wasn't broken until several cows had been milked.

"I knew there would be trouble once that bloody gin turned up."

"Well, what happened?"

"Like I said, the buck's got full on plonk and the gin sooled them on to fight over her. Jimmy grabbed the rifle, his mate grabbed the spears and they took off into the scrub. The trigger got caught in Jimmy's pants and the rifle went off. He's been a police boy and he knows he shouldn't drink grog or have a rifle so he smashed it over a rock and gave it to me. I threw it down an old mine shaft and sent him on his way."

"Do you think his mate was really going to spear me?"

"Nah; of course not. But I wish I could have seen that punch you threw at him."

"It was a good 'un, Boss."

We were having a mug of tea after I had returned from the round.

"Had some more fun while you were out," he said. "That bloody gin came back to the camp. She stood there calling out and trying to get them to fight again. She was standing against one of the tanks so I put a shot through it just above her head. She took off into the bush like a bolting Brumby. We won't see her again."

We finished our mugs of tea and I stood up to go over to my humpy for a sleep.

"Er, by the way, there's no need to mention this to the missus, is there?"

"Nah; she'll be right, Boss."

I felt I was growing up.

Mr Hilliard had a sun-shrivelled, muscle-and-sinew-type mate who can only be described as "Tough!" He appeared from somewhere out of the goldfields vastness about a fortnight after the wife and children had returned from Kalgoorlie. He stayed a week, during which time he and The Boss consumed considerable quantities of alcoholic and spirituous liquors as well as chopped the tourer about and converted it into a utility.

The mate moved on again.

A few days later, as I drove the horse and cart into the dairy yard, I was surprised to see The Boss loading the family possessions on to the newly-created utility.

"I'll give you a hand with the milking this arvo," he said by way of explanation, "then, when it gets dark, after tea, me and the family are shooting through. We're going back to Kal. I reckon I can get a job on one of the mines down there. In the morning, when you get to Mr Harris's place, you can tell him I've gone but you don't know where I've gone. All right?"

Around 8 o'clock that night, when the cool of darkness had settled itself upon the immensity of the land, they climbed into the old vehicle and set off along the red dust track towards Laverton and beyond Morgans, beyond Leonora, beyond Malcolm, beyond Menzies, beyond Broad Arrow to Kalgoorlie where, "I reckon I can get a job on one of the mines down there."

Mr Harris met me at the door next day.

"And I suppose you're going to tell me that your Boss did a moonlight flit to Kalgoorlie last night?"

Struth! How the hell did he know?

We arranged for me to run the dairy until he could get one of his sons in from an out camp.

A long, hard fortnight followed then my services were no longer required.

However, I was fortunate enough to get a job as the dishwasher at The Lancefield Mine Mess House in Beria. The mess hut was a big, galvanised iron shed with the kitchen attached, and the building had the reputation of being ten degrees hotter in the summer and ten degrees colder in the winter than the ambient temperatures. The men's quarters were Hessian walled, tin roofed shacks holding two men each and they stretched out behind the mess hut in a manner reminding me of a goods train crawling across the countryside on unseen rails.

I had my own Hessian-walled, tin-roofed room with a cement floor, a bed, and a dressing table with two drawers and a mirror. The wages were two pounds ten shillings a week plus keep and I reckoned I had never had it so good.

My job was to get out of bed at 5am, light the kitchen stoves, chop sufficient wood for the day's cooking, peel a bag of spuds, wash all the pots, pans and crockery used in each meal and keep the copper boiling for the washing up water.

The female staff were all older than I so I was polite to them in the way my Mum had taught me to behave towards ladies. Consequently, I was fed good meals, clean sheets and pillow-slips were regularly placed on my bed and my scant washing and ironing were looked after.

Meanwhile Dad had lost his job at the hospital.

Apparently there was a bit of a confrontation with The Matron and the doctor was obliged to allow Dad to withdraw his services.

A new mine was opening in the district. The manager's house was complete but his wife and family were still in Perth. Dad was employed as a houseman-cum-gardener to the manager.

Sunday, as usual, was my day off after I had washed the breakfast things. Dressed as presentable as my meagre wardrobe permitted, wearing boots and a wide-brimmed hat, I would set off across country to visit Dad. This was not such a bright idea as it was waterless, scrub country and, by 10am, the sun became quite hot and several of the mine workers had expressed concern to me but 'Dad's mine' had a tall chimney clearly visible whenever I topped a rise so there was no need to worry.

I was seventeen! Nothing can go wrong when you're seventeen!

But my Dad was beginning to puzzle me. I began to ask myself why was he working as a house servant when he had once had his own business and employed men and what was he doing so far away from my Mum and sisters. He seemed to be frailer than I remembered him as a kid; his face was pallid yet his cheeks looked rosy and healthy although he had developed a bit of a cough.

I had been visiting him for about six weeks at this new mine when 'Tuggy' White, the mess hut manageress, informed me she had received a message from the local grocer, who had a telephone, that my Dad was back at Laverton Hospital but this time he was in one of the hospital beds.

I borrowed a pushbike and rode in to see him. He was sitting up looking bright and cheerful when I arrived covered in dust and sweat.

"What are you in here for, Dad?"

"I was feeling a bit off colour so my boss sent me in. The doc has put me in a bed for a while until he checks on this cough. I should be out of here by next week-end."

He was still there when I called a week later.

"Er – the doctor wants me to go down to Perth with a letter to The Repatriation Department. I think I shall have to take his advice and I'll be leaving next week. You'll be all right on your own for a while?"

"Sure, Dad. I'll be all right."

Dad returned to Perth and he never really worked again

Life seemed a bit flat after Dad left and I, more or less, became a dedicated dish-washing, spud-peeling, fire-lighter.

A new waitress arrived and captured my heart. Nothing physical, just pure adoration. I doubt if she ever regarded me as anything but "Arthur".

A mine engineer returned from his annual holiday bringing with him a new portable gramophone and a stack of records. Mr O'Hare will never know the emotional hunger he satisfied when, on some nights, he would bring the gramophone and records to the empty dining hut where the staff gathered to hear Jan Peerce sing "Blue Bird of Happiness", Jan Salzki sing "My World Is Gold", Richard Tauber sing "Silver Hair And Heart Of Gold", Joseph Schmidt sing "Tiritomba" – and Strauss Waltzes! Oh, how they lifted me up inside!

Mr Headley delivered loads of spindly wood on the most

dilapidated truck I have ever seen. It was nothing but four wheels, an engine, a steering wheel, a seat and a flat tray. The mine's earlier fuel demands had skinned the surrounding country of any worthwhile firewood and garnishing a truck load of wood in that flat, hot, scrub country required considerable effort and determination, and, when he did find a presentable stand, he acted as cunning as an old fossicker who stumbled on a fortune.

His truck chugged its way to the woodheap near the kitchen door. I jumped on to lend a hand once and was promptly told to "Piss off! You're in the flamin' road." The load was chucked off, the motor coaxed into noisy life and the truck made its dusty way along one of the many dirt tracks leading nowhere to eventually disappear in that direction leaving a big red cloud of dust in its wake.

Mum wrote to me regularly. She had moved into a house in Broome Street, Highgate, and was taking in boarders. Dad had been sent to Edward Millen Hospital where he was receiving treatment. The hospital was in Albany Highway on the outskirts of Victoria Park where she tried to visit him daily but by the time she caught a tram into town, caught another out to Victoria Park terminus, spent an hour or so with Dad and returned home, there wasn't much time left of the day.

I endeavoured to get a job on The Lancefield Mine. The manager, Mr Fox, thought it over for a week before regretfully advising me that he couldn't see any place for a junior worker and there wasn't any opening for an apprentice even if I could qualify for it.

I don't think I was becoming depressed but I suspect I was beginning to feel isolated within my youth. The human environment, without teen-agers, was all mature masculinity. The men living at the Mess Hut were considerate in their attitude towards me but if I played football or cricket I found them too powerful or boisterous whilst their drinking sessions, to which I was welcome, were far beyond my capabilities or inclination.

Perchance this sense of loneliness crept into my writings because I received a letter suggesting I return to Perth.

"- and I don't think it is necessary for you to stay up there and Mr Candlish, one of our boarders, will see if he can get you a job where he is working. So why not come home?"

A week later I was on the train heading for Kalgoorlie.

My companion in the 'dog box' was going to Perth on his annual holiday. He was an underground shift boss who came from "it auld country" and his conversational ability was nil. He closed all the windows to "keep oot it draught" and, for the rest of that long, miserable day, he smoked a large, foul-smelling pipe and gradually filled the compartment with smoke from the strongest, vilest tobacco money could buy.

I was soon crouched over the pedestal in the toilet, looking through the hole in the bottom, watching the ballast go noisily past and being violently ill.

I crept back into the compartment, stretched out on the seat and, in between vomiting bouts, slept all the way to Kalgoorlie.

As I stepped out of that chamber of horrors, and into the clean air, the long silence was broken.

"Eh, laddie, 'tis no wonder thou art sick. Thou sleepest too much."

I strolled around the town for a couple of hours and, after a feed of steak and eggs, returned to the station where I booked a second-class sleeper for the remainder of the journey. There were three other men in the compartment but fortunately I had a top bunk and was soon fast asleep – again.

The train was approaching Northam when I awoke. I managed to dress in time to participate in that crazy scramble for a pie and coffee in the refreshment room but, this time, I took a couple of pies back to the train.

The porter, meanwhile, had stripped the beds and dropped the top bunks to transform them into seats. I sat by the window eating pies and marvelling at the massive green-covered hills, the luscious green grass, the tall green trees – green – green – everything was green.

Oh! How beautiful it was!

A few hours later I was one of the people stepping out of The Kalgoorlie Express on to Perth Railway Station to be greeted by my kid sister who just smiled through her horn-rimmed glasses and held my hand while Mum kissed me, hugged me and kept saying how big I had grown.

"Gee, Mum. I've only been away six months."

Chapter Seven

The house in Broome Street wasn't very big. My two sisters slept in one room, mum slept in the other, Mr Candlish and I slept in a sleep-out on the back verandah.

My young sister, Pat, was a quiet girl who seemed to be sitting around wherever I happened to be during the day. She was still going to school and, to me, she was just my kid sister. I'm afraid I never really appreciated the depth of her affection.

Mum clucked around me like an old hen that had just found a lost chick

Dad was undergoing treatment for his 'chest problems'. The hospital was an establishment exclusively for treating old soldiers who had the same complaint as Dad and it was rather full. They were cheerful patients with friendly natures reaching out towards me whenever I called.

A vacant bed, during weeks of visiting, would prompt an enquiry as to the man's whereabouts only to be told, "He's gone."

This information temporarily saddened me but it was happening to other people and it wouldn't happen to Dad whose health improved during periods of treatment. He came home all fired up looking for a light job until the relentless passage of time forced him back into hospital again; and I was a youth engaged in pursuits extending beyond puberty into masculinity and never comprehended the seriousness of the situation.

I'm afraid I was never the companion he needed and his ill-health prevented him from being the father he wanted to be.

My brother, Syd, according to his letters, had nearly saved his fare and would be coming to Perth before very long.

Ralph Candlish was a stocky, muscular Scot without an ounce of fat on him. He was a boilermaker employed as a Leading Hand by The Structural Engineering Co. (W.A.) Pty. Ltd; a structural steel firm currently adding extensions to the rear of East Perth Power House.

One Friday evening during mealtime, Ralph asked, "Do you know anything about rivet heating?"

Of course, I didn't.

"It's quite simple," he explained. "You keep turning the handle working the blower on the hand-forge. The draft makes the coke red-hot and the rivets are in there. When the man on the gun wants a rivet you lift one out with the tongs and chuck it to him."

"So?"

"So you get down to the job at a quarter to eight Monday morning and ask for Mr Scott. He's the foreman. Tell him I sent you and if he asks about rivet heating tell him you've had some experience with oil-heaters on the goldfields."

I couldn't imagine how I could possibly get away with this explanation.

It was one of Ralph's idiosyncrasies to always arrive at work 10 minutes late to exemplify his status as a Leading Hand as well as to demonstrate his independence at a time when structural steelwork was in the doldrums.

Mr Scott's office was a tin shed erected on one side of the site yard. Half of one wall swung outwards where it was held in place with a stick. A workbench, made of packing-case timber, was nailed to the uprights near the 'window', a stool, made of the same material, completed the office furniture.

A mass of blue-prints, rolled or flat, was stacked high all over the workbench whilst the sand floor was covered with bags of nuts, bolts, rivets, spare air-hoses and other equipment peculiar to construction sites.

I put my head inside the door and politely asked for Mr Scott. He promptly told me to wait outside until he was ready to come out.

The men, who had been standing around prior to commencing the day's work, drifted off towards the structure and were absorbed into the steelwork.

Mr Scott came out of the shed.

"You done some rivet-heating?"

"Yes; a little."

"Well, we'll see how you shape up."

He set off towards the steelwork with me trotting at his heels like a bewildered pup that had just attached itself to a new owner. I followed him down some rough-cast steps and across the basement of the structure to where two men were laying out some air-hose.

"Hey, Jeff!" he shouted above the noise, "Here's your rivet-heater. See how he goes."

He commenced to walk away, paused for a moment, and came back.

"It's his first day!" he bellowed at Jeff, letting his true character break through the rough exterior, "So look after him!"

Jeff watched Harry Scott walk away then grinned at me.

"Sure, I'll look after him. You a mate of Ralph's?"

"He boards at our place."

"Good bloke, Ralph."

It became obvious over the next few months that Ralph was 'a good bloke'. Men on the job, and outside acquaintances, spoke to him and about him with respect. Not only was he a very capable tradesman who had served his time in the shipyards of Glasgow but he was also a courteous, considerate person who would go out of his way to do a man a good turn.

He wasn't perfect. There was a story going around about a fight at

The Big Bell Gold Mine at Cue; The local police sergeant, when it was over, suggested that Ralph get the next train out of town. I don't know what it was about and I had enough sense not to ask.

Meanwhile Jeff, after classifying me as a 'no hoper', had managed to train me to the stage where I could light a fire in the hand-forge, heat a few rivets and, most importantly, boil the billy; an activity carried out under the threat of instant dismissal if discovered.

I was gradually getting the hang of the job and becoming accepted by the workmen; that is, accepted within the limits of how much a 'boy' was accepted by mature men in those days. You were a 'boy' and had to be kept in your place. This was achieved by deriding your accomplishments, belittling your efforts, ridiculing your innocence or by verbal outbursts of aggression well knowing a 'boy' couldn't defy a man without losing his job.

Jeff, Gus and I worked as a riveting crew on this job for the next eighteen months during which time we riveted together a steel smoke-stack standing on top of the steelwork and rising another hundred feet above the structure.

This smoke-stack stood as a Perth landmark until it was eventually dismantled, along with the rest of the powerhouse, over sixty years later.

The next four years were spent as a Junior Worker with The Structural Engineering Company and, when not employed at the Welshpool Fabricating Shop, I was the storeman and time-keeper on various outside construction jobs.

Mum had moved to a bigger and better house and taken in another couple of boarders and our family was beginning to lift up its head. We weren't prosperous but we were no longer broke.

My brother, Syd, had arrived in Perth and was promptly employed by Musgroves Ltd. and given the job of manager for the Kalgoorlie branch. They gave him a little Standard 8 horsepower van, filled it with radios and record players, showed him on a map where Kalgoorlie was situated and told him to get on his way. He tipped the van over in the long, sandy stretch of the highway on the other side of Merredin and was back in Perth within a few days.

No; he wasn't sacked. These things happen.

This was a growing period in my life – not only physically but emotionally.

I desperately needed a job and this one had been handed to me on a platter. I took it because a person grabbed any job he could in those days and whatever future was in that job became his future. Oft times the job he grabbed as a boy became the path he trod for the rest of his life.

Although I was physically capable of meeting the demands of the job I was too innocent, too sensitive and too emotionally fragile for the type of human environment into which I was now thrown. The coarseness of the language, the cynical envy of another's ability and the smug satisfaction over his minor errors were facets of life entirely new to me and I was acutely conscious of it all.

Fortunately, during that four years, I lost most of my youthful snobbishness; I began to understand and appreciate men as individuals but, at this stage, I was only a boy who had some painful 'growing up' to do.

I came home from football one Saturday afternoon to find a freckle-faced, ginger-haired newcomer in the kitchen. Mum and Aunty May had spent an hour in the local pub and found this young fellow in a corner of the bar. He was a teen-aged stockman from some cattle station up north spending his annual holiday in Perth where he didn't know anybody his own age so he was having a quiet drink on his own.

"Well," says Mum, "you had better come home and meet my family. They'll look after you."

His name was Ivan Francis and he became my mate for the next fifty years. Ivan was eventually nicknamed 'Kay' after the Hollywood film actress, a name that stuck till the end of his days.

My sister Joyce was also maturing and developing into an attractive sort of female. She dressed well, made her own dresses and carried herself with dignity. She had a terrific sense of humour and we enjoyed each other's company.

Saturday afternoons were periods of teenage, feminine activity as her latest long evening dress was ironed, one of her numerous pairs of high-heeled shoes was polished and her hair set. Amidst all this routine my suit was pressed, a shirt ironed and instructions given to make sure I cleaned my shoes and chopped enough wood for the chip bath-heater. The ironing was done on a large table in a big kitchen while Mum cooked the Saturday roast. I'd carry in my Brunswick portable gramophone, set it on a box in a corner and play records of Bing Crosby, Deanna Durbin or Bobby Breen as we chatted away about the happenings of the week.

7 o'clock would find us dressed in our best and scurrying, arm in arm, along First Avenue to catch the tram in Beaufort Street. Another scurry along St. Georges Terrace to Anzac House where we danced Old Time Dancing until midnight.

Another rush to catch the last tram home or, if we missed it, a gang of us would walk home or wait until 12:45am when the Rattler came past.

We were young and Perth was a homely town to live in.

Chapter Eight

Mum took in two more boarders who were brothers. The eldest was of mature age and, obviously the guiding influence upon his brother Garry.

Garry, studying to become an architect, was employed as a draftsman by a firm in town. His nature was quieter and more studious than ours and, although he boarded with us for more than twelve months, he seldom joined in our activities until he finished his apprenticeship.

His elder brother was transferred to Canberra and soon after this Garry applied for a job in Melbourne. He moved east promising to correspond with our family, mainly through Joyce, on a regular basis.

This arrangement was maintained over a prolonged period until Joyce, now a mature teen-age woman, stated she wanted to go to Melbourne to be with Garry.

She went with the family's blessing.

My oath, I missed her.

*****

Mum and Dad, being Londoners, had raised their children to believe England was the head of a mighty empire and anything 'not British' was inferior. Always there were photos of St Paul's Cathedral, The Marble Arch, Westminster Abbey and Buckingham Palace hanging on the lounge-room walls. They were there from as far back as I can remember; certainly before I commenced school.

A pile of yellow-covered copies of *The Daily Mirror*. (Overseas

Edition)' as well as numerous editions of *The Illustrated London Gazette* were on bookshelves beneath the photos. They were avidly read, time and time again, by us children. *The Daily Mirror* kept us informed of the most gruesome murders and we gazed with awe at photos of King George the Fifth and Queen Mary attending the flower show at The Crystal Palace in The London Illustrated Gazette.

Thus we kept in touch with our Motherland England, Head of The British Empire, shown in red on an insurance company's calendar hanging on just about every kitchen throughout the land.

Our education system, too, was 'England and The Empire' orientated. The birthday of Her Late Most Gracious Majesty Queen Victoria was called Empire Day. The British Empire was a great empire because our sailors ruled the seas and our soldiers had gone out and conquered these countries (shown in red) and set them free. England and The Empire had shown we loved freedom when we crushed the wicked Kaiser in the 1914-18 War called 'The Great War' and, because of this victory, there would be no more wars and Australia had shown we were a nation on England's side whenever she needed us.

All this before I was ten years old!

The influence of this segment of my education was still with me when the newspapers announced the formation of The 16th Battalion (Cameron Highlanders of Western Australia).

What could be more British than a Highland Regiment?

When recruits were being enlisted I was at Francis Street Barracks on the first night. My military knowledge was somewhat limited. I simply knew if I joined 'They' would tell me what to do.

The medical examination proved rather embarrassing as I was required to pee into a milk bottle and discreetly cough while the same doctor held my testicles. I was then told to follow the man ahead of me; a routine gradually developing into a tour of the adjoining tin sheds. We came out of the first shed carrying a fatigue uniform and a pair of boots. I had trouble getting a pair of size six boots. We came out of the next hut carrying an oily, grease-covered Lee Enfield 303

Rifle with instructions to proceed into the third hut and clean the rifle before leaving the premises.

I squatted on a bare floor amidst a group of chaps and commenced rifle-cleaning; a routine with which I was to remain familiar for the next eleven years.

A softly-spoken chap nearby asked, "What section did you join?"

"Eh?"

"What section did you tell them you wanted to be in?"

"I told them I wanted to be in The Cameron Highlanders. They'll tell me what section to be in."

"They'll put you in a rifle company."

"So?"

"They're just getting organised. You can join any section. Why don't you get into Headquarters Wing? Get into The Intelligence Section, The Mortars, The Signals, The Transport – anything but a rifle company. Can you ride a horse?"

"Sure. I worked on a farm for ten months."

"Then join The Transport Section. I did. They have horses in transport. They ride everywhere. It's better than marching."

I got up, went back to the Orderly Room and told the agitated Adjutant I wanted to join The Transport Section because I could ride a horse.

Returning to my rifle-cleaning I announced, "I got them to put me in The Transport Section."

"Good-oh," said this bloke as he prepared to leave. "Then I'll see you next Monday night."

"O.K. By the way, what's your name?"

"Benson," he said, "Geoff Benson."

Our friendship lasted right up until the time of his death some forty years later.

I came in contact with many magnificent men during the growing years between 18 and 21. Men like The Commanding Officer Major Louch, the 2 I/C Major Lloyd, and Captain Sandover, the officer commanding A Company – all of whom eventually became Brigadiers.

Sergeant Majors Dowling and Lowden of The Permanent Military Forces, whose task was to train us in squad drill and gunnery, were men of precision and bearing.

I greatly admired and respected all these men. I did my best to conduct myself according to their example and I know they had a tremendous uplifting influence on my personal development.

Some men have that influence on others; especially upon young, maturing men who are unconsciously seeking icons.

Monday nights were parade nights.

I hurried home on my pushbike after work, showered as quickly as possible, (I didn't have to shave) gulped down my meal and dressed for the evening parade. I virtually marched down the street to the tram. Not only was I a soldier of The Australian Forces like my Dad had been but I was also a member of a Highland Regiment which had a couple of hundred years of tradition behind it.

Burgeoning manhood has to have something to believe in or the man is living without purpose and, so far, my life had been without a sense of direction.

The Transport Section, in addition to a weekly night parade, had horse drill every fourth Sunday. Most of the men travelled by train to Guildford Station and walked the mile or so to South Guildford Remount Depot where we carried out horse training exercises through scrub country now occupied by Rosemount Golf Course.

There were several militia units in Perth but The Defence Department's finances could only support a limited number of horses and they were ridden every week-end by different riders from various units. They were 'Army' horses and knew the drill routine better than we did.

Invariably my mount for the day was a massive, shrewd gelding standing fifteen hands high. My eyes were roughly twelve inches lower than his backbone when standing beside him and he was so broad across the back that my hip joints ached when sitting in the saddle.

You don't just get on your horse in the army. There is a drill for it. The horses are stood with fore hooves in a straight line – riders toes in line with the hooves – right arm extended holding the rein close to the bit to ensure the horse kept its head up–

"Prepare to mount!"

The rider turns right about – holds a shortened rein in the left hand and grasps the pommel – he also grasps the rear of the saddle with his right hand – places his left foot in the stirrup – and awaits the order to mount.

This was a pain-wracked position for me. I could barely reach the pommel and the rear of the saddle at the same time, the stirrup was so high from the ground that my foot was in line with my chest whilst my knee was in the vicinity of ear-hole and my foot kept tickling the horse's flank – much to his annoyance.

"Mount!"

The rider throws his right leg over the saddle, automatically finding the stirrup, lowers himself gently into the saddle, drops his right arm to his side at the same time holding the tightened rein in his left hand at waist height.

Nine times out of ten my right foot wouldn't make the distance and thud into the horse's flank causing it to snort, arch its back, and shy away to the off side and give the horse beside it a solid bump. The bump was transmitted all the way along the line causing chaos and consternation within the ranks.

The problem was solved by putting me on the extreme right end of the line allowing my horse and I to fight out this business of mounting in the wide, open spaces beyond.

We had, on another parade, some fifteen horses standing in line with me in the centre. I had successfully mounted this monster which promptly snorted, pig-rooted out to the front of the line, pelted me off, walked around to the rear, took up its position back in the line and stood there looking at me sitting in the dirt.

This beautiful animal and I must have provided quite a bit of comic relief in our battle of wills and it wasn't until our annual camp on Rottnest Island that we become better acquainted and settled down to a period of tolerant co-existence.

Rottnest Island could best be described as 'a barren island off the mainland' but that was where the battalion assembled for its annual camp in that magical year of 1938. The only buildings were at The Settlement around the foreshore of Thompsons Bay; there were no roads, the big naval guns had not yet been commissioned and their installation supplies were transported on a light-gauge railway running from a foreshore jetty into the distant sand hills.

The army had carried out considerable preparatory work prior to our arrival. Tents were on site but not erected; equipment and stores were already in sheds on the area now occupied by the aerodrome. The horses, harness, limbers and feed had come across by barge during the previous week.

The light-gauge railway ran around the edge of the low sand hills forming the perimeter of the campsite.

Our horse-lines were some distance away behind low sand hills hiding them from the sight of the camp; a situation we used to our advantage; besides, it was rumoured that horse manure, horses and horse drivers bred flies. We had 25 horses of varied quality and doubtful lineage which had to be cared for 24 hours a day and this, during the night, required a night patrol of two hours on and four hours off.

The drivers teamed up in pairs and were allocated two horses that became their prime responsibility for the duration of the camp although we, as a group, were responsible for the welfare of all the horses.

Benno and I promptly paired and, needless to say, the team we drew consisted of that great, big, four-legged, passive resistor to military good order and discipline accompanied by a mean, cranky mare with grandiose visions of one day winning The Melbourne Cup.

The horses, after a few days in camp, began to know who was in charge and the irksome horse picket was not without its moments of oneness with the environment and creatures other than human. Often, when awoken around 2am, I'd stroll across to where a dixie of coffee was hanging over a fire and, sitting on a bag of chaff, I drank slowly and listened to the sound of waves folding on to the beach on the edge of the bay, their sound magnified by the stillness of the night, whilst the stars shone brightly in a limitless sky stretching away into infinity. Several quokkas slowly hopped out of the surrounding scrub to sit in a semi-circle within the firelight. I held out a piece of biscuit to each. They demurely took it and the group of us sat munching around the fire.

Eventually I stirred myself, stepped through the ring of quokkas to stroll down the horse-lines checking the tethering ropes and generally ensuring there were no problems.

From the far end of the line, despite the hour of the night, there came a deep-throated chuckle from that mountain of a horse which knew I had oats in a mess tin. He snuffled his way through these then, having finished munching, he nudged me several times with his nose. I put my arms around his muscular neck, scratched him between the ears – and we knew each other.

Much of this sense of companionship vanished the next day as I shovelled heaps of manure into a limber and carted it away to bury in a valley among the sand hills.

A limber is one of those unique pieces of equipment peculiar unto the army. It is comprised of two springless, box-like, two-wheeled carts pulled in tandem. The front cart has a long wooden pole projecting forward; the horses were harnessed one on each side of this pole. The 'near side horse' was ridden with the other as a lead horse. The remaining human member of this combination usually sat on the tail-board of the rear unit to act as a brakeman when going downhill; a most precarious position as the brake crank-handle jutted out to the rear below the floorboards. The army, in its wisdom-laden text books, states that the brakeman marched behind the limber to apply the brake when necessary – but things didn't always work out that way.

Benno and I were attached to a Vickers Gun Platoon for manoeuvres on a pitch-black, moonless night. The platoon marched ahead on a compass bearing; Benno and I followed with the Vickers Gun boxes in the limber.

The platoon concertinaed to a halt and the officer came back to speak to Benno.

"This upward slope we are on is about a quarter of a mile long and goes to the crest of the hill you can just make out against the stars. If you can get the limber up there my men will follow and it will save us lugging the guns. Reckon you can do it?"

"Sure," says Benno in that unmilitary-like manner for which he eventually became noted. He was a much more daring and better horseman than me but I was appalled when he hit the rump of that mad lead-horse, dug the spurs into The Monster, loosed the bit and shouted, "Go!"

They went!

I grabbed the carrying-ropes of the gun boxes and hung on for dear life as we thundered past the scattering platoon and hurtled up the slope. The limber bounced, jarred and jolted over the saltbush. I hung on and hoped Benno could see where we were going because my vision was lost in the sand thrown up by the iron-shod wheels.

The top of the hill was a plateau about an acre in area. We arrived at a flat gallop and scribed a dust-raising circle around its perimeter before coming to a halt facing the way we had come. The dust eventually subsided to reveal two sweating, panting horses, one exultant driver and one very angry brakeman.

"You bastard! You bloody near killed me! What did you gallop them like that for?"

"Steep hill. Had to give them their head or we wouldn't have made it."

"What was the smart idea of swinging around in a circle?"

"Had to or we would have gone over the edge."

"What edge?"

"Didn't you see it? There's a precipice all around us. The only way out of here is the way we came up. I wouldn't like to be manning a machine gun up here."

I walked to the edge and looked down into nothing!

The platoon arrived. "Terrific," said the officer, "Splendid driving."

"It's all part of the service," said Benno.

The men hoisted the boxes out of the limber, lifted out the guns and assembled them in the dark with a speed that surprised me.

We had a small horse with us on this camp. It had a sore on its back near where the saddle numnah pad fitted so only a light person was permitted to ride it. I was that 'light person' and did a tour of duty as the colonel's despatch rider.

There was only one fly in the ointment.

The horse was noted for its capabilities on the polo field. It was flighty, could take off like a rocket, turn on threepence and stop from gallop to zero in no time flat.

A company had gone off on a route march accompanied by a limber team half an hour ago when The Colonel decided to send a message.

I tucked The Colonel's message in the top pocket of my tunic, swung into the saddle and trotted sedately out of the camp.

As we leisurely cantered along the lake's hard-packed sand perimeter I could pick out the company sitting under some trees in the distance. The horse spotted them, too, and straightway went into a flat gallop. It fairly flew around the lake edge taking me with it. There is no other way to describe my status as the horse headed for the centre of the semi-circle where the captain was addressing the troops.

The horse propped about ten feet away from him.

The horse stopped but I didn't!

I was thrown violently forward. I wrapped my arms around the animal's neck, my feet were tossed clear of the stirrups and I landed on the ground clinging to its mane to prevent my trembling legs from folding under me as I withdrew The Colonel's message from my tunic pocket.

"Message from The C.O. sir."

The Captain took the message whilst looking long and hard at me.

"Very impressive," he commented. "You were one of the drivers attached to the Vickers Gun crew last night?"

"Yes, sir."

"Well, try and remember these are military manoeuvres and not a rodeo. Next time show a bit more caution when approaching a body of men. You could injure someone."

"Yes, sir."

I trotted the horse back to camp where, upon re-entering the horse lines, I was reprimanded by the sergeant for riding the horse so hard it was in a lather of sweat.

"Right between the eyes," I thought. "That's how you kill a horse. A 303 bullet right between the eyes."

Of course I could never have shot a horse. I had shot rabbits on Mr Collins' farm but a horse is something different. A horse is an animal that whinnies when you walk down the lines at two o'clock in the night.

A military camp of this nature just has to have a full-dress Regimental Parade; an awe-inspiring event in any regiment but in a Highland Regiment it is spectacular!

Rows of white tents aligned to perfection, platoons 'falling in' to be inspected by the two terrorfiers from The Permanent Military Forces Sgt. Majors Dowling and White; the skirl of the bagpipes penetrating the shimmering air as Pipe Major Watson led The Regimental Band onto the parade ground; the splash of colourful kilt; the precise movement of white spats; the glint of polished emblems and the flash of sunlight on rifles as companies moved off to The Regimental Parade Ground.

It all created a scene to race the pulse of any eighteen year old lad.

Our horses were groomed until they shone; the harness and saddles polished and the limbers were hosed down. Even our uniforms were clean.

I was the driver of the day and Benno was my brakeman. Our team was to lead The Transport Section on to the parade ground and take up a position at the rear of the regiment.

If we hadn't of been the leading team it may not have happened!

Suddenly, without any warning, The Monster and The Mad Lead Horse bolted!

Riding a bolting team is a rather horrifying experience. You don't have a great deal of control until they start to tire, but to be in the saddle of a bolting horse with a snorting horse beside you, a long wooden pole banging away between them and threatening to amputate your leg with every stride, two limbers bouncing along behind you, your mate hanging on and yelling, "Ride 'em, cowboy!" and the whole combination bearing down on a regimental parade is the sort of thing to wake you up screaming for weeks afterwards.

The distance between us and the parade was rapidly diminishing so I headed for a laneway between two companies where there was plenty of room but the troops didn't appreciate the sight of this piece of animated destruction hurtling towards them; nor did they take kindly to the shower of sand as we shot past to disappear behind the buildings at the eastern end of the parade ground.

We passed under a clothesline between two sheds as I tried to swing them around to the right with the idea of getting away from the parade and into the sand hills where they must bog to standstill.

The problem was the light gauge railway line running along the foot of the sand hills. The horses cleared the line in their stride, the first limber bounced over it, the trailing limber bounced three feet – Benno soared gracefully into the air and landed on his head in the sand!

The horses stopped before an implacable wall of sand. I jumped off, tied the reins to a bush and raced back to Benno who was walking around with his pith helmet jammed below his eyes and squashing his nose.

"You all right?"

"I'm all right but I can't get this bloody helmet off my head."

I couldn't get it off, either.

Lieutenant Orgill arrived. He couldn't get it off.

Our Transport Sergeant arrived. He was a big man who had been in His Majesty's Household Cavalry. He grabbed the rim of the helmet and lifted Benno off the ground.

I was told to look after the horses while they led Benno away to The Medical Officer's tent.

The M.O. couldn't move it either but he was a knowledgeable man who had been to university so he borrowed a hacksaw from The Quartermaster and sawed the helmet in half thereby permitting Benno to view the world once again as well as straighten his nose.

The regimental camp, like all good things, came to an end.

The horse lines were dismantled, the battalion's tents were dropped and stacked, the miscellaneous military gear was piled in heaps for transport back to whatever mysterious army source they came from and the troops returned to the mainland, there to disperse and pursue their various callings – and Benno was docked the sum of two pounds twelve shillings and sixpence from his pay for the destruction of army property; namely – one only pith helmet.

Ah! If only, in the days of our youth, we had an inbuilt device to shout: "These are the good days! Treasure them now! Not later!" But we have no such device and, in those halcyon green years, none of us visualised that, before the next decade passed, many would die in the realistic game of soldiering upon which we now expended so much of our carefree, youthful vigour.

Chapter Nine

Jimmy Chandler owned a semi-rater boat named *Radiant*. Benno knew Jimmy from schooldays and, as our friendship grew beyond military activities, he involved me in sailing.

The boat was 18 feet long, made of marine-ply timber and carried a terrific amount of sail for a craft of its size. Our crew numbered from 8 to 10, depending on who turned up, and we were all under the age of twenty-one years which made us the youngest crew in the club. I can't say we were a dedicated crew nor were we serious contenders for 'line honours'. The majority of us worked until 12 noon on Saturday so we assembled as early as possible after lunch for the afternoon race.

The Radiant was kept in the Australian Natives Association's boat shed built over the water at the foot of Barrack Street and we usually arrived at The Narrows start line just in time to be greeted by megaphone-amplified annoyance from the starting official and the derisive comments from supporters on the spectator ferry.

We usually managed to muster a few supporters to follow the race. They mainly consisted of girl friends, girl friends of girl friends, young brothers of crew members or occasionally a parent; all of whom took great delight in relating to us the critical, and oft times caustic, comments concerning the way we handled the boat that came over the ferry's P.A. system.

The real pleasures of sailing were on Sundays. We assembled at the boatshed around 9am and, having rigged the boat, we loaded our girl friends and their picnic hampers into the craft and set sail down the river. Most of us had girl friends at this stage and the regularity with which they were invited for a Sunday's sailing was in direct proportion to the quality and quantity of the food in the accompanying picnic basket because, in those days, there weren't any Kentucky Fries, Pizza Huts, Chicken Inns or Hamburger Stalls. Domestic refrigerators were unknown so a girl had to cook the day before or get up early to cut fresh sandwiches.

The overloaded *Radiant* usually managed to move away from the boatshed around 10am to catch the morning land breeze and make its way to Point Walter. The tea rooms, where we purchased boiling water to make tea, was a vast, cavernous, wooden structure enmeshed in lattice-work overgrown with creeper. Bottled milk, lemonade, orange drinks or ginger beer could also be purchased there – and threepence back on the bottle, too!

The sea breeze had come in hours before we set sail back to Perth and often, as we approached Pelican Point, it would drop as twilight slowly changed to night and we practically drifted towards The Narrows now hidden in the surrounding darkness.

These were the good moments!

A boat crowded with teenagers becalmed on The Swan River as the distant city settled down to rest. Benno sitting on the floor, leaning against the mast, softly playing "When My Dreamboat Comes In", "Home On The Range", "The Beautiful Lady In Blue" on his mouth-organ and we sang while slowly gliding along in the darkness.

> Soft the sound of lapping wave,
> No bow wave, wake or foam,
> So tall the mast, so loose the sail
> While we were drifting home.

A few cars humming their way around Mounts Bay Road; a trolley bus winding its way around the foreshore to disappear behind the brewery and emerging again to pursue the tail lights of the disappearing cars; an occasional call from someone fishing at the water's edge to applaud or condemn our singing; lights blinking in the distance; The State War Memorial floodlit stark against Mt Eliza and the star-covered sky beyond.

Who could begrudge us these moments of serenity?

Out of that boat's crew Doug became a bomber pilot, Bernie joined The Police Force, Owen served in The Navy, Des was killed in Tobruk, one drowned in a river boat accident, Benno and I served in North Africa, Greece, Crete and Syria, Jimmy Chandler joined The Army; the *Radiant* was put on blocks in his backyard and, during the following years, the blocks slowly sank in the sand. White ants ate away the transom, as well as some planks, and the *Radiant* never sailed again.

The Australian Natives Association boatshed was burnt to the water in the 1960's.

*****

Transport to the fabricating shop at Welshpool was difficult. The tram terminus at East Victoria Park was a couple of miles from the place so the most common means of travel was by train to Welshpool Station followed by a walk to work. Cars were rare. The accountant in the front office owned a Vauxhall and the workshop timekeeper owned a Morris soft-top of doubtful vintage; they both brought a car-load of mates to work who chipped in five shillings a week to help cover running expenses.

The blacksmith owned an Austin 7 which we never clapped eyes on because, to quote his words:- "I don't want to wear my bloody car out coming to work. I'll never be able to buy another one."

This was understandable because Gus Levitzke's new Ford V8 Roadster cost him around four hundred and fifty pounds. Gus was an enthusiastic motorist and I have always felt pleased he owned that V8 because he later went down aboard *The H.M.A.S. Sydney*.

I purchased a pushbike costing two pounds ten shillings. I could ride it from Mt. Lawley to Welshpool within half an hour and often, on the way home, I'd pull out and pass the timekeeper's laden Morris as I bored down the hill past The Broken Hill Hotel. This worried him and, next day, I would receive the standard lecture on the dangers of getting caught in the tramlines and falling off in front of his car.

The Works Manager was massive in stature with a voice to match. He had learned his trade in the shipyards, or steelyards, of England and I don't doubt he was a well-qualified, capable tradesman who had come up through the ranks but he had the inbuilt attitude of 'status within the workforce' and a junior worker was at the bottom of the hierarchy.

Stanchions, from the moment work is commenced on them, are numbered to designate their location on the construction site. This number is of prime importance and never painted over. The standard colour was 'battleship grey'; a popular colour around the suburb of Queens Park where several houses were painted a similar hue.

I approached a staunchion's number with my paintbrush.

"You paint over that number and you'll bring coals of f……….. fire about your bloody head!" roared the voice from the massive frame which had appeared from nowhere. (Frighten and dominate him! He's only a boy.)

I straightened my aching back and smiled, "I won't paint over them, Mr Foster."

"It's no bloody laughing matter! Get on with it!" (Crush him completely.)

He was a hard man who knew most of the unskilled workers were afraid of him and he was aware this sense of fear grew from apprehension. The spectre of unemployment was always in the back of everyone's mind. Work was available when the firm won a contract; boilermakers, welders, labourers and unskilled workers were employed but when the job cut out they were dismissed with 24 hours notice. There weren't any apprentices because they were indented for five years. The firm employed 'Junior Workers' who could be fired along with the rest.

I seemed to be more fortunate than most because, when the firm contracted to build seven big oil storage tanks for The Commonwealth Oil Refineries at North Fremantle, I was sent there as timekeeper/storeman; an enjoyable task after all the tension within the fabricating workshop. Furthermore, the Site Foreman was a considerate character who treated me with respect and had considerable influence upon my personal development.

This job was followed by another twelve months at Welshpool where some changes had taken place. Mr Foster had passed away after a long fight with cancer and Ted Malland, the Site Foreman from the C.O.R. job, had been promoted to Works Manager.

Ted, in keeping with his new status, purchased the latest model Ford ten-horsepower Tourer. It had a canvas fold-down top, cut-away doors designed to fit the driver's arm and was painted a brilliant yellow.

Truly a beautiful machine!

The firm won the contract to supply and erect the steelwork for three aircraft hangars on an aerodrome the government was building at some place called 'Bullsbrook'.

Ted had driven to Bullsbrook on several occasions to check out the site and determine the availability of accommodation for the workforce.

A certain character named Mr Smiley was licensee of The Bullsbrook Hotel and his wife ran a boarding-house in an adjacent, timber-framed, asbestos-walled building. Ted had surveyed the place, decided who was sleeping where, ascertained the cost of weekly board, returned to Welshpool and told us, individually, what he had arranged and what the boarding-house charged – and that was that!

Nobody argued. If you didn't want to go to Bullsbrook you were out of work. Fortunately, a weekly bus service enabled workers to get to Perth on Friday nights and return on Sunday evenings.

Life at Smiley's Boarding House wasn't too bad. Mrs Smiley was a pleasant woman who cooked appetising meals and the quarters were up to the standard of most boarding houses. I shared a room with a chap who had been to university but this is where he was now.

Pearce R.A.A.F. Base hadn't been named; it was simply known as Bullsbrook Aerodrome and consisted of a few brick buildings such as the guardhouse at the main entrance, living quarters and administrative building.

Several prefabricated, transportable hangars housed our most modern aircraft – five Avro Anson Bombers and two Hawker Demon Fighters as well as a couple of trainer biplanes with rotary engines and fabric skins. They, too, were made by A.V. Roe.

There weren't any airstrips or runways. The landing field was one vast, grass-covered paddock.

We had a site office. I recognised the tin shed from East Perth Powerhouse. The 'furniture' was the same bench and stools made from old pine packing cases with plans and blueprints stacked in a heap on top of the bench; consequently, the whole heap was rummaged through whenever a specific print was required. Also, within this shed, were stacked bags of bolts and nuts, cases of electrodes, rope, pulley blocks, paint and all the other paraphernalia of a construction site.

I managed to keep a couple of feet of the bench top for my work. Besides timekeeping I had to do a weekly stock take of the shed's contents and account for all consumed electrodes, oxygen, acetylene, petrol etc. This was a nerve-wracking job, the tension being created by the Welshpool administration staff constantly querying figures in order to justify jobs in the hierarchy. It was of no concern of 'The Office' if, while I was out on the site, a welder wandered into the shed and picked up a packet of electrodes in order to get on with his job or a labourer dumped an empty oxy bottle among the full ones and walked off with one of the latter. Nor was it appreciated how petrol from the hand-pumped bowser evaporated in quantity between the bowser and the motor-driven welding plants on the site.

There was no lunchroom or washing facilities. Men sat around in the open to eat their lunches. I was also 'the billy boy' entrusted with the important task of boiling a 4 gallon kerosene tin full of water on an open fireplace made of rocks scrounged around the site; and many a time I had arguments with the management explaining why I had chopped up a dry, pine electrode case in order to boil water so the saturated workmen could have a hot drink while they stood crowded in the tin shed because rain had been pouring down for hours and they couldn't work in the quagmire surrounding the job.

Construction progressed for the first few months. Stanchions were erected and fabricated trusses were lifted and bolted on to them.

Then the weather worsened! Heavy rain fell ceaselessly for days, to develop into the wettest winter in living memory!

The whole aerodrome became a plain of soft, water-logged, clay-like mud. The only firm area was a strip running past the end of our partially-constructed hangar. Each day a Hawker Demon roared along this strip to climb and disappear into the dark clouds then reappear half an hour later to disappear into its hangar and not be seen again until the next day. I understand it carried instruments to assist in weather forecasting but I could have supplied The Royal Australian Air Force with that information by looking through the shed doorway.

Such was the condition of our front line air base when war was declared on 3rd September, 1939.

It was an interesting day. We were standing huddled in the tin shed listening to the rain pelting on to the roof when a Vickers 'Walrus' Amphibian thundered down out of the low clouds and landed with a splash of mud before disappearing into one of the prefabricated hangars.

My word! This war was hotting up!

Rain continued for weeks, the job was closed down and I was unemployed. There wasn't sufficient work at Welshpool to employ me and, worse still, I reached the age of 21 years on the 8th September, 1939, and I was now entitled to an adult's pay.

Consequently, I was beginning to cost too much to employ.

My 21st Birthday Party was held in the Mt Lawley R.S.L. Hall in

Grosvenor Road. We lived in a small upstairs flat in this building where Dad was employed as the caretaker. All my relatives, friends from The Cameron Highlanders and the yacht crew gathered to make it a memorable event that lasted until midnight when everyone had to catch trams to get home.

21 eh? Gee! I now had the right to go into a pub and order a beer. I also had the right to vote and I tended to regard both these privileges in that order of priority.

Now that war had been declared, numerous strategic points around Perth had to be guarded 24 hours a day against fifth columnists and enemy parachutists.

Our Commonwealth of Australia had no permanent army of the size necessary to carry out this commitment so, obviously, the vital task of guarding the nation's security would have to be carried out by The Militia; not all The Militia, just those members available.

The 16th Battalion's Transport Section Officer (Lieut. George Orgill) sorted out some of the nation's defence problems at the next drill night by ascertaining who was unemployed and looking for a few extra shillings. "It won't be permanent guard duties but only for a fortnight, then we'll give the other blokes a bit of a go. When their fortnight is up we'll see if we can fit you in again."

This was fair enough. After all, we were all in the same boat and it seemed only right to share the war with your mates.

Our battalion was given the responsibility of guarding Swan Barracks in Francis Street where I duly reported for duty to find several 'other ranks' and a sergeant already billeted in one of the tin sheds. A few of us had never done any formal guard duty, being horsemen, so a few hours were spent instructing us how to change guard 'at the post' before introducing us to the monotony of 2 hours 'on' and 4 hours 'off' which went on 24 hours a day for a whole fortnight!

Our drill routine improved rapidly, spurred on by a desire to impress the civilian population with our efficiency and make it aware there was a war on and we were ready! We did our best, during the day, as we marched up and down the tin fence in Beaufort Street. We probably did look impressive, too, dressed in full highland uniform with a rifle and fixed bayonet. We had no ammunition because, in this situation, it could become dangerous. Besides, someone might take it off us.

I am not an aggressive person and I still wonder what I would have done if I had been attacked by a couple, or even one, belligerent drunk in the early hours of the morning. I reckon Swan Barracks would have been occupied without a great deal of resistance.

Saturday nights were hardest to accept.

The Unity Theatre was a dance hall popular with the more mature citizens and commonly known as "The Homewreckers". It was diagonally opposite our beat and we came in for a good bit of ribald humour when the place emptied and the patrons dispersed at midnight.

Glamour died at midnight.

So did Perth. Trams, trains and buses stopped. All dance halls closed. Traffic ceased. Few people owned a car and everyone, it seemed, went home. The Police Department's Bentley commenced prowling around the streets; a few late revellers who had missed the last tram would pass by with a "Good Night" greeting – then all was quiet until around 6am next morning.

The fortnight passed without any concerted enemy attacks on Swan Barracks and I was 'stood down' to give someone else a chance to earn a bit of pocket money.

Life was beginning to look up. I had three pounds ten shillings in my pocket and, after I paid Mum two pounds, I was rather well off!

The next strategic point requiring my protective influence was Maylands Aerodrome, away out of town, at the end of Peninsular Road. It was a bleak place with no passing traffic to break the monotony of the routine and nowhere to go during the 4 hours 'off'. Just a few hangars with "Australian National Airways" painted over the doorway of one and "McRobertson Miller Airways" painted over the other. A couple of smaller hangars, where The Royal Aero Club housed its Gypsy Moths, completed W.A.'s air terminal.

Army Headquarters (wherever that was) decided we weren't taking our duties seriously enough. We needed discipline and toughening up. Daily periods of physical training and half an hour's squad drill were recommended.

H.Q. also issued a Password to enable us to distinguish 'Friend' from 'Foe' at night.

"Friend or foe" out there in the bush beyond Maylands?

The decision to instil discipline and to make us more aware of our responsibilities was, no doubt, justified, but putting it into practice was another matter. Our meals were cooked in some obscure, central army cookhouse, put in large dixies, placed in a newly-invented container called a 'hot box' then transported to the aerodrome in a utility. A lieutenant accompanied the driver and the meal usually arrived in the dark.

I was on guard one evening and, having had a morale-boosting lecture during the course of the day, decided to put the routine into practice.

The utility's headlights cut a swathe through the darkness as the vehicle made its way along the five-strand wire fence leading to a horizontally-swinging pole titled "The Gate".

The vehicle's two lights were full on and dazzling me as two doors slammed when the officer and the driver alighted and commenced unloading.

"Halt! Who goes there?" I challenged, coming to the 'on guard' position.

"Eh?"

"Put those lights out!"

"Bloody hell!" A door opened. The lights went out. A door slammed.

"Are you friend or foe?"

"Friend," answered the officer, entering into the spirit of things.

If he had been a 'foe' he could have shot me quite some time ago or, if he had answered 'foe' I suppose I would have been obliged to shoot him. Fortunately, a military crisis was averted by The Sergeant of The Guard coming out of the shed to give them a hand to unload.

The driver, as he passed me before leaving, commented, "Don't be so bloody funny tomorrow night if you want any dinner."

The war, it seemed, was becoming serious and somewhat confusing.

The tour of duty cut out at the end of the fortnight and I was unemployed again.

*****

It was a depressing period in my life. I was 21 years old and had no trade, I was not contributing to the family income, Joyce was in Melbourne, Syd had arrived in Perth some eighteen months ago and was now managing Musgroves store in Kalgoorlie, Patricia was still going to school, Ralph had married and Mum had decided against any more boarders in order to devote more time caring for Dad.

That's why we were living in a small upstairs flat in The R.S.L. Hall and I suspect the sub branch gave Dad the job as caretaker in order to give us somewhere to live.

Dad wasn't very well. He coughed all through the night and spent weeks at a time in The Edward Millen Home For Repatriated Soldiers; and I was so damned dumb I didn't realise he was dieing even though all the indications were there right under my nose.

Perchance I knew it but didn't want to admit it to myself. Death was unknown to our family.

I still think of my Dad and wonder if this son was ever a source of pride and comfort to him.

I shall never know.

*****

The headlines of *The West Australian* newspaper proclaimed:-
A.I.F. CALL.

The Commonwealth Of Australia was calling for volunteers for The 6th Australian Division of The Australian Imperial Forces.

There is something about a war that fascinates men!

Otherwise, why would twenty thousand Australians go tearing off to the recruiting offices?

We all had our reasons and I doubt if any two men had the same reasons. Patriotism, inherited from our ancestors and boosted by our education system, may have had some part of it and my reasons were as varied as the rest.

I had uncles, aunts and cousins in England whom I had known about all my life and here was a chance to meet them. The first A.I.F. had gone to England and with luck we might get there, too.

My Dad and all his mates had been soldiers and I wanted to carry on their traditions and reputation as well as make them proud of me. Those dirty Germans had started another war and if they wanted a fight us Australians were just the blokes to give it to them.

But predominate of all my reasons was the simple fact: "The Motherland was in trouble and needed help".

I was at the drill hall in Nicholson Road, Subiaco, on the first day, enlisted in The 2/11th Battalion (City of Perth Regiment) and given the Regimental No. WX1042. My mate Benno was there too, and received the Regimental No.265.

Enlisting in The A.I.F. wasn't very difficult. In fact, it was a bit of a fun thing. The drill hall had partitions erected complete with signs directing recruits to follow along a passage like sheep in a race. I can't remember the sequence of events but clear in my memory is the act of urinating into an ink bottle and trying to stop urinating when the bottle was full.

Several 'Old Soldiers' were assisting in the recruiting procedure and one such character was endeavouring to put an early stop to my military career by objecting to my height.

"You've got to be five feet four inches. You're only five feet three and a half inches."

"Aw; come off it!"

"Nah; that's the rules. I can't 'elp you!"

Fortunately, at this stage, Captain Sandover, complete in Highland Uniform and accompanied by Captain Jackson of The 11/44th Battalion, breezed into the drill hall.

"Hullo, Leggett!" calls Capt. Sandover in his delightfully English accent. "Joining up?"

"I'm having trouble with his height," says the Old Soldier.

"I know," replied The Captain. "He's exactly five feet four inches. We measured him for The Cameron Highlanders years ago, you know. Put him through, old chap."

This, of course, was bullshit. Capt. Sandover was in a different company and I was surprised he even knew my name. Thus did he flamboyantly seal my fate for the next six years.

The word got around that Major Louch, the C.O. of The Cameron Highlanders, had been promoted to the rank of Lieut. Colonel and appointed C.O. of the yet unformed 2/11th Battalion. This greatly influenced men of The 16th Battalion and a considerable number joined The A.I.F. to be in 'his battalion'. These men already had three years militia training and quite a few of them were given NCO rank. Many others who came from similar militia units were treated in a like manner. This was necessary in order to get a chain of command in the formation of the new battalion. Nevertheless, these appointments did create a certain amount of umbrage, particularly among new recruits who had had no previous military experience and who tended to regard such appointments as favouritism. This attitude was gradually eliminated over the next few months as men with leadership qualities began to emerge, particularly among the group from the goldfields who joined the battalion a few days after we moved into Northam Camp.

These men were different. They were physically tough, they swore fluently, they drank a lot of beer and if they couldn't fight someone else they would fight each other. It was quite some time before they began to conform to 'military good order and discipline' and I, in my youthful ignorance, regarded them as people with whom I didn't wish to mingle; little realising that their sense of mateship was as big and as rugged as the goldfields themselves.

I received a letter soon after my medical examination instructing me to report to Perth Railway Station at a certain time on a definite date for transport to Northam Military Camp. Several hundred men gathered on the station platform that day. Some were straight out of civilian life and carried suitcases, there were a few 'old soldiers' who had been in the first A.I.F. and there were a considerable number of ex-militia men dressed in the uniforms of their former units and carrying rifles and side arms.

The assembly was a moving mass. Everybody knew someone else and some groups of mates had enlisted 'en bloc' to ensure they would be in this thing together. We milled around greeting each other and trying to appear unconcerned at the situation into which we were gradually being organised.

The train shunted into the station bringing with it our first taste of military authority.

"Do not get in the train! Do not get in the train!"

The compartments of the 'dog box' carriages held 9 men so we had to be placed in groups of 9 facing the doors along the side of the carriage.

Then came someone's big moment in this escalating war:- "Entrain! Entrain!"

I turned to Benno. "What does 'Entrain' mean?"

"Get on the train."

"Well, why didn't he say so? Who is he, anyway?"

"Dunno. Never seen him before."

The journey to Northam took several hours and we arrived in the heat of the day. Some ill-disciplined characters opened doors and stepped out on to the platform only to be blasted back into the carriage and told to await the official order. As soon as they were back inside The Man In Authority bellowed:- "Detrain! Detrain!"

Doors opened like the starter's gate at the races allowing Australia's Answer To The Call to flow out on to the platform where it looked even more bedraggled as individuals threaded their way through the mass of kitbags, suitcases and backpacks to greet acquaintances who they 'didn't know were in it'.

"Pick up your gear!" commanded The Man In Authority.

We did that.

"Get into rows of six."

The amount and variety of luggage spread over the platform tended to turn this simple request into a major military effort. The compartments held 9 men so this luggage-laden mass not only had to become denser it also had to become longer; a manoeuvre not accomplished without considerable cross-talk and shuffling until a state of orderliness gradually appeared amidst the throng.

There were no buses or trucks waiting at the station. It became obvious, as we snaked our way off the platform, we were to march to the camp approximately three miles out of town.

Some of us were carrying gear in army haversacks but the majority were in civilian clothes and carrying suitcases. A considerable number had celebrated the previous night in wassail and merriment; an evening now demanding its physical price.

This motley mob, in the heat of the day, plodded along the uphill road leading to the camp whilst The Character In Authority moved briskly up and down the outer perimeter calling "Left! Right! Left! Right!"

Chapter Ten

The next few weeks saw this assembly of men gradually moulded into the basis of a battalion; by now we were about a thousand strong and allocated to companies and platoons.

The issue of army gear meant civilian clothing was no longer required. The garments worn into camp were packed into suitcases and placed in The Quartermaster's Store to be returned to the soldier's home address and one cannot help but ponder upon the family's emotions when those suitcases were received by mothers, fathers, sisters and brothers.

Former members of The Cameron Highlanders were told to report to The Quartermaster's Store to hand in their uniforms. We had become rather proud of those uniforms during the past three years and the number of items missing on this parade was somewhat surprising.

"Aw; come on!" I heard The Quartermaster say to one chap, "you can't have lost your kilt! I saw you wear it into camp. Come on, hand it over!"

I had taken the badge off my sporran and it wasn't noticed due to the volume of gear being tossed on to the counter. I carried that badge with me all through the war and, 65 years later, I am still the owner of an original 16th Battalion Sporran Badge.

Rumour solidified into fact and within a few weeks we were packed and ready to be on our way to the eastern states by ship.

Our movement was classified as 'Top Secret'. We went straight from Northam to the ship without farewells from families or friends but, somehow, a big crowd had gathered at Fremantle to see us off aboard the 'S.S. Duntroon'; one of the three ships plying the interstate trade with 1st, 2nd and 3rd class passengers.

The administrative problem of deciding which company was to travel which class was settled by The Company Commanders tossing a coin. Capt. Sandover won and Headquarters Company travelled 1st Class to Sydney.

This was a good way to start in a war. The ship hadn't been converted into a troopship at this stage so we travelled in luxury with linen and silverware on the tables, a steward to wait upon us and a full menu with every meal. Another steward made our beds and cleaned our two-berth cabins.

The ship arrived at dusk in Adelaide but the R.S.L. had managed to organise a function with only a few hours notice; a gesture which indicated the warmth and friendship for which this city became noted throughout the war.

We also called at Melbourne where I spent a wonderful day with Joyce and Garry. Joyce was heavily pregnant and was expecting their first baby within a few weeks.

The 'S.S. Duntroon' steamed into Sydney Harbour in the dead of night and we promptly "entrained" for Rutherford where a convoy of trucks was waiting at the rail siding to transport us to the camp.

Very impressive new, green-painted trucks. Gee! Trucks to carry troops!

Rutherford was a terrible camp from a hygienic point of view. A type of fever began to rage among the troops until we moved to a new camp at Greta and Rutherford was eventually condemned.

Our training intensified. Squad drill became a daily routine to smarten us up in our platoon movements on the parade ground and to make us more familiar with the Lee Enfield 303 Rifle with 1918 stamped on it. Officers and NCOs were established throughout the companies and platoons and authority began to exert its influence and become conscious of its power as the regiment firmed into a military unit. A general overall desire to become efficient soldiers pervaded the various segments of the battalion but I doubt if anyone gave much thought to the act of actually killing. True, the Colonel had been in The 14/18 War and quite a few 'old soldiers', scattered throughout the regiment, had had experience now dimmed with the passage of time.

Perchance it was Patriotism.

This stimulating emotion, coupled with a strong, indoctrinated sense of duty towards The Motherland and The Empire, was very real during this period of our history. Align this emotion with that peculiar Australian attitude of "wanting to be one of the boys over there" and you have the ingredients to create a most formidable force.

Some were misfits. Their lives, hitherto, had lacked discipline or restraint and they had a hard time facing up to these new circumstances but the majority, in time, became magnificent soldiers willing to fight anyone and later, when it came to front line action, they transferred their aggressiveness in that direction.

It was also interesting to note how men of similar nature and characteristics gravitated to each other. I had many inferior attitudes. (I still have but they are different to the ones I had then.) I was slow in making new friends and reluctant to accept friendship when it was offered to me. Looking back, I realise I was a bit of a snob. I was appalled at the lack of manners of some of the men at the mess table. They reached across in front of others to get the salt, they didn't hold their knives or forks correctly and some even spoke with food in their mouth.

Nor was I happy in the Transport Section. Most of the men were older than I and a large proportion of them had been truck drivers or had driven vehicles on the sheep or cattle stations from whence they came whereas I was trained in Horse Transport and, obviously, there wasn't going to be any horses.

I applied for a transfer to The Signal Platoon. It was promptly granted and, thus, was my three years training in the militia washed down the plug hole.

I had no knowledge of signalling; neither had any other members of the platoon except the three recently appointed Non Commissioned Officers.

Lieut. Laughton was an efficient soldier who had been a Sgt. Maj in The Permanent Military Forces before enlisting in the A.I.F. He probably had an idea of the signal platoon's responsibilities within a battalion's structure but I doubt, at this stage, if he had a comprehensive knowledge of signalling.

Corporal Lew Gracie had been in the first A.I.F. A dyed-in-the-wool Aussie who seldom spoke unless he was spoken to was a bit cynical about our capabilities and our future.

Corporal Sam Penn had held the same rank in the Signal Platoon of The 16th Battalion. He had also been in The British Army in India; an efficient, quietly-spoken man who never raised his voice to anyone – not even to give command on the parade ground.

Sergeant Don Baker was a stocky, barrel-chested, bald-headed Pommy with a voice that could be heard anywhere and everywhere – and it was! He must have put his age back because he had been in the trenches in the 14/18 war and he knew what it was all about. He had no illusions of grandeur. He knew!

He roared, bullied, cajoled, threatened and bellowed as he nudged our training along in the direction it was supposed to go.

So, initially, it fell to the lot of this three NCOs to introduce 30 raw recruits into the mysterious procedure of becoming signallers.

We were issued with Don3 Field Telephones which, like every other piece of equipment, had 1918 branded on them. The Don3 also had a Morse Code key and our first requirement was to learn the Morse Code.

We sat around in groups; each man taking a turn in sending simulated, coded, military messages whilst the rest wrote down the information received. It was a pleasant way to spend a morning, sitting under a gum tree in the wide, open spaces around Greta as we endeavoured to interpret the noise coming from the buzzer and trying not to be unduly perturbed by Sgt. Baker's snorts as he moved among the group discovering each man had written a message different to any other individual and pointing out that the dots and dashes being transmitted in no way resembled the Morse Code.

His bull-like voice dropped 'aitches' with scant regard to the English language.

"Wot was the last letter yoo sent?"

"C, Sgt."

"Han' wot does C sound like?"

"Dahditdahdit, Sgt."

"Well, yoo sent dahdit dahdit witch his too Ns. Wot would 'appen hiff yoo was attached to a company hin the front line han' the Colonel wanted them to hadvance han' yoo sent Ns instead hov Cs? Wot would yoo do, heh?"

"I'd hand the company commander the phone and tell him the Colonel wanted to speak to him."

"Yoo are supposed to be sending yaw message hin Morse Code. Now git hon wiff hit."

I sincerely hoped the fate of the regiment didn't depend on whether I sent Ns or Cs in Morse Code.

When assembling the heliograph upon its tripod we received these instructions:- "Yoo will hextract the 'eliograph from the case wiff your finger an' fumb keeping your fingers hoff the mirror. Yoo will place hit hin position hon top of the tripod and turn the base screw hanticlockwise until yoo 'ears a click. Yoo will then rotate the base screw clockwise han' tighten hit down which will secure the 'eliograph to the tripod."

The heliograph sends Morse Code by reflecting the sun's rays with an oscillating mirror. Gradually, during an exercise, the beam tends to get off target.

"Hi can try to teach yoo 'ow to use the 'eliograph but Hi can't stop the bloody sun from movin' hacross! Hadjust the mirror while yoo are sendin'!"

Night exercises aimed at making us familiar with the Don3 telephone, on a party line, also presented problems.

The exercise was simple. Two men hammered in a ground pin and attached a phone to it and to a reel of cable. This was H.Q. supervised by Sgt. Baker. The platoon then moved off into the darkness, reeling out the cable, with instructions for two men to 'tee in' every hundred yards and report, in Morse Code, back to H.Q. thus establishing a series of stations on a party line.

The first party made contact with the message, "Get f----d!" (In Morse Code, of course.)

A roar goes out from The Voice. The second station reported in with the same message; by the time the fifth station reported in with the similar advice Sgt. Baker was going through a real song-and-dance routine. He took off, following the cable, into the gloom.

While he was between the first and second stations someone sent the letters 'GB'; the signal to 'close down and reel in'. The sergeant going out met the platoon coming in and the serenity of the night was shattered by the roaring threat:- "Hi'll 'ave yoo hall on the fizzer hin the mornin'."

The platoon, strange as it may seem, attained considerable proficiency in Morse Code during the following months. Some even became efficient enough to send and receive at the rate of five words a minute; thereby qualifying as 'Specialists' and a pay increase of a shilling a day. The prospect of additional wealth spurred us on quite a bit.

Thus we gradually became efficient with the obsolete equipment with which The Australian Army was going to fight a modern war and never once in advances or retreats on the field of battle did I ever send a message in Morse Code.

*****

Individual traits of character, inbuilt by nature or circumstances, long before the army exerted its levelling influence, occasionally came to the surface in a man's attitude to this new type of existence. Some accepted the fact that senior rank carried authority whilst others found it difficult to adapt to the changed circumstances to their lifestyle.

Owen was a belligerent bloke who had spent the early part of his life in an orphanage where defiance of authority seemed to have been the order of the day. He was extremely tough and had a voice sounding like a car tyre moving slowly down a gravel driveway. He also had a strong sense of loyalty to anyone he regarded as a mate but, from a military point of view, he was headed for disaster.

I took him under my wing in an effort to guide him through the elementary stages of 'military good order and discipline'. It wasn't an easy task. For example, he didn't seem to accept the fact when The Platoon Sergeant shouted, "On Parade!" he was supposed to be immediately on parade and not arrive in due course. Also, he was not entitled to invite the same sergeant to "Step outside" at the end of the day because the sergeant had shouted at him for being late on parade. I felt he was gradually responding to training when he began to accept there was no 'after hours' or 'off the job' in the army and striking an NCO would land him in the guard house on a court martial charge.

It would have been a good fight though. Sgt. Baker was also a tough man!

Sunday leave into Newcastle was granted regularly. The greater portion of the battalion boarded the train at Greta siding and arrived in Newcastle around mid-morning.

Sunday morning in Newcastle in 1939!

The place was dead, the pubs were closed and the streets deserted!

Owen and I, walking aimlessly along the main street, stopped three well-dressed young ladies walking towards us.

"G'day," says Owen in his best gravel-like voice.

Much to my surprise they stopped and said, "Hullo."

"Does anything happen here on a Sunday?" he asked.

"Not a great deal."

"We come from Perth," says Owen, thereby breaking every military admonition about 'the enemy is listening'. "How's about showing us around the place?"

Not exactly backward was Owen when it came buttering up sheilas.

The three girls went into a huddle and came up with the query, "Why not?" or words to that effect.

I reckoned it was time I took part in the conversation.

"I had a holiday in Newcastle once. We stayed in No. 8 Parnell Place but I can't remember where it is. Somewhere near some tram sheds, I think."

I knew exactly where the tram barn was. It was a bit of a walk towards the ocean side of the town and would give us a chance to enlarge upon the conversation.

They took us to Parnell Place and showed us all over Newcastle until late in the afternoon.

"Hey! Can we take you to tea?" asked the diplomat.

"No; we have to be home by tea."

I was thinking fast. "S'posin' we phone your parents, tell them who we are, tell them we've met you and we want to take you to tea, our train leaves at 9 o'clock and we'll put you in a taxi and send you home when it leaves."

We did that and I have no doubt this permission was given with considerable apprehension but we kept our agreement to the letter.

Later, during the train journey back to camp, I said to Owen, "We should write to those girls and thank them for an enjoyable day."

"Yair; I s'pose so."

We wrote to the three Newcastle girls and they replied to our letters.

That was sixty years ago. We don't write to them anymore; we simply pick up the phone, dial their respective numbers and have a yarn about the weather, or our children, or our grandchildren. You know; the usual stuff.

*****

The battalion moved to a new camp at Ingleburn where, soon after our arrival, we were vaccinated.

The Medical Officer set up his table, complete with all the necessary equipment, at one end of a hut. We entered from the other end, thus forming a long queue extending the full length of the hut and out into the surrounding area. The slow shuffle towards the M.O's. table was not without its nervous tension and drama. A considerable number of 'Furphies' had been going around about this parade. Some said the needle penetrated to the bone, others implied the needle became blunt after the first ten injections and hurt like hell or, worse still, it created a festering sore and you were scarred for life.

Apprehension increased as the distance between the soldier and the needle decreased. Some stood there stoically during the brief pin-pricking operation then walked out of the hut; a few went faint as soon as the operation was completed and were set in chairs conveniently placed to cope with such a circumstance while good-natured comments were passed up and down the line until the newly-appointed medical sergeant exerted his authority by saying, "Hey, chaps, break the noise down a bit, will you?"

The vaccination made its presence felt the next day when several men fainted on parade and, eventually, a nasty sore did appear on our arms and took several weeks to clear.

*****

Camp Guards of 24 hours duration were mounted at sundown each day. The Changing Of The Guard entailed considerable drill precision and was usually carried out by platoons from the rifle companies. who vied with each other in the precision of the formality. Somehow, The Signal Platoon had the impression it was exempt from guard duties because it was comprised of "specialists" who were not to be involved in such mundane activities. The Company Commander soon dispelled this illusion when he received orders for his company to supply The Camp Guard for a week

We were No.1 (Signal) Platoon so we got the job on the first day!

This allocation resulted in a crash course in guard drill vigorously supported by Sgt. Baker's booming voice supplemented by the demanding knowledge of our Platoon Officer (Lieut. Laughton).

The Changing Of The Guard was impressively carried out and guards were placed at vulnerable points around the camp such as Battalion H.Q., The Quartermaster's Store, the canteen etc.

The purpose of such duties was not only to conform to military routine but also to instil a sense of discipline and responsibility into the individual. The former I was aware of – the latter I lacked.

True, I had garnished some idea of discipline in the militia but that was all good fun with horse riding every fourth week end, annual camps at Rottnest Island, a weekly parade night and an Annual Regimental Ball but standing 'at ease' in full uniform with a rifle and fixed bayonet outside the guardhouse of a slumbering Ingleburn Camp between 2am and 4am tended to be somewhat disillusioning.

"Jeez, Sarge. What do I have to stand here for? Nothing's happening."

"Yoo are guarding the camp hagainst possible fif columnists han' yoo will remain halert hat hall times. Hif Hi finds yoo slackenin' Hi'll 'ave yoo on the fizzer!"

Worse than this, when I completed my 2 hours and was 'stood down' I wasn't permitted to get into my pyjamas but had to 'rest' fully clothed in case there was an emergency.

I had only slept that way once before and that was when I had come home drunk from a party. Mum didn't approve of it, at all.

This period of adjustment firmed with training and the passage of time.

Quite a number of officers were promoted to senior rank and set about the task of becoming proficient in the duties relative to their position. Former militia NCOs received similar consideration and their numbers were supplemented by men who displayed leadership qualities. The NCOs became aware, and accepted, the responsibilities and authority which their rank carried and gradually began to exercise it. This was not always an easy adjustment to make. We had all enlisted from the same town or, at least, from the same state and we all practically knew each other. A strong sense of mateship prevailed and extended beyond the distinction of rank.

The 'other ranks', in time, accepted the situation. These senior ranks had to be filled and, obviously, the best men were being picked for the job. We, too, had a good idea who would make a fair sort of an NCO.

Thus, The 2/11th Battalion (City of Perth Regiment), under the command of Lieut. Colonel Louch, was beginning to shape up as an efficient unit of The 6th Division.

*****

Pay parade was every fortnight and week-end leave was generously granted. This meant every second week-end I was rich with three pounds ten shillings in my pocket.

A bus ride to Liverpool Station, a train into Sydney and a ferry to Manly where, within minutes, I was in the company of my former schoolmates and their families. I stayed with Gordon Haygarth on numerous occasions and, more or less, made his home my base, which was very helpful; especially on the non-paid week-ends when I was nearly broke.

I began to have the comfortable feeling that it was good to be in the army and to have week-ends amidst the scenes of my childhood and within the company of my boyhood companions.

It all ended abruptly!

We were returning to Perth for pre-embarkation leave.

Luck again favoured our Company Commander in the coin tossing routine and we journeyed 1st Class back to Perth. The ship also carried cargo and we pulled into Melbourne for 24 hours.

Leave was granted and I made my way to Joyce's house.

She took me to a room, reached down into a cradle, lifted a big bundle and proudly placed it in my arms.

"His name is Garry," she said.

I looked at this nine pound human being and tried to comprehend the significance of the moment.

This was the product of my sister's marriage. Her body had created this baby!

He was the first of a new generation within our family!

I was conscious of all these emotions as I held this child and I had a strange feeling of isolation from the sister who had always been my companion. No more Saturday night dancing at Anzac House. No more hikes around John Forrest National Park. No more ferry cruises down The Swan River with the gang.

She was married. She belonged to her husband and their baby.

"But gee!" I thought, "I'm an uncle."

And I never visualised the influence this child and I were to have upon each other for the remainder of the century stretching ahead and beyond into the next.

The regiment, after disembarking in Perth, was camped at Claremont Showgrounds where the days were spent in squad drill and practicing the Morse Code. Overnight leave was restricted because many of the boys seemed to have trouble getting back to camp in time for the morning check parade. However, there was a hole in the fence near our quarters so this restriction was not a big problem.

The Signal Platoon suffered its first casualty during this period in Perth.

Our Platoon Officer (Lieut. Laughton) lived in Bunbury and, whilst driving home on leave, he was killed in a motor accident.

The platoon was taken over by Lieut. Len Dowling who was no stranger to us.

The regiment had a week's exercise in the open bush country between Fremantle and Rockingham. The manoeuvre was to go forward for a given distance then carry out a strategic withdrawal. All our training, so far, had been in the form of strategic withdrawals.

"Any battalion can go forward and everything follows," stated the C.O. addressing a regimental parade, "But to withdraw in an orderly manner requires training."

The weather was stinking hot and the sandy soil made hard going. Ray Kennedy and I were attached to a rifle company and our task was to relay messages back to Battalion H.Q. using Morse Code on the field telephone or the Lucas Lamp.

Company Commanders didn't have much time for signallers at this stage of our training. We came from another company and, therefore, our use was of dubious value. We weren't too sure of ourselves, either, so we went wherever the O.C. Company went and tried to look efficient.

The 'strategic withdrawal' part was all sand, sweat, swearing and flies!

Ray and I had to reel in the cable as the troops withdrew and a company can withdraw faster than two signallers can reel in cable. We'd be reeling whilst standing in a theoretical 'No Man's Land' while the Company Commander bellowed at us to, "Get a bloody move on!"

It was all right for him. We couldn't leave the cable there. It was in short supply and Sgt. Baker would go crook at us. Reeling in cable when you are carrying a rifle, a Lucas Lamp and stand as well as a field telephone and two flags while your eyes are filling with sweat and dust isn't exactly easy.

Maybe the Colonel was right, after all.

*****

I spent considerable leave time with my parents and my young sister Patricia. They were still living in The R.S.L. Hall in Mt. Lawley. My brother, Syd, was still in Kalgoorlie.

Dad was now on full War Service Pension and I still didn't realise how sick he really was. He had a bad cough because his lungs weren't too good.

I must have been one of the most naïve characters who ever joined The A.I.F. and the memories of Dad still hit my conscience with remorse tinged with a sense of guilt.

I simply didn't know!

I doubt if my brother or my sisters were aware of the seriousness of Dad's health, either. Nobody ever told us and the subject was never discussed.

"Just a bad cigarette cough," said Dad, "I'll be all right in a minute."

*****

I had a girl friend. We shared many interests such as Sunday morning church service, orchestral concerts in the Capitol Theatre, Old Time Dancing in Anzac House, sailing with the yacht crew in summer and bushwalking in the winter. It had been that way for over three years so I asked her if she would marry me when I came back home again. She accepted my proposal but I added a proviso:- "I don't know how long I shall be away at this war so if you meet someone else try and let me know. I'll understand."

Oh! Brave swashbuckling words of one of the nation's heroes!

*****

The Pre-embarkation Parade through Perth was the kind of event that makes men want to go to war!

We formed up in companies, in the new formation of six abreast, outside Perth Railway Station and, with the band playing "Sussex By The Sea", marched through the centre of the city.

The streets were packed! Not just crowded but packed!

The trams and trolley buses were stopped and there was just room for us to pass down the centre of Hay Street; the crowd overflowed from the footpaths on to the roadway. Some people were actually crying, especially amongst the older, middle-aged women although I noticed some of my Saturday night dancing partners, who worked in Woolworths, holding each other and crying. They weren't crying for me but for all of us.

What the hell are they crying for? This is a great day!

"Good on yer, boys!" shouted some of the older men.

"We'll join you later!" called several unenlisted men as we progressed down the street lined with a crowd exhibiting every kind of emotion between enthusiasm and misery.

The Empire was at war and we were going to live up to the traditions we had unknowingly been absorbing since the day we commenced school.

I had another week-end leave prior to embarking for overseas service.

Night had fallen before I left home to return to camp. Mum, Dad and my sister came out on to the footpath to say farewell.

I kissed Mum and Pat, shook hands with Dad, walked 50 yards to the end of the street, turned and tossed my family a casual salute then disappeared around the corner.

Years later I learned Dad had shaken his head and said, "Poor little bugger. He doesn't know what he has let himself in for."

Chapter Eleven

We climbed along the gangway leaning against the "S.S. Nevassa", disappeared into the bowels of the ship to dispose of our gear then re-appeared to line the rails and shout or wave to relatives and friends. Train loads of people had come from Perth to see us off and the wharf was crowded.

Dad was there, looking frail and grave whilst Mum and my kid sister repeatedly wiped their eyes.

"Hey!" I shouted, "Don't cry! I'll be back one day! You wait and see."

How many confident men shouted similar words to become cries in the void?

The ship, amidst an increase in volume of the crowd's farewells, gradually drew away from the wharf, moved out of the harbour into Gauge Roads and dropped anchor!

We couldn't believe it!

Fremantle was just over there and we were stuck out here!

The rest of the convoy arrived next morning. Half the ships moved into the harbour to give the troops a day's leave.

It didn't take us long to familiarise ourselves with the ship. The conditions, after our luxury voyages to the eastern states and back, were a bit of a shock. The 'Nevassa' was a genuine British troopship which had been scheduled for the scrap heap but the war came along and she was kept in service. There were no cabins below. The decks were cleared from bow to stern and we could see from one end of the ship to the other; long tables and forms projected from the ship's sides all the way along the deck – and there were several decks. Each table was numbered and titled "Mess No.----". Hooks were welded to the sides and framework; upon these were slung the hammocks at night and they were crammed so tight it appeared if a man turned over in his sleep, without falling out of his hammock, several other sleepers in the vicinity would be obliged to turn over as well.

Air-conditioning was unknown; the port-holes were permanently closed and the only ventilation was provided through wind-chutes. The wind, for weeks at a time, was a following breeze and the airflow was non-existent so the troops were allowed to sleep on deck where, before daylight, they were hosed down by the grinning Indian crew who smilingly agreed with the nomenclature hurled in their direction.

There wasn't much doing during the first day anchored in Gauge Roads and, to break the monotony, the troops had a go at fashioning fishing gear from string, bent pins or any other adaptable material. The mullet were biting and soon the decks were littered with fish.

The second half of the convoy crept into Fremantle Harbour for a day's leave and we watched them go with mixed feelings.

The ships entering the harbour yesterday were now in Gauge Roads. Apparently they had decided to do some boat drill and rowing exercise. The lifeboats were filled with troops and lowered to the water. They rowed over to the 'Nevassa' to inform us Perth was a beautiful city and they had enjoyed our women immensely. A cascade of mullet threatened to fill their boats before they managed to row out of range.

The convoy sailed next day.

The speed of a convoy is dictated by the fastest speed of the slowest ship which happened to be His Majesty's Transport 'S.S. Nevassa' plodding along at a steady 12 knots in a straight line with 'H.M.S. Ramilles' watching over us like a mother hen whilst the rest of the convoy carried out the standard zigzagging, anti-submarine course.

We were at sea on Anzac Day 1940.

H.M.S. Ramilles, that impressive representative of The Royal Navy, steamed up between the two lines of the convoy, all hands on deck and dressed in white, to give three cheers as they sailed past.

The convoy pulled into Colombo to refurbish the bunkers and to take on supplies.

We were given a day's leave.

Many years had passed since Colombo had seen days like this one. Within hours the streets were flooded with khaki-clad Australians who consumed alcohol in quantity, who conducted rickshaw races down the main streets with the bewildered native owners sitting in the conveyance and who, much to the delight of the street hawkers, beggars and shop owners, had money which they seemed eager to dispense amongst the local populace.

We returned to the ship at the end of the day to find the decks, the handrails, window ledges and every other flat surface covered in a thick layer of coaldust created by native labourers passing bags of coal from the lighter below, up the gangway, across the deck and down into the bowels of the ship.

That day, from a 'Pukha Sahib' point of view, was a disaster and, next day, the C.O. assembled the troops on the welldeck and delivered a severe reprimand concerning our behaviour.

The convoy ploughed onwards and we settled down to the monotony of the voyage. The upper decks of the ship were not strong enough to allow physical exercise by a large number of men so time was spent sunbathing or sitting around in groups yarning away about nothing in particular. Games of 'Two Up' as well as 'Crown and Anchor' flourished. Boxing tournaments were organised but these tended to become dangerous; especially if the ship rolled just as a punch was being thrown. The unexpected advantage could be disastrous to the man on the receiving end.

The weather remained calm and the sea docile so sleeping on deck became a normal routine but it meant bringing up a hammock and laying down on your favourite piece of deck as soon as the sun went down; a tricky manoeuvre when hundreds of men had the same idea and deck-space became a little cramped.

Bodies were sprawled everywhere; a circumstance creating problems when I wanted to go to the toilet during the night. Every body between me and the toilet had to be carefully stepped over, which wasn't difficult, but finding space to put my foot was. Whilst balancing on one foot as I carefully raised the other to pass it slowly over a body then slowly lowered it on to a miniscule area of deck required a considerable amount of skill. The ship usually rolled at this critical stage resulting in a foot being stamped on to someone's anatomy.

The toilets were enclosed wooden structures built out over the side of the ship. They gave some privacy from outside viewers but they didn't give much privacy inside. The seat was a long, wooden plank set out over the ocean and although thin partitions divided its length into compartments they were without doors; a circumstance which became somewhat disconcerting when one of your mates decided to stand there and have a yarn while you were endeavouring to communicate with nature. This 'free-communication-between-clients' type of toilets, minus the dividing partition, was standard for the rest of my military career and by the time I was discharged some six years later I was almost accustomed to them.

I slung my hammock one night between two uprights of the deck railing; an excellent position out of everyone's way but, during the night, a slight sea arose causing the ship to roll. When the ship rolled one way I was inboard but. when it rolled the other, I was hanging out over the dark, hissing sea. On the next swoop inboard I rolled out of the hammock to land on Tom Arlidge. The resulting argument awoke the surrounding troops who threatened to carry out the action which the squall had failed to accomplish. There was no more available space so I crept away to spend the remainder of the night in the stuffy decks below.

The convoy pulled into Aden with no shore leave. Italy was rattling the sabre and looked like coming into the war. Its colony of Eritrea bordered The Red Sea so we steamed into The Suez Canal to anchor in The Bitter Lakes for a couple of days; a welcome relief allowing the troops to have a good swim before moving on to Kantara where we disembarked, once again 'in the dead of night'.

We were treated to a terrific meal before entraining for Palestine where we set up camp at Kilo 89 near Gaza.

Chapter Twelve

The camp at Kilo 89 was situated about 5 miles north of Gaza and about the same distance from the sea. It was typical of numerous British camps established along the length of Palestine. The Orderly Room, cookhouse, Quartermaster's Store, The Wet and Dry Canteens were of timber; the company mess tents were complete with tables and forms; showers were available at all times and a picture theatre was nearby.

The troops were billeted eight men to a roomy tent equipped with bed boards and mosquito nets.

A barber's shop and a laundry, run by Arabs, were immediately adjacent to the camp, laid out on a gentle slope with a bitumen road running past the bottom boundary; a road which ran all the way north to Haifa, Jerusalem and a myriad of places with magical names that had intrigued me since my childhood.

I don't know who put up the buildings or the tents. They were there when we arrived and, like all good soldiers, we accepted the situation and simply moved in.

We billeted at Kilo 89 for over six months while the war went from bad to worse for our side. The Germans over-ran Belgium and France and belted The British Army off the continent through Dunkirk; Italy came into the war on Adolf's side and The Battle of Britain was in full swing.

The anticipated equipment we expected to be issued upon our arrival in Palestine didn't commence to trickle in until around November when the Transport Platoon received some trucks, a few sedans and other vehicles; the companies received Vickers Guns and Bren Guns; The Signal Platoon was swamped with flags, Lucas Lamps, telescopes, heliographs, the latest D5 telephones, telephone exchanges, message pads and miles and miles of cable.

Morse Code could be sent on D5 telephones and, while Europe crumbled, we spent many a pleasant hour sitting in the mess tents practicing Morse Code.

The weeks in camp soon became boring as we smartened up on our squad drill, listened to lectures, became familiar with our equipment and suffered guard duties.

Smartening up on our squad drill commenced at the 8am platoon inspection carried out by the bellowing Sgt. Baker before handing over to The Platoon Commander.

Lieut. Dowling checked rifles for cleanliness, equipment for efficiency and men for smartness. He also closely checked faces to determine if a man had shaved before coming on parade; a challenging procedure as some of us had discovered we didn't really need to shave every day to appear clean shaven.

"Sig. Leggett. Did you shave this morning?"

"Yes, Sir!"

He then had to decide if I was lying or had shaved with a blunt razor. A prolonged pause before he moved on to the next man.

He told us, at a regimental reunion many years later, we weren't putting anything over him but the paper work involved in placing us on a charge "for conduct prejudicial to military good order and discipline whereas we had omitted to shave before morning parade" was more demanding than proving we hadn't shaved.

Squad drill at times became a little hectic as Tom Arlidge and Val Thomas, our two new Corporals, endeavoured to come to grips with the awesome task of squad drilling 30 men around in a restricted area.

Signallers are not only expected to become efficient soldiers but they are also responsible for communication within the battalion.

Lectures on these two topics were delivered by The Platoon Commander or an NCO who had obtained a Training Manual the night before and now delivered his new-found knowledge with aplomb.

The Training Manuals, too, were interesting. Printed in 1918 they precisely stated how a war was to be conducted. Telephone cables, for example, were to be hung in the hedgerows where they would not be broken by vehicular traffic or men marching on duckboards.

Becoming familiar with our equipment was entered into with gusto. We spread out over the countryside and sent messages with flags; messages with heliographs; messages with Lucas Lamps; messages with telephones – all in Morse Code, of course.

Camp picket duties involved patrolling around the outer perimeter of the camp and through the lines to keep Arabs from casually strolling through and picking up anything not anchored down. The Arabs, it seems, were a bit of a problem. I didn't, and still don't, understand the intricacies of 'The Arab Situation" but the British had been occupying the country for some considerable time. The Arabs, apparently, objected to the British being there at all and had a strong desire to support that objection by purloining as much military equipment as circumstances permitted.

Our rifles obviously would be a prime target so they were chained to the tent post. But an Arab might sneak in with chain cutters so the rifle bolts were withdrawn and kept in The Orderly Room. We couldn't patrol the picket lines with a rifle because, individually, we could be overpowered by a group of Arabs who valued a rifle more than a human life.

We guarded the confines of the camp with pick handles.

Sgt. Baker's voice could be heard to bellow at regular intervals: "Yoo do not send Morse Code wiff a pick 'andle! Yoo are supposed to be guardin' the bloody camp wiff hit!"

The platoon was issued with picks and shovels for a day and we engaged in the military exercise of how to dig a slit trench in accordance with The Instruction Manual. The chosen site was a small hill overlooking the camp. This hill had been in existence long before Samson had destroyed the temple at Gaza and the soil had had sufficient time to pack down into a fairly solid section of the earth's stone-impregnated crust.

The Army Manual's instructions were: "Lift, swing, strike, break and rake"; commendable advice for a beginner but Nugget Evans wasn't impressed.

"Bloody stupid," says he. "You don't dig a hole like that!"

"That's the way The Manual says han' that's 'ow yoo will do hit," says Sgt. Baker.

"Aw," says Nugget, "I've swung a pick 'n' shovel for The Main Roads Board back 'ome -"

"Han' Hive swung a pick han' shovel for the bloody Main Roads Board too!" bellows Sgt. Baker. "Han' the foreman used to tell me to get hon wiff the bloody job an' hime the bloody boss 'ere so get hon wiff hit! By Cripes, Hiff the henemy was shellin' yoo right now yoo wouldn't be standing haround harguing. Han' that goes for the rest of yoo! Git hon wiffit!"

Enemy? What enemy? The enemy was hundreds of miles away on the other side of Egypt.

*****

There is a lot of barren country around Gaza. It stretched out beyond Beersheba and we became familiar with most of it during our stay at Kilo 89. It wasn't sandy desert; it was dust that had been worked for thousands of years, and it stunk, but a week's desert training in that country was accepted as a far better alternative to the boredom of static camp life.

A week out there was hard going. Twenty mile route marches, under a hot sun, on half a bottle of water a day was very demanding in the early stages but, over a period of time, we became physically tough and accepted it as 'part of the routine'.

Lunch rations were issued by Doughy Taylor, the company cook, before commencing the day's activities. Lunch, whilst on exercises, consisted of two thick slices of bread liberally coated with a layer of butter and between these was slapped a complete McConochies Herring in Tomato Sauce. This contribution to the war effort was then put into our aluminium dixies and placed in our backpacks.

The re-opening of our dixies, after 4 hours in The Southern Palestinian Summer Sun, revealed a concoction of grease-soaked bread encompassing a fish which gave off an odour peculiar to its species after a prolonged period of neglect.

Very few lunches were eaten but they were not wasted.

It was an accepted desert phenomenon that, no matter how long our route marches or how remote our activities, an Arab was never seen across the flat expanses or deepest wadis but as soon as we rested on a march, or took up a position, an Arab would mysteriously appear out of the wilderness with a camel-load of watermelons, a broad grin and the standard greeting of: "Saida, Aussie. You want to buy watermelon?"

Titch Carrol promptly swooped up the contents of our dixies and became engaged in an animated, bargaining dialogue resulting in the exchange of several watermelons for a quantity of Doughy Taylor's Desert Diet.

Eggs, too, occasionally became available in this manner. Cooking eggs was a simple process. A shallow hole was dug with bayonets, a small fire of scrub straw was lit and the eggs were baked. The cooked consistency of the eggshell's content was directly related to the heat of the fire multiplied by the duration of the egg's immersion in the ashes – so a certain amount of skill was required.

The training manoeuvres were conducted as though we were in touch with the enemy. This required The Signal Platoon to establish telephone contact between Battalion H.Q. and the outlying companies at the end of the day. Two men would reel out cable across the flat terrain to some spot where they hoped to meet the two signallers attached to the company.

While the prolonged twilight settled upon this ancient land, as it had done since the beginning of recorded history, the company's trucks, carrying a hot meal for the troops, would appear at Battalion H.Q.

"Where's B Company?" asks the driver.

"Out there at the end of that telephone cable."

The driver, having graduated from a farm tractor, a Perth taxi or a long-haulage truck, straddles the wire with his front wheels and follows the cable to its end where, we trust, he will find two signallers having a smoke by a telephone in a wadi.

Henceforth all vehicles, wheeled or tracked, seeking B Company followed the original wheel tracks straddling the cable.

There were times when we suspected The Army Manual wasn't quite up to date.

The enemy was using aircraft in this war and anti-aircraft defence was included in our training whilst on route marches.

"Aircraft Alert!' shouted the NCO.

This was the command to unsling our rifles and put a round up the spout. We weren't issued with ammunition but we worked the bolt.

"Aircraft right!"

We swung to the right with our rifles pointing up at the regulation angle which was governed by the training edict translated by Sgt. Baker:- " Yoo do not let the left helbow come down below the left shoulder hotherwise yoo could blow your mate's bloody 'ead hoff!"

"Aircraft left!"

We swung around to the left working the rifle bolts furiously. Thirty rifles firing rapidly should frighten any plane off if we didn't bring it down!

A long day's route march back to camp usually completed a week 'out there'; a march which produced blisters needing attention, a dust-covered sweaty body needing a hot shower and a thirst needing a cold beer. All of these requirements were available as well as clean clothes and a straw-filled mattress to lie on.

The nightly picture shows were presented to a packed house and who can ever forget the enthusiastic but rather ribald advice given to Errol Flynn as he led "The Charge of the Light Brigade?"

*****

Leave became available. It usually covered two nights, giving us three days out of camp. Palestine is not a big country by our standards and within a few hours a bus load of us could be transported up to Jerusalem to stay at King David's Hotel; a beautiful building set up for troops on leave.

We were guided around the most sacred places on earth without really appreciating the sanctity of the ground we were standing on.

The Church of The Nativity, The Mosque of Omar, The Garden of Bethsemanie, Calvary Hill, The Wailing Wall – they are all real and I was there!

But, in my ignorance, I was not really aware of where I was.

I had learned of these places in Sunday School but that was a long time ago. Right now we were soldiers on leave and more interested in beer bars and the women who frequent such places.

These topics were new to me. I didn't have much capacity when it came to drinking beer and sex was a subject of considerable discussion in the camp's tents after 'Lights Out' when a man's activities on leave attracted detailed cross-examination upon his return to camp. Any boastful statements had to be confirmed by one or two of his mates who were on leave with him.

It was a delicate topic to be discussed with strange ladies in a bar. How did you approach them? What was the polite phrase to open the conversation?

A couple of Tommies who had been in Palestine a year or so, and with whom we were drinking, undertook to open the conversation for us.

One of them walked across to the ladies, leaned across their table and, with all the refinement of 'a fine old English gentleman' enquired, " 'Ow much will it corst?"

Simple. The ice was broken, drinks were ordered and arrangements made.

Whilst on this intriguing subject there is one circumstance worthy of comment. One of these ladies of a thousand delights had a technique of sinking her finger-nails into a man's shoulders at the most exciting moment and dragging them all the way down his back leaving red weals resembling ski tracks down a snow slope.

When under the showers, back in camp, efforts were made to calculate how much money she had made over the past few days.

*****

South of Kilo 89, close by the Egyptian border, stands the Arab town of Raffa. It featured dramatically in the battle history of The 10th Light Horse during The 1914/18 War. Nowadays we view it with a gentler eye.

The 6th Division's Signallers had set up a listening post under some palm trees and scrub in the sand hills several miles beyond the town.

This outpost of The Empire was manned 24 hours a day by two Divisional Signallers and two signallers supplied from the infantry battalions.

The purpose of the listening post was to rapidly inform Divisional Headquarters, by wireless, of approaching aircraft; a duty regularly carried out every morning at 8am when a de Havilland Rapide twin-engine biplane made its way up the coast from Egypt to Palestine.

A posting to this duty was considered as being somewhat akin to banishment to Shangri-la for a week.

Jesse and I were detailed off for the job. We reported to the Lieutenant in charge of the accompanying rifle platoon, threw our meagre gear into the back of the truck and climbed aboard.

Our arrival at Jaffa was the curtain-raiser to a scene in which camels snarled, donkeys brayed, horses neighed and Arabs shouted as all our gear was unloaded and packed into panniers hung on cranky animals in preparation for our trek to the oasis somewhere out there across the sand hills.

Agitated haggling took place once the gear was loaded. I needed an animal to ride and, obviously, the quality of my steed would be in relation to my ability to argue and fix a price with an Arab who had spent all his life arguing and fixing prices.

"Aussie! You want a camel? I have the best camel for you. Right here! Look at him!"

I surveyed a cranky, snarling creature that seemed more interested in biting a chunk off an adjacent cactus hedge than in boosting his master's income.

"No! I don't need a camel. I want a horse."

"A horse! My brother has a magnificent horse! Wait! I will get him for you!"

He added to all the noise by bellowing something in Arabic. A dusky colleague, leading a rangy animal of dubious heritage, made his way through the dust-raising mass of kneeling camels and braying donkeys; but it was a horse complete with saddle and bridle.

A bargain was struck and all haggling was cut short by the officer shouting, "Come on, you blokes! Shake it up. There's a bloody war on!"

Camels rose complainingly, donkeys stopped braying and the mass of animals, men and material moved out and away from the village.

The owners of the various animals walked beside them and led the creatures, thus changing the hirer's status from a rider to a passenger. I felt this was degrading and argued with the horse's owner to let go the bridle.

"No, Aussie. He walks beside this other horse."

"Why the hell does he have to walk beside the other horse?"

"Because they are brothers, Aussie."

"Bullshit! Let go or I'll kick your teeth in!"

"O.K. Aussie."

I yanked the rein out of his hand and trotted up to the head of the column, swung around and trotted back again but, on the way, every foul-breathed, yellow-toothed, bad-tempered, snarling camel snaked out an elongated neck in a determined attempt to tear a chunk out of me or the horse – preferably the horse.

I arrived at a spot in the column that happened to be beside my mount's brother.

"O.K. Aussie?" enquired the grinning Arab.

"You bastard!"

"Yes, Aussie," says he, still grinning, "Me wog bastard."

We chatted on a more friendly basis until we arrived at the oasis, to be greeted by two Divisional Signallers who had been at this listening post so long we had trouble distinguishing them from the local inhabitants.

The radio transmitter/receiver was set up in a clump of bushes struggling for existence some distance away from the main platoon because the battery charger's motor was a source of annoyance; a circumstance expanded beyond the limits of reality by the two characters permanently attached to the equipment.

The signaller's quarters was a tent which proved handy to throw our gear into but from the moment we arrived our dress was shorts and a hat. We slept in the sand beneath the infinity of star-studded space.

Sometime during the week an officer from Battalion H.Q. rode into camp and, in a serious manner appropriate to the event, set up a Polling Booth and requested us to vote for our candidates in The Federal Parliament back home.

I was over 21 so I cast my first ever vote amidst the sand dunes near The Egyptian Border and The Returning Officer rode off into the sunset. Rather romantic, I thought.

We lived a halcyon existence for a week; on the seventh day black specks appeared on the distant sand hills, grew larger and evolved into the same snarling camels, the same braying donkeys and the same haggling Arabs, all of whom combined their various talents to create the same dust and noisy chaos at a spot which, an hour earlier, had been a tranquil oasis in the desert.

A relieving platoon and signallers took over; we departed leaving behind two Divisional Signallers sitting under a palm tree and looking more like Arabs than they did a week ago.

*****

Changes had taken place during our absence.

The tents were no longer white and in line. The probability of enemy aircraft attack was minimal but the possibility did exist. The tents had been dismantled and set up in a staggered manner so as to prevent enemy aircraft from taking a sight on a straight line of nice white tents which were now a dirty brown colour having been saturated and dirt thrown over them as camouflage. The tent floors, in addition, had been dug out to a depth of eighteen inches and the extracted dirt piled around the tent perimeter.

All very impressive but, as we later learned, would have been completely useless had an air raid taken place.

Water flowed down the hill when the rains came and filled all the tents to a depth of eighteen inches but, by then, we were on the other side of Egypt and had our own problems.

Chapter Thirteen

Burg-el-Arab is out in the desert about 30 miles west of Alexandria. Our campsite, about a quarter of a mile from the railway line, had roads, some tin sheds, and a few water taps were spread around the area.

There were no amenities and it was a boring camp.

The boredom, at one stage, was relieved by a Divisional Exercise. The plan was for our brigade to act as the enemy under attack from the other two brigades and part of the issued instructions was to make it as realistic as possible. Rain fell heavily while we were spread out over the desert on the night preceding the exercise. The desert dirt became a slippery, sticky mass of mud that clung to our clothing in chunks and built up on our boots as we walked. Tempers became as foul as the mud; consequently, when opposing platoons met on night patrols, physically aggressive situations developed that were only curtailed by officers exerting their authority.

Later, at de-briefing, we were informed the exercise had been a success and much valuable experience had been gained but, from our point of view, we had spent a night in pouring rain and mud. Worse still, several hundred yards of telephone cable had been lost.

Leave was granted into Alexandria. Leave was always welcome but it did have its problems. The regiment was a Western Australian regiment and there was a tendency to remain insular and to regard eastern states regiments with a certain amount of aggressiveness; an attitude returned with an intensity tending to increase in proportion to the amount of alcoholic or spiritous liquors consumed. Some terrific street brawls blew up but Benno and I kept away from these. The Pommy Military Police had a habit of rounding up everyone in the vicinity and you don't muck around with Pommy Military Police. They play it rough.

The Alexandria Railway Station, at the end of such a day, became the assembly point for a multitude of soldiers from various units spread out along the railway line snaking into the desert. Some were sober, some were happily drunk, some were horribly intoxicated and some had overstayed their leave by 24 hours, run out of money, and were now trying to return to their units; a circumstance which grossly overloaded the train and made scrambling aboard a somewhat hazardous activity.

We noticed one of our platoon mates sitting on a seat and staring unblinkingly at some distant object known only to himself. Benno and I stood him up, put an arm each around our necks and dragged him on to the train where we managed to keep him upright between us on a seat built for two people. Andy sat that way until the train stopped at Amiriya to allow the inhabitants of that camp to get off. Suddenly he came to life with a yell of "Wog Whiskey!!" and seemed to float through the open window to land in the dirt.

Jumping to his feet he took off across the desert at a flat gallop with Benno and me in hot pursuit and the trainload of characters cheering us on and calling out all kinds of advice, none of which was applicable to the current cross-country event.

We caught Andy and brought him down with a Rugby tackle but there was no way we could restrain him as he ranted and threw his arms about.

A couple of chaps turned up to assist. One of them swung a punch connecting with Andy's jaw and he lost interest in the proceedings.

We pulled him off the train at Burg-el-Arab to be faced with the task of getting him to the Orderly Room tent to hand in his Leave Pass, otherwise he would be reported 'Absent Without Leave'.

Night had fallen hours ago so, with an arm around each neck, we proceeded to drag him through the darkness in the direction of the camp.

Andy was about twelve inches taller than either of us. His feet made a long lizard-like track across the ancient soil of Egypt as we lumbered on to arrive at the Orderly Room tent in a lather of sweat. We staggered up to the table where, in the dim light of a hurricane lamp, Bill Bryden sat collecting Leave Passes.

"Cripes, Bill, we've had a hell of a time getting here. Cop these passes and let's get to bed."

An officer materialised from the gloom within the tent.

"Stand to attention, you men! This is an Orderly Room!"

Benno and I jumped to attention. Andy made a slow topple forward. He hit the ground sending up a cloud of dust.

"Get that man out of here!"

We grabbed an arm each and dragged him outside where we left him slumbering under the stars.

Next morning he appeared at the platoon tents asking the time-honoured question, "What happened?"

Army mateship, at times, requires a lot of understanding.

Sergeant Don Baker had been 'feeling crook' for quite some time. His bull-like voice had developed a bit of a wheeze and, over several days, he reluctantly reported on Sick Parade. We were sitting around our tent area in the twilight of an evening, yarning about nothing in particular, when he joined us. He sat there for a while, saying nothing, when he suddenly made a statement.

"They are going to send me back to hospital tomorrow."

"Eh?"

"No joking. They're sending me back. Me chest is crook."

"Jeez, Sarge. We could be in action any day now."

"I know. And I'm not going to be there with you."

"Cripes, Don, that's tough."

"My bloody oath it's tough! I'll catch up with you all later."

He got up and walked away with tears brimming in his eyes.

Five years were to pass before I saw him again.

I had practically no knowledge of the current military situation. In fact I now realise I was a very ignorant individual. As a schoolboy I had been a fairly competent Boy Scout and, later, I spent three years horse riding in The Cameron Highlanders and it is quite probable I regarded this soldering business as an extension of The Boy Scout Movement. It was many years later that I read of the circumstances that took us into battle.

Up until this moment I hadn't given fighting much consideration except to become an efficient signaller.

The Italians, having come into the war, decided it was time to throw their weight around by crossing The Egyptian Border from Libya and had progressed as far as Sidi Barrani in their advance to The Suez Canal. They were held up at Sidi Barani by The 4th Indian Division which had been keeping an eye on them. This Indian Division was to be transferred to Abyssinia and our division was to take over its position; but, before leaving, the Indian Division decided to stage an attack on the Sidi Barrani stronghold.

They took 35,000 prisoners, as well capturing a considerable number of field guns and tanks.

This episode convinced The Top Brass that we should have a bit of a go ourselves and assumed The Italians would abandon the town of Bardia when it was threatened by our advance.

The town of Bardia, with its small harbour, would have to be occupied and the best way to get a large body of men there was to send them by ship.

Our battalion packed hurriedly and was transported to the harbour at Alexandria where we sat for the remainder of the day before being taken back to Burg-el-Arab.

The Italians were going to make a stand and fight for Bardia.

The battalion was on 'Stand By' so there was no leave. Several days passed and, with Christmas fast approaching, The Colonel decided to celebrate The Festive Season a week before it was due. I don't know how he managed it but the meal was an excellent menu of vegetables and very tasty Australian lamb with peaches and cream and a bottle of beer per man.

Several more days passed and there was still no word of movement so we had a similar dinner on Christmas Day, 1940.

Within days we received movement orders. A convoy of trucks appeared. We loaded our gear, climbed aboard and headed for the war that was somewhere out there in the desert.

We camped overnight at Mersa Matruh and, next day, took up our positions outside Bardia.

The Signal Platoon is based at Battalion Headquarters with two signallers attached to each rifle company. The duty is to establish and maintain communication between Battalion H.Q. and the forward companies. I was stationed at Battalion H.Q. to operate the telephone exchange.

We moved to our positions in the dark and dug in, making as little noise as possible.

Corporal Lew Gracie, a veteran of The 1914-18 War, crawled over to my slit trench.

"They reckon there is going to be one of the biggest barrages in history go off tomorrow morning. I've seen a few and I want to see this one. Wake me up at 0355hrs."

I crept over to his trench at five minutes to four. "Hey, Lew. You still want to have a look at this one?"

We quietly moved back to my slit trench and stood there looking back to the rear.

The artillery barrage commenced promptly at 0400hrs. We could hear the thunder of the guns and felt the percussion in the air but we couldn't see a thing.

Lew slowly turned around and stood staring towards the front.

"Bloody hell! It's over there!"

Between us and the enemy, stretching from one end of the horizon to the other, were cannons belching flame and noise in a magnificent manner.

We were about ten miles behind the artillery and the artillery is usually about fifteen miles behind the front line.

Lew and I didn't know we were the reserve battalion of the reserve brigade and the battle for Bardia was taking place away up there somewhere.

Bardia was a fortified Italian port just over the Libyan, or Italian, side of the border with Egypt. It had an anti-tank ditch about 30 miles long right around its inland perimeter and this was liberally reinforced with an abundance of barbed wire.

The idea was, after the artillery barrage, for a brigade to break through the barbed-wired perimeter and fan out. The remainder of the division was to follow and engage the enemy wherever opposition presented itself.

We eventually received the order to move forward.

The task of a signaller, as I stated earlier, was to maintain communications and, to meet the demands of this commitment, a considerable amount of equipment had to be carried as laid down in the manuals dated 1918.

I moved forward into The Battle of Bardia carrying a field telephone exchange, a Lucas lamp and stand, a telescope and stand, two signalling flags, a quantity of cable, a satchel c/w message pad and pencil as well as my rifle and ammunition. I looked like a mass of signalling gear, with a tin hat on top, moving across the face of the desert and I reckon the Italians could have hit me with an anti-tank shell and it would have bounced off.

By the end of the day we had passed through the artillery lines and arrived at the break in the barbed wire.

But the battle was over except for a pocket of resistance at the southern end of the defences where two Italian divisions were still holding out.

Next morning (15th January) the battalion received orders to attack in a southerly direction and clean up any opposition.

The first part of the attack was a march down a long forward slope under full view of the enemy; a situation making us a possible target for artillery fire.

The battalion commenced its advance into its baptism of fire and across the desert could be heard the song: "We're off to see the wizard! The Wonderful Wizard of Oz!"

Judy Garland would have loved that!

Battalion H.Q. is usually back from the forward company's but our Colonel wasn't there. He was down the front with The Adjutant.

If The Colonel is forward then his H.Q. has to move up, too.

Lieutenant Dowling told us to throw our gear into his utility, climb aboard and hang on. The utility roared up to the crest of the hill, over the top and down the long slope towards the advancing troops while we hung on expecting to be blown to pieces by artillery fire at any moment.

The shelling never came!

The only thing that came towards us was a mass of the enemy surrendering in thousands!

It was a very awesome sight.

I can't say I experienced a feeling of conquest. I had contributed nothing towards a victory that took a fortified port and captured some 30,000 prisoners but I did feel proud in belonging to an army that had done it.

After the battle comes the spoils! Benelli motorbikes were all over the place. Charlie Drake, Scotty Williamson, Chris Blackford and Jack Wooding were all experienced motorcyclists and several other signallers could handle a bike as well. We now had a squad of despatch riders to make our platoon more efficient in the desert.

The recent battle had revealed how inadequate telephone cables were in the mobility of desert warfare. Cables, in theory, had to be laid out to forward companies when they went to ground, or bivouacked for the night, then reeled in again when companies moved on. And cable was always in short supply.

We never had time to use telephones in The Battle of Bardia.

As a matter of fact we weren't used as signallers at all. The battalion was constantly on the move and time was not available to establish a signals pattern.

Company Commanders received their orders from The Colonel, who was always prowling around the front, and got on with the job which usually involved movement over a considerable area.

Besides, outside of all this waffling – Benelli motorbikes! Wow! Noise! Dust! Speed! Scrub Jumping! It was all there!

The Sig Officer couldn't approve of 25 despatch riders out of a platoon of 30 men so the number was whittled down to 5 or 6; a number approved by The C.O. providing they found their own fuel and oil. This was no problem. Drums of petrol and oil were all over the place.

A variety of trucks, ranging from small utilities to giant Fiat 10 tonners were also available.

The Signal Platoon commandeered a light, covered truck and converted it into a signals office and thus eliminated the problem of setting up a signals office for the remainder of The Western Desert Campaign.

We didn't hang around Bardia. The next day we were on our way to Tobruk eighty miles along the road towards Benghazi.

Tobruk, from our point of view, was similar to Bardia. It was a town snuggling around a harbour below a 300 foot high escarpment. It was fortified by an anti-tank ditch, supplemented by barbed wire and an occasional booby trap, stretching around the town's perimeter and along the top of the escarpment.

The British Armoured Division had already made a sweep from Bardia and was now astride the road leading to Derna on the other side of Tobruk.

Our division's task was to keep the enemy bottled up and to watch its movements until sufficient supplies became available to mount an attack. Road haulage of supplies over such a vast distance was a problem and a fortnight elapsed before an attack could be mounted.

Obviously, the capture of Tobruk would provide a port and eliminate 300 miles of road haulage.

It was interesting to note, whilst travelling from Bardia to outside Tobruk, a peculiar type of Pommy unit which seemed as much at home in the desert as the Arabs. It existed in small groups and had its own transport consisting of a couple of small utilities per group. They didn't seem to belong to anyone in particular and were always squatting about 50 yards from the roadside drinking tea. If they weren't drinking tea they had just put the billy on to make a brew.

It wasn't until we had been sitting for about a week outside the defences of Tobruk we learned they were units of The Northumberland Fusiliers; a Vickers Machine Gun Battalion which had been split up and attached to regiments for machine gun support.

Our Battalion H.Q. knew who they were but we hadn't used them so they were a source of curiosity and interest to the rest of us and all kinds of rumours circulated concerning them.

It was generally accepted that they were permanent British Army chaps who had been stationed up near The Kyber Pass in India.

(All British Army chaps had been stationed up near The Kyber Pass in India. Over a period of time I formed the impression that The Kyber Pass must have been fairly swarming with permanent British Army chaps – all led by Errol Flynn, of course!)

Apparently two of their officers had been murdered one dark night so the regiment surrounded the nearest village and belted up every male inhabitant. This sort of conduct, of course, was not British nor was it the right and proper thing to do so the battalion was sentenced to seven years in The Western Desert of Egypt.

They had been there years before we arrived and, consequently, felt quite at home sitting by the roadside brewing tea.

Water had become quite a problem and we were restricted to half a water-bottle per day for drinking purposes. The other half went to the cookhouse.

The Western Desert is not sand. It is soil similar to The Nullabor Plain or The Goldfields. It gradually attaches itself to clothing and skin so, after Bardia and sitting around outside Tobruk for a couple of weeks, we not only looked dirty, we were dirty.

The battalion was now in a static situation and telephone lines had to run out to companies spread over the countryside; usually a laborious task involving considerable physical effort carrying reels of cable and paying it out as we trudged towards a forward company hidden in the shimmering distance.

But Signaller Tom Smith had other ideas.

Somewhere out of the vastness of that country and amidst the spoils for the victor he had acquired a motor tricycle. The front portion was built like a motorbike but the rear end had two wheels with a differential and above this was a tray carrying a framework supporting a large reel of Italian field cable with two extra reels of cable. The idea was for Tom to ride the tricycle while I sat on the tray, behind the framework, paying out the cable.

We set off at a rattling pace, bouncing and thumping our way over the scrub. Nothing could be easier. Unfortunately the internal end of the cable was firmly tied to the reel.

The reel became empty!

The reel, the framework and I scribed a picturesque arc through the air. I landed beside the equipment and, except for a few scratches, was uninjured; a fortunate circumstance because Tom couldn't do anything for laughing!

We ran the cable out to one company then repeated the process, minus the flying trapeze bit, to the remainder.

Around sunset the trucks came in from "B" Eschelon, where the cooks functioned, with the evening meal.

"Where's "C" Company?" asked the driver.

"At the end of that telephone cable."

The driver straddled the cable with his truck and proceeded onwards leaving a wheel track on either side of our cable which, according to The Manual dated 1918, should have been hanging in the hedgerows or tree branches away from vehicular traffic.

Henceforth, all vehicles travelling to "C" Company followed those tyre marks and gradually increased their depth and pulverised the dirt into bulldust until our cable slowly disappeared.

The Signals Officer, at this stage of the campaign, decided to switch his subordinates around a bit so that we would all gain experience in the various aspects of our duties.

Ray Kennedy and I, owing to circumstances beyond our control, found ourselves attached to the H.Q. of "D" Company under the command of Captain Egan, a very capable soldier who was bit of a disciplinarian but commanded a very efficient and aggressive company.

The battle plan for Tobruk was similar to Bardia. The 16th Brigade was to go through the defensive perimeter then fan out left and right. Our brigade was to follow them through and go straight ahead – three battalions abreast – and make our way to the edge of the escarpment some five miles beyond.

Crossing the anti-tank ditch was no trouble. A massive rock formation just below the surface had restricted its depth to a couple of feet although the Italian artillery were shelling the area and causing some embarrassment.

Italian artillery shells had a distinctive peculiarity.

They came with a roar, they exploded with an ear-shattering noise and gut-jarring percussion but they broke into big pieces – four or five to a shell.

I agree; if one of these pieces hit you it could cause a serious problem but they are not nearly as dangerous as a shell bursting into thousands of pieces and hurling shrapnel everywhere.

The progress to the escarpment was a long walk without much hindrance from the enemy although I later learned the two battalions on our left had met with some stiff opposition.

We lay for several hours on the crest of the escarpment looking down upon the harbour and town of Tobruk. Several big oil fires on the far side of the town were sending a big black cloud of smoke up into a clear blue sky.

We moved forward early in the afternoon and took a position in the sand hills overlooking the harbour where the Italian warship, *S. Gorgio*, was aground but still firing her guns. The Italian defence was caving in and the *S. Gorgio* blew herself up during the afternoon.

Tobruk surrendered next morning.

"D" Company moved down to the harbour and occupied an Italian Army Storeroom where all the equipment was neatly arranged on rows and rows of shelves. I have often pondered upon the emotions of the Italian Quartermaster Sergeant as he walked away from it all. Quartermaster Sergeants are a peculiar type who zealously guard the equipment they so reluctantly issue to 'Other Ranks' and always with the threat of dire penalties if it is not returned.

But this Italian character had to simply walk away from it all. The misery and anguish of such an experience probably prevented him from ever applying for a storeman's job again. It can be so frustrating!

Whilst billeted in these buildings we received word some prisoners had to be brought in from the other side of the harbour. Capt. Egan detailed half a dozen men, complete with Bren Gun and ammunition, to go around and collect them.

I was sitting outside the shed when, half an hour later, I went inside to address the captain.

"Sir, I think you might like to have a look at this."

"Something wrong?"

"Not exactly. But it's interesting."

He came outside.

Stretching along the roadway skirting the harbour came a long blue line of Italian soldiers preceded by half a dozen khaki-clad members of "D" Company.

The captain stepped out on to the roadway and pulled them to halt as they approached our H.Q.

"I told you to bring in a few prisoners! Where did this lot come from?"

"I dunno, Sir. They came out of buildings and from behind walls and holes in the ground so we let them come along."

"Why are they carrying your Bren Gun and ammunition?"

"They offered to carry them, Sir, and they seemed such a friendly bunch I didn't think it would do any harm."

A dressing down followed, the Bren Gun and ammunition were returned to their rightful owners and the long column moved on to the P.O.W. Compound.

Another one of the spoils was the capture of the town's military brothel complete with its 50 workers. They were moved back through our battalion lines and rumour had it that they were placed under the care of The Regimental Padre but I doubt if The Colonel's droll sense of humour would have sanctioned such an arrangement. I suspect they were sent all the way back to Alexandria where, in all probability, they applied the skills of their trade for the duration.

We rested at Tobruk for a few days. Then the transport arrived and the battalion moved on towards Derna; a picturesque seaside town nestling on the shore of the Mediterranean with the escarpment as a backdrop.

The transport column was halted by Staff Officers at a spot not far from an aerodrome established on the flat country above the escarpment. Apparently the hangars were still held by the Italians equipped with some artillery and machine guns but, in view of our previous experiences, prolonged resistance was not expected once pressure was applied.

Our battalion had been pulled up to apply the pressure. "C" Company was to make a direct assault across the flat open aerodrome; "A" Company was to take the left flank and "D" Company, complete with Ray and I attached, was to go out on the right flank.

Our company moved off at 1400hrs and made its way right around the perimeter of the aerodrome under cover of a heavy cloud of dust blowing our way from the 'drome.

I didn't know it at the time but "C" Company was being pounded by very heavy artillery and machine gun fire from a very determined group of Italians within the hangars and this 'dust storm' was the dirt flung up by the artillery fire.

A very fierce and bloody battle was taking place.

We later learned "C" Company had driven the Italians out of the hangars after some very grim fighting and "B" Company had passed through its lines with the intent to proceed along the road leading down the escarpment to Derna but had temporarily withdrawn under heavy shellfire from a nearby fort.

Our company, while all this was going on, had reached the edge of the 600 feet high escarpment where we camped the night.

Next morning we managed to clamber down a steep gully and out on to a 200 yard wide flat area between the escarpment and the sea.

It stretched all the way to the delightful, picturesque town of Derna!

The platoons spread out across the flat and advanced towards the town.

Little lights flickering across the boulder-strewn ground and accompanied by a sharp crackling sound was the first indication of machine gun fire.

Capt. Egan's shout of "Get down!" was followed by a low, earth-shaking rumbling noise as an artillery barrage commenced creeping towards us.

It didn't actually creep! It stomped its way along the flat with thudding, aggressive steps that sent shock waves through the earth upon which we lay.

I lifted my head up to see if I could spot a ditch in which to crawl. My eyes fairly popped out of my head as I saw this impenetrable wall of dust bursting out of the earth and increasing its volume as it thumped towards us.

The Italian machine gunners couldn't see through it either and had ceased firing.

I reckoned this was a good time to move. Nearby was a pyramid of rocks about 4 feet high with a hollow behind it. I dashed across and dived into the hollow. Ray followed.

"Hey! Do you blokes know you are hiding behind an artillery ranging marker?" shouted a nearby soldier.

"Good," replied Ray. "You can bet the bastards won't blow it over."

The barrage's progress was preceded by large chunks of artillery shells buzzing through the air or bouncing along the ground.

Then it arrived and stayed a thousand years!

Shells landed with a roar, explosions cracked like nothing had ever cracked before, the ground shook and bounced as a great cloud of dust rose from the earth and blotted out the sky.

Ray and I, and everyone else, lay there expecting to be blown to bits with every shell. It wasn't a very pleasant experience.

The barrage moved on another 100 yards then it came back again!

It kept moving and eventually ceased for lack of targets.

A thick pall of dust hung overall and night was falling.

We made our way over to Capt. Egan. We should have been with him all the time but he had ordered us "down" and then ran around making sure everyone else was down.

Sgt. Major Sneddon was laying nearby and moaning about being cold.

"Is the Sar' Major hit, Sir?"

"Yes. He was hit in the head. As soon as it gets dark we'll get him out of here."

Jock Sneddon hit in the head! Jeez! We had been three years in the militia together. Played in the same Rugby Team!

We lay in the dirt until darkness before moving around again. Derna obviously could not be taken by a single company on this front so Capt. Egan sent his runner to tell the forward platoons to close in on his position.

Four of the men fashioned a stretcher out of rifles and groundsheets to carry The Sar' Major then set off along the flat before ascending the boulder-strewn slopes of the escarpment. The night was pitch-black and rain was falling. It must have been an horrendous climb with such improvised equipment.

We lost seven men, including an officer, on that flat.

The company assembled and we moved back before entering a gully. We clambered up the northern side and rested just below the crest. The Italians were sending over an occasional shell in our direction but they were landing harmlessly on the other side of the gully.

It was not a comfortable rest. Rain fell heavily and we had only our ground sheets to keep it off. You can cover yourself with a groundsheet but you can't stop the rainwater from flowing down the slope you are sitting on.

"You can come out of there," said a familiar voice, "I know who you are."

I poked my head out from under the groundsheet.

Jim Fraser was standing there with a reel of cable hanging on his side.

"Where the hell have you come from?"

"Over there," he said, pointing into the darkness with his nose like an Aboriginal from one of the nor' west cattle stations where he used to work, "Hook your phone on to this and you're in touch with Battalion H.Q."

"How did you know where to find us?"

"Lieutenant Dowling said you were over this way somewhere so I came looking for you."

We connected the phone while Ray went scrambling around looking for Capt. Egan.

Jim drifted off into the darkness trailing the cable between his fingers as a guide.

The captain finished his conversation with H.Q.

"There is a low stone wall at the top of this gully running out to the roadway. We are going to move out to that junction. Captain Woods is going to meet us there with a hot meal. I want you to connect the phone to the cable up there."

We advised the signallers at H.Q. of our plan, disconnected the phone and, with the rest, made our way through the pouring rain to the spot where the wall joins the road.

Ray and I grovelled around in the mud, in an ever-increasing radius, groping for the cable.

The road ran towards Derna. The wall was at right angles to it. Any normal person would have laid the cable in the ditch beside the road until he came to the wall then turn and follow the wall along the top of the gully.

But Jim was a bushman from 'up north' and he reckoned the shortest distance between two points was a straight line and, with that uncanny instinct peculiar to the breed, he had cut diagonally across country and laid the cable in the mud as he went.

Ray and I extended our searching further into the night. It was dark. Terribly dark. The Italians had shifted the ranging and were lobbing an occasional shell in our direction. They were fascinating to watch. They came from below the horizon to climb away above our heads into the sky then, suddenly, they came down into a vast, sloppy area where they exploded with gusto.

Unfortunately the vast, sloppy area happened to be where we were scratching around searching for an invisible telephone cable.

We watched the shells until they commenced their dive. Then we dived.

The cable was eventually found a hundred yards away and dragged back to the junction by the two filthiest signallers in The A.I.F. who were reprimanded by the captain for taking so long and abused by their mates at H.Q. who were becoming worried over the delay.

Our hot meal had gone cold, too.

The company crouched up against the wall to gain some protection from the wind and rain. It was a long, miserable night followed by an equally miserable dawn when Capt. Egan received orders to proceed and take a fort standing on a bend in the road leading down the escarpment into Derna.

Ray and I were given the most welcome of instructions: "Stay here with the phone until I send someone back for you. At least I'll know where you are then."

The company spread out and moved forward. The fort, constructed mainly of mud and rubble, was taken without much resistance although one of the men trod on a landmine killing himself and injuring several others.

Stretcher bearers carried the body back and left it on the roadside near our telephone position.

I wasn't feeling too good. I didn't seem to be as emotionally tough as the rest. The strain of being caught in the artillery barrage, the climb up the steep side of the gully during the night, the slopping about trying to find the cable in the pitch-black darkness under shellfire, the knowledge that I wasn't shaping up too well as a signaller because contact had been established with H.Q. and I had lost it for over an hour, I had had very little sleep in 24 hours and now a dead man was lying over there on the roadside.

I was aware that everyone else had been through the same experience. I didn't know how they felt but that is how I felt at the end of my first combat experience.

Maybe the war had suddenly become serious and I wasn't adapting to the circumstances.

The Regimental Medical Officer (Capt. "Killer" Ryan) soon arrived in his truck to pick up the wounded and they took the body away with them.

The fall of the fort meant all the enemy had been cleared away from the top of the escarpment and, except for some occasional shelling, the day was fairly quiet.

Fires were burning in the town that night.

Next morning we were informed the Italians had withdrawn from the town.

They had blown the road winding down the escarpment but it was already being repaired. "D" Company made its way around the crater to enter the town where we took up residence in a neat, two-storied hotel.

Considerable rubbish and litter had been strewn throughout the place so a few prisoners were brought in to clean the building. They were a most obliging bunch; all smiles and not at all perturbed about being prisoners. The only problem was when one particular chap went past pushing a broom all the rest stopped work and stood to attention. Obviously he was an officer willing to share the good with the bad along with the rest of the troops. I took him along the hallway to where the Captain had his quarters and, after explaining the situation, left him there.

Meanwhile, the company cooks had arrived and set themselves up in the kitchen. The hot water system was fired up and Life began to look pretty good.

One of our duties, as town garrison, was to prevent looting by the Arabs. Patrols were sent around the town for this purpose and kept the place in order until a well-stocked wine cellar was found. One of our chaps, a bit of a no-hoper, got as full as a boot and placed under arrest.

He was put in a room on the first floor and a sentry placed in the hallway at the locked door.

We also had to guard our own personnel and equipment from thieves or looters; this meant guard duties and I found myself involved in the old 'two-on four-off' routine. I was on guard duty at the hotel entrance when, around 3am, I recognised a drunken figure coming down the street at a fairly fast pace. He walked straight past me, climbed up an ornamental pillar to the first floor, clambered over the balustrade, opened the French window and disappeared into the room guarded by a sentry standing in the hallway beside a locked door.

When I was relieved at 4am I reported "All's well".

The 2/4th and 2/8th Battalions moved through the town to pursue the enemy along the road to Benghazi but our duties enabled us to live in luxury for four more days. The town's Arabs had eggs and vegetables to barter or sell for Italian money. We had, somehow, garnished an abundance of Italian money along the way so our menu improved considerably. The Arabs also made fresh, appetising bread but our R.M.O. was dubious about the places used for the storage of its ingredients and suggested we give it a miss.

Hot showers were available, the beds were comfortable and the persistent rain was a phenomenon viewed with disinterest.

It all came to an end.

Trucks arrived and we set out along the road to Benghazi.

It was a miserable, cold, wet drive lasting until midnight with instructions to be ready for an early start in the morning.

The next couple of days were no better.

I didn't know it at the time but the main road, snaking up and down the escarpment had been blown in several places. We were on a gravel sidetrack which had deteriorated rather badly and was causing our transport drivers considerable anxiety.

We eventually rejoined the sealed road near Benghazi, to pass through the outskirts of the town and continue southwards; apparently in hot pursuit of the retreating Italians.

But it was all over!

The 7th Armoured Division had made one of the most spectacular cross-country dashes in modern history and had cut off the Italians south of Benghazi.

A rather fierce tank battle ensured but our side won.

The battalion was detailed off to guard the prisoners.

What a miserable afternoon!

25,000 to 30,000 prisoners standing in a mass in the featureless desert. Tired, battle-weary, dispirited men who had very little desire to be in North Africa in the first place. They were packed so tight very few of them were sitting. Wounded men could be in their midst but there was no way of extracting them at the moment.

We patrolled a given beat around the outside perimeter. I suppose we tried to look menacing but the rain poured down, the mud beneath our feet became more gooey, our clothing gradually became saturated and a cold wind blew as victors and vanquished shared a mutual misery.

The Northumberland Fusiliers took over our duties before nightfall.

The battalion moved back a few miles along the road to spend a long night in the scrub before moving back to Tocra, some 30 miles along the coast north of Benghazi.

Tocra was an old, dilapidated Turkish fort although I understand it was quite a town 2,000 years ago.

Battalion H.Q. managed to set itself up in the main building and the rest of the troops were spread around the area. I was back at H.Q. again because the fighting was over and the platoon was re-assembled as a unit for administration purposes.

We cleaned out the former stables and made ourselves comfortable.

The cooks were again under cover and, for the next fourteen days, produced three meals a day as well as an occasional extra dixie of coffee. There are always sardonic comments made about army cooks but these chaps had done a terrific job throughout the campaign. They, like the rest of us, travelled long stretches in the back of a truck then when we stopped, oft times late at night, they set up their camp stoves to boil the billy and prepare a hot meal of bully beef and dehydrated vegetables. They may not have been the most appetising of meals but they were most welcome.

Interesting events took place during our brief occupation of the ancient townsite of Tocra.

Now we were stationary for a while, and in order to keep the troops occupied, the Colonel ordered the mounting of formal guards. This caused consternation among the ranks. We had been living in our uniforms for three months and they were tattered, torn and dirty. Formal Guards are subject to minute scrutiny of dress with no excuse for slovenly appearance. Dirt had to be scraped off collars, dried mud had to be scratched off uniforms and some sort of shine restored to boots, rifles and bayonet scabbards.

The Australian Canteen Service had also caught up with us and amongst its merchandise was one solitary box containing 30 Freddo Frogs!

How do you distribute a box of 30 Freddo Frogs amongst a battalion of battle-hardened troops?

The Colonel solved the problem by declaring they would be awarded to the smartest platoon at the formal guard mounting and, thereafter, when anybody did anything worthy of comment, a voice would invariably cry:- "Good man! Come and get your Freddo Frog!"

Unbeknown to us, whilst we were scraping dirt off our gear, decisions were being made by men who controlled men and I emotionally carried the eventual outcome with me for the rest of my life.

Chapter Fourteen

It seems Mr Churchill was dead keen on sending a force into Greece to stem the Italian Invasion and, perchance, fight its way up through The Balkans. Apparently he had forgotten a similar venture back in 1915.

The G.O.C. 6th Australian Division (Maj. Gen. Blamey) informed our Prime Minister (Mr Menzies) that he had no hope of maintaining a force in Greece. Or words to that effect.

Mr Menzies flew to England to inform Mr Churchill of this circumstance and, on his way, pulled into North Africa to tell us how proud the nation was of us.

Upon arriving in England he was informed Mr Churchill was running this war and Mr Menzies' time would be better spent in Australia. Or, again, words to that effect.

Of course we didn't know this at the time. We were standing on parade at Tocra listening to Mr Menzies.

We stayed at Tocra for some fourteen days. This gave us time to do some swimming as well as wash our clothes and sun bake in the nude while they dried. Our clothes, badly worn and tattered, had to be treated carefully to preserve them. Indeed, the pants of Jack Wooding (the Colonel's Despatch Rider) were so torn and worn that the Colonel gave him his only spare pair of pants.

The next move was back to Ain el Gazala, a flat area of sand and scrub near the ocean. Building material and sandbags were scattered all over the place. Several makeshift buildings and humpies began to appear as the troops used their ingenuity to make themselves feel "at home".

The Signals Platoon built a substantial hut out of sandbags with timber rafters and a galvanized iron roof. We set up our signals office within its walls and, for the next two weeks, lived quite comfortably.

But, in due course, the canopied trucks arrived. We clambered aboard and drove off towards Bardia.

A sandstorm blew in from nowhere. It wasn't a dust storm. It was a fair dinkum desert sandstorm.

The truck drivers couldn't see 20 feet ahead and had to crawl along, feeling their way, and constantly braking as the rear end of the preceding truck suddenly appeared, life size, right in front.

The troops, sitting or laying on the floor of the trucks, could do nothing as they became slowly buried in dust. Some held cloths over their faces and some even donned their gas masks. I don't remember passing through Tobruk but once we climbed the escarpment, the dust thinned out a bit and we made better time. But the back of the trucks, up to the top of the sideboards and tailgate, were level with a load of dust through which protruded heads and odd limbs here and there.

We halted to camp for the night by the roadside near Bardia.

The truck driver exclaimed, "Hey! Come and have a look at this!"

The whole of his truck front was burnished right down to the shining metal!

A couple of days later we arrived at Mersa Matruh to be billeted in Egyptian Army Barracks and issued with new clothing. The Carrier Platoon were delighted to receive six new Bren Gun Carriers and I believe the rest of the battalion's weaponry was brought up to full compliment.

The 9th Australian Division had arrived in Egypt and was in the process of moving up to garrison Tobruk, The 2/28th Battalion was billeted around the other side of the bay.

The 2/28th Battalion was another Western Australian regiment and the meeting of the two battalions was like a Western Australian

Re-union with men greeting companions whose friendship extended back to schooldays.

It was all part of The Great Adventure!

Letters from home had informed me that my old mate, Ivan Francis, was among them.

We had several pleasant afternoons together. He was, as always, so fresh and full of enthusiasm for whatever he was doing at the moment. We drank a few beers, swapped a few cigarettes and talked of Perth and the people we both knew; my parents, his parents, my sisters, his brothers. He even assured me that my fiancé was being faithful to me.

"I know she is," he said, "because I pitched her a sad tale about going overseas and I might not return but she still knocked me back."

It was comforting to know I had a friend like Ivan.

"See you later, mate, and look after yourself."

"Sure; I'll be O.K."

His regiment moved up to within the perimeter of Tobruk. Our regiment moved down to a miserable, tented staging camp named Amirya.

Amirya was situated about 20 miles from Alexandria. Leave was granted. We all had money.

The scenes at Alexandria were, to put it mildly, a real eye-opener. The beer bars did a roaring trade with men determined to demonstrate their ability to consume vast quantities of alcohol; the houses of a thousand delights were filled with men determined to prove their virility and "goodie-goodies", like Jess and I, went to the museum and the pictures.

Actually, I didn't want to be a "goodie-goodie" and I desperately tried to throw myself into a period of leave with all the careless, successful abandon of my mates. I just wasn't good at it.

I'd stand at a bar and try to match them drink for drink but I would be blind drunk and falling asleep just when they were beginning to hit their straps.

My capability in a house of a thousand delights was also the subject of good-humoured derision but I think anyone will agree it is hard to complete an act of sexual intercourse when your mates are sitting around on the same bed giving words of advice and encouragement.

Staying sober had its problems. Your drunken mates attach themselves to you and rely on you to get them back to their quarters before the Pommy Redcaps picked them up and slung them in the cooler for the night.

One thing we all agreed on: Pommy Redcaps were bastards!

But, once again, it all came to an end.

Germany declared war on Jugo-Slavia and Greece.

Four days later we were crammed into a troopship and sailed for Greece, there to create a slight dalliance for Hitler's Armies before they commenced their eastward roll into Russia.

We sailed from Alexandria in the company of *S.S. Cameronia* escorted by *H.M.S. Coventry* and three destroyers.

The voyage to Greece was uneventful. Just four days crammed aboard a former Dutch passenger ship converted into a troopship but I did have some culture shocks.

I was on a cookhouse fatigue entailing some work in the ship's galley staffed by Dutchmen.

Most of them spoke English!

They spoke two languages! I was astonished. They didn't appear to be intellectuals; they were cooks but they spoke two languages without any effort!

I thought about this for days and, with the thinking, came some kind of revelation.

Australians live in a vast country with state boundaries but no borders; we can travel all over it from one side to the other and never be asked for identification papers. We are completely surrounded by great oceans, we speak one common language and, at school, we were taught the only other countries of importance are those belonging to

The British Empire.

Come to think of it, I wasn't quite sure where Greece was located.

It seemed, in that ship's galley, as though a mental door opened to let the cold blast of my ignorance blow all over me.

Another shock came when Tom Smith and I were on the ship's bridge. Signallers, in pairs, were detailed to attend the ship's bridge where we stood with a hand-held Lucas Lamp to take any messages coming from the escorting destroyers.

The convoy was a day out from Greece when an aircraft appeared and circled low down before passing up between the lines of ships.

A Bristol Blenheim! A twin-engine bomber! It looked magnificent as it passed at eye level!

The only planes we had seen, so far, were Westland Lysanders and an occasional Gloster Gladiator.

"Look at that!" I cried to The First Officer, "A Bristol Blenheim!"

He gave a contemptuous sniff and grunted, "Obsolete."

*****

Our arrival in Greece was not exactly a grandiose entry. Piraeus was the port for disembarkation at Athens but an ammunition ship had been bombed at the dockside a few days earlier and the explosion had wrecked the whole harbour.

We were ferried ashore in fishing caiques and camped the night amidst pine trees.

We left Athens by train the following afternoon. The Athenians lined our course out of the city to cheer and wave; an unexpected and stimulating demonstration.

The country was enchanting. Green covered slopes leading away to towering, granite-faced mountains in the near distance; a pleasant contrast to the barren, sandy wastes of southern Palestine and The Western Desert.

The train clattered on through the remainder of the afternoon, and into the night, carrying us through a land steeped in mystical tales and ancient history of which I had no knowledge.

Late afternoon of the next day found us at Larissa where we 'detrained', climbed into trucks then transported to Kalabaka to cover the withdrawal of The British Armoured Division and to stop the enemy advancing on Larissa.

The retreat down the length of Greece and the evacuation was already under way before we even arrived at the front line!

The battalion took up a position overlooking a railway and road defile with a river on the far side.

Refugees were streaming back in thousands!

A constant shuffling stream of poorly-clad, weary, demoralised, humanity flowing twenty four hours a day. Horse-drawn carts – silent women and children – carts pulled by humans with all their worldly possessions piled high behind them – occasional Jugo-Slav and Greek soldiers, their uniforms contrasting with the drab colours of the other shuffling creatures – all of them moving in a silence broken only by the weary, rhythmic, plodding sound of hooves on the gravel road, the constant creak of cart-wheels, the ceaseless shuffle of feet which had shuffled for days, and the occasional cry of a wrapped babe.

I was stationed at Battalion H.Q. and, during the course of the afternoon, reported to The Medical Officer with a boil on my leg and visions of being sent back to Egypt. "Killer" Ryan took a look, slapped a plaster on it and said, "You'll be right in a couple of days."

That night I was detailed to run a telephone line out to "B" Company where my colleague of Derna days was attached to the phone. The distance seemed surprisingly short after the endless miles of the desert.

"Where have you been?" asked Ray Kennedy and Dan Smith.

"Crawling around in the dark looking for you bastards."

"We've been here all the time."

"Well, see that you stay here and, if you do come back, bring the bloody cable with you."

"She'll be right, mate."

I limped back down the hill.

Next morning The British Armoured Division commenced coming through our position. The battalion stayed there for another twenty-four hours with plans to move out the following night.

We moved out on foot in the early hours of the morning to march to Kalabaka where we boarded canopy-enclosed trucks for transport to Larissa.

'Troop-carrying Trucks' is another title needing clarification. They were simply trucks with a canvas canopy and crammed choc-a-bloc full of troops. There were no seats and the troops made themselves as comfortable as possible; usually by sitting with a back against the side of the tray and falling asleep.

Not much of the war can be seen from within and reliance had to be placed on a 'look-out' standing on the rear tailboard and hanging on to the top of the canopy. We had no air support. Not a damn plane of ours anywhere.

It was a long, hard day.

We had been trained in Palestine in the technique of "anti-aircraft defence whilst on the move" but in Greece the routine was somewhat different.

"Get to bloody hell out of here!" bellows the look-out. "The bastards are coming again!"

The truck thumps to a halt. We burst out of the back and take to the countryside, putting as much distance between ourselves and the roadway as the available time allows before burrowing into the earth and making ourselves as small as possible.

A Stuka attack is a nerve-wracking, morale-destroying experience.

They appear like the swarm of locusts in the film "The Good Earth" complete with all the noise and destructive power. They are completely unopposed and, if the target is a convoy, they fly along its length dropping bombs and machine-gunning. Then, having completed their run, they bank away to the far end of the convoy and have another go until the swarm of them form a noisy, chilling circle of sustained destruction.

If the target is a bridge, or a building, they form a circle above it like a string of wasps; the leader dives his plane straight down at the target, releases his bombs and swoops away to allow the next plane to repeat the attack. The roaring planes and exploding bombs are also equipped with wind-activated, ear-piercing, nerve-straining whistles which increase in volume and intensity as they descend.

Add to this an occasional bomb or burst of machine-gun fire aimed specifically in your direction and you are going through a rather horrendous experience.

Next night the convoy passed through Larissa, which had been heavily bombed and appeared deserted except for a solitary Military Policeman armed with a torch and directing traffic.

The retreat through to Brallos was another rugged day. The road, after passing through Lamia, went across open country. It was built up like a causeway and the trucks had no hope of getting off it.

The enemy aircraft, this time, were twin-engine Dornier Bombers. They came singly and in relays, bombing the vehicles and machine-gunning the roadside where the men lay. They had the sky to themselves and were without fighter escort. As one bomber completed its run and disappeared over the mountains ahead another appeared over the hills behind and repeated the action. In this manner they could keep a convoy pinned down for hours.

Laying in a ditch, and working on the theory that no two bombs land in the same spot, I noted where a bomb had just exploded. I raced across and dived into the crater.

It was boiling hot!

"Bloody Germans," I thought, "They think of everything."

Within ten seconds flat I was back in the ditch where I started.

We did see a Spitfire one day. It came around a spur in the hills chasing a Stuka. It fired a two-second burst and chopped the Stuka in half then swooped away. It was lucky. We weren't used to seeing our planes and Bren Guns were firing at it from all angles.

Our section of the convoy gradually crawled its way off the plain and into the hills to bivouac at Brallos for the night.

The car of our Commanding Officer (Colonel Louch) had been shot up by enemy aircraft during the course of the day. The driver had been killed, Capt. Ainslie had been wounded and although The Colonel had not been physically injured he was badly shaken.

That evening, after a conference with the company commanders, the strain of the preceding days, plus the loss of his driver and his own near miss, caused him to fold up and he was ordered to hospital.

The command of the battalion was handed over to Major Sandover who promptly set about organising companies to take up defensive positions, with New Zealanders on our right, to form The Thermopylae Line stretching down to the ocean.

The German advance was to be halted and the position held until 9:30pm.

Lieut. Dowling had been transferred to Battalion H.Q. to act as Liaison Officer and the new Signals Officer was Lieut Millett.

Members of The Signals Platoon at Battalion H.Q. were ordered to run telephone cables out to the forward companies. Two of us ran a cable to "B" Company where we were again greeted by Ray Kennedy and Dan Smith, but this time there was no light-hearted banter. The game was getting serious.

Once the phone was connected to H.Q. we scampered back with a funny tingling feeling in our backs. The terrain was uphill and fairly open. The enemy, to the best of our knowledge, was within firing range and preparing to attack.

"The battalion," as Major Sandover records, "was astride the road about four miles north of Brallos. The companies were positioned in the surrounding slopes with "D" and "B" Companies forward of a long spur which ran across the valley."

Tired men waited for a superior enemy to commence the battle.

It began with a barrage of mortar fire on our front in the late afternoon.

Our machine guns and artillery opened up with great accuracy; the artillery shells rustling the grass on the slopes as they climbed over hillcrests to land on the enemy.

"The MG and artillery fire was so accurate it caused the enemy to deploy," records Major Sandover, "and whilst holding a front, to engage in an encircling movement."

"D" Company was being outflanked on the left and the phone line to "B" Company had been cut.

The line to "B" Company was causing us some worry. It kept losing contact and, on several occasions, we were preparing to send a line party to check it out but, each time, it came back on the switchboard again.

All this was taking place under heavy machine gun and mortar fire in the twilight of the evening. Our troops were giving the Germans a rough time but we had no mortars and our artillery lines were in danger of encirclement. We were in a rather precarious position.

I was keeping my head down and trying not to panic as I operated the telephone exchange at Battalion H.Q. It wasn't easy. The funny thing was I kept reciting a passage from Shakespeare's 'Julius Caesar' to myself: "Cowards die many times before their death. The valiant taste of death but once." Obviously, I wasn't very valiant.

Again quoting from Major Sandover's account: "'A' Company (which had been held in reserve) was moved forward whilst 'B' and 'D' withdrew and were re-organised on a ridge to the rear by Capt. Honner. The 2/8th Battalion's detachment was called in and "C" Company withdrew – delaying a little to get the wounded out. Em-bussing in Brallos village was hair-raising – Very Lights going up on both flanks – but The Germans, too, were exhausted."

Sounds simple, doesn't it?

Major Sandover conducted himself that way.

But it was bloody awful!

We were damn near surrounded in the dark of night and, if a light showed or excessive noise was created, we came under mortar fire.

'Em-bussing' meant scrambling into the back of a truck with its motor already revving and rearing to go!

I was pulled into the back of a truck and banged the back of my leg. The pain was terrible but, somehow, I had forgotten all about that boil!

The truck carried a few wooden crates and was packed with men. I sat on about six square inches of crate corner for the next eight hours as we bumped and thumped our way through the night to a spot on the coast named Megara.

We spent the next day destroying trucks and other equipment that we couldn't carry on our backs, Setting fire to trucks was forbidden as the smoke would reveal our position to marauding aircraft so it got down to the simple process of unscrewing the sump plug, draining out the oil and revving the motor until it seized.

Many of the drivers walked away once they had started the motor of the truck they had cared for all through The Western Desert, and the withdrawal through Greece, trucks they had come to regard as "my truck".

We also wandered around looking for mates and the platoon was gradually assembled. We didn't have much equipment between us. A few telephones, an exchange unit and, dammit, a couple of small reels of cable.

Whilst looking for members of The Signal Platoon I came across Ray Kennedy who had been attached to "B" Company. Just looking at him told me something was wrong.

"It's Dan," he said. "I had to leave him. He's dead."

"Jeez! How'd it happen?"

He told us about it.

Our platoon had been formed in Australia and Dan was our first casualty. His death weighed heavily on us all.

The following night, after destroying all personal gear and carrying whatever equipment we still possessed, we moved down to the water. I remember being taken in a crowded fishing caique out to a large boat, which had mysteriously appeared through the darkness, and climbing up a scrambling-net wearing an overcoat with a rolled blanket, a rifle, a field telephone and a telephone exchange swinging from my shoulders.

HONOURS AND AWARDS.
MILITARY MEDAL.
SIGNALLER RAYMOND JOSEPH KENNEDY. (WX 1063)
CITATION.

At BRAYLOS on 24th April, 1941, the withdrawal of the brigade was covered by two companies of the 2/11th Battalion, which had been in contact with the enemy for several hours, and pressure was being rapidly intensified, shortly before the withdrawal of those two companies on a timed programme, communication with one company was interrupted by the wire being cut. As the other company was being outflanked by the enemy there was grave danger that both would be encircled. SIGNALLER KENNEDY, whose companion was killed beside him, set out to repair the line under extremely heavy machine gun fire. On his return he found the line had again been cut, so he again set out to a more exposed position under the same heavy fire, repaired the line and communications were again re-established.

PRIVATE KENNEDY'S complete disregard of danger and devotion to duty enabled a plan for the two companies to be co-ordinated, thereby averting what could certainly have been considerable casualties.

THE UNOFFICIAL VERSION.

On 24th April, 1941, two of the battalion's signallers, Ray Kennedy and Dan Smith, were attached to "B" Company, under the command of Captain Archie Jackson, at Brayloss Pass.

The Company H.Q. was dug in about three quarters of the way down a steep slope with a platoon on its right flank; the other two platoons were dug in on its right and left rear flanks.

Another company, also covering the brigade withdrawal, was on "B" Company's left flank. Both companies were connected to Battalion H.Q. by a common line running up the slope behind "B" Company's position.

This cable lay-out enabled both company H.Q.s and Battalion H.Q. to converse on a party line.

The company's position directly overlooked a railway and a village in the left foreground.

Already two events had occurred which were to have considerable bearing on the coming battle. The artillery had pulled their guns out of a position approximately 150 yards on "B" Company's right and retired 2,000 yards leaving their observation posts behind where they could overlook the battle area.

This piece of strategy paid off in two ways. The Stukas came over and bombed the artillery's original position and would have destroyed the guns had they still been there.

Secondly, the artillery was able to inflict heavy casualties on the enemy by bombarding the village while the enemy was gathering in force. This was particularly good shooting; the shells rustled the grass as they travelled up the slope and over the top to land on the target.

The enemy attacked at 1208hrs and the companies were to hold them until 2100 hrs.

The first attacks were weak and "B" Company managed to hold probing frontal attacks but they gradually built up in intensity.

Enemy troops were moving into the village and, at this stage, were subject to heavy artillery fire.

Around 1800hrs, when the attack was at its height, the company appeared outflanked and the enemy was infiltrating the position so Capt. Jackson decided to phone Bn. H.Q. and discuss the situation.

Ray Kennedy was unable to raise Bn. H.Q. or the other company H.Q. The line was dead. He concluded it was cut between "B" company H.Q. and the T junction.

He told Capt. Jackson he would go out and fix it. Archie queried whether Ray could do it in the circumstances but Ray pointed out it would take too long for someone to come out from Bn. H.Q. and, as the line was only broken a short distance away, he would have a go at fixing it.

He left the slit trench, dashed along the line and discovered a break about 150 yards up the hill. He joined the cable but not, as he admits, in accordance with the instructions laid down in The Signals Manual. The insulation on the strands of the broken wire was torn off with pliers and the bared wire knotted together. He even commenced winding insulation tape around the join (as per The Manual) but decided The Signals Corporal wouldn't be along to inspect the line so he gave it away and scrambled back to the slit trench.

The enemy was still heavily machine-gunning the area although the mortar, which had cut the line, had lifted further up the slope.

When Kennedy arrived back at the slit trench Dan Smith informed him the line was still dead. He immediately jumped out and ran up the hill again. This time, he later told me, he was scared.

Approximately 15 to 20 yards above the first break he found another which was repaired rougher than the first. He then dashed back towards the slit trench.

Capt. Jackson's head and shoulders appeared above the slit trench.

"Hurry up! Hurry up!" he bellowed.

The reply he received entitled him to put Kennedy on a charge for insubordination but Archie Jackson wasn't that kind of bloke, either.

The phone was functioning and a co-ordinated plan was arranged between the two companies and Battalion H.Q.

The enemy maintained its infiltration as "B" Company began withdrawing up the hill in the twilight. It was a helter-skelter, haphazard affair. Ray and Dan soon found themselves alone. They made it over the crest of the slope and went to earth wondering where the captain was because he set out immediately behind them when they commenced to withdraw.

Enemy machine gun fire was skimming dangerously close to where they lay so they decided to withdraw further.

As Dan Smith rolled over to stand up he was hit by a burst of machine gun fire and apparently killed.

Ray endeavoured to pick Dan up and carry him but Dan was over six feet tall and lifeless. The task was beyond Ray's ability.

The machine gun fire was getting heavier and the enemy was obviously closing in.

Ray had no alternative but to lay Dan down and make his way to the transport at the pre-arranged withdrawal point.

*****

The Germans picked up the mortally wounded Dan Smith and transported him to hospital in Athens where he subsequently died.

Chapter Fifteen

The evacuation at our embarkation point was orderly. The cheerful, confident attitude of the ship's crew as they pulled us aboard contrasted with our depressed state of mind. I remember one of them saying: "Good on yer, Aussie. You've done a good job. Get below and we'll get you out of here." He had a broad accent and I was too tired to care where he took us.

3,500 men were crammed below the decks of the *Thurland Castle* where most of us fell asleep. When I awoke we were at sea with an escort of 2 destroyers and the cruiser *H.M.S. Coventry*.

My few square feet of floor space was right beside the ladder leading up to the deck; a handy place in such circumstances. We had been warned to stay below decks in the event of an air raid because of the danger of machine gun bullets, shrapnel, deck wreckage etc. I couldn't stay below and crept up to the deck to have a look around.

The day was beautiful with a clear sky, a calm sea and the convoy making white bow waves upon the ocean's blue surface.

I noticed an Italian Breda Anti-Aircraft Gun mounted forrard with an alert crew in attendance; in the near vicinity was a chap lying in a type of lounge chair and looking through field glasses into an empty sky.

Suddenly *The Coventry* opened up with its heavy A.A. guns. At first I couldn't see any enemy aircraft but, when the shells burst high above, planes could be seen heading our way.

They loosed their bombs from a height. The chap in the lounge chair waved his hands to starboard, the ship swung that way and the bombs fell where the ship would have been if it hadn't changed its course.

Another plane came in at a lower altitude and raked our ship with machine gun fire.

I slid down the ladder but kept my spot near the bottom just in case.

The destroyers and the cruiser were putting up a heavy barrage but planes kept coming in at low altitudes. They came in a determined manner, machine gunning the decks and dropping bombs meant to blow us to hell but landing close by in the ocean. They exploded with a concussion that shook the ship; in one particular salvo they caused the paint to jump off the internal side of the vessel and shower itself over the troops.

The noise and excitement of battle can only be tolerated, as a spectator, for a short time.

Despite the doubts of a dubious ship's captain, Bren Guns were hauled up from below, their tripods lashed to the ship's rail and defiant gunfire was hurled at any plane coming within range.

It was effective!

Several planes came in too close then staggered away to crash into the blue, sunlit waters amidst a wall of spray and a cheer of exhilaration from the troops lining the rails.

The noise of light and heavy weaponry, diving planes, exploding bombs and human yells of battle erupted continuously throughout the long, zigzagging day as waves of bombers attacked the convoy fighting its way to Crete.

Our admiration of the navy, which had always been high, broadened with the duration of the voyage; a sense of respect becoming mutual when our Bren Gunners received a signal from *H.M.S. Coventry* saying, "Well done."

The navy doesn't waste words.

The *S.S. Thurland Castle* berthed in Suda Bay. We streamed ashore, sorted ourselves out into battalions and moved off the wharf away from the sheds.

The 3 inch A.A. guns on top of the headlands opened up as a flight of bombers made the last raid of the day.

We scattered into the country surrounding the port. It seemed to be more of a nuisance raid and wasn't carried out with the ferociousness with which we were becoming accustomed.

The Blam! Blam! of the guns, the roar of the planes and the explosion of bombs abruptly ceased as the aircraft flew off and, for brief pause, a heavy silence reigned.

Capt. Woods attempted to re-assemble his company.

"Sar' Major Curtis! Sar' Major Curtis!" he called.

"Sah!" bellowed Sar' Major Curtis.

"Come and get your Freddo Frog!" yelled a voice from somewhere in the background.

We re-assembled and, before moving off to a nearby staging camp, our platoon was told to put our field telephone exchange and phones in a wharf side shed. They would be delivered to us when we arrived at our destination, wherever that may be.

We never saw them again.

Our battalion's signalling equipment now consisted of a few hundred yards of cable and the couple of phones that we had decided to hang on to.

More troops arrived with men of different units all mixed together and the sorting out took a little time.

The 6th Australian Division had been through an evacuation and, at this stage, it looked rather ragged. Some from the *S.S. Costa Rica* lost everything when the ship was sunk; they were now without boots and only had the clothing they wore. There was an acute shortage of clothing, food, weaponry and all the essentials necessary to make an army an efficient unit.

Not all the troops from our battalion arrived on Crete. Some had scrambled aboard navy ships and were taken to Egypt. One of them was Geoff Benson, my horse-transport mate from militia days. He boarded a destroyer and finished up in Alexandria. He took part in The Syrian Campaign and was eventually returned to Australia where he married my kid sister like he always said he would.

The Adjutant (Capt. Ainslie) was missing and Lieut. Dowling took over his duties.

Other officers began to trickle in so we moved out of the staging camp and walked to the township of Georgiopolis.

It wasn't a march. It was a walk.

The men, ill-clad, tired and hungry, followed goat tracks over steep hills towards an obscure destination.

Some British Army blankets had been issued but we still had only one blanket and a greatcoat each and the nights were very cold. Men unashamedly dragged their meagre covering over themselves and slept in pairs to keep warm.

Jesse Varvell and I were to spend many a night in this manner.

It took us several days to reach the airstrip beyond Retimo and move into the adjacent hills to dig in under the olive trees.

Ours was not the only battalion in the area. I know The 2/1st, The 2/8th and a couple of Greek Battalions were spread out along the slopes overlooking the airstrip but the immediate subject of interest was our battalion, our company or, more specifically, our platoon.

The whole battalion was in a bad way and our platoon was no different to the rest. Our clothing was dilapidated and, whilst causing no problem during the day, it afforded little comfort against the cold of night.

We still had a rifle each but ammunition was in very short supply, especially for Jesse's Bren gun. We also had a Boys Anti Tank Rifle complete with two rounds.

Food was terribly scarce and cooking equipment 'make-shift'. The battalion was so spread out that company cooking became a problem.

Our platoon appointed its own cook and we cooked for ourselves. Our principal cooking utensil was a 4 gallon petrol tin into which was tossed our rations of bully beef accompanied by occasional fresh vegetables purchased under the barter system from the local villagers.

The Kiwis had managed to purloin all our signalling gear from the wharf shed at Suda Bay; communication within the battalion was mainly by company runners.

Our platoon, from a military point of view, was under the command of Lieut. Millett. We 'paired off' and dug slit trenches underneath the olive trees on the slopes overlooking the airstrip stretched out between us and the sea.

Jesse and I dug a slit trench which was to be our home for the next hectic month.

Early in that month we had a visit from General Freyburg who told us exactly what to expect. It wasn't good news. We were to be bombed and strafed by enemy aircraft before an eventual paratroop landing designed to capture the airstrip.

Our job was to endure the bombing and strafing and, when the paratroops came, stop them.

Our side was still using the airstrip. Every evening, just on sundown, two Gloster Gladiators appeared from nowhere, landed on the strip, stayed overnight and took off at daylight.

Twin-engine Dornier photography planes flew up and down the island, without opposition, from day one.

Our orders were, upon hearing aircraft, to get under an olive tree and freeze; in this manner we hoped to conceal the number of troops in the area. We also camouflaged our slit trenches as best we could.

The month progressed.

Food was never enough. Trading with the locals produced some vegetables but they never had much to spare. Meat was scarce. A tin of cubed pineapple was issued one evening; a welcome addition of two cubes per man.

The nights were always cold.

Single-engine Messerschmitt Fighters now began to patrol the area. They flew around machine-gunning suspected targets or anything that moved. We had orders not to fire on them so our only defence was to crouch in the bottom of the slit-trench and pray the plane's eight machine guns weren't aimed specifically at us.

Sometimes they flew at eye-level between us and the sea; this greatly annoyed Jesse who was keen to have a go at them.

The day came when temptation was just too much.

Jesse was standing underneath an olive tree with his Bren gun mounted on its tripod when a Messerschmitt passed a bit too close at eye-level.

Jesse gave him a burst.

The plane rose steeply, banked around at the top of its climb and came roaring back with its guns blazing. Jesse smartly moved around to the other side of the tree, held his ground and kept firing.

The plane zoomed past and kept going.

"He's got me! He's got me!" cried a grief-stricken voice from an adjacent slit-trench.

We raced over to help the wounded man lying in the bottom of the trench holding his shirt and trying to be brave.

Lieut. Millett jumped into the trench to assess the damage. No bullet holes could be seen but half a dozen hot cartridge cases, ejected from the Bren gun, were still rolling around inside the man's shirt.

It took him a while to live that down.

We lived beneath the olive trees, we cooked our food in the four gallon tin and waited – waited – waited.

I was sent into Retimo for a week to operate the telephone exchange with Cpl. Meredith. It was a welcome break from the dirt. Our quarters were on the second floor of the building and we slept on army stretchers.

In the twilight of the first day I heard an unusual noise in the street below. I dashed out on to the balcony and looked down on a unique scene. The street was crowded with hundreds of people simply shuffling up and down its length.

The air raids of the day were over and the population had come out for exercise and gossip.

Each day, at 10am, I was relieved for morning tea. I'd scamper off to a nearby cafe and, in my best Greek (gleaned from a book titled "Greek phrases for soldiers overseas") order a cup of tea with milk and two cakes.

The Greek proprietor would smilingly oblige. I assume the 'oblige' bit was standard for business whilst the 'smile' was secret amusement at this character trying to speak Greek with an Australian accent.

The Greek put up with this for several days and finally said, with an American accent, "O.K. I've worked out what you're asking for."

My replacement arrived at the end of the week and I returned to the platoon under the olive trees leaving Cpl. Meredith in Retimo to wallow in luxury.

And the photographing Dorniers flew up and down the island.

Enemy aircraft patrols and machine gun attacks increased on the morning of 20th May as a group of some 20 Junkers troop-carriers came in from the sea. We thought they were heading for the airstrip but before crossing the coast they turned away and headed for the western end of the island. Another mob came in around mid-day but they turned east; apparently heading for Heraklion.

It wasn't hard to work out where the next lot was going to land.

Around 4pm a whole swarm of fighters and light bombers began to pay considerable attention to our area by intense bombing and strafing; but we were dug in and stayed under cover with the olive trees hiding us from observation – and the whole battalion waited.

They first appeared as black dots superimposed above the horizon separating the blue sky from the blue ocean.

Not just a few planes but a whole armada of Junkers three-engined troop-carriers!

Then the noise of their motors became audible; a gentle throbbing which increased in volume until it became a vibrating, drumming sound of menacing portent.

They swung eastward and, as they crossed the coastline, commenced flying along the coast towards the airstrip directly in front of the battalion's position.

It was an awesome sight as doll-like figures began jumping out of the planes to fall a short distance before their 'chutes opened and floated them to the ground.

The 2/8th Battalions Bren guns opened up with a sharp crackling noise as the carriers flew past their position; a cacophony of noise to which was added the battle-sound of our own Bren guns and rifles as the planes approached to unload their cargo.

We recovered from our initial surprise and directed our fire at the planes before the troops jumped.

Live men commenced throwing dead, or wounded, out of the planes in order to make their own exit.

The 2/8th's fire drove one flight up higher and the paratroopers jumped above the airstrip. The next flight came in at the correct height and ploughed through them.

We cheered at the chaos and laughed at the sight of some planes heading back to Greece with parachutes tangled around their wing tips and tailplanes while men swung at the end of their 'chute cords. Some paratroopers landed within our lines, or in the immediate vicinity, and were promptly despatched; but most were jumping from planes coming in at eye level and descending into the vineyards on the flat ground in front of our elevated position.

Jesse, at last, was using his Bren gun with good effect. He definitely knocked big chunks off the near-side engine of a troop-carrier and, no doubt, caused a lot of worry inside its fuselage.

Some planes were already on fire as they approached the drop zone in front of us but they held their position in the group until the paratroopers were out before banking away to crash into the sea or disappear towards Greece leaving a trail of smoke behind them.

Jesse had only one barrel for his Bren gun and it was getting hot. He grabbed our four gallon cooking tin full of drinking water, plunged the barrel in to cool it, re-assembled it on the gun and kept firing.

The Boys Anti-Tank Rifle was near my slit trench. I jumped out of the trench, picked it up, hooked the barrel-stand into the fork of a tree, took a sight on a Junkers and pulled the trigger.

I don't know if I hit anything. I landed flat on my back about twelve feet away. My mates cheered but I think it was mainly in appreciation of some comic relief.

But I do know Lieut. Millett muttered about using up half the platoon's anti-tank ammunition and threatened to put me on a charge if I did anything like that again.

"F-k' im" said Ray, "I saw a big chunk fly off the engine of that plane and it went down out to sea."

"You sure?" I yelled.

"Well. One of them crashed out there but I don't know if it is the one you aimed at."

"Gee! Thanks Ray."

The troop-carriers stopped coming and the throbbing roar of their motors faded away.

The rifle platoons had been acting independently during the landing and many individual heroic actions and tragedies took place.

The Signal Platoon's position was on a kind of headland, or spur, and gave a sweeping view over the vineyards in front and down to the airstrip and the sea beyond. It also gave clear sight westwards and across the flat country to the nearby village of Perivola.

Now that the landing was complete the enemy planes could not bomb or strafe for fear of hitting their own troops.

The platoons attacked through the vineyard and mopped up the area.

Our platoon was not involved in the action. Our task was to do whatever was necessary around Battalion H.Q. so, for the time being, we were static.

Jack Wooding, earlier in the day, had been stationed down by the roadside to receive any dispatches that may have come our way. He reckoned the whole of Hitler's Paratroop Army had landed between him and our position. He crawled along a dry creek bed and turned up later in the afternoon to proudly display where a bullet had neatly gone right through his buttock.

Corporal Meredith wandered in from Retimo. When he saw the paratroopers landing he immediately took to the mountains and made his way back through the foothills.

The sounds of battle gradually diminished with the day. What remained of the paratroopers had consolidated itself in the village of Perivola.

We commenced moving around. Our volunteer cook concocted a stew and was roundly abused because it tasted of cordite.

"Don't you bastards go crook at me", he bellowed, "You have a go at Jesse. He's the joker who kept dropping his Bren gun barrel in my bucket of water!"

"Well, what was I supposed to do?" asked Jesse, "I was busy shooting Germans. Did you think to throw the water away?'

"Of course I threw the bloody water away; but the tin's ruined for cooking."

"Aw, you won't know the difference in a few days."

A long night followed.

The standard guard routine of '2 on and 4 off' was established. We didn't know the exact location of individual paratroopers who had become separated from their units so the '2 on' meant laying for two hours close to a bush or olive tree, shivering with cold, and keeping a tense look-out for any movement in the immediate vicinity. The '4 off' was equally cold and apprehensive.

The sunlight of the following day was welcome.

Prisoners had been taken and were held in an area behind our lines.

Major Sandover could read and speak German so, under his direction and in accordance with the instruction manuals landed with the paratroopers, the correct markers were laid out for drop zones and our supply of arms and ammunition increased considerably.

Companies still had to send groups to nearby wells to carry water. I was told to report to Company H.Q. for water-carrying fatigue. Upon arriving there I was nonplussed to see six German prisoners sitting in a group.

Our platoon had not been engaged in the fierce hand-to-hand fighting which had erupted yesterday and, to me, Germans were something to be shot at from a distance, but here were six of them, right there within twelve feet of me.

The Company Sargeant Major pointed and the prisoners picked up a nearby heap of containers.

"Now you," he said, "take these prisoners down to the well and get some water."

We commenced to move off when he abruptly pulled us up and took me aside.

"For Chrissake!" he hissed, "Will you get it into your head that these are the f- - - - - -g enemy! They could kill you and escape if they wanted to. Now, fix your bloody bayonet, put one up the spout, don't get too close to them and look as though you mean to kill the bastards!"

I did as he instructed and, carrying my rifle at the port, followed the single file of prisoners down the track.

They seemed quite relaxed as they spoke and joked amongst themselves. Obviously the humour of my interlude with The

Sar/Major hadn't escaped them.

The containers were filled and we returned to Company H.Q. without losing a man.

But I was shaken! The Company Sar/Major was right! It could have happened!

Over the next couple of days we began to move around with a little less caution; the enemy had been cleared from the immediate vicinity and was bottled up in Perivoli.

Lieut. Millett, Corporal Arlidge and I were standing in a group beside my slit trench when it happened.

It wasn't the sharp, crackling sound of gunfire directed at us that made us duck for cover; it was more of a hissing noise like spent bullets at the end of their trajectory that kicked up dust all around us.

The Lieutenant and I arrived at the trench together but Corporal Arlidge lay prone on the ground yelling in agony.

"Cover me!" shouted Millett.

I cocked my rifle, stuck my head above ground, swivelling around in all directions looking for a target.

Nothing! Absolutely nothing!

Lieutenant Millett vaulted out of the trench, squirmed across the ground to Tom, grabbed him by the armpits and dragged him back to the trench where we laid him along the bottom and tried not to stand on him as we looked for targets.

Nothing! Still nothing!

"We need the doctor!" bellowed Millett.

"On me way!" cried Ray Kennedy as he took off through the olive trees.

The doctor arrived within minutes to jab a morphine needle into Tom's arm. The agonising yelling stopped. Stretcher-bearers came and took Tom away to The Regimental Aid Post.

What a hell of a mess to be in.

The Regimental Aid Post is supposed to be the depot where wounded were taken for preliminary attention before being loaded into an ambulance for transport to an Advanced Dressing Station and hospitals at the rear.

But we were on this bloody island and there was nowhere to go beyond The Advanced Dressing Station set up behind our lines by The 2/7th Field Ambulance. No ambulance and no hospitals. Simply a Dressing Station with no tents for the wounded, no surgical equipment for emergency operations and practically no field dressings. Just a doctor with a hypodermic needle and a group of orderlies doing their best amongst the wounded laying around in the open.

Corporal Tom Arlidge died two days later.

The equipment dropped with paratroopers included sniper's rifles; beautifully made weapons complete with telescopic sights and all the adjustments necessary for accurate shooting over long distances. Signaller Andy Mulgrave was a small arms enthusiast and reputedly the best shot in the battalion.

Each morning, before daylight, he and Sar/Major Mitchell disappeared into the foothills behind our lines and made their way to a hamlet overlooking the German lines.

According to Andy they made themselves comfortable on beds on the second floor of different houses and, armed with a telescopic rifle each, spent the day sniping and creating casualties amongst the enemy.

A flight of Stukas came over near the end of the week and circled around, obviously in contact with the embattled paratroopers. The circle grew tighter. They dived at Andy's hide-out and completely destroyed it!

A mood of misery descended upon the platoon for the remainder of the day but Andy's long, skinny frame turned up through the gloom after twilight.

"It was close today," he commented. "Bloody hell it was close!"

Bill Bryden, equipped with a pair of German periscope field-glasses, had set up an advanced observation post near the end of our elevated spur overlooking the country between us and Perivoli. His job was to report any undue or excessive enemy activity.

It was necessary to have a telephone at this look-out and, not being a hero, I set it up in the hollow trunk of a very old olive tree.

There were an estimated 500 German Paratroopers trapped in Perivoli. They were well equipped with machine guns, automatic pistols, rifles and trench mortars. They were experts in their use and this factor, coupled with unimpeded, constant air support, made their embattlement a very formidable garrison.

The stretch of country between our position and theirs was comparatively open with dry creek beds, low bushes and an occasional undulation.

Our companies, supported by a couple of light tanks manned by men from our battalion, attacked.

The tanks were knocked out by mortar or artillery fire, the infantry was pinned down all day by withering fire from the dug-in paratroopers while enemy aircraft dive-bombed and machine-gunned troops spread across the attacking zone and reducing movement to a minimum.

The men regrouped at night and attacks were repeatedly carried out over the following days inflicting heavy casualties on the enemy – but at a terrible cost.

More machine-gunning, more dive bombing, more strafing and mounting casualties.

On 23rd May we learned from The Greeks, who were pulling out, that a large number of German motorcycle units, several tanks and artillery had reinforced the paratroopers in Perivoli and they were preparing to attack in force.

Obviously the battle had been lost at Canea and the Germans were over-running the island.

The attack commenced soon after daylight with an artillery barrage followed by an all out assault as seemingly dozens of motor-cycles endeavoured to carry out an encircling movement supported by tanks and infantry.

Our troops, in the face of such overwhelming odds, had to withdraw from the flat country in front of the enemy and fought a desperate rear-guard action.

Trench mortars commenced blowing the tops off trees adjacent to Bill and I as we dived into the hollow trunk of our favourite olive tree. The Germans also had us covered with tracer and explosive bullets.

The phone buzzed.

"Get out!" ordered Lieutenant Millett, "And try to get back here!"

We ran zigzagging through the trees until we reached Battalion H.Q.

A few battle-weary men were standing in a group around Major Sandover.

"The island has capitulated," he calmly said. "I'm afraid it's every man for himself. You can stay here and be made a prisoners-of-war or you can follow me. I'm heading over the mountains to the other side of the island."

The Battle of Retimo was over.

The 2/11th Battalion (City of Perth Regiment) had lost 53 (killed), 126 were wounded and, eventually, 423 were made prisoners-of-war.

Chapter Sixteen

Several members of the Signals Platoon, including Jesse and I, joined the group and headed for the mountains; on the way we smashed our rifles and hurled the bolts into the bush. It was one thing to be caught with arms in the field of battle but, once the island capitulated, we could be classified as armed bandits and shot on the spot.

This prospect didn't appeal to me even though there were genuine tears in my eyes as I smashed the rifle over the parapet of a well and dropped it down into the depths.

My predominate thought, at the time, was, "How am I going to tell Mum?" but my immediate need was survival.

We followed a kind of goat track up into the heights, diving for cover amidst the rocks or in the crevices whenever a searching plane came within our vicinity.

We had climbed thousands of feet above sea level by sundown and it was becoming obvious we were in for a long, cold night when a Cretan appeared. He was clad in well-worn clothing with baggy pants as in Turkish style and across his shoulders he carried a shotgun of a bore that would have blown the front off a tank at close range. He was an old man yet he indicated we should follow him.

He danced from rock to rock following a barely discernable track leading all the way up the mountain and down to the coast on the other side of the island where we arrived in the early hours of the morning.

Hundreds of men were already there and rumours were rife.

The navy was coming in at night to pick us up.

Arrangements had been made for submarines to come in and evacuate us during the night.

The R.A.F. was going to drop food supplies that night.

None of it came to pass.

We sat there for several days. Food and water was becoming scarce and the shortages were beginning to cause considerable anxiety.

A German Officer, accompanied by an interpreter, casually strolled in amongst us one afternoon and asked for the senior officer to whom he indicated numerous positions amidst the surrounding bush-covered hills.

"We have mortars there, there and there. We have machine-guns there, there and there. Your men are completely surrounded. If you want a fight you can have it but I suggest you decide to become prisoners of war. I will return in two hours for your decision."

He returned in two hours with a squad of men.

We were lined up, counted and marched off.

It was as simple as that!

We marched far into the night, the Germans passing us from one group of guards in a village to another squad in the next village. This entailed hungry, ill-clad men standing for long periods in rows of ten during counting, checking and re-counting before being hurried on into the cold night like a flock of wayward sheep.

There was no physical abuse from the guards. They were young and physically fit. They had just won a battle and their 'espirit de corps' was at its zenith whereas we had been cold and hungry for a month and now felt abandoned by all the British beliefs and traditions that had been instilled into us since early childhood.

The route was not back over the mountains but around them and our first rest was well after midnight in a flat, open field. Jesse and I huddled together for warmth and took turns in lying on the windward side with our backs to the cold breeze.

There was no issue of food so we scrounged or went hungry. One brief roadside pause was by a garden containing a laden cherry tree. We stripped it clean.

Our second night was spent laying in the soil of a vineyard below our former position overlooking the Retimo Airstrip where so many men had died for so little purpose.

A loud, prolonged screaming awoke us at some obscure hour of the night. Germans came grunting in from the perimeter seeking the screamer and flashing torches everywhere. Vic Petersen had been bitten on the neck by a deadly snake and was in agony. The Germans picked him up, placed him in a vehicle and raced him into Retimo.

Vic told me, several years later, the German doctor had said, "Five minutes later and you would have been dead."

We tramped into Canea at the end of the day and were billeted in the civilian prison. The cells were constructed of iron bars allowing a view through them from one end of the building to the other and we filled them to capacity. We slept on the bare, concrete floor but the number of bodies tended to create warmth and we were sheltered from the cold wind. Oh, that was a blessing!

The building was locked at night but the cell doors were left open to allow ready access to the toilets; not that this mattered very much – we had scarcely eaten anything during the past four or five days.

Civilian criminals mingled with us during the day but were locked away elsewhere at night.

The Germans made a great show, on one parade, by telling us we were going to be fed. We would receive 200 grammes of bread and a bowl of stew each day.

"How big is 200 grammes of bread?"

"I dunno."

The 'stew' was made by pouring the correct amount of water into the cooking urns; a few vegetables of doubtful quality were tossed in. The result was a very watery stew completely devoid of any nourishment.

Keeping clean became a problem. Water was permanently turned off at the ablution block and was only available from a single tap in the exercise yard. A very long queue slowly progressed towards it all day long to fill water bottles or tin cans.

We began to lose weight.

Rumours flourished on conjecture without substance. Food became the chief topic as our hunger increased. We remembered the Sunday roast and the conviviality around the family dinner table or the steak and eggs available in any restaurant back home. We had given up hope of any rescue and sat around in this manner for weeks.

Movement orders were issued. We were lined up without warning, marched through the town of Cania to Suda Bay and crammed into the hold of a very ancient, dirty, Greek coastal freighter.

I don't remember much about that voyage. The sea was calm and once we reached the Grecian coast we crept along between islands to disembark at Salonika.

The guards were changed. Hitherto we had been guarded by our former battle opponents who were young men of the paratroop regiments or Austrian Alpine Troops and appeared to appreciate our circumstances but our new guards were older men. Most of them had a moustache like Adolf Hitler and they were all bad. Once the seemingly endless counting and checking was over, and we commenced to move off through the streets of Salonika rifle butts to the ribs became regular aids to progress. If a man dropped through pain or malnutrition he was kicked to his feet and pushed on by a shouting, abusive Hun.

What a humiliated, degraded mob we must have appeared to the civilian population standing silently on the footpaths as we were pushed, shoved, kicked, rifle-butted and abused along the streets.

Our uniforms, filthy from ship's dirt, hung on our thinning bodies like rags.

Some men never had sufficient clothing to cover their bodies and clumped along the streets in worn-out boots with towels or rags wrapped around their waists as a gesture towards preserving some sense of dignity.

A woman bystander leaned forward and offered a loaf of bread. She was immediately grabbed by two guards, dragged to the head of the column and hauled along screaming to the guardhouse of the Greek barracks where we were to be imprisoned.

We don't know what happened to her.

Our new quarters consisted of several very old two-storied buildings. A high, double, barbed-wire fence had been constructed around the outer perimeter and also enclosed the parade ground.

Lavatories, about 50 yards away from the buildings, were crude. Two raised sections marked the position for feet and we squatted over a six inch diameter hole descending to the main sewer. There was no water available for flushing. The design didn't worry most of us but many men had dysentery and scraps of paper suddenly became valuable.

Body washing and keeping clean was a constant problem. Water was available for a brief period each day and the taps were again focus points for long queues.

The possibility of having a shower was zero so body cleaning consisted of a wipe-over with a rag dampened with precious water.

We were crammed on to both floors of the buildings, grabbing sufficient floor space to lie on. Six members of The Signal Platoon had managed to keep together and we dropped our meagre belongings against the wall as a claim to territory.

A strip of timber, about three inches wide and at waist height, ran right along the wall. Its original purpose was not clear but it was currently the home of millions of bugs and I tremble to think how many gallons of blood they extracted from our emaciated bodies as we lay in semi-conscious sleep during the following months.

The prisoners are best described as 'anything that was captured', and a few of the groups took some adjusting to.

There were several Spaniards who had been on the losing side of The Spanish Civil War. I don't know how they arrived here but they were hard, callous men completely indifferent to death or to the consequences their actions may bring to others.

There were Cypriots who squatted in a circle all day and gambled with dice although they had nothing to win or lose.

The Argyle and Sutherland Highlanders became dirtier and dirtier.

The New Zealand crew of a Wellington Bomber, forced down on Crete, seemed to regard their bad luck as one of the hazards of the job. One of them had a slight knowledge of the German language and, on the rare occasions when a guard was amendable, managed to be of help to us in minor ways.

Barrack searches became a regular event. The guards swept into the building, roaring and kicking, to order everyone with their gear out on to the parade ground to be counted and re-counted before being left in the sun for the remainder of the day.

These parades had a debilitating effect on starving men upon whom the effects of malnutrition were becoming very obvious. The sun was hot and there was no shelter from it. No one could go to the single tap in the corner of the parade ground so, if you didn't have water, you went thirsty or shared with your mates.

Dysentery didn't mean a thing. Nobody was allowed to move from where they stood or sat; a callous method of demoralizing the troops and further reducing the physical condition of men who were already starving. After a few weeks of this treatment I reached the stage where, if sitting on the floor, I would have to crawl to the wall, climb up and hang on until the vice-like pain in my head relaxed and my eyes could focus again. I had also developed large sores on both my hip bones and at the base of my spine through sleeping on the cement floor.

We were woken one night by a rifle shot followed by loud, sustained, piercing screams.

A guard, patrolling outside the wire, had shot a dysentery-infected prisoner who was on his way to the toilet block.

No reason. He had simply shot him.

The German-speaking Kiwi stood at the barrack door and shouted a request to go to the man's aid. A bullet thudded into the brickwork above his head and several shots were fired through the unglazed windows.

Nothing could be done.

The man screamed for an hour before dying or lapsing into unconsciousness. Two German guards eventually carried him away and I never did learn his fate.

May The Almighty forgive me but I didn't really care very much.

Our journey to Germany began at night. We were given two round loaves of bread and a tin of meat and told this was the food for our journey. We marched from the camp to a railway siding, assembled in groups of 40 men then crammed into filthy, enclosed cattle trucks. We managed to delay entry long enough for a couple of the more agile men to scoop up dry cattle dung and throw it out before we were pushed inside.

The door slid shut and was bolted.

We commenced sorting ourselves out in the dark. We found, by laying head to toe along the truck's length, there was just sufficient space for each man to lie down and stretch out amongst the filth on the floor.

The only ventilation was a small opening at each end of the wagon and these were heavily shrouded with barbed wire.

The train moved off through the night and into the next day.

Our world was now confined to 40 men with two loaves of ersatz bread and a tin of meat each; all suffering from malnutrition and locked in a noisy, dirty cattle-wagon.

The fact that the wagon was part of a train carrying us into Germany played only a small part in our thinking. Our world had shrunk to the size of the inside of a cattle-wagon.

An unusual sense of companionship was strong within the wagon.

It had to be in order to sustain our mates and to tolerate the others.

An all-consuming hunger made the contemplation of our sparse food supply constant. There was a tin of meat loaf to last each man six days. If we opened a tin a day and shared half the content with three mates each day the meat should last the distance without going bad. The bread consumption was the problem of the individual.

Toilet facilities were non-existent. Fortunately, men are equipped with a handy gadget which enables them to lie on the floor and urinate between cracks in the floorboards but some were suffering from dysentery or diarrhoea. Shirts were torn into pieces and space made available on the crowded floor while an embarrassed, apologetic, miserably sick man dealt with his problem. When this was over the four corners of the rag were brought together and the bundle lifted and poked through a space in the barbed wire covering the opening. Socks and donated rags were eventually used after the final scraps of the individual's shirt had disappeared through the opening.

Mess tins, jam tins and hats were held outside the wire and carefully emptied; a manoeuvre that was not always successful.

Occasionally some of it blew back through the opening or, worse still, the wind caught up the contents and wafted it on to a guard riding in the guard box outside on the end of the wagon.

When next the train halted, the door would be violently slid open, several Germans would rush angrily into the carriage, shouting, kicking and rifle-butting, to crush us all into a mass at one end of the carriage before grabbing us individually and bashing us into semi-consciousness before throwing us into a heap at the other end of the carriage.

This was an horrendous experience, particularly at night, when starving men were woken from a partly unconscious sleep without being aware of the reason for the brutality. The Germans wore a bright torch buttoned to the front of their tunics. It blinded us and left their hands free to wield a rifle. There was no way we could see where the blows were coming from and no way we could stop them if we could see them.

The German uniform also has a bright belt-buckle upon which is embossed an eagle, with wings outstretched, standing on a wreath-encased swastika. Around this emblem is the motto: "Gott Mit Uns".

"Strange," I thought, "I was under the impression He was on our side."

The train, after some days, arrived at Belgrade.

It was night and The International Red Cross had set up a soup kitchen for us. We were allowed out of the train, one carriage at a time, to be shoved along the platform to the issuing point.

It was a pathetic sight. We could hardly walk and had no hope of complying with the command of "Hurry! Hurry!" and became the recipients of numerous thumps and kicks. Some men had to be assisted by two mates who were not in much better shape themselves; some were pitifully embarrassed to appear in front of female Red Cross Workers with so much excreta coating their buttocks and legs; some endeavoured to walk upright in front of "these f-----g Huns" but they staggered and swayed as they progressed; some shouted hurried encouragement to their mates as they passed different wagons and some had to be guided along the platform to receive soup and a slice of bread before being pushed back into the wagon again where the door was slid shut with a bang accompanied by the sound of locks engaging and the contemptuous expression:- "English swine!"

This title annoyed me. We weren't English, and we might be a bit down on our luck, but we were bloody Australians!

A few questions arose as we slumped down on the wagon floor.

"Where is Belgrade, anyway?"

"It's in Yugoslavia."

"You mean the place where the Slavs come from that work in the mines around Kalgoorlie?"

"That's correct."

'Well, where the hell is it on the map?"

The chap giving all the answers turned out to be a schoolteacher; a short lesson in geography followed before we lapsed into semi-conscious sleep again.

The train rocked and rattled its way onwards towards Germany for several more days.

Stalag 7A was adjacent to the town of Moosburg, about 40kms from Munich, and we arrived there at night.

Doors banged open. "Out! Out!" yelled the guards.

I sat on the edge of the wagon floor, dropped to the ground and finished up flat on my face.

"Up! Up!" roared some German pig.

I lifted my head and stared straight into the eyes of a snarling Alsatian dog straining on a leash held by an equally snarling German guard.

I couldn't imagine how I managed to fall flat and why I was having trouble getting to my feet. A couple of mates picked me up and we wended our way along two rows of shouting guards restraining snarling dogs and passed through the gates of Stalag 7A.

We moved into barracks holding about 250 men. Three-tiered bunks provided beds for everyone. The door was locked, the gate in the barbed-wire fence surrounding our compound was locked and a guard placed on the spot.

Next morning was all hustle and bustle with guards all around us. We assembled and marched to the delousing and ablution blocks which, to our surprise, was manned by French NCOs who managed the internal administration of the stalag.

Our hair was cut off, our clothes taken away and then – Oh; wondrous joy! – hot showers!

We scraped our skulls clean, washed off the filth and laughed at each other's emaciated bodies.

Clean clothing was issued and we emerged from that building looking like a bunch of characters from some weird movie. The clothing was comprised of bits and pieces of uniforms from French, Yugoslav, Polish or any other army over-run by Hitler's marauders. Those of us who had boots worthy of the name were allowed to keep them whilst others were issued with wooden clogs and pieces of rag to act as socks.

Registration consisted of recording names and receiving a P.O.W. number stamped on an aluminium 'dog tag' to be worn round our necks at all times.

Thus did I become Kriegsgefangen Nummer 92135.

We returned to our barracks wondering what was going to happen next. It proved to be unexpected.

Frenchmen wandered in with pockets full of biscuits for which they had scant regard but, to us, they tasted more delicious than Mum's Sunday roast.

These 'flour and water' biscuits were made in France and issued to the French Ps.O.W. on a regular basis. They seemed to use them as a form of currency on the black market that flourished throughout the whole camp – except within the Russian compound.

The Russians were treated like mongrel dogs.

A thirty feet high barbed wire fence separated our compounds. A single wire at knee height and six feet away from the fence was a 'warning wire'.

Step inside it and you were dead!

No warnings. You were dead!

Elevated guard towers armed with machine-guns and rifles were erected at strategic points all over the stalag and searchlights constantly swept the compounds during the nights.

The Russians wore the clothes in which they were captured and obviously hadn't had a shower since that day. Many times we heard shots during the night and, upon emerging from our barracks for the morning check parade, we were presented with the sight of Russian bodies hanging on the wire fence or slumped in death at its base and the remainder was standing in line, out in the open, for counting. They had been there all night and they would be there all that day without a man being allowed to move for any reason at all. Some would collapse during the day and some would die from malnutrition and exhaustion.

Russia was not a signatory to The International Red Cross and, despite our desire to assist, we could do nothing.

The lavatory proved to be an interesting structure. It was really a big, below-ground, cement tank. Toilet pedestals were set in rows on its top surface. They ranged singly along its outer edge and back to back down the centre with a superstructure overall. Whilst they offered shelter from the elements they gave no privacy at all except from the guard towers.

The nations gathered there in numbers to stand around at the end of a day to trade, swap rumours, fight lost battles or just yarn. Some even came to use the toilets where they sat to yarn with their mates as they sat in rows within the building.

The numerous national idiosyncrasies became manifest in this building. Some dropped their pants and sat, some produced a page from an ancient German newspaper and wiped all around the pedestal, some arrived with a cloth and a jam tin of water to wash all around the perimeter; but there came the day when one arrived with a large sheet of newspaper which he fashioned into a quill. He lit the end with his cigarette lighter and proceeded to cauterize the pedestal. The butane gas in the cement tank went: "Woof!"

A flame shot out of every pedestal and we were treated to the uproarious sight of men from all over Europe dancing around with their pants down and bellowing abuse, in their native tongue, at this one individual whilst whistles blew and dogs barked as guards hurried to the building to eventually join in the laughter of the onlookers.

Our food was mainly boiled potatoes in their jackets. They were issued to barracks then further broken down to groups. When the dixie arrived at our group we placed our receptacles on the floor adjacent to our bunks and the spuds were proportioned out as fairly as possible.

We climbed back into our bunks, peeled the potatoes and ate them slowly, relishing each mouthful. The peelings were then eaten with equal relish.

A rumour ripped around. Red Cross Parcels were to be issued!

Someone had actually seen the trucks arrive at The Camp Admin Office and, in due course, we were issued with one parcel between four men.

Oh, the uplifting magnificence of that parcel's contents!

Chocolate, butter, biscuits, tea, powdered milk, soap, cigarettes – all the magical items to make us realise we were not forgotten or abandoned.

It was our first encounter with The International Red Cross and, for the next three and a half years, we were issued with one Red Cross Parcel per man per fortnight. Without these parcels many of us would have come out of the war in a much worse state of health and certainly many more would have perished.

The fear of sudden death gradually diminished as our health improved although brutality could erupt without warning. I can't say we began to put on weight but we began to feel better within ourselves.

The Frenchmen had an orchestra which played classical music, the British had a concert party as well as a theatrical group presenting some excellent plays, and Life, such as it was, began to become acceptable to most of us although we knew we would eventually be sent out to work to assist The Fatherland's war effort.

"You will be sent into Munich," said one of our English-speaking French colleagues.

"Munich? Where's Munich?"

"About 30 to 40 kilometres from here."

This didn't help much because we weren't too sure where "here" was but the Frenchman's information proved correct.

The German Guards lined us up with our scant belongings and arranged us into groups from lists which they had previously made –

and I was separated from Jesse!

I appealed to the German Interpreter and copped a rifle butt in the ribs.

They counted us numerous times then marched us through the gate to a nearby railway siding to board the train to Munich.

Chapter Seventeen

West End Prisoner-of-War Camp was not a big camp. It held about 500 men and consisted of four barracks, ablution blocks, a cookhouse, an entertainment hall and the guard's barracks.

We also had a small hospital, our own doctor and a couple of orderlies.

The barracks were divided into rooms holding 30 men in three-tier bunks. A long wooden table and forms went the full length of the room.

Around the camp was a 3 metre high wire-netting fence with three strands of barbed wire on the top and a knee-high warning wire roughly two metres from the fence but there were no machine gun towers or traversing searchlights at night.

We simply moved in and sorted ourselves out within the barracks. Five of The Signals Platoon kept together within a room with several men from our battalion as well as men from other Australian and English units.

Within a few days we were organised into work parties and allocated to various firms or organisations around the city and its suburbs, the number in the party depending upon the requirements of the firm.

Twenty of us were allocated to the town's asphalt works.

Next morning, clad in our weird assortment of uniforms from various nations, we assembled in the dark, were counted, re-counted and, accompanied by two guards, marched out the gate and boarded a tram taking us across the city to The Stadt Asphaltwerk.

The guards escorted us into a well lit, clean mess-room complete with tables, forms and lockers around the walls.

A big, middle-aged German entered the room. He was obviously the foreman and somehow, by using an impressive mixture of sign language, pantomime, an odd German word and observation, he sorted us out.

"Who is the oldest?" he asked in German which none of us understood.

Pantomime and sign language followed. He suddenly hunched his shoulders, stooped and commenced counting on his fingers: "Thirty-one, thirty-two, thirty-three."

We got it and one very old Pommy bloke, who was every bit of thirty-one, stepped forward.

The foreman led him towards the door, opened it and bellowed, "Hans!"

Hans appeared out of the darkness.

"This one."

Hans took his charge by the arm and they disappeared across the expanse of cobbled yard.

We didn't know it then but Hans was a truck driver and this chap was to be his off-sider.

Colin Murray was given a similar job. Jimmy Spurge and Ernie Maisey, having had some experience in lathe work, were allocated to a machine shop and the remainder, with the exception of Charlie Drake and myself, were employed around the yard.

Charlie and I, during the foreman's interrogation, had picked out the word 'specialist'. We didn't know what it really meant but we liked the sound of it and decided we were specialists.

The foreman took us down the yard and ushered us through a doorway. Three German workers stood there. They looked at us. We looked at them. The foreman spread his hands, shrugged his shoulders and left us to it.

The Germans spoke softly to each other and shook their heads.

The language barrier prevented them from communicating with us and the day was spent without a great deal of physical effort.

I found a broom and swept the floor, commenting to Charlie, "I started working for a living by sweeping the floor. I don't seem to have got very far in the last seven years."

Charlie spent the day unnecessarily wiping down some machinery.

There was a number of French Ps.O.W. working around the plant also. Three of them worked in this same workshop.

The guards, whom we hadn't seen since our early morning distribution around the place, assembled us at the end of the day, counted us, re-counted us and returned us to the barracks where many and varied were the tales of the day's activities.

The evening meal was a very fluid potato and cabbage soup but it was food.

Gosh! Was there ever a time when I wasn't hungry?

However, the camp had a clean toilet block and hot showers, both of which are advisable when men are living in close contact with each other.

The bunks had straw-filled mattresses and each man had a blanket.

We slept deeply until aroused before daylight.

Breakfast consisted of brown bread and black coffee; the principal ingredient in each, we asserted, was finely ground jarrah sawdust.

Blue overalls were issued at The Asphalt Works next morning before commencing work. No markings or brands on them. Blue overalls the same as everyone wore.

Another surprise awaited us that morning. The Germans, during the morning coffee break, offered us cups of ersatz coffee and a couple of slices of brown bread.

Both these items were rationed and suddenly the thought behind the gesture became apparent.

Our physical appearance and our apparel, which we had unconsciously come to accept, had appalled them and this was their way of expressing their concern for us – the enemy.

*****

The quality of P.O.W. life began to improve once we settled in at West End Camp.

A few British and Australian Warrant Officers and Sergeants had volunteered to be allocated to the camp for the purpose of setting up and maintaining the camp's internal administration; cooks were given the thankless task of trying to make something out of the limited ingredients; a sick parade was available at the end of a day and it was conducted by an Australian doctor whose rank was acknowledged and respected by the Germans.

Once inside the gate we could roam around within the camp until 'Roll Call' at 8pm and the counting was done within the rooms.

Sundays were non-working days which allowed us to do our washing and, with the passage of time, eventually permit us to indulge in all manner of hobbies and other activities.

The International Red Cross established and maintained a regular supply of food parcels – magical parcels containing such wondrous items as powdered milk, two ounces of tea, tinned butter, a block of chocolate, tinned bully-beef, cigarettes, soap and other "goodies", the likes of which we had long since forgotten.

Individually we were issued with one parcel a fortnight so the lurk was to share one with a mate who ever afterwards was known as your "mucker".

British Army clothing, after several months, also became available through The Red Cross. Boots, woolen socks, long underpants, flannel shirts, a pullover, battle dress jacket and trousers, an overcoat and a forage cap; all arriving before the fast approaching European winter.

We began to physically fill out and emotionally settle down to the routine of P.O.W. life as we waited for the final victory which seemed very obscure in the far distant future.

We were prisoners in the hands of the enemy yet things happened in Munich which, for the remainder of my life, has endeared me to that city although I have never seen it again.

*****

The Bavarians are different and they seemed rather proud of the fact.

Whilst some of the work parties experienced moments of aggression – in the form of vocal volume in a language not understood – the majority of the civilians accepted our presence as a circumstance associated with the war.

The trams and trains carrying men to and from work also carried civilians and, when marching through the streets, we were never abused.

We gradually picked up a smattering of the language. Our vocabulary was never voluminous and our sentence structure occasionally caused laughter from the listeners but we were able to communicate.

Many months later Hans The Tractor Driver explained to me how Adolf Hitler managed to keep the crowds enthralled with his vocabulary. The verb comes at the end of the sentence in the German language and the crowd was never too sure what he was going to come out with until the sentence was completed!

The Germans in the north were under the impression they were going to win the war. The Bavarians had little respect for them whilst The Austrians seemed to have scant regard for either of them.

But, as they explained, "We are at war and we must stand united behind Unser Fuhrer."

Nobody ever mentioned The Gestapo or The Nazi Party. We didn't know anything about them either although the chauffer of 'Herr Direktor' seemed to command respect because, it was rumoured, he was a member of the Nazi Party.

*****

The winter of 1941 made its entry gently.

A group of us were sitting around in our room playing cards, reading a book or yarning when Alf looked out the window.

Alf, who is best described as 'a rough diamond', was a timber-worker from down the south of Western Australia.

"There must be a bushfire somewhere," he commented. "There's ash falling all over the place."

We sat there for a while contemplating this unexpected phenomenon.

"Bloody hell!" yells Alf. "It's snowing!"

We all rushed outside to witness snowfall which, to us, was a unique experience. We held out our hands to watch it fall into our palms; it settled on our shoulders, it piled up on the window-ledges, it settled on top of posts, it gradually covered the ground and the rooftops.

Snow! Beautiful, clean, white snow! How wonderful!

*****

A rumour became a fact. Half of the camp's occupants were moved to another camp in a different suburb. Our work party was among them.

The new camp bore the impressive name of "Waldfriedhof Kriegesgefangenlager" which, very loosely interpreted, means "The Woods Cemetery Prisoner of War Camp". The cemetery was behind a belt of pine trees on the other side of the road.

The camp was brand, spanking new. Accommodation consisted of three barracks, a cookhouse, an entertainment hall and a toilet block. Constructed of pine, the barracks had internal toilets for night use and were divided into rooms holding 16 men in two-tiered bunks. Each room had a small stove for warmth in winter and double-glazed casement windows for fresh air in summer, although wooden shutters were secured over the windows after the evening count.

The method of securing the shutters was simply to swing an iron bar across and drop it into a hasp on the outside thereby preventing them from being opened from the inside.

The German guards' barrack was also inside the barbed wire and immediately adjacent to the gate.

On the other side of the wire was open space big enough for several football fields.

This camp was about as good as you could get in P.O.W. life.

*****

Guards woke us in the mornings by noisily opening the window shutters and shouting "Raus! Raus!"

The guards, incidentally, were mainly middle-aged men who came from anywhere within Germany. Consequently, some of them were good blokes and others had a tendency to be a bit rough on occasions but, over a period of time, we came to know their individual first names and addressed them as such.

One of our chaps remarked, "They are necessary to have around the place in order to keep the civilian population away from our Red Cross Parcels."

The Asphalt Works Party assembled at the gate in pre-dawn darkness and, accompanied by one guard, marched to work.

It became a pleasant twenty minutes walk in summer's early morning sun but, in winter, ice covered the road, the wind was cold and, oft times, a snowstorm blew up.

We had our own lunchroom at work. It was complete with a stove and, once there, the guard settled himself down by the fire's warmth and we seldom saw him again until the end of the day.

The Asphalt Works yard was an extensive, cobble-stoned area with several open sheds protecting quantities of blue metal, sand, and other road-surfacing material from the freezing effects of snow or frozen rain.

Asphalt Works Team: Standing L-R: Chris Kealley, Doug Burling, Bill Franklin, Unknown, Unknown, Unknown, Unknown Ray Kennedy, Jim ?

Front L-R: Scotty Williamson, Colin Murray, Arthur Leggett, Frank Anderson, and Alf Passfield

We had our assigned tasks. Frank was the gardener. He disappeared towards the garden shed and somehow, during the spring, vegetables grew. Scotty and Chris drove electric trolleys carting blue metal to the mill whilst others lent a hand with a shovel.

Charlie and I made our way to the workshop to be greeted by Sebastian The Electrician and Hans The Blacksmith.

The three Frenchmen had also arrived and, once the forge fire was glowing, we stood around keeping warm and talking amongst ourselves in that peculiar language by which mixed nationalities communicate.

The mill was a giant crusher that crunched reclaimed road bitumen to be recycled. High within the building housing this machine was a revolving shaft with pulley wheels. Long belts swooped down from the pulleys to urge this dormant mass of metal into life. Each morning, as the shaft started to revolve, the belts squeaked out their initial command before strengthening their grip and applying pressure. The mill, groaning its objection to any movement, slowly stirred and picked up momentum with a developing roar that drowned any conversation – then out of the building's dark depths came Karl The Miller; a short, shrivelled, bent man dressed in an overcoat with a collar that wrapped around his neck and climbed half way up the back of a head surmounted by a cloth cap. He would observe us standing there, turn and look at the mill then survey us again before spreading his mittened hands, looking at the roaring mill once more then smiling as if to say, "Well, it's going. My, aren't we all surprised?"

Herr Strassel commanded respect by virtue of his status as manager but we soon gave him the nickname of 'Snaggletooth'. He had his own office in a separate building from whence he periodically emerged to check on nothing in particular while he endeavoured to impart an impression of aloof superiority but, as our German vocabulary improved, he unwound to tell Charlie and I some military anecdotes from The 1914-18 War. He had been captured by The British in Africa and had spent three years within a barbed-wire enclosed P.O.W. camp erected at Sidi-Bish in Egypt. They lived in tents. Treatment was rough and conditions harsh. I couldn't imagine anything worse than having nothing to do and living three years within a compound out in the desert country of Egypt. He hadn't learned to speak English but he had an impressive knowledge of British foul language that occasionally erupted complete with a Cockney accent.

*****

The winter's snow continued to fall copiously and, despite the abundant sprinkling of unrefined salt, the streets gradually became deeply smothered in the stuff. The combined manpower of both West

End and Waldfriedhof was assembled to scrape the snow off the roads and pile it on the edge of the footpaths.

We were warmly clad by this time and the whole task, more or less, became an enjoyable activity. It presented us with the opportunity to mix with mates from the other camp, smoke Players Cigarettes in front of cigarette-starved civilians and occasionally eat a piece of chocolate in a disgustingly flamboyant manner.

The guards, who had been doing the old '2 on and 4 off' during the night, weren't very enthusiastic about the activities of the day and the application of a few cigarettes made them less interested.

Some streets contained a cosy pub and, on numerous occasions, mid-day breaks became quite bizarre with a guard standing at each end of the street and another standing outside pub's door whilst we sat in a bar-room, warmed by an open fire, enjoying the hospitality of 'mine Bavarian host' while a group of Welshman sang around a piano as the barmaid wept behind the counter.

*****

Many weeks during winter, however, were spent in the workshop of Das Asphaltwerk.

The workshop had a window-wall that looked out on to the street running alongside the factory. Butted up against this wall was a workbench where Charlie and I fiddled about all day, usually making bits and pieces for the camp. These "bits and pieces" started off as hooks upon which to hang hats, clothes hangers, cup hooks etc but eventually developed into spikes to hold down wire fencing, false nail heads to fit into loosened boards plus a few pliers, screwdrivers, hacksaw blades and so on.

Gradually, as we worked away, it dawned on us that a very attractive young lady went stepping through the snow at the same time each day, right past our window.

She was dressed in a fur rig-out; a fur hat upon her head and she wore a fur overcoat which fitted like a glove down to the waist then flared out just like the coat Sonja Henie wore in "Million Dollar Legs". Her hands were hidden in a muff. Knee-length leather boots, matching the coat, completed a picture that awoke hitherto dormant emotions,

It was exciting just to watch her walk past.

There were notices in every P.O.W. camp warning of extreme penalties for any fraternisation with German women but there are some things a man cannot fight.

Next day a tap on the window and a hand-wave brought a smile; the following day won another smile and a return wave. Within a week she was appearing at lunchtime going the other way then re-appearing an hour later,

"Charlie," I said, "we've got to get to know this lady."

"Ja," said Der Karl, demonstrating his knowledge of the language.

The challenge was to be on the other side of that wall at lunchtime.

Next day, as we approached the factory, a good look along the street showed how to go about it.

A door was in that long wall, and it was an exit from an empty room right next to our window! A locked door faced the factory yard. A locked door faced the street.

The next few days were spent in manufacturing a key by the "trial and error" method. They were big, old-fashioned locks and soon responded to our efforts.

We had our own lunchroom. The German workers withdrew to their canteen for lunch where they were joined by the guard.

Slipping out of the lunchroom with the comment "Going for a leak", I made my way down to the empty workshop, unlocked the door, slipped inside, locked the door, unlocked the street door, held it open and waited like a spider that had spun a cunning web across a bush track.

She came along the street, saw the open door and stepped inside!

We stood there for quite a while just looking at each other.

I don't know what she saw in me but I was looking at something truly beautiful.

A film of snow covered the top of her fur hat, the shoulders of her fur coat and the collar wrapped around her neck and face as protection against the cold wind. Her smile would have warmed the heart of a snowman let alone a hungry P.O.W. This mutual admiration routine was becoming too prolonged so I decided to try out my smattering of the language.

"Wie heist Du?' I enquired.

"Ellen."

"Ellen?"

She laughed with a sound like music.

"Nein. E--llen. Aber, wie heist Du?"

"Ich heiste Arthur."

"Ar – tew – er," she pronounced.

I don't think my name had ever sounded so musical and I promptly decided not to correct her, which was fortunate because I later learned that Germans have a hard time trying to pronounce 'th' the way we do and you don't have to be a Rhodes Scholar to work out the trend of our conversation. My German came out of an Englische/Deutsche Buch that Hans The Blacksmith had bought me and, if you are a student, you will have already realised my knowledge of the language wasn't too good. But, just then, it seemed to be eloquent.

Ellen was a typist working nearby and she daily went home for lunch. By the end of the following week my face was buried amongst the snow and the fur and the perfume as we embraced for a few platonic moments each day.

The embraces were platonic because we only had a few moments each day – dammit!

Hans The Blacksmith and Sebastian The Electrician were delighted at the speed my language improved over the next few weeks and I assured them it was all for a good cause.

*****

I wasn't the only P.O.W. who got into that street. A number of German schoolboys used to throw snowballs at us while we were working so Doug ran around the corner and commenced a snow-fight finishing up with Doug rolling around in the snow with the kids in wrestling bouts that became regular events.

Hans, Sebastian and several others would watch through the big window and laugh at the ebb and flow of the spectacle.

"Why are we at war with each other?" asked Sebastian. "We seem to be getting along all right."

How do you answer a question like that at such a time? Tell him we are part of The British Empire and we are supporting England in her fight against oppression and The Motherland brought freedom to the world, then he could counter with The Treaty of Versaille, the need for German expansion and how The Fuhrer was going to lead them into a great and glorious future.

Nah, we were just a couple of blokes living a day-today existence; don't let's get involved in politics.

*****

I received a letter, through The International Red Cross, from my Mum. This one told me my father had died.

I knew he was a sick man but I didn't expect this. I was going to get back home one day and we would all be together again but now, no matter when I returned home, he wouldn't be there and I would never have the chance to be a mature son to him.

After the initial shock had subsided I felt a terrible anger well up inside me. Damn and blast the bloody Germans! They gassed my father in the first war and now they had me cooped up in a P.O.W. camp in the second war and I could do bugger all to help my mother and sisters when I was needed!

Next day I was sullen and morose at work. Sebastian The Electrician came up to me and, in our peculiar language, asked, "What is wrong today?"

"My father is dead."

"How old was he?"

"53."

"Not old. How?"

"He was gassed in The 14-18 War."

Sebastian swung on his heel away from me.

"Herr Gott Sacrament!" he exclaimed.

He then came back, put his arm around my shoulders and, with a tone of voice and clear pronunciation anyone could understand said, "Artewer. I am very, very sorry for you."

*****

Spring arrived with all the magic of a European Spring.

The snow disappeared, the ground softened, flowers appeared, the country turned green and Bavarian womanhood blossomed forth in all the exciting colours of their national dress.

How far away was my own country in Springtime? How far away was the girl to whom I was engaged? How far away was my Mum, my sisters, my brother and would I ever see them again?

We never doubted we were going to win this war but, in 1941 and 1942, the end seemed far away and we wondered how much of our country we were going to lose to the bloody Japs before it was all over.

*****

There was trouble in the workshop.

Charlie got into an argument with Snaggletooth who became angry and called Charlie a f------g, b----y British prisoner. Charlie implied that Snaggletooth was a similar kind of German but born out of wedlock.

Charlie was banished out of the workshop and into the work's yard.

I can't remember what the argument was about but I must have felt Charlie was in the right because I quit the workshop and joined the boys working in the yard.

I suppose we should have both been punished for this attitude but, as I stated earlier, Bavarians are different. Snaggletooth's status had been maintained, Charlie had been admonished and if I cared to join him that was my decision.

This decision eventually turned out to be a lucky break. We now came under the control of the yard foreman who assigned me to work with Ray Kennedy.

*****

Das Asphaltwerk produced a mixture of molten tar, blue metal and gravel for general road maintenance; this mixture was conveyed to the road-gang in a couple of trailers pulled in tandem behind a tractor driven by gas contained in two bottles secured to the side.

The trailers were of unusual design and looked like two steam-engine boilers mounted on wheels. They had a firebox underneath with an internal shaft to which was attached paddles. The paddles were driven by a chain coming from the rear wheels; in this manner the tar mix was kept hot and plastic during transit.

Each wagon had a seat high up with a handbrake lever beside it. Apparently the law demanded someone must ride on these trailers in order to apply the handbrake in any emergency. This job was entrusted to two trustworthy Ps.O.W. namely, Signaller Kennedy and my humble self.

A whole new world opened up!

A considerable stretch of road repair was going on right in the centre of Munich. The road gang came from West End Camp so we knew most of them. Occasionally we passed messages on behalf of mates within our camp; this wasn't dangerous as communication between the two camps was accepted. But we also came in contact with civilians on a regular basis and Munich became a familiar city to us.

Toilet facilities become a necessity when a gang is working in one area over a period of time. Nearby was a large, underground toilet and the use of this convenience was quite an experience. The sum of five pfennings was required but we weren't permitted to have civilian money so we signed a book; a routine helping to justify the employment of the plump, middle-aged, cheerful frau who officiated within its confines.

Upon descending the stairway I was greeted by this smiling lady who escorted me to a cubicle, preceded me into it, wiped the seat, made sure a sufficient quantity of toilet paper was available, and graciously bowed her way out again. The sound of the toilet flushing brought her to the cubicle door from whence I was led to the basin to wash my hands before proceeding to the autograph book. One day, after we had been working in the area for several weeks, she shook her finger under my nose in the manner only Germans can shake fingers and, turning page after page of her precious autograph book said, "Nicht mehr Winston Churchill oder Ned Kelly! Nicht mehr!"

Incidentally, the road-working gang came to regard her as a kind of 'mother symbol' and she did quite well with occasional cigarettes, soap or tea. She should have finished the war as a wealthy woman providing she wasn't killed in the subsequent air raids.

Ray and I had a pleasant summer driving around Munich on these tar-wagons.

The tractor driver, also named Hans, was a cheerful chap with a terrific sense of humour. He was also a keen photographer and, with our help, developed a nice old racket on the black market as our chaps in the camp were always eager to have photos enlarged or refurbished in exchange for the scarce items which we received in our Red Cross Parcels.

Tea was a negotiable commodity.

One of the men in our room worked on the local rubbish tip and he gradually equipped our room, and the camp, with all manner of peculiar objects. A very useful article was our teapot. It was about 4 inches in diameter but stood around 12 inches high. Its exterior was covered with cherubs and seraphims, dressed in many hues, dancing and cavorting in an elegant manner and its lid was a joy to behold.

Tea came in 2 ounce packets glued at both ends with a sticky label. The labels were steamed off the packets and the contents poured into a glass jar. The packets were also placed in jars to prevent them becoming damaged.

The lurk was to add tea to the pot every time we made a brew. When the pot became full of tea-leaves they were emptied out, dried in a dish over a slow fire, returned to the packet, glued down again and traded to the Germans for a kilogram of sugar.

Complaints concerning the quality of the tea were rare; this made us suspect it was mainly used as currency on the black market. Whenever an adverse comment was made we would hunch our shoulders, spread our hands palm upwards in the German manner and say, "England kaput."

"Yes. Yes. I understand."

We knocked off work at mid-day on Saturday and, as far as P.O.W. life was concerned, summertime weekends within the camp were pleasant periods. There were plenty of internal activities to occupy the time of the individual.

I joined the repertory group. Scripts of full-length plays had become available and learning lines for these performances became a challenging past-time.

Our work party labours were paid for in token money of no value outside the camp but, through the camp's administration, it could be used to hire costumes, make-up grease and scenery paint. We charged the troops five camp-marks to see the shows.

I played the part of the leading lady in several productions. Someone had to do it and it was not without its shocks. The pommy make-up artist finished making up my face for one particular performance and stepped back to admire his work.

"Hey; have a look at that!" he exclaimed as he held a mirror in front of me.

There, looking back at me through the mysterious Time behind the surface of the mirror, was my sister Joyce!

Suddenly the pointless emptiness of my present existence was there right in front of my eyes.

"What's wrong with you?" asked the make-up artist, "You're making all the greasepaint run!'

Another time I made my entry and, after the usual whistles had died down, the continued discussion among a group of Welsh coalminers concerning what they could do with a 'woman like that' was not only disconcerting – it was downright horrendous!

Naturally I came in for considerable, good-natured banter around the camp and I entered into several boxing competitions to counterbalance any funny ideas.

The first time I entered the ring the M.C. announced, "– and over in the blue corner we have The Leading Lady who will fight for her honour!"

Those Welsh bastards again; "– an' wot 'appens if she loses?"

Fortunately the referee always made sure I won or the bout was a draw.

The camp was encompassed by a four metre wire-mesh fence capped by four strands of barbed wire with the usual 'warning wire' about a metre and a half from the fence. There were no machine-gun towers on the corners and only two guards, (moving in opposite directions), who patrolled the outer perimeter of the camp. They weren't really interested in what went on inside the camp and this attitude, plus the visual obstruction of the barracks, allowed other activities to make steady progress.

Snakes and ladders was a popular game. Four players set a board on the grass near the warning wire. The game was surrounded by as many as twenty enthusiastic onlookers who cheered, shouted or abused as fortune favoured or deserted the players. The guard, of course, would be intrigued by the noise and come down along the fence to determine its source. After being greeted by his Christian name he'd stand there for a while and, having determined it was not a riot but only a game of snakes and ladders, he would continue his patrol shaking his head and re-affirming 'all Englishmen were mad'. Ten minutes were to pass before he came this way again; sufficient time to allow a prone body to crawl to the fence, cut the bottom straining wire with a pair of pliers and return to the enthralling game of snakes and ladders.

The cut wire, now held in place by spikes made in our workshop, was not discernable amongst the weeds but the fence could now be lifted sufficiently to allow a body to wriggle through.

Close examination of the barracks revealed the ceiling, only a metre from the top bunks, was made of pine-wood panels about one and a half metres square. These could be prized loose allowing access into the rafters and neatly dropping back into position again.

The ceilings in the toilet block and ablution block were of the same design and put to the same use.

Once the day was over we would be lined up in the barrack's lengthy passageway to be counted by Max, the German Sar'major. As he counted and passed by we'd peel off into our rooms with the result, when he came to the end of his count, there was only half a dozen chaps still in the passageway. But the count was correct, he was satisfied and all was well. The Germans then locked the barrack and there we were until morning.

Charlie, Colin Murray and Arthur Huggins decided they were going to have a night out in Munich. I've no idea what they expected to do on a Saturday night in a blacked-out town in the middle of Germany during a war but they were going just for the hell of it.

Before the evening count they climbed into the ceiling of the ablution block, replaced the panel and sat on it to hold it firm.

The count within the barracks was proceeding according to plan.

As soon as Max had passed and the men peeled off into the rooms, five men clambered on to the top bunk, removed the panel, climbed into the rafters, replaced the panel, crept along the length of the barrack, came out into the end room and took their place on the end of the line.

Unfortunately, too many men were involved and Max came up with an excess of two men.

"Everyone out! Recount!"

This time he was three men short!

The barracks were locked, the guard marshaled, and for hours afterwards, we could hear them thumping and grunting around the place as they searched for three men who must still be within the confines of the camp because the outside guards had not yet been called in.

The noise eventually subsided and we slept until around 3am when the iron bar across the window shutters was lifted, the shutters opened to allow the three night-owls to clamber in through the window and pull the shutters close again.

The two prowler guards patrolling around the barracks within the barbed wire later found the iron crossbar dangling outside our window. We heard them conferring in their grunting language before replacing it and moving on.

Perhaps they thought it had been overlooked at roll call or perhaps they decided to replace it and say nothing because they had had enough trouble for one night. I simply don't know but let me say this;- They were all middle-aged men, some of them obviously of peasant stock, who were on permanent guard duty (2 hours on – 4 hours off 24 hours a day) while we apparently had plenty and were enjoying life. We knew them all by their Christian names and there was very little animosity between us. But don't get the opinion that Germans are stupid. Far from it. There were some very intelligent people among them just as there were some vicious, sadistic bastards who were constantly on the look out for an excuse to destroy a man and any of these incidents could take place in Munich early in the war.

The tale our three mates later related was quite amusing. They had sat on the pinewood panel in the ablution block during the search while the guards prodded the ceiling with bayonets fixed to loaded rifles. Eventually the search was called off and the guards returned to their barrack leaving the standard two prowler guards to patrol around the camp.

The rest was easy. When the guards passed the ablution block the boys slid out of the ceiling, made their way to the cut straining wire and they were on their way. Munich was blacked out and, not knowing where to go or what to do, they hung around the town until the early hours of the morning then returned to camp.

The correct number assembled for every work party next morning. No doubt some head scratching went on in The Kommandant's office and the broken wire was discovered a couple of days later.

The enthusiastic playing of snakes and ladders within areas immediately adjacent to the fence was forbidden from that day onwards.

Escapes were fairly regular in Munich. The Germans were inclined to regard escaping as a soldier's duty just as it was their duty to prevent it. However, it was an unwritten law among ourselves that escapes were not to be done from the P.O.W. camp as it would only make life tougher for the rest of us. Besides, escaping from a work party was a piece of cake.

Alf Passfield escaped from our work party at Das Asphaltwerk and if you want to share in all the emotions of being an escaped P.O.W. in Germany procure his book titled "The Escape Artist" from the public library. You will also learn that this tough, determined character was about the biggest headache the Germans ever captured.

*****

Our conduct, at times, would appear rather irrational to people outside the fence but, on occasions, we had to deal with emotional problems for which we were not responsible and over which we had no control.

The chappie who worked on the rubbish tip had brought in a rather impressive bronze bell which was hung in the recreation hall for a specific purpose. I had received a letter and, upon reading its content, made my way to the recreation hall to ring the bell in the manner I had seen them do in a picture titled "Lloyds of London". A group of men quickly assembled.

"Dear Arthur," I began.

"Cheers! Hooray!" yelled the mob.

"I truly hate myself for writing this letter," I continued.

"Boo! Shame!"

"But when you left you said if I met someone else I was free to make a choice –"

"Oh, noble gesture!" – "You silly bastard!" etc.

The letter continued, with appropriate interjections, to finish with this line, – "so I am writing to ask what can you do to help me."

The advice I received from the group was not the advice one puts in print but it was generally agreed that I couldn't do very much on account of the barbed wire fence. However, if I was so inclined, I could apply to The Kamp Kommandant for compassionate leave of absence but its approval was rather doubtful.

My Dad was dead.

My fiancé had dumped me.

Singapore had fallen.

The Germans were pouring across Russia.

The Japs were boring southward.

Life wasn't looking too good.

*****

Air raid sirens often sounded in the night but raids did not eventuate because, as the German workers informed us, Munich was in the southern centre of The Fatherland and bombers had no hope of getting this far. Admittedly the sirens disrupted their sleep but after a while everyone went back to bed.

One day 'The Munchener Beobachter' carried a full front page photo of a shot down Lancaster Bomber.

"Look at that!" they exulted. "Ninety of them were shot down last night!"

We looked all right. We had never seen such a massive plane. Four engines, all metal, a wing of impressive dimensions, perspex domes and machine guns with a tail gunner!

Bigger than The Blenheim! Bigger than The Wellington! Oh Ho! This would make The Jerries sit up and take notice! We were still in the war!

As for shooting down ninety of them in one night? That was obviously bulldust and you couldn't believe German propaganda anyway.

Oh God! How isolated and insular we were!

Ninety planes had been shot down and nine hundred airmen had been killed, wounded or captured – and we sat around in our little cocoon of a P.O.W. camp and joked about it.

What else could we do?

We heard the sirens one night but took no notice laying there in the hush which follows an air raid alert.

A single plane!

We could tell by the sound of its motors it wasn't German. Anti-aircraft guns opened up and rattled the windows. Just one plane. We listened to the heart-warming sound of its motors gradually fading in the distance.

"Just one aircraft," said Hans The Blacksmith next morning. "One aircraft isn't much."

But the facade of The Gestapo Headquarters, right in the heart of Munich, was blackened with oil from some dirty type of bomb.

I saw it with my own eyes as the tar-wagons went past. It was beautiful!

Someone was out there on our side and they were still trying!

Soon after this episode we had to dig open air raid shelters within the camp; good slit trenches about two and a half metres deep and lined with timber. The guards enjoyed hustling us out at any hour of the night during false alarms gradually becoming more numerous as the winter of '42 progressed.

*****

Travelling around Munich on the open-air seat of the tar-wagons in mid-winter was a cold job.

Snow blanketed the streets, the roofs, the lamp-post tops and any other exposed, horizontal surface. Thanks to The Red Cross we were, by now, well equipped with winter clothing and able to cope with such harsh conditions.

Ray, finely tuned to the natural instincts which course through the body of a young man in good physical condition, found out the location of the brothel.

This information was quickly transformed into "The Project of the Moment".

Hans The Tractor Driver, after a couple of weeks of negotiation, agreed to have a mechanical breakdown outside the building for the price of one tin of 50 Players Cigarettes.

We promptly paid Hans his fifty smokes and anxiously awaited the day.

It came!

We had delivered a load to the road gang and, on the return journey, Hans swung into Senefelder Strasse and organised a tractor breakdown simply by closing off the gas bottles.

He grabbed a spanner out of the toolbox, gave us a curt nod, and disappeared under the tractor.

Ray and I jumped off the wagons, ran up the steps, gave the big, double, swinging doors a push and stepped inside.

It was a large room furnished with several lounge suites. A counter was just inside the door. The cash register and a receptionist were, in all probability, situated there in more prosperous times.

The disconcerting part of the scenery was half a dozen members of Rommel's Afrika Korps talking to a group of the girls at the far end of the room. We hadn't considered the possibility of German soldiers being on the premises. After all, there was a war on and we assumed they would all be at The Russian Front or in North Africa.

We stood in embarrassed silence; neither of us willing to retreat while the situation remained calm.

After a while two massive examples of The Afrika Korps rose and strolled across the room to stand directly in front of us. They slowly looked us up and down from head to toe.

"You're not German."

"No, we're not German."

"You're not Dutch."

"No, we're not Dutch."

So! What are you?"

Such a question can start a fight in any brothel.

"We're f-----g Australians!"

"Australians!"

"Yeah, Australians."

"Have you been in Tobruk?"

"Yeah, we've been in Tobruk."

"S-o-o-o-o!"

He stuck his index finger into his mouth and, with spittle, drew the outline of Tobruk defences on the adjacent counter.

"We were here," he said, dropping an extra large blob of spittle outside the perimeter. "Where were you?"

"We were outside Tobruk, too. We took Tobruk from The Italians."

"Oh, The Italians!"

Eyes looked to the ceiling, hands were thrown upwards as though imploring Heaven's forgiveness that The Fatherland should have associated itself with such an ally.

A lengthy discussion followed, in broken German, concerning the failings of Italy in general and its soldiers in particular.

Suddenly one of The Afrika Korps broke off in the middle of a sentence.

"You want a woman?"

It was a delicate topic but, finally, it had been broached.

"Yes, we came in here for a woman," I confessed.

"Blonde or brunette?"

Ray doubled up with laughter.

"What is wrong?" woofed The Afrika Korps.

"Geez," said Ray, "We haven't seen a white woman for three years. Any colour will do."

A roar of laughter followed. So help me, there we were – four soldiers laughing our heads off over a common topic. The German turned to face the group in the far corner to hold a thumb and forefinger aloft as he bellowed: "Two women!"

Two of the girls obligingly came over and we followed them up the stairs with the wishes of "Good luck" from the six members of The Afrika Korps penetrating through the thumping sound of my heart and the roaring noise in my ears.

We separated at the top of the stairs and went into different rooms. I shan't record the rest of the affair except to comment on the uncontrollable laughter of the woman laying on the bed waiting for action while one of our nation's heroes went through the routine of peeling off 1 pair of army boots and socks, 1 pair of blue workers overalls, 1 battle dress, 1 pullover, 1 grey flannel shirt (oversize), 1 pair long woolen underpants etc. etc. etc.

Ray and I met again at the head of the stairs and made our way hurriedly to the doors, calling "Auf Wiedersehen" to The Afrika Korps as we passed through the lounge room. We were worrying about Hans lying under the tractor during a snowstorm.

As we descended the outside steps Ray asked, "What did you give her?"

"A two ounce packet of tea."

"Me too. And I got five marks change."

"So did I. God bless the Red Cross."

"Yeah; God bless 'em."

*****

Air raid alarms and the compulsory turn out to the slit trenches was becoming a fairly regular source of annoyance until, once again, the war suddenly became serious.

The air raid defences of Munich had a large, powerful, blue searchlight probing the sky for aircraft that seemed to come over singly. A plane caught in its beam appeared like a toy on a black background. The other searchlights immediately fastened on to it and all the A.A. guns blazed away in its direction as the massive, four-engine plane weaved and gyrated in its efforts to escape the situation before dropping its bombs and disappearing into the night sky.

Cleaning up bomb debris next day was not a very enjoyable experience.

I had unconsciously become very fond of The City of Munich and its traditions extending back over many centuries; to see it being blown away in this manner had a most bewildering, emotional effect upon me.

Obviously I had been away from the front line too long.

P.O.W. life sheltered me from destruction of the air raids on

London, the methodical process of exterminating the conquered Polish Nation, the merciless rape and plunder of Russia and denied me the knowledge to predict our own fate if our side didn't execute this "Total War" to its fullest extent.

I expected some hostility from the civilian population but it didn't happen and, when one of our barracks was set alight by an incendiary bomb and burnt down, the workmen at Das Asphaltwerk commiserated with us.

Colin Murray and his mate, Doug Burling came from an artillery unit. They were completely opposite in nature but, bound by that sense of 'espirit de corps' which united all men from the same units, they were good companions.

Doug had a strong Christian family background and would, on occasions, burst forth into song to sing us hymns when we least expected it. His placid, tolerant attitude would only become ruffled if he felt an unjust act was being perpetrated.

Colin, in civilian life, worked for Mick Simmons Sports Store in Sydney and had all the dynamic attributes necessary for the rough and tumble game of salesmanship. His job in Munich was off-sider to a truck driver who seemed to drive around all over the city. Part of their daily routine was to drive up to the camp to pick up a canister of soup for our daily lunch.

One day towards the end of winter in 1942, when snow was still patchy on the ground, he returned at lunchtime full of excitement.

"We're moving!" he exclaimed. "Everything is being packed up! Tomorrow they are sending us off to Poland!"

"Bullshit!"

"You're kidding!"

"They can't do this!"

But they could.

"When you get back to camp to-night," Colin convinced us, "you will have to pack all your gear and be ready to move off in the morning.

The admin staff is flat out packing right now."

"My God," I thought. "This is awful. How am I going to tell Ellen?"

We discussed the problem. Charlie had been accumulating some civilian clothing with the intent of making a break in the spring but this idea was now shot to pieces so I could have his green Tyrolean hat, complete with colourful feather, as well as a jacket.

The plan was for me to jump the back fence of Das Asphaltwerk and meet Ellen on her way home from work then return to camp later.

Meanwhile the boys were to carry on working as though they knew nothing about the move which was "top secret"; then at the end of the day, when the news was broken to them, they were to mill around shaking hands and saying 'good-byes' and endeavour to move off without a count being made.

Later in the afternoon I donned my hat and jacket, clambered over the fence and made my way into a nearby pine forest where I hid inside a building used as a bowling alley on the weekends. The pine forest was familiar to us, having daily walked through it on our way to work in the summertime. The building had been noted then.

Around knock off time I heard voices moving through the forest. I hastened to a window in time to see a heavily-laden working party heading back to camp. When things quieted down I clambered out of the building and walked across to the street, where I knew Ellen would pass, and stood on a corner adjacent to the block of flats where she lived.

Ah; the best laid plans of mice and men etc. etc. etc.

A snowstorm blew up from nowhere. Ellen had apparently gone home by another street. I was standing on a corner in the snowstorm with a curious woman gigging at me from behind the curtains of a nearby window and daylight was fast fading.

I had to make a move. Ellen had previously indicated to me where she lived on the top floor of the three-storied building so I climbed up the stairs and knocked on what I hoped was the correct door.

A pleasant-faced woman opened the door.

"Ja?" she enquired.

I was about to try out my best German.

"Is Ellen at home?"

"Yes, but what do you want?'

Ellen appeared in the hallway.

"My Australien!" she cried. I was taken by the arm and led inside. My Tyrolean hat, complete with coloured feather, was hung on the hallstand. The snow was shaken off my jacket and hung beside my hat. I was ushered into the kitchen and sat in the warmth by the stove.

Ellen's mother obviously knew about me because they laughed and joked with each other during this routine. My knowledge of the German language wasn't good but it was sufficient to communicate and my grammar caused many an amusing moment. We must have chatted away for over half an hour as tea was prepared.

A sound at the front door caused mother to hurriedly leave the kitchen.

"Who's that?" I asked.

"Father."

This was unexpected. Like The Afrika Corps, he should have been elsewhere.

I could hear mother talking rapidly to him before he entered the kitchen.

Father was a big man! He had a big fist, a big smile, a mighty grip and a voice to match.

"Welcome to my house!" he bellowed as he opened a bottle of beer and filled two glasses.

A bewildered Australian Prisoner of War sat down to a meal with a rather wonderful German family.

We "chatted" away for several hours about Australia and Germany in peacetime and carefully avoided the current situation, but eventually it became time for me to go.

I said "Farewell" to Mum and Dad. Ellen saw me to the door. We embraced for a few moments.

Auf Wiedersehen, Artewer."

"Auf Wiedersehen, Ellen."

I never saw any of them again.

Ellen Schlaghaufer 1941-42

Now that Love's Farewell had been spoken the immediate future did not look very pleasant; in fact, as I crunched along the dark, snow-covered road back to camp, I had to admit it looked decidedly grim.

The whole venture had been filled with excitement creating happy memories for years ahead but, when viewed in the light of what could happen within the next hour, it tended to lose some of its lustre.

The Germans had a statement on the camp notice board: "The intimate association of Prisoners-of-War with German women is regarded as a serious crime and, in some cases, is punishable by death."

I had been belted several times; the heavy military belt with its buckle inscribed "Gott Mitt Uns" playing havoc wherever it landed but, somehow, this side of Life had slipped my memory until now.

The camp, as I crunched towards it, appeared to be a hive of activity. Instead of the usual two-man picket patrolling around the locked barracks the whole guard was moving around flashing torch beams on every shuttered window and minutely examining every locked door. So intent were they upon their duties that I was obliged to vigorously shake the gate to attract attention.

Max, The German Sgt. Major, came over.

"What do you want?"

"I'm a British Prisoner-of-War. Can I get bed and breakfast in there?"

He unlocked the gate and bowed in a mock manner.

"Welcome home," said he. Then, with all the majesty of The German Wehrmacht behind his voice: "To the office of The Kamp Kommandant – MARCH!"

We clumped along the corridor of The German Barrack to the door of The Kommandant's office. It was pushed open and I found myself inside blinking under the sudden brilliance of the electric light. I have never worked out if the door was opened and I was pushed inside or whether I was pushed and the door, fortunately, came open. Anyway, my arrival was abrupt.

The office seemed crowded. Our English Sgt. Major was there; so was an armed guard, the German Interpreter and a very worried-looking Kommandant.

Silence reigned as The Kommandant looked me over for a million years.

"Nammee und Nummer?" he roared in German.

"Name and number?" shouted the interpreter in English.

"Leggett. 92135," I answered in despair.

"Where have you been?" screamed the German voice followed by the English echo.

"Sir, it is the duty of every soldier to escape and I have been planning for weeks to escape in the spring and make my way to Switzerland. But I heard we are being moved to Poland in the morning so I escaped today. However, the snowstorm outside is too much for me. I'm nearly frozen stiff already. (Indeed, I was. Cold with fear and stiff with fright.) I couldn't find anywhere to sleep so I came back."

Herr Kommandant exploded with a roar like a twenty-five pounder.

"Liar!" he hollered as only a German can holler. "Liar! Liar! Liar!"

I came to the conclusion he didn't believe my story. He made a grab for a drawer in his desk and pulled it open. I closed my eyes. Rubber truncheons can really hurt. The sound of rustling paper caused me to open them again.

Der Offizer was examining a long piece of paper.

"92135!" he woofed.

"92135." I whined.

He scanned the list on the paper then raced his pencil vigorously to and fro along the lines obliterating the words. The action was followed by a verbal broadside directed at the interpreter who, in turn, swung upon the British Sgt. Major whose presence I had forgotten.

"'Arry," said the interpreter, "take 'im to 'is barrack."

I turned to leave the room but was promptly swung around again and told to salute The Kommandant. I complied and, for a moment, I thought I saw the stern features relax a little.

"What do you think will happen, Harry?" I asked as we shuffled towards the barrack.

"Nothing."

"Don't be silly. This is serious. I'm in real trouble."

"So are the other nineteen if the old man likes to cut up rough."

"What other nineteen?"

"Altogether twenty of you lovebirds shot through from working parties today. The old man was furious and called me into his office. He was going to call out The Gestapo, The Military Police as well as The Civilian Police to round you all up and someone was likely to get shot, especially if The Gestapo got cracking. I calmed him down and gave him my word you would all be back in the morning. This didn't help much because if you didn't come back he would be severely punished for having such a thing happen to his camp and for not reporting the escapes as soon as he knew about them. Then he had a brilliant idea.

"Arry," he said, "if they are not back by morning I will accuse you of taking advantage of your position as Camp Leader and helping them to escape. You will probably be shot."

"He was obviously scared of being punished and so was I. But it's all right, now."

"Do you mean they have all returned to camp?"

"No. There are still two missing but we know where they are. The Kommandant has sent a couple of guards down to Senefelder Strasse to bring them back."

The quiz programme which followed my entry into the barrack was far more detailed and probing than the interview in The Kommandant's office but I wasn't saying much.

I had had a wonderful evening and I wanted to keep the charm of it alive within me.

Next morning we were marched to a nearby rail siding to board a train. This one had seats in it. Quite a contrast to our previous train journey.

But the surprising scene was the sight of several hundred or so citizens of The City of Munich who had come to wave us 'farewell' as we commenced our journey across Germany.

*The Germans provided a military funeral for a British Prisoner of War.
Munich 1941-42*

Chapter Eighteen

The Germans railed us back to Stalag V11A at Moosburg to be counted, recounted and shuffled about for a few days. We had improved both physically and mentally and were no longer the dirty, under-nourished, bewildered mob that had been shoved into the place 18 months ago; a circumstance of which the numerous English-speaking guards seemed aware. They no longer shouted at us and their attitude, in a military sense, was more courteous.

Mind you, you couldn't trust the bastards and there was always the nasty character willing to support his comments with the application of percussion per medium of a rifle butt.

The "gathering together" enabled us to meet mates from whom we had been separated when dispersed into Munich, and Jesse rejoined the group from The Signals Platoon that had managed to stick together.

This large Stalag, holding thousands of men of all nationalities, was an unpleasant place to be incarcerated. The high, barbed-wire fences dividing the different nationalities, the warning wires running parallel to the fences, the patrolling armed guards, the machine-gun towers and searchlights dominated everything and reinforced the impression that you, as an individual, were nothing.

Conditions for the Russian prisoners-of-war hadn't changed. They were slowly starving to death and the treatment handed out to them was brutal. The Germans still chased them out of their barracks at any hour of the day or night for roll call and counting. These starving, weakened creatures were still kept there for hours long after the count was completed.

Bodies were still to be seen hanging on the wire in the morning and these men were not trying to escape – they were trying to get into our compound for the food we weren't permitted to throw to them in the daytime.

Any attempt to communicate, or throw them food, was punishable by death – and this time Fritz wasn't joking!

Eventually a train ride took us right across Germany to Stalag XIIIC at Lamsdorf near Upper Silesia. Living conditions in this Stalag was no better than the previous one but the inmates were different; several hundreds of them were a 'newer' edition.

Non-commissioned aircrews were kept in a separate compound. Many of them had recently been shot down in bombing raids and seemed determined to escape in order to make their way back to England or to engage in acts of sabotage.

Consequently, the old Fritz was equally determined to make escape impossible. We weren't there long enough to learn all the tricks they were up to but the Australian and New Zealand Infantry Ps.O.W. managed to swap identities with quite a few of them by exchanging identity discs and uniforms. This allowed the Air Force characters to be available for a work party and possible escape.

The Ps.O.W. taken at Dieppe were also there. Apparently the Germans had captured a British Order stating that German prisoners taken at Dieppe were to be handcuffed and sent back to the beach. The German media made great propaganda out of this and claimed it clearly showed the British marauders treated honourable soldiers like common criminals.

The British prisoners captured in the Dieppe fiasco were therefore compelled to wear handcuffs "like common criminals" from check parade in the early morning until check parade at the end of the day. This order was quite acceptable because the men soon found out the key from a tin of milk powder supplied in The Red Cross Parcels also unlocked the handcuffs. When guards entered the compound the word was quickly passed around and the handcuffs were clamped on again. The old Fritz didn't seem to wake up to this until the day a prowler guard found a naked chap under the shower wearing handcuffs.

Within a short space of time a couple of hundred of us were despatched to a small camp at Dombrova but, in the shuffle, I lost contact with Charlie, Doug and Colin although Jesse and I kept together with other mates.

The camp was partially occupied by troops from The British Expeditionary Force who had been captured at Dunkirk and who had already been working in the coalmines for some considerable time.

It wasn't a big camp. It had a couple of barracks divided into rooms holding 12 men in double bunks. A wooden table and forms occupied the centre of the room. Also, inside the barbed wire fence, was a barrack for our administration personnel including a doctor and a hospital ward. The guards' quarters were made of solid brick and stood outside the fence.

The surrounding skyline was ragged with spinning wheels on top of poppet legs and the nearby countryside was grey with slag-heaps and presented a dismal picture.

I had never been underground, nor ever contemplated working below the earth's surface; this lack of knowledge, coupled with the horrendous tales recounted by 'The Dunkirkers', made the future appear somewhat daunting.

We were a bit crooked on the Poms, too.

"Coal mining is a war industry," we said. "Why the hell did you all volunteer to work in the coalmines?"

"After Dunkirk," they said, "we were marched right across Europe with what we stood up in. They knocked us around a bit and crowded us into Lamsdorf where the barracks had no windows and no doors. If they had any Red Cross food or clothing they never issued it. Then winter came and the icy cold wind blew snow through the barracks. The Germans used to announce: "The barracks and food will be better and clothing will be made available if you volunteer to work in the coalmines." We hung out for several months then some of the men volunteered. You can't blame them. Things were bloody tough."

"Good-oh!" cries the old Fritz, "The British are volunteering to work in the coalmines! Everybody be ready to move early in the morning!"

"But, it's not too bad here. We've been in worse places," we assured them.

The camp guards were not the same as those in Munich. The majority was middle-aged with a cruel streak in their nature and they shouted and pushed without provocation.

The notice board soon displayed a paper giving names, the mine section to which that name was allocated and the shift; either day shift or afternoon shift.

They marched us across to the mine to be issued with work clothes, a pair of boots, a leather safety helmet, a carbide gas lamp and, of course, a number.

They sent us down below – a long way down below. The skip stopped. The Polish skipman, who had talked to us in Polish all the way down, opened the skip gate and we stepped out into a tunnel of surprising dimensions. It must have been twenty feet in diameter, cement lined with a small gauge railway line running along its floor and disappearing into the darkened distance.

A number of Polish miners were standing nearby and, when all the Ps.O.W. allocated to that section had arrived, we were further split into smaller groups and attached to a Pole who greeted us with "Hoj!" and we followed him along the tunnel.

It is not the purpose of this journal to go into details of the techniques of coal-mining in Upper Silesia (of which I have scant knowledge) but it is pertinent to comment that the mine appeared to be divided into sections with a German shift boss at the head. Each section was further divided into sub-sections with a Polish shift boss in charge of each sub-section. All the workers were Polish and the demand was twenty wagons per man per day. Each wagon held two tons. Additional men meant additional output and we became introduced to the coal-face and the shovel.

The coal-face, where I was shovelling, was at the end of a tunnel cut into the coal deposit. My knowledge of coal mining came from descriptions in books by D.H. Lawrence where men crawled along cramped tunnels scratching at coal seams but here the volume of coal was immense.

This tunnel had a sand floor but both walls and the ceiling were coal and the blowing down of the coal-face took it deeper into the distance. Later, at some predetermined stage, railway lines, electric cables and as many timber supports as safety permitted, were all withdrawn; the mouth was timbered up and the whole tunnel filled with sand. This was achieved by running in a mixture of sand and water. The water ran off to be pumped up to the surface whilst the sand gradually filled the tunnel right to the roof. Another face would be opened up further along the deposit and it, too, would eventually be sealed and filled. The coal between the two sand-filled tunnels was then taken out.

Some of our chaps, in other sections, were not so fortunate. The coal-face was the wall of the tunnel and when it was blown, a vast quantity of coal had to be shovelled on to a conveyor belt running the full length of the tunnel. The other side of the conveyor belt allowed the German shift boss to roar up and down the line abusing and threatening as he demanded greater effort.

The Polish miners were a friendly mob who watched over us like a group of hens with newly hatched chicks and over a period of time, as our P.O.W. language began to include phrases in the difficult Polish language, we worked in well together.

Upon reaching the surface at the end of a shift, we returned our lamps to the lamp room and showered in the change-room. Our clothes, coming or going, were hung on a hook and hauled up into the high ceiling by a light rope fastened to a wall bracket with a number on it.

The hot shower was always welcome after 10 hours underground.

We lined up outside the change room to be counted before commencing the half mile walk back to the camp gate and counted again before being turned loose inside the wire.

Shift work had its problems. Jesse was my 'mucker'. I had the top bunk, he had the bottom bunk. We shared Red Cross Parcels and every other item we could garnish by rackets or black market. But he was on the opposite shift to me. Consequently, when I was preparing for work he would be asleep and when he came in I would be asleep. We weren't able to hold a conversation until the shift change on our 'free' day every three weeks.

The free day was a day of mixed activity depending on individual inclinations.

Numerous soccer games were played on the small, black dust-covered parade ground from whence the players returned looking like a troupe of nigger minstrels.

Clothing worn underground had to be washed and dried.

Many hours were spent in just sitting around yarning about our respective homelands; a very educational and horizon-widening past-time because we were a mixed mob.

Some of the English chaps came from the deepest dark depths of London and told tales which seemed to come straight out of Charles Dickens's writings whilst others were of farming stock and spoke of farming techniques which intrigued us.

A considerable number of The South Africans were descendants of The Boer Vortreckers and, at first, were a bit hostile and hard to get along with. They were big men and there was no point in arguing with them. They just didn't like Dear Old Mother England. Two of them were Rangers in their country's national parks and there was no way we could convince them that all us Aussies were cattle station owners.

Incidentally, one of our chaps WAS a cattle station owner's son. He had a few excellent photos of the double-storied, weatherboard homestead as well as several additional photos depicting station life. Whilst in Munich we had numerous copies made and handed around. Reluctantly we would display them to our German workmates and shyly confess it was "Meine Hause".

I became involved in the camp's entertainment group. The desire to entertain was always running like an undercurrent amongst chaps who could 'do something'. Perhaps to simply blow a tune on a mouth-organ, twang a guitar, plonk away on a mandolin. Such instruments had been acquired in shonky deals in Munich or from contacts currently being established underground. Their owners were spread throughout the camp and the idea was to form an entertainments committee and get them together.

I was made president with another chap as secretary. I had no knowledge of music or how to organise a concert so if someone expressed a wish to 'have a go' I simply gave him his head and loosed the reins a bit.

The Germans never asked difficult questions about musical instruments. They would stage an occasional search looking for hoarded Red Cross food, civilian clothes, photographs of local acquaintances or illegal letters but they simply passed over instruments obviously acquired by illegal means.

One of the chaps even had a portable gramophone and a stack of records openly kept in his possession from Munich. A warm, sunny afternoon on a free day often found a group of us sun baking and, lost in our own thoughts, silently listening to Joan Hammond singing 'One Fine Day' from Madam Butterfly and 'Musetta's Waltz Song' from La Bohemme.

Jesse had a talent for music. He could play a mandolin with considerable skill and handle other stringed instruments with no trouble; but he had aspirations to play a violin.

He made a contact with a Pole underground. I don't know what the deal was, or how he smuggled it into the camp, but one free day he reaches under his bunk and drags out a violin in a wooden case.

Living in a barrack room with a chap trying to get the hang of how to play a violin can become a little irksome so we regularly chased him out and into the empty entertainment hut until his teething troubles were over; but he did get the hang of it and thereafter contributed to the camp's entertainment in an efficient manner.

Working in the mine entitled us to be paid but, again, we were paid in worthless P.O.W. money. Nevertheless, if we presented a roll of it to the Kamp Kommandant with a list of goods we required for the theatre it was changed into marks and, when available, the goods were supplied.

We charged five marks entry into our shows and, in this way, managed to accumulate sufficient funds to meet the theatre's needs. With this money we hired costumes and wigs as well as purchased make-up grease from a shop in the nearby town. We were unable to obtain scenery because transport was a problem but paper and paint were available and impressive scenery was created by chaps who were "willing to give it a go" and some excellent shows were presented.

I once wrote and directed a Christmas pantomime of 'Cinderella' in which some Welsh coalminers formed their own ballet group titled 'The Hairy Fairies'. I had no hope of controlling their activities but they brought the house down.

The humour, the drama, the monotony of our existence rolled on through Time.

The rackets, the black market and all other forms of bribery and corruption commenced as soon as we could see an opening. The magical influence of English cigarettes, chocolate, soap and tea began to exert their influence upon the German shift bosses and the Polish foremen.

My first job underground was shovelling coal on to a long conveyor belt at the coal-face. Within a month my job was to make my way to the electric motor driving the belt. When the coal-face was blown I pressed a black button on a switch to set the belt rolling. When the shift finished I pressed a red button to stop it.

I wrote "Cinderella" and read many books sitting with my back against that post.

I struck a bargain with a Polish shift boss. Half a dozen eggs for two ounces of tea. I had a French Army dixie of a style much deeper than ours and I carried the eggs out in this. The usual body search was conducted at the camp gate so I stood there with the dixie in my hand and my arms extended. The guard never thought to look in the dixie.

Next day the shift boss was really going crook. He was so upset I couldn't follow his words. Fortunately one of the Dunkirk chaps was handy and I asked him what was wrong.

"That packet you gave him yesterday. He says it's the worst tobacco he has ever smoked!"

Another time I was sitting with this chap and yarning in our peculiar language as we waited for the miners to come on shift. Ps.O.W. were always sent underground ahead of the rest. One of the Polish miners handed him a chit of paper from a doctor stating he was to be on light duties because of some health problem.

The shift boss flew into a tearing rage and, basically, told the miner if he couldn't do a day's work he could go back up top and work somewhere else. He could do that or pick up a shovel and take his place at the coal-face with the rest of them. Please yourself.

The miner had no way of going up top so he picked up a shovel and disappeared down the tunnel.

When he was out of sight the shift boss asked me for a cigarette.

"Not on your life, mate. One of your own countrymen sick and you're making him shovel coal all day. I'm not giving you a cigarette."

He sat there for a while trembling and trying to control himself. Eventually he heaved a big sigh and quietly said, "Zigarnik, I went to school with that man. Now, for every man in this section I have to send out twenty wagons of coal. What do you think would happen if I didn't do that?"

"I suppose you would get into trouble with the Germans."

"No! I can still work. They would take my wife and my children and I'd never see them again."

I gave him a cigarette, lit one myself and, while we sat there in silence, each lost in the misery of his own thoughts, I had a sense of being lost in a situation I couldn't understand. I felt so helpless and far away from home as I wondered what might happen to my Mum and sisters before this war ended.

*****

One Polish miner, about my age, was a tall, big-boned man but he seemed to lack flesh on his bones; his skin was quite sallow and he moved around in a disinterested manner.

Months later I heard his story.

He had finished afternoon shift and was on his way home when The Germans swooped on about thirty men in his immediate vicinity and carted them off to Auschwitz Concentration Camp. No reason. No suspicion. No crime. Just a swoop on the community.

At Auschwitz they were all shoved into a bare, cement cell with hardly room to lie down. The low ceiling prevented them from standing upright and the floor had half an inch of water all over it. The door was shut and the place was in total darkness.

The psychological effect of this sort of sustained terror upon the community of an occupied country is not hard to imagine. A man simply disappeared off the streets on his way home from work. Families were never notified. The worker had no idea why he was picked up and taken to Auschwitz but, in due course, a bewildered, broken man returned home to go down the mine and pick up his shovel again – or else!

And this threat hung over the community 24 hours a day!

*****

Ten months underground and I commenced to have painful sinus problems. My shoulders, too, made a crackling noise when I moved them so our camp doctor arranged for me to be examined by a German doctor with a view to changing my workplace. This would not take place for a couple of weeks so I studied and polished up my German. The lurk is to occasionally use German words and convince them you are becoming assimilated. Some German military doctors had a strong awareness of rank and insisted on military courtesies such as salutes, standing to attention whilst being examined and so on.

I entered the surgery with trepidation, stood to attention, saluted a rather young doctor and in my best German said, "Good morning, Herr Doktor."

He returned my salute with a hand that displayed only the thumb and index finger and replied in his best German, "Oh, shit! Sit down."

I later learned he had been wounded on The Russian Front.

He checked me over and allocated me to permanent surface work!

The magic of permanent surface work! The sky, the sunlight, the distant horizon, the wind in your face, an occasional tree, fresh air. Shangri-La!

The new work group was called 'The Electrical Party'. A mixed crew of Australians, Englishmen, South Africans and a Kiwi, with a German civilian in charge as well as a couple of Polish workers. Herr Katonski must, of necessity, remain a little aloof but, as a group, we got along very well together. We were employed in the area beyond the mine boundary and the work consisted of 'odd-jobbing' around the place. We occasionally dug a trench or laid out cable but we never came in contact with electricity itself.

A guard took us to the mine where we had our own little nook to wait for our work boss but, from then onwards, we never saw the guard all day.

This situation obviously lends itself to escape – but where could a man go?

We were at a mine called Dombrova somewhere in the area of Gleiwitz and Kattowitz across the Polish Border. The Russians were thousands of kilometres to the east and the Allies an equal distance in the opposite direction. We had been about two and a half years behind the wire and those who hadn't made some attempt at escape seemed resigned to sit it out because of the hopelessness of trying to escape.

A dentist in Gleiwitz attended to our dental requirements.

Periodically an appointment was made when our Camp Doctor had found sufficient tooth decay to rustle up a party to be escorted by an armed guard into the city. These visits often presented the opportunity to meet with Ps.O.W. from other camps and to keep in touch with mates who you hadn't seen for eighteen months or more.

A "dental party" came back to camp one evening in a sombre mood and bristling with indignation at news they'd received from other camps.

"They've shot Doug Burling!"

"Doug?"

"How did the bastards do a thing like that?"

"He was one of the best! Remember how he used to wrestle with the kids in Munich?"

It seems the boys had come up at the end of a shift and were in the change room when some altercation arose and a guard started to bash one of our chaps. The guard had him down on the floor and was thumping him with his rifle butt when Doug came out of the shower and intervened simply by taking possession of the rifle.

There isn't much a naked man in a shower-room can do with a rifle when he is a P.O.W.

Doug gave the rifle back to the guard who went out through one door to re-appear at another.

He shot Doug through the head.

He was left lying there twenty-four hours before his mates were allowed to move his body.

*****

Communication with your mate, who was on the other shift, sometimes meant leaving a note for him to read when he awoke. One of our room-mates had smuggled in a kilogram of sugar and, in compliance with the accepted principle, half of it was his 'muckers'.

This chap left a note reading, "Be warned! Use more than one spoonful per cup of tea and you will become a victim of The Claw!"; and he reinforced the warning with a drawing of a very hairy, long-fingered, long-nailed, grasping claw.

This line of humour 'took on' and little notes began to appear all over the place.

"Be ready to play soccer at 0900hrs next Sunday or you will become a victim of The Claw."

"Concert rehearsal tomorrow at 1900 hrs. Be there or you will become a victim of The Claw!" and so on.

This sort of humour was all right within the camp but it got underground. Some character left a message for his mate, written with the carbon from his lamp, on the wall of a cement-lined tunnel:- "Jackson. 20 wagons today or you will become a victim of The Claw"; and it was signed by that horrendous hand.

The Polish miners viewed it with a certain amount of fear. We didn't know it but The Polish Underground Movement also pushed people around a bit in a similar manner.

The Germans took it seriously.

Next Sunday we were all ordered to dress in uniform and "fall in" on the parade ground.

A German Colonel, accompanied by an interpreter, strode in through the gate to address the parade.

His comments, basically, stated although we are prisoners of war we are still soldiers the same as the soldiers in The German Army. It was against the principles of The German Army to have anything to do with secret societies but it was apparent that a secret society was forming within the camp and threatening us Ps.O.W. It was his duty to stamp out this society. Now! Step forward all those who are victims of The Claw!

Military discipline prevented the parade from dissolving in laughter but, after three and a half years behind the wire, we reckoned we were all probably victims of the claw.

*****

The Concert Party's finances were booming.

The organisation which printed The Camp newspaper, as well as our token money, had been bombed out of business and, consequently, we were now paid in real German money.

Our rate of pay was only a few Marks a week but there was nowhere to go and nothing to buy so the five Marks charged for admission to the shows was chicken feed. However, if you have 200 men willingly paying five Marks over several shows you soon accumulate a wad of dough well over and above requirements and beyond the legal limits.

The secretary and I kept this circumstance to ourselves. We feared, if some determined character wanted to escape, we could be robbed and if the escapee was recaptured with a roll of wealth on his person some heavy interrogation could follow.

The war wasn't going too good for The Germans.

Their propaganda informed us they had withdrawn from North Africa after inflicting humiliating losses upon The British whose advance, at times, was so slow they lost contact with The German rearguard. The German Army had been betrayed by The Italian Capitulation so they had staged a strategic withdrawal in order to set up a line of defence across Italy before driving the invader back into the sea and, in addition, they had halted the enemy's advance on The Russian Front.

The enemy's advance on The Russian Front?

The Russians, we had always been told, had been slaughtered like cattle as they retreated in chaotic panic right across Russia to the outskirts of Moscow, Leningrad and Stalingrad; three cities which had staunchly resisted the advantages of being liberated from the communist yoke.

This was the first news we had heard about an advance!

A peculiar characteristic of a soldier's life is the manner in which the demands of his own immediate vicinity isolated him from the overall view of the major events. We didn't live a complacent life but, amidst the life-destroying turmoil raging all over the world, we lived a somewhat isolated and sheltered existence. Radios were forbidden, our English language P.O.W. paper contained only what The Germans wanted us to know and think, whilst our irregular letters were heavily censored from both sides.

We never doubted 'our side' would win and, one day, we would be back with our own folk in Australia but, at times, I felt very lonely and I'm sure most of the boys had similar periods of emotional hopelessness.

Consequently, we grasped at any item or event conveying hope.

*****

The winter of 1944 arrived suddenly on gusts of icy winds coming all the way from Russia. They swirled snow across the rooftops and the grey countryside to lay a white blanket of cold misery overall.

Fortunately we were warm-clothed and well shod. The Red Cross parcels plus the German rations, such as they were, meant we had one good meal a day. The underground mine temperature was constant though occasionally requiring a pullover in cooler spots. Some days the above-ground Electrical Party were out in the snow-covered open but most of the time was spent in some building crouched over a fire and swapping yarns about South Africa, England, Australia, New Zealand or some other native land made all the more magical as time and distance increased.

It was an unusual winter. The low rumbling of distant thunderstorms could be heard when lying quietly in bed at night. Thunderstorms don't usually occur in winter but this was quite distinct.

The next night it sounded louder.

"Jeez! Did you hear that! I don't think it's thunder! It's bloody guns!"

"Aw; bullshit. The Russians are nowhere near here. We would

have heard about it if they were."

Next morning our Camp Leader came around the barracks.

"No work today. We're leaving in 24 hours."

"Bloody hell! Where are we going?"

"I don't know. All I know is you have to pack whatever gear you can carry and be ready to move tomorrow morning."

A frantic day of sorting, discarding and packing followed. Being restricted to only what we could carry meant so many little treasures, garnished over the years, had to be abandoned. Books, drawings, drawing material, pots, pans, favourite tea mugs, plates, letters from home, blankets, the gramophone and all the records – anything and everything which was not absolutely essential.

"You've got to carry it, mate, so if you don't need it – chuck it away."

Food and warm clothing were the main concerns. The clothing requirement was easily dealt with. Wear everything you possessed; woolen socks, long johns, flannel shirt, pullover, battle dress, overcoat and a warm hat. "It's damn cold out there."

All the musical instruments were left behind; that is, all except one and that happened to be a violin in a wooden violin case belonging to Jesse.

An extra Red Cross Parcel was issued per man; an act reinforcing the seriousness of the situation and, at first, created a bit of a problem. The additional quantity of food and the necessary clothing, crammed into a haversack, was damned heavy.

The camp's wooden stools were broken down, sawn, shaped and made into small sleighs complete with a box into which was stacked a man's worldly possessions.

This was to be no orderly movement of Ps.O.W. within The Third Reich. It was a full scale retreat before the advancing Russian Army!

The entertainment committee's British, public-school-educated, secretary had a problem.

"Look here, Arthur," he said, looking at the 4 inch diameter roll of notes. "All this money. We should hand it back to the chaps, you know."

My Australian attitude came to the fore.

"I reckon we should split it in half and buy whatever we can for the boys along the track."

The track went out the camp gate, through the buildings of the nearby township and into the cold, misty, snow-swirling distance beyond.

Chapter Nineteen

Four weeks into the march and it was becoming a bitter experience.

We marched five abreast with guards flanking both sides – and these older men weren't enjoying the situation either – as we trudged along hour after hour, while the cold wind swirled the falling snow across the countryside. Some of it landed on the narrow road, to be trampled underfoot and stamped into the snow packed solid by thousands of boots.

Soft snow was often inches thick when movement commenced in the morning. It clung to our plodding boots where the warmth of our feet melted it to gradually saturate our boots and soak our socks.

There seemed to be some order within the chaos. Each day we arrived at a village or a hamlet where a large barn was prominent. We were herded into the barn and the door shut with a guard on the outside. We burrowed, at first, into the straw to keep warm but men soon began moving around to check on their mates and generally yarn over the situation.

The aggressive attitude of The Germans gradually diminished as the march proceeded and time increased. Strangely enough, this circumstance was brought about by food.

They didn't seem to have an established supply line for rations and we usually scrounged potatoes, carrots, turnips or an occasional cabbage from the local inhabitants. These were all dumped into a farmyard copper and brought to the boil; a procedure resulting in a vegetable soup noted for its warmth and water rather than its vitamin content.

The consumption of our Red Cross Parcels was purely a personal thing to be worked out between a mucker and his mate. We eked out our stores with considerable restraint. We had all been hungry before and this was no new experience. Most of us restricted ourselves to one "good" meal at the end of a day by having half a meat loaf between us. Keeping meat loaf in an opened tin was no problem because it was frozen solid with ice crystals all through it.

Our Camp Leader was a South African Sgt. Major named Sullivan. I don't know what he thought of The British but he certainly stood up to The Germans. He demanded we be allowed to cook our Red Cross food at the end of a day.

The Germans, knowing we were without cooking gear, said, "Go ahead."

Within a very short space of time small campfires were smoking all over the open cow yard as men commenced cooking bully beef, crushed biscuits, powdered eggs and similar ingredients in utensils of all shapes and sizes.

No meals had ever tasted so delicious but we were all slowly starving and losing weight without really being aware of it.

Herded back into the barn as darkness approached, we took off our boots and socks, buried them in the straw then, in pairs, buried ourselves to try and keep warm.

Next morning the socks crackled and the boots were stiff with a thin layer of ice inside them and these we pulled on before moving out into the stream of refugees shuffling into the unknown future.

Somewhere up ahead a bullock, or a horse, was bleeding from the hoof. Big blobs of blood had dropped at precise intervals on to the iced roadway for several days and I found myself wondering how much further it could travel in such a condition and, if it died from malnutrition and exhaustion, what would happen to the refugee's treasured possessions piled up on an overloaded wagon.

The cold wind swirled the snow around us and I didn't really care, anyway.

A group of political prisoners was also up ahead.

Sometimes, usually in the afternoon, when I felt I couldn't go much further, we would pass a political prisoner.

He'd be lying in the roadside ditch with a bullet hole drilled neatly in his forehead. His thin coat, wrapped around his gaunt, bone-protruding body, was occasionally wind-ruffled before it, too, was frozen and buried beneath the blanket of whiteness stretching to the horizon.

Ah, well; what's another body? They're all over the place.

The column occasionally ground to a halt. God knows for what reason. It simply stopped and the cause could not be discerned through the misty snowstorm. We squatted on our sledges with our backs to the wind.

Then this arrogant, young German NCO put on his act.

He swaggered up the centre of the column waving his hand and shouting, "To the right of the road! To the right of the road!"

We had no option but to move our aching bodies and sleighs to the right of the road.

The theory was, if any motorised vehicles came through, the centre of the road would be clear. But we were on back roads and hadn't seen a truck since the march had commenced but this arrogant, little upstart went through his routine every time we halted.

"When we get out of this," vowed Jacko, "I'm going to kill that bastard."

"Bloody good idea. I'll give you a hand."

And we meant it.

*****

The distance covered varied from 15 to 25kms daily as we shambled on for another couple of weeks. Although distance had its fatiguing influence the biggest problem was being exposed to the merciless winter weather all day; this, coupled with the lack of nourishing food, began to build a subtle tension within the individual.

Big arguments didn't break out but little niggles kept cropping up.

Some of the men had frostbitten feet and cheekbones. Faces were becoming gaunt and considerable flesh had disappeared from our bodies; an obvious circumstance witnessed whenever we peeled off our stiffening clothes to have a quick sluice in a sheltered trough or under a flowing tap. Our socks were beginning to show holes and our clothing was gradually becoming worn and grubby after a month and a half of sleeping in hay-sheds, cow barns, horse stables or any shed offering shelter. We probably stunk, too, but as we were all in the same condition, we didn't seem to notice.

Our trek had taken us ever westward, across the Oder River, across Czechoslovakia, through the mountains separating that tiny country from Germany and back into Bavaria.

The winter's fury had abated considerably. Snow still covered most of the countryside but it was thinning out on the roadways and gravel tracks as a prelude to the coming thaw.

The sleighs had been abandoned and gear was carried on our backs. This was no great burden as the remnants of our Red Cross food had been consumed long ago.

I had become sick of the sight of Jess's wooden violin case bobbing along in front of me day after day and that German NCO still smirked and called "to the right of the road" whenever we sank wearily into a heap during a halt in the ceaseless onward shuffling.

And, by cripes, there was bloody big war going on somewhere nearby!

Aircraft sightings were becoming more frequent and they weren't German planes, either!

First it was a twin-engine, double-fuselage, silver plane swooping unopposed around the sky at an amazing speed.

They were exhilarating yet frightening to watch. We had never seen anything like them before!

The Germans had anti-aircraft guns on their trains and the plane's target was the engine. It bore down through the flak to point straight at the engine; then, when it was close enough, it released a mass of firepower which completely put the engine out of action.

And courage! The pilot swooped high, swung around and, ignoring the flak, raked along the length of the now stationary train before disappearing into the overcast sky.

The first time I witnessed one of these attacks I was shocked and afraid. Shocked at the proximity of violent death and destruction once again and afraid because, obviously, our day of liberation was getting close and I was filled with a fierce desire to end it all in one piece.

A few days later the atmosphere vibrated with a new, deep, thunderous sound. The vibrations multiplied as the sound increased – then they appeared!

Flying Fortresses! Not just one or two but hundreds and hundreds of them! They stretched across the blue sky, glistening in the sunlight, from one horizon to the other!

We knew not where they were going but they were ours! They were on our side! Go to it, you little beauties!

We plodded on with a sense of uplifted morale and, with the temperature rising slightly, conditions were becoming easier. The guards, with whom we had shared much misery during the past months, showed no animosity despite the obvious destruction through which we daily passed. We had started off this march as guards and prisoners but had gradually become a conglomeration of humanity existing from day to day.

Then a wonderful thing happened at the little town of Krippaw. I can't remember what the town looked like but I remember the event clearly.

We had been resting in a barn for a few days after trudging an estimated 680 kilometres by the end of the sixth week. Suddenly an International Red Cross Truck appeared from Switzerland and unloaded food parcels!

Food! Good wholesome food!

Oh; the advice we gave each other. "Don't eat too much or you will be ill. We're not used to it." – "Be careful with the cigarettes. Half a one at a time, eh?"

"Tea! You put the billy on; I'll mix up some milk."

The "mucker system" still applied. Jesse and I drank tea, ate bully beef and munched a few biscuits.

There was no guarantee when the next lot of parcels would arrive but now The Red Cross had established contact, and the weather seemed poised between receding winter and approaching spring. The never-flagging conviction our side was going to win seemed about to become a reality.

We plodded on for another two weeks along ice-free roads snaking through the still snow-covered countryside.

Occasional hills. Occasional pine forests. Camping in barns, cowsheds or other farm buildings at night. Our clothes becoming dirtier. Our socks wearing out.

Day after day we trudged on. Sometimes we saw American planes; oft times we heard the thumping of air raid bombs in the distance but nowhere did we see soldiers of either army.

We rested in Weidon for a couple of days before being loaded on to a train.

Packed tight with scarcely space to squat down and travelling in open freight wagons wasn't exactly first class but it conformed to the army expression:- "A third class ride was better than a first class walk."

The train trundled along all night. Some of us slept; some of us stood up most of the night. Next day we were unloaded at the village of Obertraubling and marched to a massive barn half filled with bales of hay. We made ourselves as comfortable as the situation allowed and, during the next few weeks, all manner of hay walls were constructed to enclose individual areas of accommodation.

The International Red Cross found us again and although food was not plentiful it sustained us and supplemented the liquid received from

The Germans who, after a few days, decided we should be working.

Regensberg was about 15kms away and there was plenty of bomb damage to be cleared.

We were daily loaded into the open trucks of a small shunting train and transported into the town. There was, indeed, plenty of bomb damage. The town had been severely dealt with and there wasn't much we could do except toss rubble off the streets and make passageway for any people who may be passing that way.

We returned to Obertraubling at the end of long, hard days; the train travelling through an extensive rail marshalling yard situated about half way between Regensberg and the village.

The barn had a large, sliding door opening out on to a small yard where we did our cooking. Immediately adjacent to this yard was the village church with a steeple where a clock bonged out the time every fifteen minutes.

Snow still covered the countryside. We noticed long mounds under the snow in the field close to the barn; a method of storing potatoes from the previous harvest.

The sliding door was shut at night and a guard placed on the outside. These guards had tramped from Poland with us and certain amount of appreciation of each other's problems had developed during the past months. We weren't mates but we had problems in common. A few cigarettes to the right guard and we commenced trickling out of the barn, a few at a time, to the potato mounds and returning to bury the booty in the straw.

Several mounds were rifled during the night.

Upon returning from Regensburg next day we faced a serious problem.

The farmer had noticed his potato mounds had been robbed. A pathway ran from the barn door, through the snow, and over to the mounds so it wasn't hard to work out where the culprits were living. Apparently the potatoes were his seed potatoes and he needed them for planting when the ploughed field thawed.

However, he stated, he knew we were hungry so if he pushed a wagon into the barn and it was filled by the end of the next day he would take no further action.

This seemed fair enough and the wagon was filled; but then The German Army poked its nose into the affair.

Several guards had been placed on the barn door during the course of the night and one of them had co-operated with the pilfering.

Who was he?

The guards weren't going to own up so it came back to us.

Who was he?

Well, we weren't going to dob in a bloke who had helped us get a few extra spuds. Besides, it is an established military principal, 'You don't dob anyone in for anything.'

All the guards appeared at dusk that night shouting "Raus! Raus!"

I sensed something was "on" so I grabbed an armful of straw as I was pushed out into the yard. We didn't need to grab warm clothes; we were wearing them.

The arrogant German Corporal lined us up in rows and announced, "You will stand there until you tell us the name of the guard who assisted you. Any man who steps out of line will be shot."

I reckoned we would be standing around for quite some time so I dropped the bundle of straw on the icy ground and stood on it.

What a predicament!

The guards had been ordered to shoot any one who stepped out of line yet we were standing there to protect one of them for giving us a hand.

The arrogant German bastard, after a while, returned to the warmth of the house where he was billeted.

"Guard," called one of the men, "Toilet?"

"Ja," replied the guard.

A constant flow of men to the toilet commenced and, in this

manner, we managed to move occasionally and get some movement into our cold, aching limbs.

We stood there throughout the long night while the church clock bonged out the time every fifteen minutes.

A wintry dawn had pushed its way into a long night when The Kamp Kommandant appeared. He stood there looking at us before shaking his head. He told us to get something to eat and to be on the train in an hour's time.

But that arrogant corporal! His days were numbered!

The latest 'ferphy', hot from The Kamp Kommandant's mouth, was "Today will be a short day because tomorrow we are moving on towards Munich."

This suited me because the air raids around the place were becoming too frequent and I hadn't lost this desire to arrive home in one piece.

We packed into the shunt train and headed back to camp in the early afternoon.

The air raid sirens sounded while we were half way between the city and the marshalling yards.

The train stopped. We waited, scanning the sky. Aircraft alerts had become an everyday event and we wondered where this lot was going and, if it was those twin-fuselage characters marauding around, we hoped they would realise who we were and give us a miss.

We saw them!

Massive Flying Fortresses coming from the other side of the city and you didn't have to be a military genius to work out where they were going!

Black objects fell from them and parts of the city disappeared in noise, smoke and dust.

They kept coming in our direction. We jumped out of the rail-trucks and spread ourselves on Dear Mother Earth.

The near side of the town rumbled and jumped before

disappearing in a cloud of dust.

Bombs could be seen leaving the planes as they passed directly overhead. I muttered a quick prayer which must have been heard because the missiles moaned their way beyond us and commenced wiping out the marshalling yards.

"Bloody hell!" commented one of the troops. "Now we'll have to walk back."

This we did, skirting the wreckage and picking our way through craters to Obertraubling.

The march recommenced next morning and it was back to the old routine of trudging all day, dossing down in barns or cowsheds at night and on again the next day.

The end of the third day found us billeted in a large barn packed with bales of hay and straw. Next morning The Kamp Kommandant had a yarn with Sgt. Maj. Sullivan which was relayed to us.

"The Germans are going to leave us here. They advise us to stay inside this barn for a couple of days and don't go outside because the German Troops coming through are nasty types and they could set fire to the barn. I suggest you all take his advice."

We did!

We spotted several individual Germans scurrying through the fields and scrub during the next two days. There was never more than two or three together and they appeared to be in a hurry as they scrambled up the slope to the roadway running along the crest of the hillock behind the barn.

One of our men, looking out of a window high in the barn's wall on the fourth morning, shouted, "There's dozens of tanks moving along the road up there! They must be Russian because they've all got stars on them!"

"What colour's the stars?"

"White!"

"Stone the crows! They're American!"

There was no cheering or shouting. I shook hands with Jesse. Everyone seemed to be doing the same and there was a lot of laughter.

Eventually common sense prevailed.

"Let's get outside and get a fire going. I reckon it's not a bad time to boil the billy."

"Bloody good idea."

Chapter Twenty

We sat around outside for some time before three jeeps loaded with Americans detached themselves from the road above and swooped down the gravel track to the barn. One jeep came straight on, one flanked out left and the other to the right. The soldiers jumped out to form a line with carbines facing the barn. A chap with two white stripes on his helmet approached us.

"G'day," we greeted him.

"Howdy," he replied.

"We've been waiting for you. What took you so long?"

"We had a few problems. Where're you men from?"

"Australia."

"I've been there. Great place, Australia."

We indicated the semi-circle of soldiers facing the barn with their weapons held in an alert position.

"Expecting trouble?"

"No, just being careful. There's a few krauts in this area so be careful if you wander about."

He turned, made a signal to his men who piled back into the jeeps and disappeared up the gravel track to mingle with the passing parade.

It took some time for the reality of the situation to sink in.

We were free!

We could get up and wander about or stay where we were! Please yourself!

We sat there for a bit longer.

"Jesse," I said, "I'm going down to that village to see if I can scrounge a bit of grub. You coming?"

"No. I'll fossick around here. There might be something over there," he said, indicating an abandoned farmhouse.

"I'll come with you," Jacko said to me. "There's a bloke I want to have a few words with and the yanks could have him down there. He can't have got very far."

"Aw; come off it. We don't have to worry about his sort any more."

"What the hell's wrong with you blokes? You've all got bloody short memories. What about the way he used to fire his revolver into the ground behind you then bray like a donkey when you jumped and fell over your mates? And what about the time he kicked old Ken in the guts when he fell over and was too weak to move? He belted all of us at some time or another and we said we were going to kill him. Maybe I won't kill him but, by Jesus, I'm going to knock him about a bit if I can find him. If you won't help me I'll do it on my own."

"Come on," I said, "I'll go with you just to see you don't get hurt."

We made our way to the nearby village where an American Sergeant called us over.

"Hey! Can any of you guys speak this Heinie language?"

"I might be able to help."

"Well, (he didn't say 'well'. He said 'Waal') "This guy seems to be the boss around here. Can you tell him we're not going to plunder the place, rape the women or burn the joint down. All we want to do is set up a command post in the school hall for a couple of days."

I managed to convey this information to "The Boss" who happily led the way to the school.

"Hey! That was good!" exclaimed the Sergeant, "Here, can you use these?"

He handed me half a dozen packets covered in what appeared to be beeswax.

"What's this?"

"K Rations. Sorry they're not dinner units but that's all we've got at the moment."

The packets were marked 'Breakfast Units' but I wasn't going to complain.

"You got any prisoners around here?" queried Jacko.

"We're holding about a hundred of them in the square. It's around the corner."

We went around to the village square where a couple of heavily armed Americans were guarding a mob of prisoners. They seemed a rather harmless lot. We strolled over there.

"You guys looking for someone?" asked one of the G.I.s.

"There's a bloke we want to have a word with if we can find him."

"Waal, look 'em over."

We looked them over. It wasn't easy. There had been times during the past four years when we had suffered rather badly at the hands of German soldiers and now we were searching through an unarmed bunch of them while the men with arms were on our side. Not a German eye wavered as we walked past them. They knew why we were looking but our man wasn't there.

"He's not here," stated Jacko. "Got any more?"

"There's half a dozen behind you washing down a few jeeps."

We turned and saw him.

Three jeeps, axle deep in water, were parked in the village duck pond. Pieces of ice clunked against the vehicles on wavelets created by Der Unterfeldwebel and his companions who, knee deep in freezing water, were swabbing down the jeeps with pieces of rag.

I was full of apprehension because Jacko was a very determined man.

He picked up a brick from a nearby heap of rubble and landed it in the pond, splashing water all over the German.

He slowly turned until he met our threatening gaze.

"So; Mr Right-of-the-Road," slowly called Jacko in German, "How goes the war now?"

The German looked around. His eyes took in the American jeeps, the freezing cloth held in his blue hands, the village duck pond, the ice nudging his knees below his rolled-up pants, the surrounding buildings of a village belonging to his Fatherland and the liberated prisoners standing at the water's edge.

He forced a smile on his lips.

"Bad," he replied. "Very bad."

"You bastard!" yelled Jacko, "I hope you die in a prisoner-of-war camp!"

His eyes, too, had seen what the German's had seen. He stood there for a while with another brick in his hand.

"You know," he said dejectedly as he dropped the brick at his feet, "maybe you're right. The game's over. C'mon, let's get out of here."

This suited me.

Although Jacko had been a tough bastard in the front line, and a good mate as a P.O.W., he obviously wasn't a murderer and I felt good as we wandered back to the barn. Furthermore, I was looking forward to inviting Jesse to a feed of K Rations.

"Anyone seen Jesse?" I bellowed as I entered the barn.

"I saw him going around the back somewhere."

I went looking for him. Nothing. Just a set of footprints printed in the virgin snow where they climbed over a bank behind the barn.

I clambered up the bank and stood at the crest to survey the scene.

Jesse sat on a rock within a natural amphitheatre of snow-covered slopes softly playing his violin while two chooks boiled in an enamelled bed-chamber resting on a rock-constructed fireplace.

I knew the bed-chamber was sterilised because Chris Keally had carried it all the way from Poland and had cooked numerous meals in it.

"Hey, Jesse!" I cried as I scrambled down the slope waving the K Rations in my hand, "Look what I've got!"

"What are they?"

"Dinner!"

He turned one of the packets over several times in his hand.

"They're marked Breakfast Units."

"So?"

"So you can't eat them now. It's dinner time."

"Pig's arse I can't! I went to a lot of trouble to get these."

"And I went to a lot of bloody trouble to get these chooks for dinner. Even found some salt to go with them."

Sometimes my mate was a bit hard to get along with.

We ravenously devoured two salt-flavoured, boiled chooks for dinner and ate the Breakfast Units for our evening meal.

There didn't seem to be any point in just sitting around the barn and, next day, the men began drifting off in little groups. No fond farewells. Just "See you later, mate" as they walked up the gravelled track to the road above.

Jesse and I, along with a few mates, set off to nowhere in particular.

We were free!

The Americans didn't seem to be concerned about us; they were more interested in crushing what was left of Hitler's Third Reich and rounding up German soldiers who were throwing in the towel in increasing numbers, so we were left to fend for ourselves.

We still had some Red Cross food and whenever an American convoy passed they threw us numerous packets of that wonderful item known as 'K Rations' for which they seemed to have no appetite for the same reason we disliked bully beef and biscuits in The Western Desert.

They were magnificent men! – vigorous in their actions, well fed, well clothed and confident in their abundance of equipment. Men who had fought in battles of a magnitude beyond our knowledge. Men who had the scent of victory in their nostrils and the light of conquest in their eyes.

We must have looked a raggle-taggle mob, in contrast, with our thread-bare uniforms covered in barnyard filth whilst our bodies hadn't known a shower in three months and, no doubt, most of us had a common skeletal appearance.

"Go to Regensberg!" they shouted. "They're flying you guys out from an airfield up there!"

Regensberg was several days away. We walked some of the way and, at one stage, commandeered a farmer's tractor and wagon.

The farmer had brought in a load of Germans who wanted to surrender. The Americans took the Germans; we took the tractor and wagon. We rode until the tractor ran out of fuel.

We no longer slept in barns. Arriving at a village near the end of a day, we would find the local tearoom and, much to the proprietor's surprise, ask him to allow us to cook our Red Cross food before we bunked down on the dining room floor for the night.

One such establishment even had some buns for sale so I purchased the entire stock with The Entertainment Committee's money. It was beginning to burn a hole in my pocket.

We arrived at Regensberg and made our way to the airfield that had obviously been one of Willy Messerschmitt's outfits. One of the buildings housed a worker's dining hall with a spotlessly clean kitchen attached. Part of the kitchen equipment was a series of huge, stainless-steel soup vats. We filled them with water and broke up furniture to fuel fires underneath them. When the water became warm we stripped off and bathed.

Most of us had Red Cross Soap and it was passed around to those without. Cracked feet were softened, scalps were soaped and scratched clean, grime-entrenched bodies were washed and re-washed, backs were rubbed by mates and, when all this routine was completed, there was the luxury of laying back in a soup-vat full of hot water.

No more bullying guards shouting "Raus! Raus!" No more rifle butts in the back. No more kicks or punches without the right to hit back. Just the sheer luxury of relaxing in hot water.

Socks, underpants, singlets, shirts and pullovers were all thrown in and cleaned. We then laid them on the cement aprons outside the hangars and, standing in the nude, watched them dry in sunlight now becoming warmer each day as Spring drove Winter away.

Later, when scrounging through the building, I came across the office and there was another luxury. Sheets of paper, a fountain pen and a bottle of ink!

The magic of sitting down and writing again!

A British Liaison Officer instructed us to get ourselves into groups of 20 men in preparation for flying out. No planes had been seen for days but the several hundred men at the airfield sorted themselves into groups and sat around in bunches resembling massive mushrooms spread over an empty paddock.

I unexpectedly found myself in charge of 20 men who looked a bit like a mob of newly-washed refugees anxious to get home to England, Africa, New Zealand, Australia, Canada and all corners of The Empire. My promotion wasn't due to any authority of rank or qualities of leadership. I had a quantity of paper and a fountain pen. Therefore I could write out a list of 20 names in duplicate; one for the aircrew and one for our records.

I hadn't the faintest what 'our records' implied and I had no intention of being responsible for these characters a moment longer than was absolutely necessary.

A flock of Douglas Dakotas appeared from nowhere and landed.

I know it isn't correct to describe Douglas Dakotas as a 'flock' but that is just how they appeared. Dozens of them swooped in, landed and trundled to a stop like a convoy of taxis looking for clients.

The clients were available. 20 of us to a plane. I led my group over to a plane where an airman was already standing by an open door. I offered him a copy of my list.

"What's this?"

"The names of the men who are in this group."

"Man, we don't want paper. We want men. Welcome aboard."

And, fair dinkum, he gave us all a stick of chewing gum as we clambered through the doorway.

The plane was obviously a paratroop transport and we sat in dished, metal seats running lengthwise along the fuselage. The plane joined the queue rumbling towards the end of the runway and took off.

Five hours later we landed in Brussels. A convoy of trucks took us to military barracks within the city and straightway we were in the clutches of The British Army.

A Pommy Corporal was waiting as we dropped down from the vehicle.

"Nah! Line up in three ranks! Dress from the right. Look smart nah!"

"Stone the crows," muttered Jacko. "What the hell is this?"

"No talking in the ranks. Nah pay attention because this is wot is going to happen. First, you will be taken to the delousing tent for delousing. Then you will be shown your quarters for the night. You may then leave the barracks and go into the city if you so desire but I am going to warn you about two things. Some of you will be looking for women. The type you are looking for have also been sleeping with Germans for a few years. And pay attention to this; you are in groups of twenty men and I want you in groups of twenty right here in the barracks at 9am tomorrow morning. If there is one man missing then that group will remain until we find him. Got that? Nah; follow me to the delousing tent."

Delousing had its bad moments.

"Strip off to the waist," said the delouser.

I stripped. He sprayed me with some air blown white powder which also contained minute granules that stung as they bounced off my bones.

"Drop your pants," was the next command.

"Eh?"

"If you want to get out of these barracks, drop your pants."

I dropped my pants. A blast of white powder nearly blew my testicles away.

"Next!" shouted the delouser.

Jesse and I didn't hang around. This bloke was dangerous.

We had been informed Deutschmarks were acceptable in the city so, on the way, I slipped into a bank with my large roll of German money and came out with a much larger roll of Belgian money.

We had arrived at the city centre around 4pm on the 8th May, 1945.

It took a while for the sight before us to sink in. Thousands and thousands of people, led by The Grenadier Guards Band, had linked arms and were marching around and around the city blocks as they laughed, sang and waved to anyone and everyone.

"What's going on?" I shouted to a Pommy soldier going by.

"Jerry's thrown it in! He's capitulated!"

Life suddenly became wonderful. We slipped into the joyous throng and did a few laps around the city centre before I realised I had lost Jesse in the multitude. I pulled out of the crowd to climb an ornamental lamp-post to look for him.

It was an impossible task. Khaki-clad soldiers, men in civilian clothes and brightly dressed women were passing by in their thousands.

Three girls waved to me. I waved back.

"Join us! Join us!" they cried in English.

Three against one. I never could fight against such odds.

I slid down the post to link arms with the merry trio and continued circling around the city to marching tunes played by the band up ahead.

A few laps and I had had enough.

"Can we get a drink somewhere?"

"Yes. Over there in that cafe."

The cafe was crowded. Not a table nor a seat available anywhere.

"We want a table," I told the waiter who spoke English. It seemed to me that everyone in Brussels could speak English.

"I can't find one."

"Listen, mate," I said displaying the roll of money, "I'm from Australia and I want to buy drinks for everyone."

A table was squeezed into a corner as drinks were distributed all around the place. I paid him with a small portion of the wad of money.

We chattered away and drank a few drinks.

"Do you really come from Australia?" asked the brunette.

"Flamin' oath!" I replied, pointing to the metal nameplates on my shoulder straps. "Our family has a cattle station down there. Look, here are some photos of our home."

Impressive! Oh; very impressive!

We chattered some more and drank some more.

"What," asked the brunette, "is an Australian doing in Brussels on VE night?"

"We've been everywhere the same as the last war."

"You are on your way home now?"

"I expect so."

She looked at my uniform again. "You've been a prisoner-of- war, haven't you?"

I confessed I had been.

"How long?"

"Four years."

It was nice to have a female shoulder to cry on and the drinks helped a bit.

"Was it bad?"

"The last three months were bad. We've been sleeping in cow-sheds, horse stables and hay barns."

"And all the time you've been sleeping in barns I've been sleeping in my comfortable bed at home."

You don't have to be very smart to work out what my next question was going to be.

"Well, why don't you take me to your comfortable bed?"

The three of them went into a Flemish-gabbling huddle complete with giggles.

The brunette's head bobbed up out of the scrum.

"Yes, you can come home to my place."

I didn't wish to give the impression I was lacking in patience but I suggested we leave right away as it was midnight and I had to be back at the barracks by 9am in the morning.

A bus took us some 15 kilometres to an outer suburb where we let ourselves into a two-storied cottage.

My companion hurried along a passage to inform her awakened parents they had a guest for the night. She then ushered me upstairs and opened a door to a bedroom.

"This is my brother's bedroom. He is in hospital with appendicitis."

She opened a drawer and handed me a pair of pyjamas.

"I think these will fit you," she said, standing in the doorway and smiling impishly. "Sleep well."

Admittedly I was far from sober but here was a pair of clean pyjamas, a real bed with crisp sheets, a soft pillow and a carpetted room with window curtains.

Quite frankly, I didn't care where she slept.

We left a still sleeping household early next morning to catch a bus that never came because it was Sunday!

I was becoming desperate by half past eight. I had a list of 20 names, in duplicate, in my pocket and 19 mates waiting for me in town. The Pommy Corporal's threat was beginning to paint an ominous picture. I had money but taxis were conspicuous by their absence.

I flagged down an American jeep.

"You fellas going into the city?"

"Yep."

"I've got to be at the barracks by nine o'clock. Can you give us a lift?"

"You're cutting it fine. Hop in."

American soldiers are obliging chaps. The jeep, guided by my companion, drove into the city at a horrifying speed, screamed around several corners and pulled up outside the barracks where one army truck containing 19 men stood by the kerbside.

A roar went up.

"You're popular," commented the Yanks.

Amidst another roar I kissed the brunette "Good-bye" and ran to the truck.

Weeks later, when writing to me while I was in England, she asked: "The last I saw of you was your backside hanging over the back of the truck and all your friends seemed to be punching you. Why were they doing that?"

Our view of Brussels was restricted to looking out of the back of the truck as it sped through the streets to the airfield where it deposited us at the end of an airstrip.

Mosquito and Lancaster Bombers were everywhere!

The aircraft intrigued me; probably because of my boyhood heroes. I had never seen so many planes in one place before and none of these had even been invented before we were captured.

I wandered off to have a closer look at a Mosquito and got talking to a bouncy, bald-headed Pommy chap dressed in khaki shorts and shirt and wearing sandals. He had two or three blue stripes on his shoulder straps but I had no idea of his rank simply because we had never met up with air force personnel before The Jerries rounded us up.

"Splendid kite, the Mosquito," he informed me, "Does a splendid job at low level. On one of our shows we had to blow the wall out of a prison full of political prisoners so we went in real low and bounced the bombs at the wall. Blew it to smithereens. Prisoners poured out all over the place."

I wasn't sure if this joker was having me on and it wasn't until months later I read about that particular "Show". I wish I had known about it then because I was actually talking to one of the most courageous men in The R.A.F. and history has shown The R.A.F. was fairly loaded with courageous men.

"Hey!" shouted my travelling companions, "if you've still got that list of names it's wanted over here!"

There, at the end of the airstrip and standing out like a bubble in a bedchamber, was an army issue folding table and an army issue folding form. Upon the form sat a British Army Issue Corporal and on the table in front of him was a stack of paper held down by a brick.

But the key figure of this tableau was a British Army Issue Lieutenant standing at the end of the table. He stood straight up and down like two metres of pump water. His uniform was immaculate, his officer's cap sat at the correct angle, his shoes shone brilliantly, his buttons and cap badge dazzled the eye and his sandy moustache was trimmed to perfection.

I approached him warily and held out the piece of paper.

"Stand to attention!" he barked.

I straightened up a bit because I didn't want to cause any problems. Nineteen mates were involved in this manoeuvre.

"You have the list of names?"

"Yes."

"Yes what?"

I thought for a second or two before it dawned on me.

"Yes, sir."

"Yes, sir, WHAT?"

"Yes, sir, I have the list of names."

I handed him both copies and hoped the extension of my right arm didn't convey the stench of my uniform in his direction. He handed a copy back to me, delicately holding it between his forefinger and thumb.

This sort of authority was going to require some emotional adjustment.

"Group 30, Corporal!" woofed the effigy from Sandhurst as he handed the paper to the NCO.

'"Group 30, Sah!" snapped The Corporal as he ticked a number and placed our list under a brick which was obviously the 'Out' file.

"That plane over thereah!" barked this stalwart of The British Empire pointing with his swagger cane in the direction of a bomber standing placidly on the grass.

We ambled across towards the plane. The chalked graffiti on its fuselage became clearer as we approached.

'The Ham Cram Spam Special! All Australians welcome.'

It was manned by an Australian crew!

There was much back-slapping and "Good on yer, mates" as the crew handed around glucose lollies.

The pilot was a stocky, freckle-faced, ginger-headed chap who, upon being complimented on his welcoming messages, said they liked a bit of a joke now and then. He also told us to get aboard and the next stop was England.

Avro Lancaster Bombers aren't exactly constructed with passenger comfort being regarded as of prime importance. They are very narrow and without windows; in fact, they are rather uncomfortable. The men were packed forward over the wing area. I was last aboard and found a seat on the rear end of the bomb bay immediately beneath the turret-gunner and facing the tail-gunner. The door was shut, the motors whirred into a cough then roared into life and we trundled to the end of the airstrip.

I had never been in such a massive plane and I didn't know much about flying but I knew the tail lifts off first and, eventually, the plane becomes airborne. Consequently, I was a little perturbed when I noticed the rear end veer a couple feet to the left followed by a swoop to the right then repeat the performance before swinging upwards in an alarming manner then crashing down on to the runway!

The rest of the plane followed. I grabbed hold of the side of the fuselage as the wing hit the bitumen with a screaming, tearing, metallic noise. The fuselage filled with dust and fumes as this massive machine of the skies tore itself to pieces skidding along the runway.

After a thousand years the noise slowly subsided and the plane came to a stop!

The tail-gunner scrambled out of his turret and tried to open the door in the side of the buckled fuselage. The skipper was pushing men out through the escape hatch in the roof.

"Come on!" he shouted. "Get out of here!"

"She's right, Skipper," answered the big, bronzed Anzacs. "Nobody's hurt."

"If you funny buggers could see these bloody motors smoking like I can you wouldn't say she's right."

The tail-gunner wrenched the door open. I poked my head out. Each motor was sending up a spiral of smoke and the whole heap of wreckage was sitting in a pool of petrol extending beyond the wing tips!

We shot through that doorway like a burst of Bren gun fire.

The fire tender arrived and buried the awesome sight in a blanket of foam.

We stood around like a group of interested spectators when the pilot came over to explain what had happened.

"Just about to become airborne when the wheel came off so I switched on the fire extinguishers and sat her down again. Simple really."

"Simple! Cripes, you frightened shit out of us."

"Ah well, we like a bit of a joke now and then."

A truck arrived and took the air force crew away. Another truck conveyed us back to the end of the airstrip where I approached an army issue folding table beside an army issue form whereon sat a British Army Issue Corporal and surrendered my remaining document of dubious authority to a British Army Issue Lieutenant.

I stood smartly to attention, just to show him I was responding to training, while he examined the paper.

"Group 30, Corporal."

"Group 30. Sah, they've gone!"

Six feet of Sandhurst Tradition, representing The Empire, looked down at five feet four of grubby humanity representing an unarmed gathering. He handed me back the list.

"You've gone!"

"Well, sir, you see that heap of crap smoking away at the far end of the airstrip? We've just come out of that."

He surveyed me and my mates as though we were so much rubbish which had blown across the airfield and arrived at his table.

So help me, to this day I am not sure if I was the victim of army humour or whether this bloke was dinkum: "Damn it all!" he exploded, "You can't do that! What about my books? I'll have to alter them all now! You stand over thereah until I've sorted it all out!"

We had had a gutful of this bastard by now so I told him in pure Australian what he could do with his books. We climbed back into the truck and the driver took us to the hangars where the Aussies were celebrating VE Day plus One.

We jumped out of the truck and stuck our heads into a noisy doorway. The aircrews were still celebrating; they hauled us inside and a beer was promptly placed in our hands. The yarn spinning, the episode swapping and the beer drinking went on for a prolonged period until an officer, with numerous rings on his sleeves, asked, "What are you blokes doing here, anyway?"

The tale we told horrified him. Within thirty minutes we were on another Lancaster in the company of a crew delighted to be heading for England on VE Day plus One and I am still not sure if our prompt departure was arranged in sympathy with our plight or as a maneouvre to conserve the liquor in The Officers Mess.

I was sitting in my favourite Lancaster Bomber seat when the turret-gunner nudged me with his foot and beckoned me to stand beside him in that cramped dome.

The coastline ahead gradually drew back and passed beneath the bomber as we flew over The English Channel.

The gunner tapped me on the shoulder and pointed ahead.

There it was! ENGLAND!

England! Homeland of my parents! Where uncles, aunts and cousins lived!

This was not my country but it was part of me! Its history, its traditions and folklore had been instilled into me since my first day at school and I felt I was part of England. And The Empire was still The Empire!

Nowadays I have trouble coming to terms with the emotions of that moment.

The plane landed; authorities spirited us away to a train and we arrived in Eastbourne at sundown.

Chapter Twenty-One

Eastbourne is right on The Channel Coast looking at France and I'll bet when Adolf Hitler and his mate, Herman Goering, were looking through their telescope they were gazing at Eastbourne.

A considerable portion of the town had been evacuated during the war and numerous houses were requisitioned in the 'Old Town' to be used by The Australian Army as billets for the Ex Ps.O.W. beginning to flow in from Europe.

An NCO informed us a meal was available and uniforms etc. would be issued in the morning.

Meanwhile an Australian Comforts Fund parcel containing pyjamas, dressing gown, slippers, towel, soap and shaving gear was issued to each man. We shaved and generally cleaned ourselves up then sat around in clean pyjamas to smoke and yarn.

A relaxed, happy atmosphere developed among us. We had been through some rather tough times but, at last, we were in England and under the command of our own army personnel. Life seemed pretty good.

One of our men. who had arrived earlier in the day, burst into the room. "Hey! Guess what?" he excitedly asked without waiting for an answer. "There's a dance hall down at the bottom of the hill and it's full of sheilas and they all talk English!"

About twenty of us rapidly dressed and, without being conscious of the appearance of the grubby, dirt-stained uniforms hanging on our emaciated bodies, made our way down the hill.

The Winter Garden is a three-storied building with a dance hall in the basement. "No charge," said the girl in the ticket office so the bunch of us moved in.

I had never seen such a place! The dance floor seemed to be a couple of acres in area! There were beer bars and snack bars with tables and chairs all around the edge of the dance floor! Colour seemed to be everywhere!

The band had just finished a tune. We stood bunched up together for mutual support on the semi-circular platform at the top of the steps leading down to the dance floor. We had been hanging together for four years for mutual support and old habits die hard.

A ripple of movement, making us bunch tighter together, slowly gathered strength throughout the building as young women flowed across the dance floor towards us. They took our hands and led us back to their tables. I know it sounds bloody silly now but I remember holding some girl's hand and wiping tears from my eyes as she introduced me to her companions.

The war, on occasions, produced some very beautiful moments.

The dance went on until midnight.

The morning parade contained a liberal sprinkling of men suffering from alcoholic remorse.

I was surprised at the patience shown by the army personnel. Most of them had been sent to England as a gesture of appreciation 'for services rendered' and many of them had had their share of action or were "originals".

The queue outside the Quartermaster's Store was rather long and forward movement slow so I slipped off to a nearby public telephone.

"Hullo, Aunty."

"Oh, dear boy! Is it really you?"

Gee! Dad's sister! I tried hard to swallow the lump in my throat.

"Are you there?"

"Yes, Aunty. I only got in last night. I just wanted to say hullo."

'When will I see you?"

"'I don't know yet. We will probably get leave soon. I'll phone you then."

There was some small talk before I hung up and rejoined the queue.

Dad's sister! Dad would have liked that.

A Sgt. Major approached me. "You! Move back to the end of the line! Where have you been?"

"I just went to the phone box to phone my aunty."

He took a deep breath. "All right; but you broke off from a parade without asking permission. You were actually Absent Without Leave and you could be placed on a charge. Don't do it again!"

Stone the crows! I never thought of that!

A bloke came out of a nearby doorway. "Serves you bloody right. If it had of been me I would have put you on a charge."

Ivan Francis! He bobbed up just as I knew he would! Gawd, it was good to see his face again! He looked a bit light on but we all did. And what a tale he had to tell!

Captured on a night patrol outside the wire during the siege of Tobruk he was transported to Italy then swooped up by the Germans when Italy capitulated. The Americans eventually liberated him. A small group commandeered a car and set off for France because they knew The English Channel was over that way somewhere. Once, when jacking up the car to change a tyre, the American M.P.s suggested they change the car instead of changing the tyre so they continued their journey in a Mercedes Benz. The going was tough after they crossed the French border. It seemed the inhabitants of every village wanted them to stay and drink champagne forever. Eventually the Americans escorted them to an airfield where Ivan disposed of the car by standing in the doorway of the plane and tossing the keys into a crowd of G.I.s.

He had arrived in Eastbourne late last night while I was at the dance.

The issue of clothing was an uplifting experience. It felt good to be again dressed in an Australian uniform complete with metal badges, colour patches and a slouch hat.

But the most delightful issue was our pay books! They had hundreds of pounds in them! We were rich!

Each morning had its muster parade but after that we were free to do as we wished.

Gowrie House, with its abundance of tea, cakes and smiling women, was a meeting place where men sat in the sunshine and yarned as they looked out over The English Channel. Some men soon established themselves in a favourite pub whilst others simply enjoyed the town of Eastbourne where everyone wanted to talk to us.

Shipping was still scarce but, whenever a ship was available, men were being sent home in hundreds. One, with a few berths vacant, was due to sail within three days after our arrival.

"I'm going to be on it," said Jesse.

"Eh?"

"I'm going to be on it."

"But we've only just got here!'"

"The war's over and I've had a letter from my girl friend. I just want to get back home and get out of the army."

Three days later he was gone! Just like that. And sticking out of the end of his kit bag was a wooden violin-case with a brass handle.

The troops, after being kitted out, were given a week's pre-embarkation leave and they scattered all over the island from Land's End to John O'Groats.

Ivan and I didn't take pre-embarkation leave because we weren't in a hurry to get home. We had written to our families and assured them we were in good health as well as having a great time and we wanted to spend time with our relatives in England. A typical serviceman's story with an element of truth in it.

We took a forty-eight hour leave to London and stepped out of the train on to Waterloo Station.

Waterloo Station! Can you beat that?

Mum and Dad had photos of Waterloo Station hanging on the walls when we lived in Moree so many years ago and now I was actually standing there!

This was one of the many emotional moments I experienced in England. It was obviously the outcome of the manner in which my parents had hung on to their London background during our upbringing; an attitude reinforced by an education system which considered duty to The Motherland more important than loyalty to the soil I stood upon.

Consequently, I felt quite at home in London. When scenes and buildings, which had hitherto appeared as sepia-coloured pictures in *The Illustrated London Gazette*, suddenly appeared before my eyes and activated my memory, I experienced a sense of 'oneness' with that battle-scarred city.

Ivan took off to track down his relatives and I caught a train to Streatham where upon emerging from the station, I spotted my uncle's real estate office directly opposite.

I entered the office. A young woman met me at the counter.

"G'day. I would like to see my Uncle Ben, please."

"Pardon?"

It never occurred to me that she wouldn't know who my Uncle Ben was. It had always been 'Uncle Ben" and "Aunty Patty" ever since I was born.

"Mr Russell. He's my uncle."

"Oh." She disappeared behind a partition to inform Uncle Ben there was a footloose Australian in the front office claiming to be his nephew.

Uncle Ben appeared and he was just like his photos. He made me welcome and introduced me to his staff who were unaware that The Boss had connections at the other end of the world.

His residence was only a short distance away so I set out to meet my mystical Aunty Patty. I owed this woman plenty. She had regularly written to me in the prison camps, had sent me photos as well as books and generally did her best to make me aware of her supportive existence.

"She's just gone around to the corner shop," said the cleaning lady, "and I'm hanging out the 'Welcome' decorations. Like to give me a hand?"

We had just completed the task when Aunty Patty arrived back.

Like I said: – The war, on occasions, produced some very beautiful moments. Thus began a very wonderful week-end. I was introduced to cousins who, until now had only been names mentioned by Mum and Dad during casual conversation.

They were here! They were real! I belonged!

The week-end seemed to fly.

I met Ivan again at Waterloo Station. Our yarning on the way back to Eastbourne was full of Pommy relatives.

The Reception Group where we were billeted consisted of three houses and a cottage used as an Administrative Office. The Admin Office put out a notice stating it could do with some 'specialist' assistance and, if anyone wanted to stay awhile, come and see the NCO in charge of Records.

We promptly applied.

Ivan, who was experienced in riding horses around an outback cattle station, was taken on as a transport driver and I, once again, became a switchboard operator.

The Entertainment Committee's roll of money, now converted into English currency, suddenly became useful. I purchased a 1929 model B.S.A. Sloper Motor Cycle. Ivan promptly bought a 1936 Ariel. They were well-worn and rough and, at times, caused many prolonged delays to a planned outing but we rode them around the town and made numerous bone-jarring excursions into the surrounding countryside.

Life was good in Eastbourne. The office closed down at 5pm and our time was our own until 8am next morning. We were on good rations and Gowrie House sold all manner of marvellous things such as chocolates, biscuits, cigarettes, pipe tobacco, writing material and quite a variety of tinned food which was not available to the general public.

Of course, The Winter Garden became our nightly haunt and the evenings had become nights of beer, dancing and chatting up girls whom we now knew by name.

Sitting on the sidelines, one night, I noticed a truly exotic-looking girl being thrown around in that rhythmic style called jitter-bugging. I was amazed. There was none of this crazy abandonment going on before we left home and if anyone had come at it in The Embassy or Anzac House Ballrooms they would have been chucked out!

This girl was full of rhythm and life!

"Cripes!" I thought, "I've got to get to know her."

So, I asked her for a dance and, whilst listening to my standard line of approach and endeavouring to follow my interpretation of a quick step, she remarked: "You ought to meet my sister. She hates Australians."

"Why?"

"One of your chaps cut up a bit rough the other night and she won't have anything to do with you lot."

"Supposing you introduce me to her and we'll see if we can change her mind."

I was enjoying this girl's company and if it was necessary to put up with her sister – so be it.

"There's three of us sitting at that table over there."

Three of them! The equation was becoming familiar. I desperately looked around for Ivan and signalled him over.

"Mate, this is Marjorie. Her sister hates Australians and she is sitting over there with her friend. Care to join us?"

Marjorie took us to the table and introduced us to her sister, Eileen, and their friend Mavis. (It is interesting to note that fifty-four years, two daughters, six grandchildren and six great-grandchildren later I am still trying to convince Eileen that we are a pretty good mob of blokes.)

We had a pleasant evening dancing, mainly with Eileen and Mavis because Marjorie seemed fully occupied. We arranged to meet them the following night – and the next night – and the next.

The Reception Group to which we were attached was closing down as it was running out of customers. Ivan and I were becoming desperate.

A month of army life such as we had never known had slipped by.

Eileen and Mavis were now our constant companions at dances, pictures, the theatre and walks along the seafront or up to Beachy Head.

Ivan and I also cooked up a bit of a lurk on Saturday afternoons by organising our own intimate tea gatherings at our H.Q. cottage. Making full use of the inexhaustible food available at Gowrie House we served caviar on toast, cheese with biscuits and cups of tea with milk and real sugar. Couple all this with motorbike rides into a countryside sprinkled with magical tea houses you may safely assume if an Orderly Officer had mysteriously appeared, blown a whistle and shouted "Any complaints?" the answer would most definitely have been in the negative.

But it gets better!

I had met Eileen's family and was now a regular visitor to their house. I had got drunk with her brother when he came home on leave. I had met his wife, too. The family was so much like my own; mum, dad, brother and sisters living in harmony with each other.

Ivan was also making progress with Mavis and her parents.

However, there was just one snag. Both girls had boy friends in The Canadian Army still in Europe. I don't know if Mavis' relationship was serious but Eileen's friend was a bit dinkum about their future. It was a problem to be dealt with when he returned to England.

Anyway, it looked as though it was all going down the plug hole. The Reception Group was closing down and its staff was being sent back to Australia.

The Orderly Room Sergeant took Ivan and I aside.

"A couple of vacancies have cropped up at H.Q.," he said. "Would you two blokes be interested?"

Would we? My hand shook as I filled in the application form!

Australian Army Headquarters was based in The Cumberland Hotel right on the ocean front. I had a room on the seventh floor overlooking the promenade and a window looking out over The English Channel.

Numerous military bands presented daily concerts in The Promenade Bandstand below and, once again, I reckoned life was pretty good. Ivan was now a driver in The Transport Section and I had managed to wangle a job on the telephone exchange.

This job was a piece of cake. The exchange had to be manned twenty-four hours a day. The army reckoned six men, working four shifts should be able to handle the task. We promptly divided the job into two twelve hour shifts. Day shift was never hard and the chap on night shift simply laid a stretcher beside the exchange and switched the buzzer on.

Nothing happened between 7pm and 7am except for the officer in charge of transport; an awfully English Captain Dingley who invariably phoned from his room around midnight.

"I say, Sig, can you put me through to transport?" he would ask in a voice loaded with alcoholic friendship which was never apparent in the morning.

He was plugged through to a newly-awakened Sergeant.

"Oh. Dingley here, Sergeant. Is everything all right?"

"Everyfings sorlrite, sir."

"Thank you, Sergeant."

"Bastard!" I would explode as I pulled the plugs out. "Bastard!

Bastard! I'd like to get you washing down jeeps in an ice-encrusted duck pond! I'd throw rocks at you, too!"

The front door of The Cumberland gave entrance to an area which was formerly the lounge room but the furnishings, nowadays, consisted of rows of desks occupied by officers of various rank processing the paper which troop movements generate; especially when the troop's arrival was influenced by a somewhat indifferent desire to hurry to England after being liberated in Europe and, when they did arrive, their departure was governed by the availability of shipping.

A former reception clerk's desk stood just inside the main doorway and behind it was the telephone exchange room; a rather den-like room where nobody sitting in the lounge area could see who was on duty. Actually, nobody cared very much as long as the board was manned.

So, the beauty of the job was, once you had done your shift, you could vanish for 48 hours!

Ivan, who was as cunning as a cage full of monkeys, also managed to get more than the usual number of free days. He had become the official driver to an A.I.F. Captain who had been in the front line most of the war and whose present attitude to The Kings Rules and Regulations can best be described as 'flamboyant'.

Furthermore, I still had a fair whack of that Entertainment Committee money, our pay books were loaded and life, as I commented earlier, seemed a bit beaut.

My favourite ride was up to the crest of Beachy Head. There I would stand, in wondrous isolation, feeling the sea breeze on my face and looking at the ocean far below. Down on the flat country, discernible in the distance, was Hastings where William The Conqueror landed almost a thousand years ago. Dead ahead, just below the horizon, was France where a recent would-be conqueror had ranted, raved and shaken his fist at England. Out there, on the now placid ocean, Sir Francis Drake had chased The Spanish Armada in a raging storm, past Beachy Head where I was now standing – and that was in the time of Queen Elizabeth!

History, which contrasted with the history of my own country, of which I knew so little.

The tour of duty at The Cumberland Hotel was a period loaded with the type of unofficial incidents which enrich army life.

Eileen was employed at a small factory currently completing its contracts for 'war work'. She operated a lathe and, during morning tea break, would rush home for a cup of tea with her mother who lived just around the corner. It didn't take Ivan and I long to work out this was a good place to be for morning tea but we soon realised tea was in short supply within the household and decided to do something about it.

Our cooks were from General Slim's Burma Army awaiting discharge. They were tough men with a tendency to flog off whatever was left lying around. We approached The Sergeant Cook to enquire if he might be able to scrounge us some tea in exchange for cigarettes. He intimated this was a possibility. Neither Ivan nor I had a realistic knowledge of the bargaining power of cigarettes (having been out of circulation for quite some time) so, instead of giving him a packet of cigarettes, we slipped him an eye-boggling carton of Players. He suggested we come back tomorrow.

Next day we appeared on Mumma Stone's doorstep with four sandbags full of tea.

"Oh, my goodness!' she exclaimed and promptly buried them in the coal heap under the stairway.

Brighton is approximately sixty miles away and the trains took only an hour to get there. Eileen and Mavis suggested we rip down there one Saturday afternoon to have a go at ice skating.

The ice rink was immense. The sheet of ice was enclosed by a low, wooden palisade to which we clung as we slowly edged our way around the rink's perimeter.

Brighton was also the recreation town for The Royal Australian Air Force.

Ivan and I made a desperate half-lap of the arena. We were in line with the bar when many hands pulled us off the ice with exclamations of: "Jeez, Digger! Let's buy you a drink!"

Several hours later we completed the remainder of the circuit but I don't remember the train ride home.

*****

The buzzer on the exchange jangled out its sleep-destroying noise long after I had dealt with The Demon Dingley.

It was Eileen's sister, Marjorie. She and some girls had been out on the town with some R.A.F. chaps who had missed the last train back to London.

"We've managed to stash them around the town for the night but we have one left over. Can you find somewhere to put him?"

"My bed is doing nothing. If you come quietly to the front door I can let him in and take him up there. Does he know the Morse Code?"

A muffled conversation took place in the phone box. Yes, he knew the Morse Code. "Good, Tell him to tap 'Vic Eddie' on the front door when you arrive."

They arrived in a clapped-out heap of tin with a hole in the muffler and made several attempts to sound a raucous 'Vic Eddie' on a reluctant car horn.

I opened the front door and admitted a tall, slim member of The Royal Air Force. The climb to the seventh floor was uneventful. I ushered him into my room and left him to it.

The day-shift operator arrived at 8am. I grabbed my eating gear and meandered off to the mess room in a nearby building. After breakfast I wandered back to return my utensils to the exchange room.

"A quiet night?" asked my colleague.

"Yeah, nothing much."

Nothing much! Stone the crows! The Air Force chap was still up in my room and the lobby was already filling with staff.

I raced up the stairs, entered my room and shook him awake.

"Hey, Mate! I forgot all about you! You've got to get going and I don't like our chances. Most of the staff are already in the lobby."

He followed me down the stairs winding around the lift well. We paused on the final flight behind the lift while I gave him some advice.

"I'm not sure what's going to happen but, once we round this corner, keep going. We might get away with it."

"Righto," he said, speaking in the way air force chaps do in pictures, "leave it to me."

He set his cap at the correct angle, dusted down his tunic, stepped down on to the landing overlooking the lobby and just stood there!

"Cripes!" I thought. "We're sunk!"

Eventually one of the officers looked up and stared at us in surprise.

The Air Force character stared back.

The Lieutenant jumped to his feet and yelled: "Attention!"

They all did that!

I followed Squadron Leader Laurie Osborne D.F.C. (plus a few other bits and pieces) of The Bomber Command all the way to the front door and didn't return until two days later.

*****

Ivan and I received leave passes for our overdue Rehabilitation Leave. We felt we had become used to living without barbed wire and guards all around us but we took it just the same.

We planned to tour the south of England on our motor bikes; an ambitious plan because these two obsolete models had a habit of arranging their own transport strike just when their services were most in demand.

We arrived in Salisbury and before we had the bikes on to their stands a married couple stopped to talk with us. They were Australians who had settled in England before the war. Of course, we must stay the night at their place. No argument. Come around. We did.

It was a pleasant evening during the course of which we helped eat portion of a wedding cake destined never to grace their daughter's wedding reception. The Americans had been this way and passed on. Some of them left a trail of dubious intent behind them.

We were standing outside Salisbury Cathedral next day when The Vicar's daughter appeared and invited us inside for an impromptu guided tour.

The feeling of awe as I entered the cathedral was powerful; probably because I had never been in a cathedral of such magnitude in my lifetime. Massive pillars towered upwards to expand and spread over the high ceiling in delicate stone lacework; picturesque lead-light windows embellished the walls whilst the whole structure imparted a sense of dignity and tradition – British Dignity and Tradition, by Jove!

Later, when standing outside on the roadway, I contemplated the force, or authority, which activated the construction of this magnificent edifice now dominating the whole countryside.

I know all cathedrals are built to The Glory of The Lord who gives us strength to conquer our foes but I hadn't yet shaken off the original sense of degradation when being called an "Englische Schwein" and belted over the head with a buckle emblazoned "Gott Mit Uns" and I wondered where The Good Lord fitted in with all the mess His Sheep were making of His World.

I hadn't lost my faith in God because I had asked Him so many times in recent years to help me survive and enjoy freedom once more, and here I was enjoying it.

But I still pondered upon the logistics and wondered from whence came the force, the inspiration and the necessary finance?

We rode out to Stonehenge and ate our lunch sitting on a stone slab. People could do that before the days when graffiti artists, souvenir hunters, pillagers and other human vermin had commenced to defile rather than revere.

Rain commenced to fall as we headed back to town. It fell all night and we recommenced our tour of southern England in a steady downpour.

An hour later we pulled up in some wayside village and entered the pub. A large fire burned merrily to warm a bar-room full of local inhabitants who insisted we also warm ourselves internally with Devon Cider and there was no way we could buy them a drink.

"The Aussies were here in the last war. Let me buy you a drink."

It's funny how a man's childhood suddenly stands up right in front of him. My Dad and his mates often spoke of the time they trained on Salisbury Plains before going to the trenches in France.

I told them of this and we drank a toast to my Dad who spent the next twenty-four years slowly dying because he had trained on Salisbury Plains before going to the trenches in France.

Devon Cider is cagey stuff. It has a beautiful golden colour that glistens in a clear glass when held against the light. But it packs a wallop – a warming wallop that warms you inside, warms you to your noisy companions and makes you feel you can tackle anything – including the rain.

We stepped out of the pub feeling externally warm from the fireside, internally warm from the Devon Cider and emotionally warm from the extended friendship, to face the cold wind and drizzle.

"Mate," I said, "I know a place where we would be more comfortable than riding a motor bike in this weather:"

"Me, too," he replied.

We arrived in Eastbourne just at dusk. Ivan vanished in the direction of Mavis' place and I spent a few enjoyable hours in The Black Horse with Eileen and her family.

*****

I was getting a bit worried about my mate. He seemed to be going a bit clucky and had a faraway look in his eyes. I should have recognised the symptoms but the complaint was new to my experience. A couple of days later it was too late.

"I proposed to Mavis last night," he calmly said.

'What did she say?"

"Yes."

I was shaken. The past few years had been chaos, destruction and survival followed by this halcyon period in England with no thought of the future except to eventually return home to my Mother and my sisters.

I suppose prisoner-of-war life affects a man that way. There is only today. Tomorrow you may be dead.

But here was my mate staking a claim on the future!

That's the bit that shook me.

I suddenly realised there was going to be a future!

"Do you know what I think?' he asked one day when we were sitting in a couple of deckchairs on the promenade and listening to the band.

"I've already worked out what you think," I replied, "but it's not on. I've got to face up to some Canadian who'll be here next week and I don't like my chances."

"Have you said anything to her about it?"

"Jeez, no! I've only known her six weeks!"

'Well, I suggest you ask her then you'll have some idea about how she feels."

I didn't know how Eileen felt but I was slowly coming to realise I didn't want to spend the rest of my life without her stimulating companionship.

I took the train to Brighton where I wandered around until I found a jewellers shop and, as a morale booster, I bought a wedding ring as well.

"I'm taking Eileen up to Beachy Head to-night," I told my mate. "I think I'll ask her."

Double daylight time was still in operation and twilight lasted until around 11 pm.

I called for Eileen after work and we rode up to Beachy Head. We parked the bike by the roadside and strolled up a grassy slope to sit looking out over The Channel. We sat there for some considerable time talking about nothing in particular. I had taken several deep breaths but questions like this one require a lot of courage.

"I think I can hear a motorbike," said Eileen.

Damn and blast! I could hear the bloody thing, too!

The Ariel coughed to a stop and parked beside my BSA Sloper. Mavis and Ivan came running up the slope.

'What did you say?" squealed Mavis.

'What do you mean, what did I say?"

"Hasn't he asked you yet?"

"Hasn't he asked me what?"

"The purpose this little ride this evening," I lamely explained, "was to ask you if you would marry me."

"Oh."

'We're going down to The Black Horse," said Ivan, sensing a problem.

I won't go into all the details but we sat there for quite a while. Eileen didn't say "No" but she didn't exactly say "Yes" either.

The poor girl was in a mental turmoil. This proposal came right out of the blue. She didn't know if she could leave her family or leave Eastbourne. And the Canadian would have to be told first. She owed him that much.

I was beginning to suspect she wasn't feeling too sure about Australia either, and I wished I hadn't given her so much bulldust about marauding Aboriginals and kangaroo stampedes.

Finally Eileen agreed to wear the ring on the understanding it may have to come off when she had to do some explaining.

We rode down the hill on a magic carpet and burst into the house.

"Look'!" cried Eileen, holding out her hand to Mumma Stone and Marjorie. Gradually the excitement simmered down.

"I think you ought to ask your father's permission," said Mumma Stone.

"Where is he?"

"Out in the garden with a torch looking for snails."

Eileen took off the ring and gave it to me with instructions to hang on to it for a while. We went out into the back garden.

"Dad, we want to have a talk with you."

'Well, I'm a bit busy right now."

"Dad, this is important."

"There seems to be a lot of snails around lately."

"Mr Stone, I want to marry Eileen."

"That's right. We want to be married."

Mr Stone slowly straightened his back. He was a mild man and I can now appreciate what he was thinking. Here was the first of his daughters grown into womanhood and seriously talking of marriage; and the man was some character who had appeared on the scene a couple of months ago and was planning to take her to some distant country called Australia.

"What about Lloyd?" he asked.

"I'll explain it all to Lloyd when he gets back."

'Well, when you've told him I'll think about it. But, until then, I can't agree."

That was that!

We went back inside to talk to Mumma Stone and Marjorie for a while. Night had fallen and the BSA had no headlights so I parked it in the hallway just inside the front door.

I bid Eileen a rather saddened good-night, placed the ring back on her finger then set out to walk to the hotel.

I hadn't reached the end of Gilbert Road when I heard female steps pounding after me. The ring was shoved back in my hand.

"He's changed his mind! Come on back and put it on my finger again."

We returned to the house where Mumma Stone and Marjorie were standing in the dining-room looking rather aggressive. Mr Stone sat in a corner looking somewhat subdued.

"I just learned you don't plan to marry immediately," he said.

"Pop, Eileen and I want to marry but I've been through a lot and I think I should go home first. There are other problems to be sorted out and when they are fixed Eileen can come out to Australia later. By then we'll know just how we both feel."

"Well, in that case I'll give my consent to those arrangements."

I gallantly placed the ring on Eileen's finger once again and, in front of her family, gave her a very sincere kiss.

"I think we ought to drink to this," said Pop Stone.

He placed a chair in front of the bookshelf and, from behind books on the top shelf, lifted out a bottle of Johnnie Walker Whiskey. I don't know how long it takes whiskey to mature but I reckon the years it had been hidden up there had added to its flavour.

I eventually drifted back to The Cumberland Hotel on clouds strung together with whiskey.

*****

Lloyd returned to Eastbourne from Europe.

Eileen had gone out with him the night before to acquaint him with a situation which had upset him considerably and our meeting was contemplated with apprehension.

He was a stocky built character who had been in the thick of the fighting and knew what war was all about.

We shook hands and proceeded to get blind drunk together. We did this on several occasions during the course of the next few weeks.

Lloyd didn't give up easily and, between us, we pulled poor Eileen this way and that. There were several times during this period of emotional stress when I thought I had lost but he returned to Canada leaving behind an engaged couple who had come to grips with the seriousness of their commitment.

He was an honourable opponent and I still have the utmost respect for him.

*****

I had arrived in England early in May. Time had now moved on to the end of July. I knew I would have to leave soon and, besides, I was becoming homesick and wanted to return to Australia to arrange Eileen's passage out.

The newspapers on 6th August announced the dropping of an atomic bomb on some Japanese city.

"An atomic bomb? What the hell's that?"

"Well, it says they have found some way of splitting the atom and it causes a big explosion."

"Must be a beauty. They say it wiped out a whole city."

"Tough, eh?"

"Yeah, tough."

A couple of days later another one put an end to the war and wassail and revelry carried on all night.

I was leaning out of one of the hotel's windows, early in the evening, shouting to Ivan and the girls that I was about to join them when I felt a tap on my shoulder.

"If you carry on making that noise," said Sgt. Major Lindsay Hassett, "I'll put you on a charge for disorderly conduct."

I suppose if you have had a hard day at the nets and there was another day's cricket coming up tomorrow you can't have your rest interrupted by a noisy character rejoicing in freedom after four years in a prison camp.

Somehow, at that moment. I kind of lost interest in cricket.

*****

The four of us had a week-end in London where we stayed with Aunty Patty and Uncle Ben. The girls had a room at the far end of a very long passage. Ivan and I had a room at the other end of that very long passage. My Uncle and Aunt were somewhere in between. Queen Victoria would have been most pleased.

Soon after returning to Eastbourne I was given my embarkation orders.

My cunning mate, despite his lowly rank, had chummed up with a certain captain who exerted his influence and convinced H.Q. that Ivan was absolutely necessary to drive him around in the course of his duties. This intrigued me because this particular captain rode everywhere on an army issue pushbike. I distinctly recollect, on one occasion, Ivan sitting in his vehicle outside The Cumberland when I stuck my head out the window to enquire why he was sitting there.

"Waiting for Captain Sergeant to go and get the pay from the bank."

Captain Sergeant arrived on his pushbike.

"What are you waiting here for?" he enquired.

"Waiting for you to go and get the pay from the bank."

"I've got the pay here," he said, indicating his bulging shirt, trouser pockets and officer's cap.

Thousands of English pounds riding along the esplanade on a pushbike! Nevertheless, Ivan managed to stay in England for another six to eight weeks during which time he married Mavis with Eileen as bridesmaid.

Leaving Eileen was not without considerable emotional stress. She was more than just an attractive, cheerful person with whom I had fallen deeply in love. Sometimes, during our outings, I could imagine her landing on the beach at Hastings, wearing a horned helmet, a sword in one hand, a shield in the other, and willing to take on all comers. She exuded an impression of internal strength and feminine awareness that influenced people around her. Also, I felt so relaxed and at ease with her family which was so much like my own.

I suppose Eileen and I would have married in England if I had of applied a bit of pressure but I wasn't as flamboyant as Ivan. I had come to realise that the future extended a long way ahead. Military activities had taken me out of circulation for five years and I felt I should go home and sort myself out a bit.

This may seem a strange statement but I lacked a sense of security within myself. I had been under the influence of military discipline. both Australian and German, for so many years that the prospect of facing the future without the army's guiding disciplinary influence tended to bewilder me.

Eileen too wanted time on her own to think over the situation. Our commitment to each other was firm, but Australia was a long way away and completely different to England and the town of Eastbourne where she had lived all her life in a loving, harmonious, family atmosphere.

But now the army, still exerting its 'guiding influence', had put me on 24 hours notice and I was going home.

Chapter Twenty-Two

The train left Eastbourne around 11:30am. The date was around 30th August, 1945, give or take a day or two. It stopped at Nottingham on its way to Liverpool. We piled out of the train to swarm around the N.A.A.F.I. for a cup of tea and a bun; Australian soldiers and airman engaged in a serious jostling game where rank carried no authority.

An Air Force Officer bumped me, causing my tea to slop.

"Oops. Sorry," he said.

I looked at his freckled face and red hair. It was him alright.

"Jeez! That's nothing compared to what you did with that Lancaster Bomber at Brussels."

We put our cups down on the platform to shake hands and laugh over the incident which, nowadays, seemed humorous.

"The officer in the control tower saw the wheel come off," he said, "so there were no charges laid. We were all flying again in two hours."

"Well, if you're going to be on the same ship as me," I assured him, "I won't be going anywhere without my life jacket."

It was after 10:30pm when we arrived at Liverpool and 1:30am before I crawled up the gangplank of the *Dominion Monarch* loaded with a pack on my back, two full kitbags tied together with string hanging from my shoulder and my hands carrying a service kitbag full of grog of a somewhat dubious vintage.

The *Dominion Monarch* had a displacement of 27,000 tons and I remembered, as a teenager, riding my pushbike to Fremantle just to see her on her maiden voyage. Here she was as big and as beautiful as ever.

The upper decks were occupied by the officers but the lower decks had been stripped clean. The 18 Australian Infantrymen returning home were allocated a mess on one of the decks devoid of any other troops except a few New Zealanders going home and some R.N. personnel going our way. We could see from one end of the ship to the other. Quite a contrast to our previous experiences on troop ships.

The ship ploughed down The Bay Of Biscay in flat calm and passed Gibraltar in a dense fog to eventually arrive at The Suez Canal where she crawled along to a fuelling point at Port Said. She stayed there, refuelling, all night.

We had been informed leave would not be granted until the ship arrived in Sydney or Wellington, a statement causing annoyance amongst the troops because we were all Middle East Campaigners and had some inexplicable sense of bondage with Egypt.

The ship was anchored about 50 yards from the wharf with a floating fuel line attached to its side. Snowy Dufall had an idea. He would go over the side, swim ashore, hire a boat and come back for his mates who would slide down a rope hanging over the stern. Snowy quietly slipped into the water, swam ashore, climbed up the wharf and was met by a smiling Arab policeman pointing a shotgun at him. Snowy swam back to the ship.

The next day, 8th September, 1945 was my 27th birthday.

A few miles further down the canal we passed an American freighter going in the opposite direction.

An American opened up the exchange with the comment, "O.K. Youse Limeys can go home now. We've finished the war down here."

A group of Aussies informed him, in lurid language, we had been going in the right direction in 1940 before they were conscripted. The American crew grinned and tossed us a packet of chewing gum. It was tossed back with advice on what they could do with it.

Our ships moved on.

We passed Kantara where, in 1940, The *Nevassa* had unloaded us for the great adventure from which so many never returned.

The ship moved on to Ismalia and hove to in a lake. We had had a gutsful of shipboard life so a mob of us dived overboard for a swim. It came to an abrupt end when one of the ship's officers announced, "If there is any member of the crew down there he'd better come aboard because we're about to move off."

The scramble up the rope ladder hanging over the side became quite hectic.

The ship moved further down the canal and passed the memorial dedicated to the memory of the members of The Australian and New Zealand Army Corps who fought in the defence of The Suez Canal during The 1914-18 War – two immense granite pillars surmounted by a magnificent bronze statue depicting a mounted 10th Light Horseman protecting a dismounted mate – an impressive memorial eventually blown to pieces in a demonstration of patriotism by a Gyppo mob.

The *Dominion Monarch* majestically floated past the town of Suez and dropped anchor in The Red Sea, a splash greeted with cheers by thousands of New Zealanders ashore and waiting to go home.

They were all aboard by 5 o'clock and, in the afternoon, we commenced moving down the bay at full speed – next stop Sydney or Wellington.

The voyage through The Red Sea and The Arabian Sea and out into The Indian Ocean was on flat, calm water and we settled down into a shipboard routine; another way of saying if you weren't on mess fatigue you slept about eighteen hours a day. The weather was hot and we took our hammocks up to sleep on the decks at night.

Below decks was now crowded with New Zealanders who 'ribbed' us Australians at mealtimes with such questions as, "How do you like that New Zealand butter, Aussie. Eh?"

"Good meat today, Aussie. Comes from New Zealand."

We hit back with the usual comments about New Zealand sheep and cattle having two short legs because they are always standing on a hillside and the general standard of living will improve now that New Zealand was just another outer suburb of Sydney.

Nightly concerts were organised under floodlights on the aft deck. Half naked troops assembled in force to squat on the decks, swarm over winch platforms, sit on stacks of rafts or perch high amidst the rigging and winch booms until the place resembled a monkey pit built around a piano, microphone and two loud speakers.

The impromptu items were quite entertaining with considerable audience participation; especially when a chap put on a Frank Sinatra impersonation and three chaps assisted with a bobby soxer screaming and fainting act.

The fact that they were 50 feet up in the rigging added to the entertainment.

Crossing The Equator brought the usual 'Crossing the Line' ceremony. Father Neptune came aboard and sat upon his throne whilst the initiates were lathered with a liberal coating of flour and water applied with a paint brush before being shaved with a massive razor then tipped over into a tank of water.

It was an hilarious affair which abruptly terminated when one of the victims turned on a fire hose and washed everyone off the deck.

I noticed the topics of conversation amongst the troops had subtly changed. Instead of recounting battle or leave anecdotes their thoughts now looked ahead and their conversation centred around their plans for the future.

I'm going to miss my Dad. I felt I now understood the reasoning behind his actions over the years and the sternness of our upbringing. But it was all too late. He was gone and we would never sit down and have a beer together.

There were times during this voyage when I felt very lonely despite the thousands of men around me. I missed the mates I had known so well in the prison camps; they had come from all over The Empire and were dispersed to whatever corner they had come from. Signaller Vic Powell was among the eighteen in our mess. Vic was one of the original members of The Signal Platoon and our friendship went back over six years. I had lost track of him during P.O.W. life and meeting him again was like meeting up with a brother. He, too, expressed concern over the future.

Things were tough in Australia before the war. Jobs were damn hard to get and, if you were a teenager, you left school as soon as you could, grabbed any job and hung in there so as to contribute to the family income because your father's job was never too secure.

The shining thoughts of marrying Eileen and sharing the rest of my life with her were slightly dulled at times when I contemplated the future.

Damn it all! I hadn't been allowed to create an original thought, and act on it without some fear of punishment, for six bloody years! Important years between the age of 21 and 27 when a man should be planting his feet on the ground; but the war had started five days before my 21st birthday and I couldn't get into the army quick enough because The Motherland was in trouble.

Now I was about to be turned loose to face a future for which I was not qualified.

Unhappy thoughts which were unwarranted – but I did go through periods of depression and doubt.

The ship's P.A. system announced on 20th September she was sailing direct to Wellington and then to Sydney. The five West Australians didn't even rate a mention.

The same P.A. system on Saturday 22nd September 1945 suddenly came to life broadcasting an Aussie Rules Football Game played between South Fremantle and Swan Districts!

Perth! It was just over the bloody horizon!

We gathered around a loud speaker and cheered with the mob at the game. Bets were laid and South Fremantle won by 4 goals so I picked up a quid. The football was followed by the first few bars of a popular patriotic song: "Australia's sons let us rejoice" preceding the ABC news. And what news it was! Dinkum Aussie stuff telling us of the probable abdication of The Mikado, the way the Aussie troops were rounding up the Japs in the islands and what The Government was doing to help England's food situation. The news ended in time to switch over to Belmont Racecourse for the last race. And we were going to New Zealand!

Five days later we passed Wilsons Promontory. There it was – my country!

It was only a mile away with waves breaking against the defiant rocks and throwing spray high into the air!

The Kiwis weren't very impressed with the scenery and passed such comments as: "Gee, why didn't they give it to the Japs and let them starve there?" "They wouldn't have starved. Look at the rabbits crawling all over the place."

We hoped, for The Kiwi's sake, the ship wouldn't arrive at New Zealand in the night because we'd sail right past the place and no one would know where we were.

The ribald banter increased as the ship approached New Zealand and our mess table became verbally surrounded like an island in a sea of boisterous verbosity.

"Today," announced one of them, "we will be finished with you bloody Australians and if you blokes are in the next war I'm keeping out of it."

"Get out of it, you ant-eating ape. You had to come into this one to get a feed. I s'pose you're the bloke who gave the captain a bar of chocolate to bypass Fremantle and head straight for Wellington because your Mummy's waiting for her little boy."

"And ten cigarettes, Aussie, and ten cigarettes."

The mess deck was crowded with New Zealanders jostling for space as they assembled equipment, packed gear, cleaned boots, shaved, showered and joined in singing songs of their homeland led by a Maori playing a guitar.

A group of us went up on deck to look at the land that was quite close as we approached Cook Straight.

"What do you think of it, Aussie?"

"Well, I haven't seen anything like it since I left the Western Desert."

"It's the best country in the world."

"You mean people actually live in that place?"

The land, looking truly beautiful, rose gradually from the sandy beaches in tiers of thickly wooded, undulating hills rising higher and higher to develop into mountains disappearing into the blue haze of the distance beyond.

We journeyed up the coast of North Island until mid afternoon when we entered Wellington Harbour. There wasn't much to be seen at first; a few houses scattered amidst the trees covering the surrounding hills.

The ship passed through a narrow defile, turned a corner and there before us lay The City of Wellington snuggling between green hills and wrapped in a thin veil of smoke rising from the chimneys of countless houses.

A large, crowded launch pulled alongside to allow numerous army officials and politicians to come aboard. Speeches of welcome were made over the P.A. system. The Mayor of Wellington spoke on behalf of The Governor and The Premier. This was followed by words from several politicians who also welcomed the country's old battle comrades and hoped we would enjoy our visit.

We knew nothing about going ashore so this little part of the welcome sounded quite interesting.

The ship moved on to a wharf where we were obviously to berth.

It was barricaded off but around the rear of the sheds and along the barricades was a vast, cheering, waving crowd which burst forth and, as our ship berthed, flowed along the wharf, around the waiting train and through the sheds to stand below us crying the names of their sons, brothers, husbands or friends and screaming hysterically when they saw the one whom they were seeking.

Disembarking was impossible under these conditions and it was only after repeated requests over the wharf's amplifiers that the crowd slowly and reluctantly withdrew behind the barricades.

It wasn't my city and it wasn't my country but the emotions of the moment almost overwhelmed me.

The waiting train was filled with men going inland and, as it drew away, the remainder went down the gangway into the shed where they received their leave passes before moving out into the cheering, flag-waving throng.

Joyous cries and shouts rose up on the stillness of the evening air as though in salute to the end of a wondrous day, a day embellished by a blaze of gold as the setting sun sank behind the rugged, proud hills of New Zealand.

A nation's soldiers had come home.

*****

A few hours later we swarmed ashore with leave passes lasting until midnight. The ship was due to sail at 6am the next day.

Gosh; it was good to feel land under my feet again.

The local A.I.F Association had hurriedly prepared a delightful reception for us and wished us all the best in the future.

A dance was being held in a nearby building and we danced until 11pm.

Snowy Dufall and I were in a taxi heading back to the ship when we pulled up to give a lift to a couple of Air Force characters. They explained they weren't going back to the ship because a couple of mature-aged ladies standing on the footpath had invited them back to their place for a feed of steak and eggs. This sounded like a good idea to Snowy and me so we all piled into the taxi and away we went, picking up a dozen bottles of beer on the way.

The Almighty created some wonderful things but I think the most outstanding are the middle-aged mothers who took strange soldiers into their homes and gave them a feed of steak and eggs.

The Air Force chaps were pilot officers who had been flying Spitfires over England and France. They claimed they were to receive a special medal when they arrived home because they had been two years in England and had never married. A commendable effort worthy of some recognition.

Around 2am we agreed we should do something about returning to the ship although we still had half a dozen bottles left. It was against orders to take beer on to the ship so we stuffed them inside our tunics where they made conspicuous bulges but, remembering the antics of Wilfred in "Arsenic and Old Lace", we faced the gangway and with a cry of "Charge!" zoomed up past the disinterested sentry, over the decks and along a corridor to the cabin of Flight Lieutenant Somebody-or-other who was promptly turned out to help us dispose of our contraband.

The three officers, all younger than me, came from Perth where our battalion originated. A lot of water had flowed under the bridge since we were cheered through the city streets in 1940, consequently this session developed into a bit of a smoko lasting until around 4am.

I returned to a mess deck resembling a Casualty Clearing Station with bodies spread-eagled amidst the rubbish left behind by the disembarked Kiwis. I laid my hammock out on the mess table and slept without pain until we were at sea.

We still had New Zealanders on board who had to be delivered to the South Island.

The ship journeyed down the coast until mid-afternoon when it suddenly turned into one of those inlets that quicken the pulse of the uninformed traveller. Headlands parted to allow us to slowly move past more headlands. It was something like sitting in a theatre waiting for the curtain to go up; you wondered what was coming next.

A headland slowly moved aside to reveal the town of Lyttelton snuggling within the shelter of protective hills where numerous trains puffed and panted along the wharves adjacent to coastal vessels moored in the small harbour.

Small, white puffs of steam kept popping up all over the harbour and railway yards.

Quite some time elapsed before we heard the noise as every ship, launch, train and motor car gave vent to the jubilant feelings of the town until the volume of sound filled the valley to echo and re-echo among the hills; a fanfare of welcome that was supplemented by the cheers of the crowds lining the wharves and quayside where an enormous banner hung from a crane to proclaim: "Lyttleton is still here, thanks to you!"

The ship berthed, the New Zealanders disembarked to board a train that chugged and promptly disappeared into a tunnel. The *Dominion Monarch* managed to go about without damaging the headlands of the harbour and headed for the open sea.

I was on my way home.

*****

Breathes there a man with soul so dead
Who to himself hath never said,
"This is my own, my native land!"
Whose heart within him ne'er hath burned
As home his footsteps he hath turned
From wandering on some foreign strand?

Sir Walter Scott.

The *Dominion Monarch* majestically entered Sydney Harbour at 6:30am on the 5th October, 1945. Manly, in the starboard distance, gradually glowed as the sun climbed above North Head to bathe The Village in radiance.

We moved up harbour for about a mile then dropped anchor to

await the pilot.

Manly ferries, on their way to the city, passed right alongside. Passengers waved hats, hands, handkerchiefs or newspapers as they cheered, shouted and "coo-eed" while the ferries blew their horns time and time again to be answered with yells and "Coo-ees" from the diggers and airmen lining the rails.

The ship commenced to move again in a slow, majestic manner, surrounded by a myriad of small craft laden with well-wishers.

We rounded Bradleys Head and commenced our journey through the shipping lane towards The Harbour Bridge and Darling Harbour. Flags and handkerchiefs waved from house windows in a galaxy of colour; the naval crews of aircraft carriers, cruisers and destroyers cheered time and time again as we passed; the whistles and sirens of dozens and dozens of ships and ferries filled the air with a discordant din of welcome which steadily increased in volume and discord as we approached the bridge where the noise of jubilation was reinforced by yells, cries, shouts and "coo-ees" of the crowd lining the water's edge around the base of the pylon.

I could only stand with my mates trying to crack hardy. Moments like this don't come very often in your lifetime.

As we approached our berth a R.A.A.F. band struck up with some lively music then an A.I.F. band took over while the cheers of the crowd in the background went on and on and on.

We diggers were assembled on the mess deck to hear words of welcome from Staff Officers who had come aboard; among them was Lt/Col. Munro who had been our CO at No3 Reception Camp in Silverdale Road, Eastbourne.

We picked up our gear, moved down the gangway and stepped ashore.

Our kit bags were thrown into a truck and the army personnel were ushered into a double-decker bus. It promptly moved off at a slow pace followed by more buses carrying the air force.

The convoy moved up into the city where every street was lined with laughing, cheering, flag-waving people who poured out of shops, out of pubs, out of buildings or packed office block windows while we, poor bewildered mugs, leant through the bus windows to shake the hands of old diggers, young diggers, old ladies, young ladies and kids who were all shouting, "Welcome home, boys! Welcome home."

Oh yes; it affected me.

I had never done anything heroic in this war. I had spent most of it in the hands of the enemy and this tended to make me, subconsciously, feel inferior as well as sustain the personal impression I had 'let the side down'.

You have to be real tough not to be emotionally affected when people push each other aside just to momentarily hold your hand.

I don't know what happened to the buses carrying the air force chaps but we finished up at Sydney Showgrounds where, within 30 minutes, the N.S.W. soldiers were given leave passes and they were gone. The Victorians were told they were leaving at 5pm that night by train.

The Western Australians were told they were leaving by ship at midnight. We strongly objected to this arrangement and forcibly stated our views to a disinterested Transport Officer. Fortunately we had two officers from The 2/11th Battalion with us. Capt. Wally Gook and Lieut. John Darling backed us up by pointing out we had all been six weeks on the *Dominion Monarch* and needed a bit of shore leave. We were granted three days leave.

Three days leave!

A train left for Newcastle that evening and I was going to be on it, you betcha!

I collected my rail warrant and was heading for the gate when I saw Ida.

One of my own family! My sister!

We held each other as I shook with emotion while she, dear soul, coo-ed like a contented dove saying, "Welcome home, dear boy, welcome home."

More surprises. June Leslie, a six month old niece named after me, and a two year old named Wendy.

We had lunch in a nearby cafe where a soldier asked if he could nurse the baby while we ate because he hadn't seen his baby son yet.

Ida was looking fatigued and I insisted she take the children home. We returned to Central Station where I held the baby while she went to buy a ticket.

The baby, sensing her mother's absence, began to cry lustily. I had no idea what to do in such a situation and was contemplating putting her down on a seat and running but I became surrounded by a group from The Australian Women's Army Service Corps who took the child from me to calm it down.

Such assemblies of service personnel happened several times during that afternoon. My khaki uniform, medal ribbons and six service stripes proclaimed I had been in the bag because no serviceman had been overseas for six years unless he had been a P.O.W. and, knowing a shipment of Ex Ps.O.W. had arrived that morning, people simply gathered around to say, "Welcome home" or "Good on ya, digger."

Ida returned to gather her children then disappeared into a train leaving me encircled by the A.W.A.S. who insisted we all have a cup of tea at the Railway Tea Rooms.

Life gets tough at times.

Ida's appearance at The Show Grounds had been completely unexpected; it was a magnificent effort on her part and it was all the more appreciated when she informed me that she and her husband were leaving Australia to do missionary work in The Solomon Islands within the next six months.

A letter from Peggy had been waiting for me at The Show Grounds so I had her number and phoned to hear a screaming voice say my name over and over again. I eventually managed to state I would be on the train leaving Sydney at 5:30pm.

There is something about the Australian countryside that is soothing to a fellow who has been away a long time. After the houses thinned out and disappeared, the countryside displayed the distinctive peculiarities of the Australian bush where gum trees, ferns, scrub, streams and mountains spread from one horizon to the other in a manner whispering "Australia", every breath of the invisible breeze encouraging colourful gum tips to wave in welcome.

Darkness fell and I spent the remainder of the journey talking with a couple of seasoned jungle fighters who occasionally laughed at my recollections of Aussie and told me of the many changes that had taken place during my absence.

The time passed quickly and it was with surprise mingled with anxiety that I saw my fellow passengers preparing to alight.

Peggy and Phyllis were at the station; two dinkum Aussie girls who didn't jump up and down screaming but quietly said, "Welcome home", as we stood with our arms wrapped around each other. There isn't much you can say at a time like this. We had only known these girls for 6 hours back in 1940 yet a friendship was formed to last and to support Owen Kenrick and I all through the past five years. They had joined The Red Cross and kept my family informed of my whereabouts as well as sent me parcels of warm clothing and, I guess, conducted themselves just like hundreds of thousands of other young women throughout the war; but Peggy, Phyllis and Nancy were looking after Owen and me and that, as far as I was concerned, was rather important.

Owen had arrived in Australia three weeks before me and had made his way to Newcastle just in time for Peggy's 21st Birthday; a circumstance which puts her age at around 16 years when we first met them. No wonder their parents had sounded a little worried when we phoned for permission to take them to dinner before catching our train back to camp at Greta.

We caught a taxi home and the talking went on until the small hours of the morning. I produced photographs of Eileen and they wanted her address so they could write to her.

Peggy was engaged to a sailor who was on board a ship bearing the unglamorous name of *Whang Pu* but he had spent considerable time on Australia's crack destroyer *H.M.A.S. Arunta* so he knew what it was all about.

Peggy had albums of photographs of her hero and, when I chided her about being untrue to me, she produced albums containing every photo and letter Owen and I had sent over the five years right up to the time I had left England.

Nancy was in Sydney for the week-end and I didn't catch up with her until Sunday night when she stepped off the train. We all trooped back to Peggy's house to talk and talk about those evergreen wartime topics titled "Do you remember when", "Oh! Look at this photo!", "What happened when –"

There were some bad moments. A platoon photograph or a snapshot of me and my cobbers on leave and suddenly I was looking at the face of a mate who no longer existed.

Midnight had long since passed when I went to bed wondering what I had done to deserve such friendship. True, it was wartime and many friendships are formed to fade with time but this one is still going over fifty years later.

My train left at 6:40am next morning and I was back at The Sydney Show Grounds around mid-day.

"You West Australians are leaving this arvo for Melbourne by train," announced The Transport Officer. "One hundred and forty repatriated prisoners of war have arrived by ship and we are bringing them up to Central Station by bus. These men have been in Jap hands and they could do with a bit of help to get on the train. You might like to lend a hand."

Each bus displayed a big canvas sign stating "8th Division Boys from Singapore" and they drove up the ramp to the cheers from the crowd of well-wishers.

We strolled over to the bus doors as they opened.

Oh, my God! Were these spectres really Australians?

They wore Australian uniforms but they were a horrible yellow colour, their eyes were sunken, and their heads portrayed the shape of their skulls more than their facial features.

We might like to lend a hand? We assisted them down the bus steps, carried their kit bags and helped keep them upright as they moved through the curious onlookers and slowly walked to the train.

"Were you a P.O.W.?" asked a bystander.

"Yep," I replied.

"You look in better nick than your mates."

"Ah well; I guess I was a bit lucky."

"Bloody hell!" growled Vic Powell, "we've been on a f.....g holiday!"

The train was all sleeping coaches with a bed for everyone; four berths to a compartment. The men turned in before the sun had set. The six West Australians wandered along the carriages to have a yarn but it wasn't easy. These poor bastards just wanted to lie down. Most of them spoke softly out of the side of their mouths without looking at me and they seemed unable to concentrate for long in conversation.

Maybe they weren't interested in this curious character, with his head stuck through the door, asking stupid questions.

Maybe they just wanted to wallow in the luxury of clean sheets, pillow-cases and blankets.

I knew the feeling but I lay awake for hours after getting to bed.

The train bore on through the night towards Melbourne.

We changed trains at 6am at Albany and had breakfast. Breakfast was in a large, airy building set out like a banquet hall to dish out steak, eggs, chops, sausages, mashed potatoes, tea, toast, oranges, apples, bananas in unlimited quantities by ladies whose one ambition seemed to be to ensure we were well fed.

The train moved on through countryside dear to every Australian's heart. It stopped at Benalla where we were fed again and handed a bouquet of wild flowers before trundling on to eventually arrive at a quiet siding on the outskirts of the city around 1pm.

First The Victorians detrained and moved out of sight around the corner of a building. The Tasmanians were next and the West Aussies followed.

The scene changed around the corner of that building!

The whole railway yard seemed filled with cars!

Someone was shouting "Throw your gear into a truck and get into a car."

The cars were owned by civilian members of The Royal Automobile Club and we clambered in, three to a car.

The convoy moved off.

The streets of Melbourne were packed with thousands and thousands of cheering, flag-waving people who shouted greetings of "Welcome Home" and "Good on yer, digger." Everyone was there; factory girls, shop assistants, A.W.A.S., staid business men, grey-headed mothers, young men, seasoned jungle fighters, all crowding the streets and just leaving sufficient space for the vehicles to slowly travel. Office workers leaned out of windows to empty the fluttering contents of their waste-paper baskets to mingle with the confetti being thrown all over us.

Occasionally the pace slowed to a halt. Then dear old ladies reached out just to stroke our arms and say "Thank you" as we leant, half laughing and half crying, through the windows.

Some men, dressed in jungle green, poured out of a pub to hand us a beer and cry, "Good on yous! You bloody beauties! 'Ere, 'ave a beer!"

The Lord Mayor of Melbourne stood on a dais, raised his top hat to us and, like every other citizen of Melbourne, shouted "Good on you, boys! We're proud of you!"

Gradually, almost imperceptibly, the crowd began to thin out to be replaced by groups of schoolchildren or factory workers and, at one spot, a glittering white array of nurses cheered as we passed their hospital.

Another crowd cheered us through the gates at Royal Park where we were driven up to Anzac Hall for a lunch few of us could eat.

Royal Park was quite a large military administrative establishment. We collected our gear and found our quarters. Six men to a hut and that suited the six of us from Western Australia.

A captain stuck his head in the doorway. "There are some girls in my office who come from Western Australia. They would like to talk to you chaps. Is it O.K.?"

"Bring them on," we said.

He did.

A pleasant afternoon followed as we individually recollected memories of Perth. They were younger than us and had only been away less than twelve months whereas we had been away five years and I had difficulty in recalling the names of some of Perth's main streets. They informed us that the sheets and blankets on our beds had been dumped there so they had made the beds for us; a thoughtful, wasted gesture because, although we stayed two nights in Melbourne, they were never slept in.

Iris suggested we go out to where she lives for a party that night. Snowy, Reg and I reckoned it sounded like a good idea. Reg, whom we had met on the *Dominion Monarch*, lived in Melbourne. He was on leave and doing the rounds with us. Vic and George decided to go their own way as they had other ideas.

Mr and Mrs Mathews welcomed us into their home as though we were their own. He had fought in Palestine and France in The 1914-18 War and he treated us like mates. Mrs Mathews played the piano and we sang until 2am when a taxi called for Snowy and Reg to take them to Reg's place.

Mrs Mathews insisted I stay the night so I slept in my underclothes under a quilt on the floor in front of the lounge room fire.

After breakfast I returned to camp to hear some sad tales as we sat around drinking coffee and waiting for Capt. Gook to turn up. Last night's taxi driver turned out to be a female so Reg and Snowy enticed her into the flat to finish off half a dozen bottles which she did in a very efficient manner before disappearing down the street in a cloud of exhaust fumes.

Vic and George had been strolling around Melbourne when a taxi pulled up.

"West Australians?" called the A.W.A.S. "Hop in. We're from W.A. too."

They apparently went on an elite sort of a pub crawl during which Vic drank long and deep. The last thing Vic remembered, before passing out, was laying in the back seat of a taxi with his feet on one girl's lap and his head on another who was stroking his head and saying, "You poor boy. You poor boy." This morning he awoke in a bed dressed in his underclothes. Upon looking around he discovered five other beds with a female body in each. The A.W.A.S. made him cover his head while they dressed before bringing him a breakfast of chops and eggs. They then took him to the door of the hut, pointed to somewhere in the distance and told him, "Your quarters are over that way. On your way, Digger." Poor Vic. He was heart-broken.

Capt. Gook arrived to inform us we had leave until midnight and exhorted us to be back in camp by 8am the next morning because we were leaving.

Vic and George took off on their own again. Reg and Snowy planned to take Reg's sister and a friend to the pictures that night; this gave them all day to book seats. I wanted a day on my own to see Melbourne. Besides, these blokes were tough and I knew I wouldn't be able to keep up with their pace.

I met, by chance, two woebegone characters in a cafe that evening.

"What happened?"

"Well, you see," says Reg, "It's this way. We had all day to fill in and we got drunk. Real drunk. Then we decided to call on the girls.

They panicked and said they wouldn't go out with us if we were drunk so we went to the pictures to sober up and fell asleep. We didn't wake up until nearly 7o'clock so we're in strife with the sheilas and we ain't got no seats booked, we ain't got no girls and we ain't got no nothin'."

"What do we do now?"

"We'll get some beer'" says Snowy, "an' go out to The Mathews and have a party."

Life was like that in those days. You turned up on someone's doorstep with some beer and a party naturally followed.

The taxi called around 3am to take the three of us to Reg's place where we bedded down for the remainder of the night.

I emerged into startled wakefulness around 7:15am next morning. I roused the other two who told me to "Piss Off!" so I did that and arrived at the barracks to find everyone assembled for moving off. I tossed my gear into a truck, yelled good-bye to Iris, and fell in with the rest of the troops.

An hour later we were still standing there; a circumstance which allowed our two officers, accompanied by Snowy, to crawl in and join the squad before it was transported to the dockside.

The *Strathmore*, heading back to England, was scheduled to call into Fremantle after delivering some former Burma Railway Workers and Changi Residents to Bernie, in Tasmania, where they were welcomed with all the excitement and joy we had already seen on several occasions.

I hadn't become indifferent to these scenes and I wondered if the physical wrecks walking down the gangway to be embraced by tearful families would ever really recover from the degradation and misery they had survived.

The Passage of Time would help and History would condemn but nothing could ever justify the treatment they had received at the hands of a mongrel enemy.

My God! What if we had lost?

The *Strathmore* only stayed two hours then headed out across The Great Australian Bight for Fremantle carrying one captain, one lieutenant and five 'other ranks' from The 2/11th Battalion (City of Perth Regiment) after five and a half years overseas service.

The *Strathmore*, with only 600 troops on board, was practically empty and living conditions were superb. We had cabins fitted with beds, complete with sheets, pillows and blankets, a wardrobe, a dressing table, a writing desk and a bedside reading-lamp.

This war was becoming quite an enjoyable experience.

I gave considerable thought to the future during the next five days. I never doubted Eileen would come to Australia and we would marry but where was I going from there?

I oft times wondered how I would shape up without someone telling me what to do. All my teenage years had been spent carrying out instructions from tradesmen and foremen who demonstrated considerable scorn for the capabilities of the younger generation. The years of military discipline hadn't encouraged individualism. The close companionship moulded in P.O.W. life was necessary at the time but now it was all gone.

All Australians, at this period in our history, were convinced we were a strong country and would have considerable influence in future international affairs so I asked myself, "Who makes this country strong and where does its wealth come from?"

The answer, obviously, was the agricultural community. Therefore, I must become employed by some firm involved with the farmers.

Thus, in this manner, was the wrong decision made by a man about to stand on his own two feet after twenty seven years of life sheltered by parents, appreciative works managers and the seclusion of military commitment.

Anyway, I had formed this opinion although it was several years before I managed to do anything about it.

Around 1pm on 16th October, 1945, a cry went up; "There she is! There's Rottnest Island!"

Gee, eh! Rottnest Island!

The ship made its way around the island to enter the channel leading into Fremantle Harbour then slowed right down to take the pilot on board.

One of the boys remarked, "Yep, this is Western Australia all right. Look at all the sand."

The pilot seemed to be in no real hurry and we cursed him as the ship crawled at a snail's pace through Gauge Roads towards the crowded wharf.

The people could be plainly seen while we were still some considerable distance out in the harbour. Quietness held everything in its sway. The troops on the ship were quiet; probably too full of emotion to trust themselves to call out. The crowd on the wharf was quiet, expectant and anxious. A tram travelling along the main street of Fremantle could be distinctly heard.

Suddenly the tense quietness was banished.

"Coo-oo-ee-ee!!"

Hundreds of voices broke out with answering 'coo-ees' to the summons, the ship's foghorn added its unmelodious blaring to the noise as it tied up wharf side.

Oh! What a sight!

Most of the crowd were women whose bright, beautiful, colourful dresses blended with waving arms, upturned faces and fluttering handkerchiefs while the afternoon sun shone in that warm pleasant way known to Western Australians.

Women seemed to be everywhere! They packed tight as they screamed, laughed, called, enquired or looked for their men folk then, upon discovering them, jumping up and down in unrestrained excitement as they pointed and called his name to their friends who, in turn, screamed his name and jumped up and down until the whole scene was as colourful as a piece of gaudy shot silk being waved under a bright light.

I looked for someone whom I might know but to no avail. Anyway, I had written and told them I didn't want any of them amongst that mob.

"Righto, men. Pick up your gear and move down the gangplank!"

I don't know how I hobbled down the gangway and staggered through the crowd which yelled, cheered, banged my back and laughed at my load before I became installed in a bus and eventually unloaded at Swanbourne Rifle range.

Many were the wonderful moments I had experienced here when in The Cameron Highlanders but so many new buildings had sprung up that I scarcely recognised the place.

George Mercer and I dumped our gear on an adjacent lawn where a few chaps were being claimed.

"Doesn't anybody love us?" yelled George.

Apparently not, so we made our way to where The Red Cross ladies were handing out tea and cakes. I could see this cup of tea right in front of me; hot, brown with milk and still whizzing around after being stirred when an indignant voice said: "Come out of it, Leggett."

I turned to see who was coming between me and this cup of tea when two, strong female arms were wrapped around my neck as my sister Joyce held me so close I thought my neck would break from the strain.

"Come on," she said. "Over here."

Over there was my Mother. We just hugged each other as a funny, trembly feeling bubbled up inside me. People seemed to shimmer and fade in the distance while Mum patted my shoulder and said, "Hullo, son."

"'Lo, Mum. See! I told you I would be back one day, didn't I? Just took a little time, that's all."

Slowly people came back into focus and I saw many of them were smiling at us so I smiled, and Mum smiled, and Joyce smiled and we just stood there holding each other and saying nothing.

Within the hour I had my 21 day Leave Pass and we were in a Red Cross sedan car driving home.

Driving through Perth was an emotional experience. Many odd corners or scenes unexpectedly appeared to awaken long-slumbering memories and there were other places I had completely forgotten.

The car stopped outside 41 Alma Road, Mt. Lawley. We stepped out, my gear was dumped on the footpath and the driver gave a wave and drove off.

So; I was home. This was the moment I had dreamed about through many lonely hours as I starved in Salonika, rotted in prison trains, sweated in coalmines or froze while massaging my toes against frostbite when we halted at some filthy farm for the night.

I was home! My mother and my sister were standing beside me, my gear was on the footpath and the house was in front of me.

"Well, what are we waiting here for?"

I gave Mum and Joyce an armful each, picked up what was left and lumbered through the gate as far as the front door when a whirlwind in the form of my kid sister Patricia wrapped itself around me and, as I held her, I extended my hand to grasp the hand of her husband – my old mate, Geoff Benson!

My sister-in-law was there, too, and babies seemed to be everywhere. Three of them, actually, but I had never seen so many babies together at one time and they were my nephews and niece.

Dinner was a wonderful affair with a linen table cloth, shining crockery and sparkling silverware. And a turkey!! It came from Mr Malatzki who owned the grocer's shop around the corner. He had been a mate of my Dad's during the first war and this was his way of extending the hand of friendship.

Eventually Mavis went off with her son; Pat and Geoff left with their son and I was left with mum and my sister. We talked far into the night. I had difficulty in absorbing and appreciating all the family events which had taken place during the past years.

The war had left its mark upon Mum and her two daughters.

Several hours later we said 'Good Night" and I made my way to my room.

It was just as I had imagined. My bed on one side with a silk cover, the wardrobe in one corner, the lowboy in the other, the dressing table near the door and my writing desk on the far side. My pictures of Nelson Eddy, Deanna Durbin and Bert Hinkler's Avro Avian hung on the walls. My text books were stacked on my writing desk shelves whilst drawing gear poked out from odd corners.

I sat in the chair and commenced to open the many letters from England while a framed photo of Eileen smiled at me from the desktop.

Chapter Twenty-Three

The 21 days leave was spent in getting to know Perth once again. So many places had been erased from my memory. I also called on relatives in other suburbs; a challenging experience carried out on trams and buses.

I visited Scarborough Beach where I just sat to gaze at the sea. This was not a good idea. I found myself pondering over mates who had been lost at sea or shot down over The English Channel.

I think many Ex Ps.O.W. had the same sense of loss because we gathered in city pubs for prolonged yarning sessions as though reluctant to let go of each other.

I also had to adjust to circumstances within a family which had seemed as solid as rock when I enlisted. My father was no longer there. Mum had now been a widow for several years and seemed to be coping. My brother Syd was still in the islands. He had married and his attractive wife and baby son had been at my homecoming. My sister Joyce was now married to an American sailor who was currently at sea. Joyce and their daughter, Diedre, were living with my Mum. Joyce's former husband had remarried and had custody of their son Garry. My old mate, Benno, after the evacuation of Greece, had done some scrapping up in Syria but, upon returning to Australia, had been classified "B" on account of his eyesight. My gawky, school-kid sister had grown into womanhood and married Benno; which made me suspect his eyesight wasn't too bad. They had a son and were expecting another child.

The Australian wartime attitude of spontaneous friendship was still a predominate spirit within the community but I experienced emotional problems in accepting the companionship of strangers.

Mum still enjoyed a few Saturday afternoon beers at The Queens Hotel and, on one occasion, she brought back three Aussies who had been Ps.O.W. in Japanese hands. One had had his tongue cut out because he wouldn't split on his mates, another had three fingers chopped off and the other acted as interpreter for the tongueless chap. They were fellow Australians who had fought a different war to me and had experienced suffering far greater than I, yet I couldn't accept their companionship and felt they were intruding in our home.

This is a terrible thing to confess but, unknowingly, I was terribly mixed up at the time. I thought I could take the future in my stride but, in reality, I could hardly jump puddles.

My leave eventually expired and I reported to Karakatta Depot for discharge.

Next day I had an enjoyable time with clothing coupons purchasing a new suit, shoes, shirt, a hat and coming home with my uniform in a brown paper bag tucked under my arm.

The following months weren't easy. I needed a job. The Structural Engineering Company was obliged, by law, to give me a job because I was working for them as a junior worker prior to enlistment and I approached them with some trepidation.

Ted Malland, the Works Manager, welcomed me with enthusiasm. He escorted me all around the works to be greeted by former workmates and to meet new people. We spent an hour or so yarning in his office – a novel experience because I had never been allowed past the door in previous years.

Of course he had a job for me. The firm was finishing off a couple of water-lighters for the navy at a site adjacent to the traffic bridge at North Fremantle.

"We need a timekeeper-storeman down there. I'll phone the foreman and tell him you're coming. You can start next week. Oh, by the way, they're working shift work so you'll cop a bit of night shift.

O.K.?"

"Sure, that'll be O.K."

The job was a piece of cake but traveling to and from work was a problem. I had to catch a bus into Perth then get a train to North Fremantle. I always fell asleep in the train after night shift and there was the possibility of awakening at some suburban station beyond Perth Central.

But it was a job and I was making money.

The next thing was to arrange Eileen's passage to Australia.

The Immigration Department, much to my surprise, was nowhere near as excited as me over this important event in my life. They granted me several interviews and gave me numerous forms which I attacked with grim determination and eventually managed to supply a disinterested representative of the department with sufficient proof to convince him I was dinkum.

"How long do you think it will take to arrange her passage?"

"At this stage," quoted the official with finger-tips touching as he leaned back in his chair, "I should say about twelve months."

"What!"

"My dear fellow, the appropriate shipping is still very scarce, there are a great number of wives to come out from England who have priority and Miss – ah," he leaned forward to read a name on a form, "Miss Stone, being a fiancé, will have to await her turn. I'm sorry, but that is the situation."

"Ah, well; I'll keep in touch."

"Please do. By the way, we require a payment of forty-five pounds. Please let us have it as soon as convenient, will you?"

"Forty five quid! What's that for?"

"Wives are transported free of charge as they constitute a family but a fiancé doesn't quite meet that criteria and there is a shortfall of forty-five pounds. You understand Miss Stone will be brought here under an arrangement whereby you undertake to marry in three weeks."

"Mister, you get her out here and I'll arrange the marriage bit."

I think he actually smiled.

I settled into a working routine, plodding along from week to week, assuming things would happen and everything would fall into place. But Life isn't like that. Things will happen if a man plods along but they may not be the things he wants to happen. A man has to take Life by the throat and shake it until he gets what he wants.

This little homily suddenly hit me in an unexpected manner.

Day shift was supervised by a site foreman who had authority over the leading hands and so it went on right down the line. The 'pecking order' within the firm was rife before the war and it was still flourishing.

Night shift was supervised by a leading-hand welder; so, once the initial paperwork was completed, I spent most of the shift curled up in a lean-to shed beside the open fire of the copper containing the hot water for the men's tea at meal break.

I was on day shift when the phone rang. It was Ted Malland, the Works Manager at Welshpool.

"Have you got a welder and a plant that can be sent across to Fremantle to do a job?"

"Hang on. I'll ask Matey. (The Foreman was nick-named "Matey" because he wasn't.) "Mr Malland wants to know if you have a welder and a plant that can be sent across to Fremantle to do a job?"

"Ask him what's the job."

"Matey asks what's the job?"

"It's none of your bloody business what's the job! All I want to know is … …" He repeated the request embellished with so many derogatory and illuminating adjectives that the original question was hard to define.

"Matey, he wants to know if you have a welder and a plant that can be sent across to Fremantle to do a job."

"Tell him 'Yes'."

"Yes."

"Thank you."

I stewed over this conversation for about ten minutes then rang him back.

"I want to talk to you about that phone call."

"All I wanted was a simple answer to a simple question."

"And you got it and if you ever speak to me in such an ignorant manner again I'll come out there and we'll see which one of us is a stupid bastard."

"What!!"

"If you think I'm kidding you try me. I've been abused and insulted for four years by the bloody Germans and I'm not going to take it now that I'm back in my own country! Just don't do it again!"

I hung up and fully expected the phone to ring and tell me I was fired.

The phone didn't ring but I had abruptly come to realise I was going nowhere and, within the hierarchy on the job, I was probably classified as "Shit Kicker. 2nd Class."

The North Fremantle job eventually finished and I was transferred back to Welshpool where, much to my surprise, I was greeted with a big grin and a thump on the shoulder; but I was back where I started in 1937.

I determined to get away from this type of work and, lacking the ability to see into the future past next pay day, I made all the wrong decisions.

An army mate of mine had started up a cake delivery service. A simple business of purchasing a variety of cakes from a pastry cook at wholesale prices and hawking them around from door to door at retail prices. He had purchased a pre-war Commer panel van from which he, and a former Air Force colleague, worked their way through suburbs on a regular basis and were doing all right.

The ingredients for making cakes and pastry were still in short supply and housewives were glad to purchase such merchandise at the door after years of being without them.

Another van and another partner would double the income and who knows how big we could grow.

I still had a couple of hundred pounds of accumulated pay from the army days so we purchased a small Bedford van and sold cakes and pastry from door to door in all the suburbs between Midland and Maylands.

They were long days commencing before daylight and finishing at dusk but we were making money.

Eileen's passage to Australia wasn't progressing. Indeed, the war brides in England were staging regular demonstrations outside Australia House in London.

Eileen and I had both engaged Australia House in a paper war and had accumulated quite a pile of correspondence that, basically, informed us shipping was not at present available; we hadn't been overlooked and we must await our turn on the priority list.

Kay had returned to Australia and he, too, was storming the bastion with paper. So was every other ex-serviceman who had a wife or a fiancé in England. I wouldn't have been on the staff of Australia House for quids.

Kay had settled down to civilian life much more logically than I. Although he had no knowledge of welding he had secured a job in a one-man welding shop situated in a conglomeration of sheds at the West Perth end of Wellington Street.

Frank Wyatt was doing very nicely welding up cracked or broken gearboxes, sumps, cylinder heads or any other automobile part made of non-ferrous metal. I think he originally engaged Kay out of a sense of patriotism. He probably needed someone to sweep the floor and boil the billy but, such was Kay's ability to convince anyone he could do anything, he was soon welding intricately shaped components and lecturing me on the use of the oxy-acetylene welding equipment, a topic with which I had been familiar since about 1938.

Mavis was advised she had been given a berth on the "Orbita"; a statement which trebled the broadsides of paper to officialdom as the four of us endeavoured to get Eileen on the same ship but to no avail.

The arrival of Mavis was a happy occasion. Kay's family and my family were at Fremantle to welcome her and guide her through the customs routine. We all went back to Kay's father's place for a wonderful meal and partied on until the last tram left Wembley for the city.

Kay kept progressing while Eileen and I battled with Australia House. He purchased a weatherboard house out in the bush at an area called Kewdale at the far end of a track named Belmont Avenue. He also purchased a motor-bike and sidecar in order to get to work because there wasn't any public transport out that way.

The house was on a quarter acre block and, in the winter, the bottom half of the block was under swamp water. Oft times, when riding home in the dark at the end of a day, he would be obliged to make lengthy detours through the scrub because the same winter swamp covered a considerable portion of Belmont Avenue; but the same quarter acre block was the venue for some terrific camp fire barbeques in summertime. Beer was still in short supply but everyone scrounged around during the week and we usually had sufficient to see us through the night.

The *R.M.S. Orbita*, having returned to England, commenced filling up again. Eileen received a telegram from Australia House advising she had six days to get on board.

This berth hadn't been easy to secure. Our newspapers had recently carried a splurge proclaiming 'love conquers all' and presented an article showing Australian ex-servicemen welcoming their German brides to their new country. A reply to aggressive letters to Australia House stated Eileen's file had been mislaid. I had accumulated a vast quantity of correspondence upon this topic and threatened to hand it over to the media accompanied by the letter relating to the missing file.

Eileen's file was found in a hurry and she had six days to get on board.

She made it!

The depth of her affection, and her willingness to make sacrifices in order to bring it to fulfillment and to maintain it, is a feminine mystery which overawes me even unto this day when I recollect how she left her family, her hometown, her friends, to sail to Australia to marry a joker whom she had only known four and a half months.

The voyage to Australia wasn't exactly a 1st Class Tourist Holiday. There were sixteen women in the cabin and Eileen couldn't sit upright in her bunk as it was too close to the cabin ceiling.

I had to get busy too, and organise a wedding, a reception and a honeymoon while my two sisters counted clothing coupons and checked out the city shops for bridal gowns and other intriguing pieces of feminine clothing.

I approached The Vicar of St. Patricks Church in Mt Lawley. He was delighted. "Come and see me when Miss Stone arrives. Then we can have the bans announced."

"Can we make a date?"

"Of course we can."

"December 7th. O.K?"

"That will be fine."

Piece of cake, really.

I reckoned I had eight weeks to organise everything but finding somewhere to hold a reception in Perth and someone to cater for it was not so easy.

An electrician friend of ours, who worked for Claude Neon Signs Ltd, told me of an American who was opening an upstairs restaurant in Murray Street so I dashed in to see him.

Apparently this American was quite a personality and seemed to be known to everyone. Formerly the Bandmaster of an American Naval Band stationed in Perth over a prolonged period during the war he had provided considerable uplifting, moral-boosting entertainment to our festivity-starved city. I don't know if he took his discharge in Perth or whether he went home and returned but Perth was now his "home town" and this restaurant was his business venture.

"Sure, for a wedding on a Saturday afternoon you can have the whole restaurant. How many people will be catered for?"

"About fifty. How much will it cost?"

"You supply the beer. I'll supply the food. A hundred and fifty pounds should cover it."

"That sounds all right to me."

"Would you like to confirm it with a down payment."

I gave him fifty pound and walked out of the place feeling a load had been lifted from my mind.

But that wasn't all that was on my mind. I had also arranged the honeymoon. Saturday and Sunday nights at The Como Hotel then, on Monday, we were to catch the train to Pemberton.

I had never been south to the big timber and I reckoned this would be a good opportunity to show Eileen some of the magnificence of her new country.

Everything was now under control. I had arranged the church, the reception was arranged, the honeymoon was organised and my two sisters were prowling through the city shops for bridal wear.

Beer for the reception was a problem. It was still scarce. Publicans sold two bottles at a time to regular customers but, as most of us had been overseas for several years, it was hard to be classified as a 'regular' at any particular pub.

The problem was resolved just two days before the wedding. Kay had a brother, Bruce, who was earning a living selling life insurance. He not only sold a policy to a publican but had convinced the man it would be a grand patriotic gesture if he supplied a 5 gallon keg for the wedding of an Ex P.O.W. whose English fiancé had arrived a few weeks ago and the wedding was on next weekend.

The keg was to be supplied on the assurance it would be returned first thing on the following Monday morning because the brewery rationed the publican and if the keg wasn't there his supply would be down by 5 gallons.

The keg was promptly taken to Perth Ice Works at the upper end of Murray Street where it was stored until needed.

I received a letter from The Department of Immigration. It was an interesting letter with "The Department of Immigration" emblazoned across the letterhead; this announcement was surrounded by an impressive array of phone numbers and state office addresses throughout The Commonwealth. It informed me that Miss Eileen Stone was a passenger on the *R.M.S. Orbita* bound for Fremantle, (I had known this for four weeks) Her passage had been arranged on the understanding we would marry within three weeks, (I had known this for eighteen months and would have gladly cut the time down to 24 hours if it wasn't for convention) and, in order to ensure prompt disembarkation of passengers, I would be unable to board the ship.

Came the great day!

I stood amidst the floodlit crowd impatiently waiting as the "Orbita" slowly approached to gently bump the wharf long after the sun had slipped below the horizon.

I anxiously scanned the rows of faces lining the ship's crowded rails.

Oh Gawd! Which one was hers? Surely I haven't forgotten what she looks like?

I spotted someone who looked like her and waved in the general direction. There was a whole line of feminine faces and I reckoned, if it wasn't her, every one of those girls would think I was waving to someone else.

The gangway was down. I had folded the letter in such a manner that it only displayed the impressive letterhead from The Department of Immigration; I poked this under the nose of the disinterested wharfie standing at the bottom of the gangway, pounded up the steps and waved it in front of the crewman standing at the top. I stepped aboard and made my way along the crowded deck.

It WAS Eileen!

She stood there for a moment, hesitant, just looking at me before rushing into my arms.

All the beauty that is womanhood wrapped its arms around me and held me close. I could only hold her and whisper her nickname over and over again.

This was my Eileen!

This was the hub around which the future years would revolve!

A thousand years passed before we drew apart. (I learned, several weeks later, she had hesitated because she wasn't sure it was me! Gee; a man can be lucky in a crowd.)

I had gone to Fremantle on my own in one of our vans so, after processing through immigration and arranging to pick up her luggage the following day, we left the wharf side to the calls of "Good Luck" and "All The Best" from friends she had made on the voyage.

The next three weeks were a bit hazy.

I had taken time off from the cake business which was in financial difficulties. The vehicles, having survived the war years, were giving up the ghost and the cost of repairs was gradually exceeding the firm's profit margin; a circumstance which my colleagues kept hidden from me because they didn't want to spoil my imminent wedding and honeymoon with such a mundane topic as the business going broke.

Eileen, Mavis and my sisters, regularly disappeared into the city for a day's window-shopping that must have been a bit like a guided tour of Alice through Wonderland. They had found a dress that seemed to be the fulfillment of all Eileen's dreams in battle-scarred Eastbourne; pure white with long sleeves and a flowing train to trail behind. Peggy, the Bridesmaid, already had a dress from a previous wedding and Mavis, who was to be Matron of Honour, found a dress of similar design.

I managed to grab Eileen, now and then, to introduce her to the neighbours and to show her around Perth which, in those days, was a lovely town and has, over the years, grown into a beautiful city.

This was a halcyon period in my life.

Three days before the wedding I went to the restaurant to ensure the reception was under control and to make final financial arrangements.

I stood at the entrance watching a sparrow-like Italian gentleman dart from table to table in preparation for the evening trade. He fluttered past me several times before I managed to attract his attention by standing in front of him.

"I'd like to see the manager, please."

"I am the manager."

"No; I mean the American chap."

"He's gone."

He skipped away to a table and smoothed the tablecloth.

I stopped him on his next pass.

"I have arranged a wedding reception here for next Saturday, all right?"

"You arrange with him. He gone. I not know about it."

'But I paid fifty quid deposit to confirm the arrangement."

"He got your fifty quid but you got no arrangement with me. Me busy man."

He flittered off. I was getting a bit angry at this stage. Bloody Italians! I had had enough of them in The Western Desert and I had a gutsful of this character, too.

These were unjust thoughts because I now believe Italian immigrants are among the best people in the country but this episode took place just after a war.

I stopped him again and angrily demanded: "Then where the bloody hell is he?"

The man suddenly seemed to realise I had a real problem.

"Look, mate, he got my restaurant on lease. He go broke. I got my restaurant dumped back on me. I busy man."

"O.K. So, where the bloody hell is he?"

He took a deep breath. "I hear he has got job of bandmaster for the Young Australia League Band. Maybe you find him at The Y.A.L. Hall. I carn 'elp you. I sorry."

I believed him.

I pounded the pavement around to the Y.A.L. Hall and found him, and the Y.A.L. secretary, in the office.

A heated discussion followed and I was offered my fifty pounds back.

"I don't want the fifty quid! I want the wedding reception you agreed to organise!"

"I went broke. I can't do anything about it."

More heated argument before the secretary poked his nose in.

"What time is your wedding?"

"3pm."

"We run a dance here every Saturday night commencing at 8pm. If you agree to be out of here by 7 o'clock you can hold your reception here."

I faced The American. "Well, what about it?"

"O.K. Buddy, you're on."

"How much do I owe you?" I asked the secretary.

"It's on the house," was his smiling response.

I paid The American some money and we shook hands all round.

I wasn't happy with the situation. This character could have written and advised me several weeks ago but there wasn't anything I could do about it now. I sincerely hoped the secretary of The Y.A.L. would exert some influence and make him live up to his end of the arrangement.

I couldn't stay at home on the eve of the wedding because Eileen was living there. I spent the evening at the house of Ivan's brother,

Bruce. The 'buck's party' was not a riotous affair. The gathering was comprised of a few ex-army mates plus some of Bruce's working colleagues. The shortage of beer toned the party down a bit; a circumstance for which I, at least, was thankful because I was still highly strung from the effects of army service and I had a tendency to suffer with a bilious attack for several days if I drank too much.

The weather was one of those warm, sunny days that bring out the beauty in everything – especially when viewed through the eyes of a groom on his wedding day.

We lolled around the house all morning then – Right! Into it! Showers, shaves, dressing – check – re-check – Got everything? – Come on! – Let's go!

The church was crowded when we arrived.

It wasn't a simple case of me marrying a girl I had met in England. I had waited 14 months for my fiancé to arrive and this situation was known amongst my friends and their families, and the friends of their families as well as by the neighbours up and down the street.

When she had arrived in Australia people came from all over Perth to meet her. Front doors would suddenly open and people appeared to speak to us whenever we walked down the street to catch a tram.

Eileen and I weren't aware of it but we apparently represented "Romance and The Future" to people who had been through six very depressing years – and so the church was crowded.

There was a rustle of excitement at the church lobby; it rippled through the congregation to the front pew, the organ began The Wedding March, we three males stood – and I waited a thousand years for Eileen, on the arm of my old mate Kay, to arrive at my side where the rustling of her flowers assured me we stood in mutual nervousness.

And the wonder of that moment has never faded!

Taxis took us to Victor Penrose's Photographic Studio in central Hay Street. We alighted from the taxi to be 'well-wished' by the clanging bell of a passing tram.

The photographs must have been good because Victor Penrose enlarged one of them and had it in his display window for months afterwards.

We entered The Y.A.L. Ballroom to a scene of splendour. The American and The Y.A.L. Secretary had come up trumps!

Perchance we had stars in our eyes but the tables were set out in order with white linen tablecloths while cutlery, glasses and dinnerware glistened and gleamed overall.

The food was enjoyable, the correct speeches were made, the 5 gallon keg was broached, toasts were drunk and friendship, mixed with happiness, prevailed throughout the gathering.

Of course the receptionist at The Como Hotel knew we were a honeymoon couple. So did the rest of the staff as well as all the whispering, wise, head-nodding guests who smiled knowingly as we dragged our cases up the stairs to the room.

The sun was still above the horizon so we walked down to the river to watch it set behind Kings Park. It was another emotional moment in a day filled with emotion. The sun setting in my country – I was safe – beside me stood my wife – this woman who had come so far to be there beside me – the sun set the sky aglow as though to enhance the beauty of the moment.

Someone had placed a bottle of port and two glasses in my suitcase. We discovered them when we commenced to unpack upon our return to the hotel and we drank a toast to our future.

I grabbed a towel and went for a shower in the men's bathroom directly across the hallway. It was a quick shower but Eileen was already in bed when I returned. I scrambled in beside her and lay there for a few moments.

The glass of port, having arrived at a pre-determined spot deep within me, met up with some of the contents of that 5 gallon keg and they decided there was only room for one of them in such a confined space.

My stomach decided there wasn't room for either of them!

I flew out of bed, wrenched open the door, raced across the hallway, shoved open the toilet door, dived into a cubicle and commenced yodeling down the well in technicolour!

Ten minutes later, looking sickly pale and hardly able to walk, I crawled back into the room to flake out on the bed – and this routine was repeated several times during the course of the night.

I awoke around 8am next morning. Eileen was already dressed and sitting in a chair doing some crochet work.

"I feel terrible," I moaned.

"Perhaps some breakfast will help."

"O.K. I'll give it a go." (6th Australian Division and all that sort of stuff.)

Gawd! What a tableau we must have presented as we entered the dining room. The bride walking upright and the pale-looking groom hanging on to her arm to steady himself. The heads nodded and the old ladies smiled knowingly to each other.

Breakfast was some kind of crumbed fish; two mouthfuls and I bolted up the stairs.

Around mid-day I returned to the conscious world and, after a big glass of milk and soda water, gradually recovered.

The train left Perth around 7am on Monday but my Mum was there to see us off. The carriage was the standard 'dog box' type with doors all along its length and windows that dropped down for ventilation. We leant out of the window talking to Mum for a while and then waving as the engine belched smoke and steam, the buffer-chains took up the slack to jolt the carriages into motion, and the train gradually crawled out of Perth.

We changed trains at Brunswick Junction because this train was going to Bunbury and we were going south.

Kay and Mavis met us on the platform. He had crammed Mavis and a suitcase into his sidecar and they were on their way to Collie to visit his mother. Our train wasn't leaving immediately so we had lunch in the station tearooms.

Numerous towns are spread along the railway line between Perth and Pemberton. The train stopped at every one of them to pick up an occasional passenger or to shunt a carriage or goods truck into a siding; thereby gradually decreasing in length until, when the journey ended some thirteen hours later, our carriage and the guard's van were the only units left attached to the engine.

The shortened train ground to a halt on a flat piece of land. The guard came walking past.

"This is it," he said. "You can get out here."

"Where are we?"

"Pemberton. We ain't going no further."

Two grubby, dust-covered honeymooners climbed out of the carriage, lifted their cases out of the dog box and slammed the door.

The guard and engine crew opened the doors of a big shed, unhooked the engine, shunted it into the shed and closed the doors behind them.

A motor fired at the far end of the shed and a car containing three men climbed up a road and disappeared into the bush.

We stood there not knowing what to do next before the fast approaching night enveloped the land.

"There must be a town somewhere around here," I said. "You wait here with the cases and I'll go and have a look around."

Eileen looked at the surrounding forest and had visions of aboriginals rushing out of the dusk to carry her off to some place where she would, no doubt, be eaten by cannibals.

"Don't you leave me here alone," she pleaded.

I was contemplating the prospect of spending the night in the stationery carriage when two headlights wound their way down the slope and the town's taxi slid to a dust-distributing halt.

"Cripes, mate," apologised the driver, "I was having a few beers with me mates and I didn't hear the bloody train come in because the bloody thing is two bloody hours late. The bloody train crew told me you was waiting down here. Get in and I'll have you up at the guest house in no time."

He delivered us to Karriholme Guest House where our host and his wife had prepared an appetising meal and made us most welcome.

We met the other guests to whom Eileen was introduced as "The English Bride". We sat around yarning for a while but we were very tired and dusty after the long train ride.

We showered and returned to our room.

The walls dividing the rooms of Karriholme Guest House were made of asbestos sheets an eighth of an inch thick and weren't exactly sound-proof.

Eileen went to the window and pulled down the Holland blind. A moth with a wingspan of four inches, having been rolled up in the blind all day, fluttered out above her head.

"Get away from me!" she cried.

Her brave, new hubby promptly grabbed a newspaper and sprang to the defence of his wife.

Bang! Thump! Smash! went the newspaper.

"Don't come near me! Get away! Get away from me!" cried Eileen as she waved her hands above her head.

Bang! Thump! Smash!

Nobody believed me the next day when I tried to explain.

Our hosts had known for weeks an English Bride was coming to the town and the news had been whispered on the winds throughout the forests.

The whispering breeze wafted towards us while window-browsing in the sloping main street next day.

"You must be the English girl," said a middle-aged lady.

"Well, yes. I must be," chuckled Eileen who was beginning to accept the title.

"My husband and I came out here after the first war to go on The Group Settlements," continued the lady. "And this is my friend, Mrs So-and-so. She came out with her husband on the same ship. We heard you were coming and we were hoping to meet you. There's been nobody come out from England for over six years now."

That was one of the magical aspects of our honeymoon. Women who had come from 'The Old Country' in the early 20's under The Group Settlement Scheme made an effort to come and speak to Eileen. Most of them had husbands working in the town's timber mill because the Group Settlement Scheme had been a bitter experience; others came out of the bush for miles around.

They were hungry to meet someone young and new who had been through the tribulations of war 'back home'.

Me? I listened and sensed that peculiar bond which holds the English together in times of stress. I heard Eileen relate anecdotes of bombing raids that were hitherto unknown to me and I thought, "By Cripes! Come to think of it – we have been through a bit."

And I heard tales from the days of The Group Settlement Scheme; tales which were told in a humorous tone to hide the heartbreak and disillusionment beneath the surface.

Mine Host of The Guesthouse had arranged for all the guests to have a day out in the bush where the timber was being felled. Cut lunches were handed out. We made our way down to the timber mill at the bottom of the hill and clambered aboard the empty rakes of the steam-hauled timber train.

The sound of the engine's whistle echoed and re-echoed throughout the valleys as it choofed its way through the forest towards the location where the timber was being felled by men who camped out there and only came into the town on weekends.

It was a dirty ride. The engine blew smoke and grit over where we sat on top on the heavy, seasoned timbers forming a cradle for logs to ride in. The empty rakes bumped and swayed along the uneven line in a manner that made us hang on and endeavour to avoid the splinters which the lurching motion and the seasoned timber constantly threatened to drive into our rolling posteriors; all to the amusement of the engine crew who had no illusions as to what was going on.

Our destination was an area deep within the forest where massive logs lay strewn around the hillside before being hauled up to the train and stacked on the rakes.

Men were working with cross-cut saws further down the slope so we wandered down in their direction.

Two of them were sawing through the butt of a massive tree. We stopped to watch these sinewy, muscled, sun-tanned men; their bodies moving in rhythm as they pushed and pulled the saw.

The tree gave a few ominous cracks.

"I think we had better move." I said to Eileen.

"No; I want to hear them sing out "Timber!" the way they do in the pictures."

Another ominous sound from the tree. The sweat-covered sawman turned and saw us standing there.

"Get to bloody hell out of here!" he bellowed. "The bastards going!"

Eileen took off up the track like a startled rabbit with me close behind.

We paused at the top.

The tree emitted a few more mournful sounds. It leaned and leaves, accompanied by a small limb, toppled from the crown. The tree leaned further, groaned in a despairingly hopeless manner, gathered speed and crashed down to thump the earth that had supported it for hundreds of years.

"Ah well," I said, "at least you have heard an Australian sing out 'Timber!'"

Logs were stacked on to the rakes with a bulldozer and the train was loaded by early afternoon.

"Climb aboard!" yelled the driver.

I looked at the long line of timber stretching back into the bush. Riding on top of that could be dangerous and I mentioned this to the driver who grinned.

"Thought you'd say that. Spread yourselves out on both sides of the engine and hang on."

We did just that!

We stood on the footplate and hung on to the handrail running the length of the engine. The chimney roared and belched smoke above our heads, the pistons hissed and panted steam below our feet, the conrod swooped back and forth past the wheels and the long, snake-like train followed us through the bush all the way back to the timber mill.

The rest of our honeymoon maintained its pace and magic.

We were taken marron fishing at night in the creek at the bottom of the hill near the railway shed. A number of half sheep-heads were tied to stakes with a length of string and anchored to the creek bank before being gently lowered into the water. A slip noose at the end of a piece of fine piano-wire attached to a stick, and a torch, comprised the rest of the equipment.

The lurk was to search in a semi-circle with the torch until the beam approached the bait where marron could be seen feeding. Touch their eyes with the beam and they vanished in a flash but carefully approach the bait until their tails could be seen, gently slip the noose over their bodies and – whoosh! – one beaut, bonza marron!

Half a kerosene-tin full then back to the boarding house for a supper of fresh bread, marron and red wine. Shangri-la!

We climbed The Gloucester Tree; we went to Windy Harbour with another couple of honeymooners who had their own car; a vehicle picked us up and a chap proudly showed us over the trout hatchery; we swam where the creek was dammed to form the town's swimming pool; we walked along some of the forest tracks and our world was full of sunshine.

It all came to an end.

We boarded a train and faced the long journey back to Perth.

Next day I went to the Commonwealth Employment Office and applied for unemployed relief.

Chapter Twenty-Four

The next few years were a bit hectic.

We lived with my Mum – it never occurred to me that we had nowhere else to live. Houses to rent or buy were simply not available. Mum had this place empty so naturally we lived there the same as my sister Pat and Benno lived with his parents at Kelmscott.

The cake delivery business had gone broke and I was re-employed by The Structural Engineering Company under The Commonwealth Reconstruction and Training Scheme whereby a man employed in a field of work prior to the war could now serve a two year apprenticeship and, upon completion, come out as a tradesman; a scheme which met up with considerable hostility amongst the established unions.

I had applied for a Boilermakers Apprenticeship.

A boilermaker's apprentice in the structural steel game doesn't necessarily make boilers but he is taught to read blueprints, mark out steel, fabricate structural steelwork and erect it on site.

When my application 'was being considered' I was interviewed by a former union official, now assisting the government, who didn't want me or anyone else getting into the trade on a two year apprenticeship.

He was a big man who leant back in his padded chair and slowly shook his head in a manner implying deep, heart-felt regret.

"Well, I'm afraid we can't accept your application as you apparently weren't associated with this type of work in the services."

"What!"

"That's what The Act says and I can't do anything about it."

"But I've been working in structural steelwork ever since I was seventeen except for my war service."

"I can only go by what The Act says."

I exploded!

"I was in the front line and I spent four years in a prisoner of war camp! Two and a half years of that was shovelling coal in Poland and you've got no bloody hope of getting me down another coal mine!"

"There's no point in getting angry. It's unfortunate but that's the situation."

I sat there nonplussed and bewildered. Ever since the war ended people had been speaking of the great years ahead and implying a buoyant sense of nationalism and confidence in the future. The politicians had even passed this Act in an endeavour to overcome the shortage of tradesmen in the community yet here was this bloke blocking me on a technical point.

"How about an apprenticeship as a Boilermaker's Welder?" I asked.

"Apparently the same situation applies."

"No; I was working with welders in Munich and in the coal mines."

"Can you get Statutory Declarations to that effect?"

"Yes."

"Well, when you've got them come and see me again."

Fortunately I had been occasionally working with welders in Munich and in the coalmines. I soon produced the necessary declarations from my mates and was granted an apprenticeship as a Boilermaker's Welder.

A considerable amount of skill is required and developed in this trade but, basically, I was welding structures fabricated by the boilermakers. The work also required me to have my head inside a welder's hood all day. This encased my head but it didn't prevent my mind from wandering, or events of the past few years crowding in, until I had to take the hood off and sit down while I brought my mind back to the present. It was during one of these depressing moments I received my first bit of Post War Counselling.

"Get on with the bloody job," said the foreman, "You're not paid to sit on your arse doing nothing all day."

Like I said; we called him 'Matey' because he wasn't.

*****

I served twelve months of my apprenticeship with The Structural Engineering Co. before I managed to transfer to Agricultural Spare Parts Supply Co. Ltd. This move was probably the outcome of my desire to be of service to the agricultural community. The internal fire of patriotism, or the desire to be of service to my country, hadn't yet burnt itself out.

Agriparts premises were in Pier Street and the firm was vibrant. It not only sold David Brown Tractors and Fiat Crawler Tractors but also designed and built bulldozer blades, tree-pushers and overhead gear for the latter. The firm had a fabricating shop as well as a machine shop and produced numerous items in demand throughout the wheatbelt.

I finished my time with this firm, qualified as a tradesman and continued working for them.

*****

Domestic life was moving along also.

Benno and Pat had purchased a quarter acre block of land half way down the big hill leading into Scarborough and had commenced building a timber-framed, asbestos house.

Mum was a bit angry with Benno for asking Pat to live down there in the scrub away out of the city.

"There are no streets anywhere. They even have to run a pipe across from a neighbour's house in order to get water to mix cement for the brick foundations and God knows when they are going to get electricity down there. Nobody in their right mind would want to live at Scarborough."

"Pretty good blocks going for forty five pounds down here. You ought to grab one of them," advised Benno.

Forty-five quid? I never had forty-five quid!

Besides, I had a block in Bayswater. My intelligence was limited by an inherited attitude decreeing I must never go into debt and success is only achieved by a hard day's work. If I had of known then how money worked I would be a millionaire by now.

But wouldn't we all?

*****

We had now been married two years and reckoned it was time to start a family. I hadn't given a great deal of thought to the subject of parenthood but, during the months following this decision, I learned to treasure the wonderful, shared emotions as a woman who loves you gradually creates your first child.

Anxiously waiting for an urgent taxi eight o'clock at night while your wife is in labour can be a very harrowing experience for a male beginner.

The only calm person in the house was Mum.

The taxi arrived and the driver, seeing the urgency of the situation and obviously more concerned for his vehicle than the plight of the passengers, roared off to St Anne's Maternity Hospital then roared off again as soon as we had alighted; no doubt wiping the sweat from his brow.

A single light globe, burning over an imposing wooden door at the top of a flight of stone steps, helped dispel the surrounding gloom of the night.

We slowly, painfully, ascended the steps, pausing after conquering each one, then pressed the white button of the doorbell.

The door gradually opened to disclose a sister in nun's attire. She smiled at Eileen, took her arm and helped her across the threshold. She smiled at me, told me to phone in the morning, and shut the door in my face.

I sat on the top step under the light globe, looked out into the surrounding darkness, and felt bloody miserable.

Our daughter was born on 2nd January, 1949, about thirty minutes after we arrived at the hospital. We named her Maureen Edith; the name of Edith being Eileen's mother's name.

And, just to prove we had got the hang of it, Eileen was pregnant again in next to no time.

This sort of thing creates a sense of responsibility and I started to once again ask myself where was I going?

We had lodged an application for a Building Permit under The War Service Homes Scheme as soon as we married. So had every other ex-serviceman and, as building material was still in short supply and rationed, permits were slow in coming.

Eileen and Mum were the best of companions but we felt it was time to be an independent family.

The magic of our honeymoon was still a shared dream and we both had a desire to live amongst the big timber. Lew Thompson offered me a job in his garage at Manjimup. A house was available with the job so I took it.

The situation seemed perfect. A job, a house, and big timber in the background. However, there were a few complications. The job was immediate.

Our second child was due within a couple of weeks so we arranged for me to go to Manjimup with the understanding I could return to Perth to pick up my family when Eileen was fit to travel.

Can you beat that?

We had one daughter under two years of age, another child was due within weeks, and I went off to the country leaving Eileen to sort it all out and to let me know when she was ready to come south.

"Of course I'll be all right," said Eileen.

It was a stupid thing to do and I'm damned if I know what we would have done without my Mum to back us up.

My departure from Perth was rather grandiose. Lew Thompson was the Holden agent. I drove a brand new Australian car to Manjimup and that's where the glamour ended.

The anticipated house still had tenants who couldn't be moved for six months but accommodation had been found in a room, a kitchen and the back verandah of a timber-mill styled house built on the site of the town's original gravel pit.

Eileen and Mum, up in Perth, were busy making plans for the arrival of the baby. Mum now had a lad in his late teens boarding at her place where he occupied a back room. The plan, when the moment arrived, was for Mum to awaken this lad and send him around the corner to a neighbour who owned a car. The neighbour was to pull on some clothes, race the car around to Mum's place, load Eileen and dash off to the hospital.

An excellent plan, actually.

One dark night, around 2am, the labour pains started in earnest. Mum woke this lad and sent him, half asleep, on his errand of urgency.

He returned twenty minutes later to announce he couldn't find the house in the dark!

More instructions, liberally sprinkled with anger and abuse, and he was shoved out the front door again. Bryn's pre-war Ford 10hp Tourer roared to the kerbside fifteen minutes later, Eileen was bundled in and the car vanished down the street with a window-rattling bellow proclaiming the purpose of its mission to all and sundry.

Our daughter, Susan Patricia, was born fifteen minutes after Eileen's arrival at the hospital on 2nd September, 1951. Her second name, "Patricia" was also the name of my aunty in England.

We had purchased a bedroom suite and a kitchen suite in Perth and, once they were made, they were railed to Manjimup where I set them up in our quarters. Several items of furniture, such as Maureen's cot, Susan's bassinette, Eileen's clothes, my clothes, babies clothes, as well as quantity of cooking utensils and bric a brac, were still in Perth and their timing of transport to Manjimup had me a bit worried. They would be needed from Day One when my family arrived.

The problem was solved by my army mate, Owen Kenrick.

Owen had taken up land under The War Service Land Settlement Scheme at Northcliffe. His block had previously been occupied by a battler under The Group Settlement Scheme. The battler had walked off the block and similar circumstances would eventually cause Owen to do the same but, at present, he was engaged in a ceaseless confrontation with massive, long-dead, ring-barked trees standing like silent sentinels guarding a sea of bracken fern.

I met him in the hotel and, over a few drinks, told him of my predicament.

"Aw shit, mate, take my truck then you can bring your family, the furniture and the bloody lot down in one hit. It'll get you there and back if you don't go over forty. You might 'ave to pump on the brakes a bit because the 'ydraulic valve needs a rebore but she's not a bad truck. Go on! Take it!"

The success or failure of Owen's property depended on that Bedford 30cwt truck yet he said, "Go on! Take it!"

Mates!

I drove the truck up to Perth, loaded it with my family and furniture and "brought the whole bloody lot down in one hit."

The job at the garage was quite an experience. A motor-driven welding-generator was mounted on the back of an ex-army Chevrolet utility and the job entailed driving to adjacent timber mills, bulldozer contractors, farms or caravan parks to weld whatever was broken. The district and its inhabitants gradually became known to me and I made a few friends.

On Sunday afternoons we dressed in presentable clothes, tucked Maureen in the pusher and Susan in the pram, then walked around the outer perimeter of the town finding pleasure in the way Susan slept and in the manner Maureen's eyes would follow the outline of the towering trees as we passed.

Our family excursions must have been the subject of considerable tongue-wagging amusement amongst the town's establishment whose older members were still 'sizing us up' as they did with all newcomers to the district.

The house became available at the end of six months so we walked up the street to inspect our future residence and our hearts sank within us!

It was an old timber-framed, plasterboard structure with a lathe and plaster interior displaying more lathe strips than plaster. The interior ceilings were holed and areas of the floor were rotten; not white ants, just rotten with age and damp. It was old, exceedingly old, and in our opinion required a lot more than tender loving care to make it habitable again.

I'm not implying Lew Thompson had deceived us. He had offered me a job with a residence and this house was of the same standard as many others in the town. The country had been through a war during which no building material was available for the construction of new buildings nor the maintenance of old buildings; years after the cessation of hostilities, building materials were only issued with a permit for approved dwellings.

We had been offered a house of a standard accepted within the locality but we simply couldn't live in it.

This placed us in quite a dilemma. We needed somewhere to live. No other house was available in the town and we couldn't continue to live in a room and a kitchen.

My application to build a house on the block in Bayswater had, with the passage of time, been approved by The Housing Commission and, after considerable discussion, we reluctantly decided to return to Perth.

A letter from Agriparts advised a job was waiting for me. Apparently the foreman had anticipated my return.

We couldn't go back to Mum's place. She now had three English chaps living there as boarders. They had recently migrated to Australia and settled in nicely. The three of them called my Mum "Ma" and, over the years to follow, they became members of our extended family. They all eventually married and one in particular produced children who regarded my Mum as their grandmother and accorded her all the respect and consideration due to such domestic status right up to the end of her days.

Benno had finished building his house at Scarborough. It had two bedrooms, a lounge room, a sleep-out and a kitchen. My sister Joyce, after living for two years in Newcastle waiting for the American sailor who never returned, had come back to the west and was now living with her two children in Benno's lounge room. His two boys slept in the sleep-out and that left the other bedroom empty.

"Stacks of room! Come and join us!"

Most of our furniture had to be railed back to Perth. Owen insisted we use his truck again to carry the children's gear and our clothing up to the city. A relative of his was coming to Northcliffe during the week and would bring the truck back. No worries, mate.

We moved into Benno's spare room. The girls had a cot and the bassinette but Eileen and I slept on a blanket on the floor for five nights until our furniture arrived and enabled us to make ourselves a little more comfortable. Besides the bassinette, we had in that room a double bed, a kitchenette, a dining suite and six chairs. Benno had made a low bed for Maureen that fitted under our double bed during the day giving some extra space.

There are times, or circumstances, in a man's life that compel him to sit down, have a good think and take stock of himself. This was another one of them.

I seemed to be running away. Running away from what?

Reality?

Obviously I was relying upon other people to present me with the opportunities to make a living; you could do that in those days. Work was in abundance and jobs were everywhere but I wasn't guiding my own ship and my wife and kids were the losers.

Perchance during the years in the prison camps, where men were punished if they expressed an unacceptable opinion, I had relinquished the desire to make a positive decision and I still carried an unexplainable sense of awe, or fear, of authority.

The war had finished, I was discharged and I was lost.

I had, during the past few years, reached this stage of emotional turmoil on several occasions and no matter how hard I tried to analyse myself I still made blunders.

I have long since come to the conclusion that I, like many other ex-servicemen, never really got rid of those emotions. You learned to live with them; endeavoured to rise above their negative influence and got on with your life.

So ... I was living in Scarborough, I had a permit to build a house in Bayswater and I had a job as a tradesman welder.

Get on with it!

Our house was to be built under The Self Help Scheme. I had, in effect, contracted to build a house for The State Housing Commission and payments were to be made as the job progressed. Upon its completion I would be the occupier with a mortgage payable to The Housing Commission. The work would be done during the weekends and in my spare time; a common practice during that period of housing shortage.

Benno was now a certified carpenter; so was his brother-in-law John Hogan and, between us, we decided to build a timber-framed asbestos house, but by the time I had signed numerous forms with The State Housing Commission, asbestos sheeting had gone completely off the market.

Cement was now available and the new decision was to construct a cement-walled house using The Condeco Travelling Mould. This apparatus was unique in its day. Once the foundations of a house were laid the mould was placed at the north-east corner of the intended structure, packed with cement and moved along leaving a portion of wall behind.

However, the trench for the foundations had to be dug. Inter-suburban transport was a problem so I purchased a push-bike. I was out of bed at daylight, swallowed some breakfast, rode to Bayswater, spend an hour digging trenches, rode to Pier Street to work for the day then back to Bayswater to dig until nearly sundown before riding back to Scarborough.

This went on for weeks.

Eventually the foundations were poured then cement went the way of the asbestos sheeting. It simply was not available.

The Midland Brick Company had commenced production at its new kiln in Upper Swan; another snap decision was made.

We'll build a brick and tiled house!

We needed a bricklayer. There were plenty of them around but they all worked under contract to builders and, although most of them did additional jobs over the weekends, they were still hard to get.

Mum found us a brickie. He was a friend of hers and 'reckoned he could give us a bit of a hand.'

His nick-name was 'Tiny'. He worked as part of a brickie's gang all week and laid bricks for us over the weekends. The walls of the house slowly rose to windowsill height before we started to have problems with Tiny's attendance on the job. Some Saturdays, instead of arriving at 8am, his clapped out Austin A30 would bellow to the kerbside like a reluctant camel around mid-day. A door would open and a long pause followed before Tiny emerged to peer at the world through bleary, bloodshot eyes. He would walk past us without saying a word and commence laying bricks. Sometimes the cement, which had been mixed hours ago and regularly turned over as we awaited his arrival, may have gone a bit hard and he would spend the first five minutes on the job cursing us and only pausing for breath as he lifted the smoke-blackened billy-can to his lips to drink the unsweetened tea which had also been brewed several hours ago.

As long as that house stands I can point out Tiny's 'bad days'.

Some weekends he wouldn't turn up at all!

It wasn't just two work-days lost. We only worked on weekends so it was a week lost. A few non-working weekends and the job was becoming a long, drawn-out process, a circumstance reinforced by a constant shortage of building materials.

The domestic situation in Benno's house was quite remarkable. My two sisters and Eileen lived in harmony with each other and the children never seemed to cause any great problems but, after eighteen months, the desire to be on our own began to exert itself.

We borrowed enough money from Mum to purchase sufficient cement blocks and tiles to build a 10 by 20 feet shed on our block. It had two windows and a door. We gave it a wooden floor and my cousin, who had a plasterboard ceiling business, put in a ceiling. Across the back wall we had a Metters No2 Stove, the kitchenette and the refrigerator. Two wardrobes divided the bedroom from the kitchen.

An asbestos sheeting lean-to shed served as a laundry and a bathroom. Quite effective, really. Water was heated in the copper then bailed into a bathtub that would, one day, be installed in the house.

It was a cosy shed. A winter's evening would find the two girls warmly tucked in bed whilst, on the other side of the wardrobes, Eileen and I sat in front of the open grate of The Metters No.2 Stove, our feet resting on the open oven door, as we listened to "The Shadow" and "McCackie Mansions" on the radio.

After four years of married life we were finally on our own.

Chapter Twenty-Five

Kay and Mavis now had two sons and they were our constant companions at picnics, parties or barbeques. We knew each other's families and friends and life seemed to have settled down.

However, Life is closely related to Time and Time creates changes as it moves on.

Kay's brother, Bruce, was a successful life insurance salesman who had topped the national sales figures for a couple of years in a row but he felt burnt-out and needed a change.

So he bought a small grocers shop in Geraldton.

He did quite well for several years but his wife, who came from the eastern states, became terribly homesick being so far away from her family. This was an understandable circumstance. Many servicemen married whilst ranging far and wide during the war years but, when it was all over, marriage in civilian life was a matter of settling down and the decision of where to settle often became a problem.

Bruce was an obliging sort of a bloke so he talked Kay into buying the grocery shop then took his wife and children east.

The move of Kay and Mavis to Geraldton took some emotional adjustment. Geraldton seemed so far away. Over 300 miles north. He had been my mate for many years and Mavis and Eileen needed each other for mutual support in the problems of marriage and motherhood in a new country.

We didn't lose contact with them and, in a way, I think I was lucky I didn't follow him.

Kay was one of those characters loaded with an abundance of

enthusiasm and self-confidence. He invariably managed to convince himself, and others, that whatever project he undertook would turn out all right in the long run.

The corner grocer shop was the family residence for quite a few years before he bought a small supermarket out of town in the growing suburb of Wonthella.

A local resident named Boueff Morgan had a couple of Reo trucks and ran a trucking business to numerous points 'up north'. Boueff began to develop a bit of a heart problem and was advised to get out of the trucking business. I don't know what legal documents were signed but the upshot was Boueff took over the supermarket and Kay took on a trucking business which hauled any kind of merchandise, ranging from drums of fuel to steel trusses, to Carnarvon, The Gascoyne Junction, and station properties spread over the vastness of the north beyond these points.

The hours were long and the going was tough. The northern highway beyond Northampton was corrugated gravel and the roads to the station properties just seemed to be tracks meandering off into the wilderness. The heat was debilitating in the summer and rain made truck driving hazardous in the winter but, for reasons beyond my comprehension, he enjoyed it!

Often, over a beer, he'd relate some life-threatening episode as though it was all part of the game. He once mentioned a bank overdraft that shocked me and I asked him, "How the hell did you get into this sort of business?"

He contemplated a glass of amber fluid before answering, "Dunno. Just lucky, I guess."

He turned up at our place one weekend in a brand new Mercedes Benz Truck. "Traded in one of the Reos," he answered, "She's cost me eight thousand quid but the bank said the money's right."

He was also building a house at Wonthella under The War Service Homes Scheme.

The north began to develop over the next few years and the trucking business became a bit competitive. Kay sold out to an opposition firm then took on the job as storeman for a Geraldton marine engineer and boatbuilder.

Whilst truck driving he had met up with Bruce Robson who, in himself, must have been quite a colourful character. Originally a fisherman from Port Fairey in South Australia, he was the manager of Yalbalgo Station when Kay met him. They struck up a friendship and decided to go into a prawn fishing partnership. They worked from Sam Creek out from Roebourne for the next four years.

Kay knuckled into this game, studied for a bit and eventually gained a coxswains ticket for "The Northern Star."

He appeared in Perth during the quiet season.

"Bought out me partner's share in the boat," he announced. "Got me own prawning boat now."

He also mentioned he owed the bank twenty three thousand pounds.

Six months later he was back in Perth flourishing an echo-sounder printout under my nose.

"See that thick black line? Well, that's prawns! It was like that for several nights. I've cleaned up all me debts, I've sold the boat and we're going to move back to Perth so we can be near Steve for a while."

Steve was their eldest son. He was in a bad way with cancer and going downhill. Tragically, it wasn't long before he lost the battle.

A newsagency in Murray Street was the next venture which flourished and was eventually sold "at a small profit", to quote my colleague.

They also purchased a duplex house in Carlisle for eleven thousand five hundred pounds which, after some years, was sold for thirty five thousand pounds.

Kay and Mavis then purchased a house in Wanneroo. Mavis still lives there but my old mate died of emphysema on 6th January, 1986.

His passing left quite a hole. I had assumed he would always be around.

*****

So, let me get back to my own story.

I had been endeavouring to gain employment on the firm's sales staff, a move supported by an enthusiastic Sales Manager.

The Managing Director summoned me to his sanctuary. "Hurrumph!" he coughed as he approached a map of Western Australia hanging on a wall, "We're going to give you a go at sales. Now, your territory will be from here (he jabbed at Perth) up to here (he jabbed again; this time at Geraldton) across to here (Another jab. Mullewa) down to here (Jab. Toodyay.) and back to Perth. That should do you. Go and see The Sales Manager and get yourself organised."

Getting organised with The Sales Manager was no trouble. Standard pep talk, pamphlets, order book and a 1953 model Chevy ute with a road map in the glove box. The road map was necessary because I didn't have much of an idea of what the country was like beyond the city's outer suburbs. True, I had worked at Mandiga and at Laverton but they were 'straight there and straight back' arrangements.

Getting organised at home was not so easy.

"Going away for a fortnight at a time! Who's going to build the house?"

"Benno, John Hogan and Tiny are building the house. I'm just labouring and pottering about the place. Benno will tell you what materials are required. You just have to order them and see they are delivered by the weekend. I simply have to take this job with the firm. It's quite an advancement."

Eileen didn't rant and rave at me. She had come to this country to marry and make that marriage work. We were in it together and this was part of the deal; and I have to admit the house-building project went ahead at a greatly increased tempo from that moment onwards.

I still had this peculiar desire to be of service to the agricultural community, a fantasy born in the depths of the Polish coalmines and dispelled in the face of reality. The farming community proved quite capable of looking after itself and my job was to make sales.

Nevertheless, I set off in pursuit of this vision leaving behind a wife with two children living in a shed with a half-built house standing on the block beside it.

A week later I arrived in Geraldton and stayed with Mavis and Kay for a couple of days; in this manner we kept in contact with each other.

The life of an agricultural machinery salesman can be a very lonely and demanding one, especially if you are operating from Perth and endeavouring to establish a market for imported machinery.

Agriparts marketed Fiat Tractors from Italy, David Brown Tractors and Salopian Ploughs from England, Claas Headers from Germany as well as numerous items manufactured in our own workshop; all good quality equipment whereas the established opposition had agents and showrooms manned by a staff born in the district. I had my share of ups and downs during the next few years but I made sales and managed to keep my head above water. I became more familiar with farming life which had indeed changed since the days on Mr Collins farm at Mandiga.

Also, on several occasions, I packed Eileen with our two daughters into the Chevrolet utility and drove straight to Geraldton where they spent a week or so with Mavis and Kay while I prowled around the district.

Occasionally, when boring down the gravel road between Mullewa and Morawa, I'd pull in to Buntine and spend an hour or two with Aunty Ivy and Uncle Ben who were the district's Sunshine Massey Harris agents.

It is not necessary in this yarn to relate, in detail, all the activities of this period but a few anecdotes are worthy of mention.

A farmer, out from Yuna, had a big property. He was a big man who thought big and did big things. He was enthusiastic about our firm and, besides buying numerous items of our machinery, he became our agent.

Overnight accommodation was never available at Yuna. The place was just a dot on the map with an uninspiring pub as its sole building. The first time I was out that way I approached the publican to book in overnight.

He was full of apologies.

"I'd love to put you up but I'm just redecorating the place. I've had to move the furniture out of both the bedrooms so as to get on with the job. Come and have a look."

He escorted me around the premises and, sure enough, floor cover sheets, paint tins, brushes and trestles were in both rooms and each room was only half painted.

I made my way out to our agent's property.

"I'll have to leave a bit early," I said, "The local pub is being repainted and it's seventy miles back to Geraldton."

"He's a bastard," said the agent. "That heap of crap has been in those rooms for years. He just doesn't want travellers to stay overnight. Anyway, there's a bed for you over in the bunkhouse."

We were sitting on the homestead's back verandah having a quiet beer at the end of the day when a mob of brumbies went galloping past.

"By Cripes," I commented, "one of those looks a bit too good to be a brumby."

"Well, there's a bit of a story about that one. I was doing all right at the time and making money so I decided to invest a bit of it in a trotter. You can't expect to make money at the trots if you haven't got a good horse so I sent to New Zealand and purchased a thoroughbred. It cost me three thousand pounds by the time I got him here. Then I spent another two thousand getting him ready before I took him down to Perth to make a bit of a clean up. I had a thousand quid in me pocket and I was strolling around amongst the bookies checking out the odds when I met a mate.

"What odds are you getting?"

I told him.

"Aw, I'll get you better than that."

"So I give him me dough. He disappeared in the crowd and comes back five minutes later with the betting ticket."

"You've done your dough," he says.

"What the blazes do you mean? The race hasn't started yet!"

"A mate of mine is a bookie. I stood there in front of him holding up the money and calling out your horse's number but he kept going past me so I sings out, "It's not mine!"

"He swoops it up and mutters, 'The wife of that horse's driver has just put five hundred quid on another horse in the same race!'"

"So, after the race was over," says my companion, "I took the driver around behind the stables and belted shit out of him. Then I loaded the horse into the float, brought him up here and turned him loose amongst the brumbies. That's a six thousand quid experiment you just saw going past. You can't trust them city blokes."

*****

The firm manufactured a well-built, sturdy scrub rake designed to rake the scrub off newly cleared country. The rake was twelve feet wide with strong, curved tines spread equally along its width. These tines were attached to a frame lifted by an hydraulic ram, an hydraulic pump was driven from the tractor's power-take-off whilst the control lever and oil reservoir, complete with breather-valve, were attached to the tractor in a position convenient for the driver.

A couple of bachelor brothers on a property well out beyond Kulin had purchased a scrub rake but had written to state it was not entirely successful on their property. They were working on some modifications and, in due course, would let us know the outcome.

Letters of this nature send shivers down executive spines.

That's how it is with farmers. People in the city can never make a machine that exactly suits their particular property so they decide to make a few modifications. Some are good but some can turn out disastrous. Then the word spreads like a bushfire through the district and your product is classified as "crook".

Kulin was not in my territory but I was promptly despatched out to the property because, as a welder, I had helped make the rakes.

I arrived on the property just as these laconic characters were about to "give her a go".

The unit was mounted behind a Lanz Bulldog Tractor. Now, if you don't know anything about tractors, let me tell you the Bulldog is a large tractor with a big single cylinder which races backwards and forwards to develop tremendous power when placed under load.

The rake's oil reservoir with the breather valve and control stick were mounted on the large mudguard beside the driver.

These bachelor chaps had certainly been modifying the scrub rake. It seems the tines were set too far apart to hold the vast quantity of small sticks that covered their recently cleared new country. If they blocked out the space between the tines, they reasoned, it would overcome the problem.

They had sandwiched each tine between two pieces of timber measuring three inches thick by eighteen inches wide by twenty four inches long; in effect they had bolted a balk of timber twelve feet long by two feet deep by eighteen inches wide to the scrub rake.

"All right?" queried James.

"All right," affirmed Alfred.

James climbed up into the tractor seat and revved the engine.

"O.K.!" bellows Alfred. "Lift her."

James moved the control lever. The Bulldog bellowed into the challenge, its exhaust roaring like an enraged bull, the big mudguards flapped like a pelican endeavouring to become airborne whilst the tractor danced up and down on its pneumatic tyres.

The hydraulic pump cried in squeezing agony as the massive piece of timber was slowly raised from the ground.

"She lifts too slow," announced Alfred.

"Can't lift her any faster," shouts James.

"All right. Drop her down."

James hit the lever. The weight of the timber caused the tines to drop at a phenomenal speed. The oil in the hydraulic ram was sent back into the reservoir under a pressure that forced it out through the breather-valve in a fine mist to cover the tractor, the driver, the scrub rake and the surrounding area with a coating of good quality hydraulic oil!

James shut off the motor.

"I don't think it will work," he stated.

"Nah; it don't look too good. Let's go and have lunch."

I followed them through the heat of the day into a hotter, tin-roofed, weatherboard house where their perambulation around the kitchen table was marked by a distinct track in the dust upon the floor.

James sat in a chair and completely withdrew from the sparse conversation; he was no doubt contemplating the next engineering project.

"Sandwich?" asked Alfred as he cut slices off a loaf of bread and opened a tin of salmon.

The tin's contents were tipped on to an enamel plate and the tin tossed through the kitchen window where it landed with a clatter. I later stole a sly look through that window and marvelled at a 3 feet high heap of empty salmon tins glistening in the fierce sunlight.

Salmon sandwiches and hot black tea were consumed in an airless house in the company of two oil-smeared men who seemed to ignore the coating and I would never have been surprised if they, one day, appeared in our showroom leaving footprints of oil in their wake.

*****

Sales meetings were held on a Saturday morning and, during one of these, The Managing Director was horrified to learn my knowledge of mechanics could be assessed as a few degrees above zero.

"Good Heavens!" he exploded, "How do you expect to sell tractors if you don't know how they work?"

"I talk to people, show them some pamphlets and let them make up their own minds. They know tractors better than I do. If they are older types I talk about the good old days when we used horses. People know who I am as well as the firm I represent and I have sold a few tractors."

This lack of knowledge appalled The Old Man; consequently, when the Chevrolet utility stripped its terracotta timing gears he seized the opportunity to embark me on a crash course in mechanics.

The firm had purchased H.V. McKay's vacated premises at Bassendean and now had a vast workshop under one roof for all the manufacturing and assembling. The ute was towed out to the workshop and deposited in a work cubicle.

"We're going to replace the big ends as well," he told me, "so get the motor out and strip it down. That's the best way to learn. Hands on under supervision."

The workshop foreman was a German migrant who had been trained in one of those precise engineering firms for which that country is noted. He did his best to provide the 'supervision' bit but he invariably left my workplace with a sorrowful look on his face, shaking his head and muttering in German, not knowing I was familiar with such words as "Sacrament!" and "Dummkopf".

It occurred to me, if I had to dismantle this motor, there was every probability I would eventually have to re-assemble it.

I took the air-cleaner off and placed it on the floor at the front, right-hand corner of the work cubicle. The carburettor was placed next to it and, during the following week, the perimeter of the cubicle became lined with row upon row of the mysterious-looking objects that go to make up a motor.

Meanwhile, The Sales Manager was putting on a bit of a song and dance number. The seeding was finished, the crops were looking good and the whole of the wheatbelt north of Perth was without a sales representative.

My induction into the marvels of the mechanical world was proceeding at a steady pace. I had reached the stage where objects known as pistons and conrods were being extracted from the bowels of the dismembered motor and placed, with reverence, upon the floor next to an impressive thing called a crankshaft when The Sales Manager's demands prevailed.

A mechanic was led into the cubicle and introduced to the chaos I had created.

I left the workshop, bound for the sales department, with the mechanic's accolade ringing throughout the workshop: "You rotten bastard!"

Next morning I was handed the keys to a brand new Holden Model FJ Utility.

A great deal of respect for The Old Man grew out of this episode. He didn't deride my lack of knowledge and he didn't sack me because I was unsuitable for the job. He did his best to bring me up to the standard required at considerable expense to the firm.

It was unfortunate the outside influences won the day otherwise I may have become quite a good mechanic. Motors seemed to be such interesting things.

*****

The house building had progressed to the stage where the kitchen, the toilet, the laundry and a room were functional.

I came home one Friday evening to find Eileen and the two girls had moved into this half-completed house.

"But the house is only half finished! You can't do this sort of thing!"

"I've done it. I'm not going to have our two girls live another winter in that shed."

"What are you going to tell the building inspector when he calls?"

"He's been."

"So?"

"So I made him a cup of tea."

The Vikings, it seemed, had landed on Hastings Beach.

*****

The house was eventually finished.

I arrived home very late one night after a long drive. The place was in darkness. I let myself in, made a cup of tea, had a shower and climbed into bed.

A dreamy voice enquired, "Is that you, darling?"

"It had bloody well better be!"

*****

I put in a couple of years on the road until the girls commenced school and Eileen found a part-time job.

I went back into the workshop as a welder but found my enthusiasm and interest in this type of work had vanished. The management's enthusiasm and interest in me had, in all probability, also vanished.

Years before I had regularly attended night school and had obtained a certificate in "Management" so, making full use of the doubtful value of this piece of paper, I secured a job as The Service Manager's Clerk at Winterbottom Tractors Ltd.

The main office was in an old, well-constructed house standing on the edge of the highway at Redcliffe. It was a romantic place with large rooms, fire-places, brick chimneys and bay windows. The grounds upon which it stood covered several acres and ran back to the perimeter of the airport.

I suggested I make a spare-time project of learning its history just for the record. This suggestion was vetoed by the manager who was a man of high moral standards; a quality which made him a good bloke but he wanted nothing to do with the building's history.

Nevertheless, I made a few enquiries and, to the best of my

knowledge, a brief resume is like this: The house was one of Padbury's buildings and he ran sheep on the extensive area behind it. When The Americans came into the war they established an air force base on the paddocks which became the present site of Perth Airport. I don't know if the house had tenants at the time (it was rumoured to be a brothel at one stage) but the building was commandeered as The Officer's Mess for The American Air Force Personnel and, in keeping with the times, its reputation became rather awesome.

No one seemed to recall the deaths, the horror, the destruction or emotional stresses of The Americans who flew B29 Bombers out from the airstrip behind the building. People only remembered the scandals created by men who lived while knowing they could be dead tomorrow.

The firm built a big glass-fronted showroom right around the house. The romantic, old building can't be seen from the highway nowadays but the glass-fronted showroom is most impressive.

We worked five days a week so I suggested I spend Saturday mornings cleaning the windows; a little job lasting many years and continued for some time after I had left the firm.

Another firm, immediately adjacent, asked me to clean its windows. I was doing this for several weeks before they asked me to clean their offices, also.

Life was all go! I was doing clerical work all day, followed by night school then office cleaning up to 11pm five nights a week.

Actually, I didn't leave Winterbottom Tractors – I was pushed. There was none of the much-needed Job Training as suggested in the night school course on "Management". The firm was governed by a head office which, in turn, was governed by accountants who had obviously all failed in the subject of "Public Relations" or "Staff Job Training". They had decided I was not necessary (probably a correct decision) and The Service Manager was obliged to request me to seek employment elsewhere.

Things fell into place. I ran the office of a small engineering firm for the next six years and did everything from timekeeping to job costing.

Time, moving ever onwards, continued to present dark patches and bright moments in the tapestry of existence.

My old mate, Benno, had been working for The Public Works Department in New Guinea for quite some years now. Every two years he, my sister Patricia and their two boys arrived in Perth on furlough.

My nephew Garry finished his apprenticeship at The Midland Workshops and went to live in Melbourne and his sister, Dee, had married.

My sister Joyce, who was my life-long companion, developed cancer and passed away.

The firm I worked for was purchased, along with several other firms of similar industry, by a group of English investors who assembled them all in a new factory at Kewdale and sold off the unwanted properties.

I was discarded along with the unwanted properties.

I was fed up with being pushed around so I gathered up all my trade papers, work records etc and went to an employment agency.

"Here's my papers. Find me a job."

Life is funny that way. Within an hour I was employed as Storeman by Henderson Instrument Company in Subiaco and, within six months, became its Purchasing and Despatch Clerk. It turned out to be a good, challenging job and I eventually had my own office with two typists as part of the team.

I settled into this job and, for the next ten years, caught the same train each morning, walked slowly through the park to work, sat in my office chair all day, walked slowly through the park to catch the same train at the end of the day and arrived home at the same time.

Eileen and I had raised two daughters. They were now married. We had two grandchildren. Everything was under control but I was simply plodding along Life's Highway without raising too much dust.

I was also putting on weight and developing a nice pot tummy when a mad, long-distance runner came to work for the firm.

He wanted to put a 'firm's team' in the next City-to-Surf Fun Run so half a dozen of us agreed to give it a bit of a go.

Life has never been quite the same since that decision.

Every evening, after work, he would have us huffing and puffing around Kings Park. This went on for weeks and gradually it dawned on me that I was no longer huffing and puffing; in fact, I was beginning to look forward to the afternoon jog.

Our team assembled with thousands of other runners in the city on the day and headed for the coast twelve kilometres away.

It was an exhilarating experience jogging along surrounded by other runners, hearing people shouting encouragement from the footpaths and occasionally waving to people I knew.

I was 57 years of age and I ran 12 Kilometres in just under an hour!

Without me being aware of it – a whole new phase opened up within my life!

Chapter Twenty-Six

The next year, under the influence of John Maddison The Mad Runner, I joined The W.A. Veteran Athletes Association as well as The W.A. Marathon Club and settled into some serious running.

The word 'serious' is perhaps a little inappropriate. If a man takes to running at 57 years of age he shouldn't kid himself and become too serious. He will never be a world champion but that doesn't stop him from thinking like one and doing his best.

The Marathon Club conducts the City of Perth Marathon annually and, on this particular day, I was acting as a course steward about half a kilometre from the finish. The job was simply to shepherd runners across the road and see they weren't clobbered by motorists. I was about to leave the post when, around the river's edge, came a lone runner. Surely the last of hundreds who had left The Esplanade five hours ago. He approached slowly, walking some of the way, and obviously exhausted. His mature years became apparent as he drew nearer.

"Come on!" I encouraged. "You're looking good. Only half a kilometre to go. Come on. I'll run it with you!"

He perked up and we ran along The Esplanade past The Rowing Club's shed. I looked around. He had dropped behind and was walking again; I waited until he had caught up.

"Just a little walk," he commented. "Mustn't do anything silly at my age."

"How old are you?"

"Sixty four."

Oh; magnificent man! I felt proud just to be running beside him. We crossed the road and commenced the last few hundred metres in Langley Park. As we rounded the sweeping semi-circle leading to the finish I peeled off and left him to face the photographers and the glory of finishing The Marathon.

Perchance it was this moment that made me commence to contemplate the marathon. I had been running some three years now and I knew people who run a marathon. It was always there – waiting and challenging.

42.2 kilometres is a long way.

The next one was twelve months away and I would need that time to improve and bring myself up to the necessary physical condition.

John instinctively knew. I never mentioned it to him but it gradually dawned on me that he referred to the marathon and I in the most casual manner, as though my participation was all within the natural course of events.

Numerous club events took place between June and December and I met with some success in these. First in my age group in the Cross Country Championships at Jorgenson Park in Kalamunda. Actually, this was a bit of a pushover because I was the only one in my age group but I clipped 10 minutes off the time taken for the same event the previous year. This statement, too, is a bit misleading. I had just been running for only a few years and a man's physical condition improves immensely during that period. Consequently, his reduction in times for events run 12 months ago becomes quite dramatic.

Andy moved into the same age group as me and we regularly battled it out around Jorgenson Park.

The trouble is, with Andy, he always got well ahead right at the beginning simply because he goes out so fast; but this is a race of attrition and the plan, on this day, was to let him burn himself up for two laps then gradually overtake and pass him in the final three kilometres.

He was 100 metres ahead and climbing the upward slope as I pounded down the forward gradient towards the first creek in the last lap; a narrow grass-covered watercourse that could be jumped if lined up correctly.

A heaving push-off from knee-high grass towards more knee-high grass a metre and a half away.

Made it! Now; where is he?

He was at the top of the slope but floundering as he set off down the track towards the second creek. I knew he was floundering because when he is tired he sways from side to side as though his leading leg is going to fold under him.

"Now, take this hill easy," I told myself as I set out after him. "Keep within your aerobics and you'll have more speed on the downward slope."

The gravel downhill track was dangerous with ironstone knobs protruding along a course lined with spiked bushes imparting a sadistic pleasure as I brushed them away from my face.

Pain! Everything was pain!

My lungs hurt, my shoulders ached and my legs protested at every jarring thud of my weary feet.

Andy was fifty metres ahead, plowing along the track, thrusting bushes aside as he turned towards the creek crossing at the bottom of the valley; a twenty metre slop through ankle-deep mud made sloppier by hundreds of running shoes.

Andy's breath was accompanied by a distressful moan every time he exhaled. I could hear it from ten metres behind as we climbed and staggered up the valley side.

Over the top and downward to the next sloppy stretch then up again to the gravelled pathway.

"Sit behind him," my mind told my body. "He'll extend himself and, at the top, you'll catch him! But keep nudging him!"

It worked!

I caught him at the top and, breathing easily, I ran for about half a kilometre beside this swaying, groaning, gasping staggerer.

It all tied in with the book on Running Psychology which I had been reading:-

"If your ability is similar to the other competitor let him exert himself and get about fifty metres or so ahead then gradually reduce the lead. This is demoralising.

Keep behind him on the upward slopes and he will extend himself to his maximum effort. When you catch him at the top, run beside him breathing easy. Such an action imparts a negative response. Nothing is more shattering than to be passed by an easy-running competitor when you have extended yourself to the limit."

Over the last three quarters of a kilometre I increased the pace by compelling my rubber-like legs to flop my feet forward at a rate quicker than Andy could compel his panting, palpitating, protesting body to produce.

I gradually drew away to a twenty metre lead.

A slight upward slope of a hundred metres then fifty metres to the finish line.

I had just commenced that fifty metres when I heard a noise reminding me of the horrendous rhinoceros charging John Wayne in "Hatari". The rock-studded earth shook with the pounding! The serenity of the environment was shattered by spasmodic, bellowing gasps hurled forth from pain-encrusted lungs as Andy staggered past roaring and waving his arms in a most haphazard manner with every roll of his body.

'As who pursues with yell and blow,

Still treads the shadow of his foe

And forward bends his head!'

The trouble is, with Andy, he hasn't read any books on Running Psychology.

I commenced serious marathon training whilst on holidays in February by jogging 10 to 12 kilometres five days a week to toughen up. During the following months I ran early in the morning, in rain, in heat, in cold. The hardest step in training is the one out the front door – and to make that step, day after day, night after night, for months on end requires self discipline.

Self-discipline is a quality to be developed and nurtured for without it you are not going to force your body to train and you are not going to finish. Developing this quality is as important as developing your physical capabilities.

My body became divided into two components; my mind and my physical self with my mind predominating.

My mind completely ignored the hour of the day and the weather. It subjected my physical self to a demanding schedule of kilometres, time checks, speed workouts, exercises and discipline.

Discipline in kilometres per week that had to be increased each week.

Discipline in times to cover kilometres.

Discipline in carriage, foot action, breathing.

Discipline in stimulation and a burning desire to conquer this marathon looming ahead.

Gradually things began to fit into place. I could now cover longer distances faster without my heart pounding or my lungs gasping because my legs had developed sufficiently to carry me without placing stress on my aerobics. Four weeks prior to the marathon I was running 18 kilometres three nights a week as well as 10 kilometres twice a week and enjoying every bonus of such an activity.

Some nights were cold and wet. The long, straight stretches of highways became very lonely and I asked myself: "Is it worth it?" and I had no answer. Other times I would see the dawn of a new day, watch the sunlight climb across the rooftops then reach down to touch the dew-soaked grass; or run when the moon was full and the air was crisp, thereby promoting a feeling of wondrous joy and a sense of oneness with the universe. Forgotten were the wasted teenage years when there were no jobs to be had; forgotten were the years in the prison camps, forgotten was the struggle to raise a family and gone were the daily problems.

I live! I am ready to run a marathon! I wanted to dance along the streets and shout, "Rejoice! The Lord is My Shepherd!"

I felt I could put my foot on the starting line, face the awesome demands of running a marathon in 3 hours 50 minutes, and say, "I'm here!"

Is it worth it?

Langley Park was all hustle and bustle with over 600 runners bunching up on the roadway waiting for the starter's gun, the sprightly steps of the first few kilometres, the stimulating view of runners stretching from the brewery around the edge of the water to back beyond The Narrows Bridge, the blue of the sky, The River Swan in placid, reflective mood, The City of Perth in the background, – my city – my country.

Is it worth it?

People manning the drinking points had been asked to dress up and impart a carnival atmosphere.

The first station was manned by my family. There were my two daughters wearing dressing gowns, with curlers in their hair, and displaying a large sign reading, "The things some fathers will do to get their children out of bed in the morning."

My grandchildren were there, too. Not my children but my children's children – part of my Life which has been handed on and will be here when I am gone.

"Come on, Pop," cries No.1 grandson in a deep, adolescent voice. "You can do it!"

Is it worth it?

Crossing over Fremantle Traffic Bridge, doing a sharp turn down to the river's edge, passing a sign which read 'Half Way', knowing I was feeling good, knowing my daughter was leapfrogging my progress in her car simply because I am her dad and knowing I was 5 minutes ahead of my planned schedule.

Is it worth it?

The long hack along Preston Point Road knowing two chaps, who regularly thrash me in club runs, are up ahead and they're aware of my proximity. The gradual whittling down of the distance between, running with them for a few kilometres, then drawing away to later learn they pulled out, exhausted, around the 35km mark.

Is it worth it?

The sharp hill in Kintail Road where I passed men who were walking only to be passed by them when I was walking. No one speaking to the other. Each man locked in his own struggle with the marathon.

Glancing at my watch, as I grabbed a plastic cup of water at the 35km mark, noticing I was 10 minutes ahead of schedule and realising, because of this stupidity, I was beaten!

Oh; the dull ache of that realisation.

I had a retreating feeling of 'letting go' and doubted if I was capable of further effort.

Where does it come from? This gathering up of inner strength which makes a man rise above the smallness of himself?

Perchance it is the mental discipline acquired during training.

Perchance it is the pre-race knowledge that he is going to reach this state of physical and emotional exhaustion.

I do know the mind is no longer running with the body; it takes over and demands the body extend itself to beyond its accepted limits because the spiritual unity which makes the man has dedicated itself to attaining this predetermined goal.

Give up now – and you fail!

The mind started reasoning: 7kms to go and 45 minutes to do it in. That's a little over 6 minutes a kilometre. Come on! You regularly run 20kms at 5 minutes a kilometre. Come on!

I made The Narrows Bridge by combining walking, jogging, staggering and, at one stage, quietly crying.

Walking over The Narrows Bridge I realised Time was running out. I doubted if I was physically capable of finishing, let alone in 3 Hours 50 minutes.

Just past the ramp on the Perth side of the bridge, by the pathway leading through the gardens, was a little sign quoting, "40Km".

Ah well; it was a good try.

Only 12 minutes to go.

12 minutes! Come on! Walk 100 paces! Run 100 paces! Count ten paces for every finger and thumb. Come on! 1-2-3-4-5 – that's it!

By the time I had reached Barrack Street jetties I had increased my jog to 400 paces without walking.

"Dad! You all right?" It was my daughter's voice.

"Yeah. I'm O.K."

A deep, adolescent voice sounded in my ear. "Come on, Pop. You can do it. I'll run the rest of the way with you. We'll make it!"

"You bet we will, mate."

We did!

I rounded the sweeping, flag-bedecked curve in Langley Park with a blurred vision of friends and colleagues leaning over the ropes and calling my name, the P.A. system announcing the arrival of the oldest person in the race and the big, digital clock displaying figures reading 3 hours 49 minutes and 30 seconds!

Success requires no apologies and failure permits no alibis!

I walked the streets of Perth for weeks after, knowing I was not an ordinary run-of-the-mill person. I had run a Marathon and for the rest of my life I shall have the knowledge I had reached for the stars and for one brief moment I held one in my grasp!

Chapter Twenty-Seven

MEMO.
TO   The Office Manager
FROM   The Purchasing and Expediting Clerk.

Sir,

Owing to circumstances beyond my control (e.g. Born 1918) I herewith request permission to retire.

I have, of late, become increasingly aware of the manner in which working for a living is interfering with my:-

(1) Hiking

(2) Camping

(3) Surfing

(4) Kayaking

(5) Household Maintenance & Domestic Commitments

in that order of priority.

Furthermore, in support of this application, I would direct your attention to a tall eucalypt growing in the adjacent street. Each day the afternoon sea breeze rustles through its leaves causing them to twist and glisten in the sunlight and I begin to wonder how many bright, sunny days and afternoon sea breezes are left for me to enjoy points (1) to (5) above.

Assuming this application is granted, and you feel the firm can carry on without me, I would like to terminate my dubious services two months from now.

Meanwhile I remain your appreciative employee

Kind Regards,

Arthur Leggett.

Of course, I didn't have to request permission to retire. I was now 62 years of age. Although, as an Ex-Serviceman, I was entitled to retire at 60 it didn't appeal to me. I had a good job that I seemed to handle to my satisfaction and I enjoyed the company of the other staff members.

Owing to the manner in which I had flitted from one job to another during my working life I would be retiring on a week's wages and month's holiday pay so the need for money, no doubt, had its influence but I thought it was time to face up to the future.

My request to retire was granted with jocular alacrity.

The Sales Manager, at the end of my final day, invited me to have a few beers with him at the nearby pub. He became quite sentimental during the 'few beers' that, somehow, developed into a bit of a session and he invited me to be his guest at the adjacent cafe for an evening meal.

I was now retired and living on a pension so I reckoned a free feed was acceptable at any time.

We entered the cafe to find it packed with the firm's staff. It was a delightful meal with the usual standard speeches and I was presented with a very nice Seiko Watch with buttons sticking out around its outside perimeter.

"Just what you need for training," asserted The Sales Manager. "You can use it as a stop watch. It will tell you a whole whack of information once you get the hang of it."

I hadn't the heart to tell the staff I don't wear glasses when I go running and I couldn't see the figures on this beaut, bonza, digital watch.

Nevertheless, it is still one of my prize possessions and I wear it on all official occasions.

So, I retired.

The first six months was a miserable period.

For the first time in my life I was no longer committed to be in a certain place at a definite time. I was no longer contributing to anything and I felt as though I was no longer necessary and the uncertainty of the future years worried me.

Nowadays I am aware this emotional turmoil was completely unfounded and the stress it caused was unnecessary.

A child is under the influence of teachers throughout his schooldays; he leaves school to commence earning a living and is under the authority of the foreman, the accountant or the sales manager; he joins the army in times of national crisis and is immediately subject to discipline and the rigours of the army; the next forty years or so he is occupied in marriage, a family, a mortgage and running a motor car.

Then, suddenly, the mortgage is paid, the kids have left home and the car has never run better.

It was easy, at this stage, to feel I was no longer necessary.

Most of the 'domestic commitments' had been attended to within three months. I didn't have a 'too hard basket' anymore so the difficult jobs had been consigned to a mental compartment labelled 'maybe later'.

I owned a VW Kombi Camper at the time and distant horizons beckoned. I loaded the vehicle on to The India Pacific and booked a 2nd Class sleeper to Adelaide.

Eileen declined to accompany me on this venture, claiming VW Kombis didn't have an en suite and she had reached the stage in life where she preferred some comfort on her holidays.

I drove around The Coast Road to Melbourne to stay a week with my nephew Garry and Marie then made my way up to Manly for a few days before driving to Newcastle to visit "The Girls".

Three months later I was back in Perth.

Hinco Engineering phoned. "The chap who took your job is leaving. Can you give us a hand for a week or so?"

Two years passed before I decided to give retirement another go – a pleasant two years despite the fact that my former typist had been my boss.

However, my relationship with "the old firm" carried on for the next ten years by doing odd jobs and standing in for people on holidays.

I settled into retirement, mainly because I didn't have much option. I secured odd jobs here and there and generally managed to live a buoyant life for several more years.

One of the factors leading to retirement is the accumulation of years or, in other words, the passage of time; and the passage of time can bring about unexpected emotional shocks and upheavals compelling you to re-adjust your life and to reshape your thinking about the future.

I had a mate named Ernie who was a Supervisor in The State Energy Commission. We had been knocking around together for over thirty years. He and I, with our wives, had trailed caravans from Perth to Cairns; had been on a ship's cruise to Singapore, Jakarta, Bangkok and Bali; pulled caravans up to Broome; spent weeks at Mandurah crabbing and fishing from his launch and sitting around an open hearth fire at night devouring the spoils and enjoying a few beers.

We had great plans for the future but he died of cancer before he reached retirement age.

Johnnie was another mate. He joined the army at the outbreak of

The 1939-45 War, was sent north and captured on Ambon.

He had been starved, bashed, abused and generally treated like a mongrel dog in the manner Japanese treated their prisoners of war.

Consequently, he was always going to die but, by 1984, he hadn't actually got around to it.

Many years before this date he had won a half gallon bottle of Johnnie Walker Whisky in a raffle. This bottle, complete with its cradle, was solemnly placed on his mantelpiece with the comment: "When I go you can drink this at my wake."

Several more years passed and the bottle began to gather dust until Johnnie decided, "I think we had better give this a bit of a nudge."

We had an uproarious Wake but only drank half the bottle which, during the course of the following year, was topped up with more Johnnie Walker.

The hectic Wakes were repeated every year until, in February, 1989, Johnnie collapsed and died of a heart attack two days after his fifth Wake.

The loss of these mates, along with Ivan Francis, was a facet of retirement I had never even contemplated. Its abrupt appearance on "The Stage of Life" created a shock that took many years to overcome.

Quite a few long-cherished, former Army mates were also slipping away and, after many days of sitting in the sand-hills and watching the sun go down below the sea, I became philosophical and decided we are all granted so many days to live; some are granted more than others and those who remain behind have to continue living and to make good use of the days they have left.

Yet, within a few months, another miserable event occurred which challenged the serenity of this philosophy.

My Mum, who lived in a Granny Flat attached to my sister Pat's residence, had developed a non-malignant cyst on her bottom lip. It had to be cut out. This minor operation was successfully carried out at Hollywood Hospital and Mum was home again within a few days.

Her health, however, started to deteriorate some three months later. She lost all desire to eat and took practically no nourishment for weeks. The doctor diagnosed that her medication was having a dehydrating effect. He also recommended she return to Hollywood Hospital to be taken off her medication and generally checked over.

Mum was placed in a ward full of elderly ladies. Some of these ladies went days, sometimes even weeks, without any visitors but Mum's friends, her children, her grandchildren and great-grandchildren swarmed through the place in a manner described by the ward doctor as 'most impressive'.

Whilst Mum was mentally bright, and her spirit was high, she wasn't physically improving. Eventually we were told her kidneys were functioning "very poorly" and the staff could do no more for her except give her fluids and whatever food she fancied. She obviously had a strong family around her and, if we wished, she could go home.

Mum wanted to go home and Pat, also, wanted her home so she went back to the granny flat.

My elder sister, Ida, flew over from New South Wales. She was a nursing sister and her presence was most opportune. But my Mum was slowly dying.

*****

I was having some hamstring problems and, on numerous occasions, rode my pushbike to the Sunday morning meetings of The Veteran Athletics Association.

A character by the name of Fred Hagger sidles up to me one morning. It seems he had entered himself as the bike rider in a three-man triathlon team within the age group of 65-70. Unfortunately he had developed a bit of an angina problem and his doctor advised against participating in the event.

"But," says Fred, "I told the other two not to worry because you would do it for me."

"Me?"

"Well, you ride your bike to our meetings and I reckoned you could do it."

"But I've never been in anything like a triathlon. Besides, my bike is built like a draft horse. I couldn't push it in a triathlon."

"Take mine! It's a brand new racing bike! Hardly ever been used! Here, when you get home phone this bloke. He's waiting to hear from you."

When I arrived home I phoned 'this bloke'. He didn't think he had heard of me. No; he didn't think he had ever heard of Fred Hagger – unless he was the chap who was going to ride the pushbike.

By the time this short telephone conversation was over I was the cycling member of a three-man team within the age group of 65-70 years. The team was called 'The Jerry Hat Tricks'.

I had never met the other members but I was determined not to let the team down. I found out the location of the cycling course and trained diligently in this area during the few weeks preceding the event and gradually whittled my time down over the distance.

The day came. Quite a large crowd had gathered at the South Perth end of The Narrows Bridge where I managed to fossick out Bruce and Peter within the mob. Bruce was a well known surf lifesaver and an accomplished swimmer and, judging by the build of Peter, a 6km run was well within his capabilities.

We walked to the South Perth Jetty to see the swimmers start then hurried back to the bridge. Bruce came ashore, we "tagged" and I set off across The Narrows Bridge to swoop around under it to the spiral approach to the footbridge spanning the highway.

I rode the bike up the spiral approach! Something I hadn't been able to do in training!

Dismounting at the end of the footbridge I jogged beside the bike up the steeply ascending pathway on the face of Mt Eliza, arriving at the top with a thumping heart and gasping lungs.

Remounting to circle The Sir John Forrest Memorial I entered

Forrest Drive, engaged top gear and bore off down the hill. Oh Boy! This was living! I had never travelled so fast on a pushbike before! Passing the lakes at the bottom of the park I engaged a much lower gear for the long, uphill climb back to Sir John; a quick swoop around his memorial then another lap around the park

No way was I going to ride the bike down that pathway. I dismounted and, occasionally buckling at the knees, I jogged and walked my way downhill. It was gratifying, as I dismounted, to see other riders just commencing their second lap of the park.

Remounting, I pedalled over the footbridge, down its spiral end, through the foreshore park, over The Narrows Bridge to "tag" Peter who set off on his 6km run. I felt a bit sorry for Peter because the day was becoming warm and the run would be very demanding; but he made it in 37 minutes; a good time under the circumstances.

Our total time for the event was 1 hour 38 minutes. Just one minute outside the state record for our age group!

Oh, that elusive minute! I seem to have been chasing it all my sporting life!

We were the only team in our age group but we received a hearty burst of applause at the prize-giving ceremony where we were each awarded 6 months free membership to a well-known Subiaco Gymnasium

"I could have taken that minute off if I had of been riding," confided Fred.

A man needs a friend like Fred.

*****

The next four days were rugged.

Mum was slowly slipping away. The Silver Chain Nurses called three times a day to attend to her and change the linen supplied by Hollywood Hospital.

I drove out to Padbury on the Sunday evening with the idea of attending to Mum throughout the night and give my sisters a bit of a break.

I made up a bed on the floor of Mum's flat and awoke several times during the night to give her a drink and to talk for a while.

Poor Mum; she knows she is dying and is bewildered by it all.

What can you say to your Mum at a time like this?

I don't know if I was much help. I later learned both Pat and Ida had frequently checked on her during the night while I was soundly sleeping.

Mum's first grandchild, Garry, flew in from Melbourne next morning. A large family group was there to meet him and take him out to Mum's bedside.

Garry has grown to be one of the symbols of unity within our family and this was the spirit which made him take time off work and fly across Australia to be with his "Nanna" just the same as he did for his Mother many years ago.

I was doing all the usual things a man does when he doesn't know what the hell to do with himself. Next morning I went to the Health Studio for a work-out followed by a Sauna and a spa bath and left the place feeling better. I arrived home at the same time as Eileen, Julie-Anne and Stacey returned from tennis. Felt a bit proud seeing one grandmother and two grand-daughters playing tennis together.

I drove to Padbury after lunch. Mum seemed to have slipped further away during the past two days. Pat had the Locum in and he had prescribed some A.P.C. that Mum had managed to keep down; consequently she was sleeping.

Garry had been picked up by his step-parents, Margaret and Colin, and taken for a drive. Apparently he had sat beside Mum's bed all night and watched cowboy movies on T.V.

I arrived home around 6pm in time to receive a phone call from Norm Crook who was in Perth for a few days.

Norm first knocked on my door somewhere around 25 years ago when he had been sent over here by his firm to supervise some construction work on the standard gauge railway. I was a District Commissioner in The Boy Scouts Association at the time and Norm, being a Scoutmaster, was looking for some scouting activity. I promptly made him The Senior Scout Leader of The North Perth (Iona) Scout Troop. He was also engaged to a lass in the eastern states, whom Eileen and I duly met, and they have been our friends ever since.

We invited him for tea the following night.

Next afternoon I attended Hollywood Hospital to ascertain the result of a prostate gland biopsy taken a couple of weeks previously. The result was "all clear" which is about the only bit of good news to come my way for some time.

I arrived home to learn Eileen was with Mum so I phoned Norm Crook and cancelled our arrangement.

Eileen phoned and suggested I go out there after tea. She came home and, while we were having our meal, the phone rang.

It was Garry.

Mum had passed away.

I made my way out to Padbury.

Mum was at peace now. So many of the lines, as well as the drawn look, had gone from her face and she lay there as though asleep. But she wasn't asleep. Her spirit had crossed over into The Great Beyond and was now in the care of The Great Architect of The Universe.

I kissed her forehead and stroked her hair for a few moments; but she wasn't going to open her eyes and give me that tired smile any more.

Farewell, my Mum, farewell.

My brother Syd arrived early next morning and spent a few minutes with Mum.

The funeral director had been advised and his crew arrived around 10am. Ida lent them a hand. Our Mum was placed on a stretcher and taken out through the door she had so often jovially said she would be taken out through.

Syd, Pat and I stood in the adjacent kitchen while this was in progress. A little group huddled together, each struggling desperately with individual emotions as we held each other in a common bond of misery.

Then came the discussion with the mortician. The unhappy tension had eased somewhat by now and we sat around in a circle, on Pat's back verandah, in the sunlight of another morning.

The first day in 99 years without our Mum to see it.

The funeral took place three days later. Dad's grave had been re-opened and we lowered our Mum into the earth with him.

We threw earth on the coffin and walked away.

Chapter Twenty-Eight

The hamstring problem, which had been troubling me for months, seemed to be clearing so I commenced jogging again with the intent of entering The Bunbury Half Marathon in a few weeks time – a rather hare-brained decision because I hadn't been running for many months and a 21:1 km event demands considerable preparation.

I went through all the routine of getting fit and drove my old Kombi Campervan to Bunbury on the Saturday before the event.

The Bunbury Marathon and Half Marathon are popular events in the running calendar and a considerable number of Veteran Athletic Association members drive down there to participate or to lend support. We gather at The Rose Hotel for luncheon on the Saturday whilst Saturday night is usually a case of early to bed in preparation for the next day's event.

Veteran Athletes are divided into age groups of five year segments with winners being acknowledged within each age group but it is just my flaming luck to be in the same club and the same age group as John Gilmore, the undisputed world champion who, on this day, had set his mind on breaking the world half marathon record for 70 year olds.

There is always a bit of humour amongst the veterans concerning this situation. I am nowhere near his capabilities. However, I am about three months older than John so, every five years, I have three months to create new club records for our age group then he turns 70 and blows them to pieces.

The run was to start next day at Hayes Park, a sporting complex of considerable dimensions so I parked my Kombi in the pavilion's parking lot and bedded down for the night wondering what the morrow would bring.

The noises in the surrounding car park awoke me around 5:30am when vehicles from all over the south-west arrived to commence disgorging rowdy individuals dressed in track suits or preparing for a warm-up jog. The volume of noise increased when a convoy of cars arrived from Perth and cheerful greetings were called to and fro across the parked vehicles.

Many of the runners were well known to me so I clambered out of the Kombi to mingle with the thickening crowd. There were the usual handshakes and good wishes sprinkled with some humour thrown in for good measure. Basically, the top runners would be competing to win but the rest of us would be competing against the doubts, strains and emotional stresses which beset a runner over 21kms.

John Gilmore and I were the two oldest runners but I didn't expect to see him during the event unless he sat down and waited for me to come along. However, I did see him before the start and wished him every success in his record attempt.

About 280 runners bunched around the start line and, at the crack of the starter's gun, we were on our way.

My hamstring was still slightly sore but I was determined to ignore it and to complete the event by easy running. Indeed, this was the first half marathon I had ever run without setting myself time targets or splits.

The first kilometres out of the park and around to the oceanfront contained a few hills presenting no problems and helped to get the heart and lungs working. The run along the lengthy, straight oceanfront was quite enjoyable. Runners could be seen stretching all along the road ahead and, I was happy to note, quite a few were stretched out behind me.

The trick here is to control the breathing and settle it down after the hills, otherwise too much energy is expended in panting.

The weather was perfect, the early morning air was stimulating, the ocean was blue, I was running within my capabilities and, by the time I had done the length of the oceanfront, I was beginning to feel lifted beyond the smallness of myself.

The course, at the end of this section, swung left and wound through the town centre for about 5kms before entering another straight stretch then commenced winding around the streets of another suburb.

The course was efficiently marshalled and there was no chance of getting lost but I found running around the streets rather irksome. They were short and, at times, nobody could be seen ahead or behind which gave the impression I was running on my own. The road camber, too, was rather steep and this tended to put a strain on my left leg.

I realised, after the event, these were trivial things and, at 15kms, I was beginning to get tired.

The course entered Promenade Road and I soon wished I was running around the streets again.

Promenade Road is a dual carriageway with a garden strip down the centre. It stretches for kilometres in a straight line going right past the entrance to Hayes Park and beyond to a turn-around point. It seemed endless and I was beginning to fade badly. I swung around the point to head back to Hayes Park, with about a kilometre and a half to go, when I was overtaken by Leo Hassen and Basil Warner running together.

Their pace wasn't much faster than mine so I told them I would try and hang in behind them and boost myself along a bit. This I managed to do for about two-thirds of the distance but it was taking too much out of me so I dropped off. They crossed the line 24 seconds ahead of me.

As I crossed the line, the P.A. system boomed : "And here comes our other 70 year old runner. Give him a big hand!" Very gratifying.

I was then ushered to the microphone for an on-the-spot interview but I was so flat that I'm afraid my main comments were, "You bet",

"Sure thing", "Aw; you know." etc. etc.

I was also informed John had broken The World Record by 9 minutes 57 seconds! His time for the 21.1km was 1hr 21mins 41secs.

I ambled in 33 minutes later, having taken 1hr 54mins 55secs; 7 minutes outside my best time for the same event made two years earlier. Considering the lack of preparation and training, I shouldn't complain and, of course, a man learns something from every run.

I have to exercise more mental control at the start. When I'm mixing with 200 plus runners I get caught up in the euphoria of the moment and go out too fast until the pounding of my heart and the shortness of breath compels me to slow down to walk for a couple of hundred metres. I also need more mental toughness. If I train diligently and correctly I can physically handle these distances but I tend to mentally fade over the last 8kms. But, most importantly, I must hold myself back for the first 10kms. Leo and Basil didn't catch me until the last couple of kilometres yet they are both 15 years younger and consistently run better than me. If I had hung back with them at the beginning I should, theoretically, have had enough around the 19kms to have taken minutes off my time.

Ah well; the world will still carry on tomorrow but, by cripes, I reckon John Gilmore's world record will be standing long after he and I have left the running field.

The following month's club newsletter contained this paragraph. I quote: A special mention to the man who also ran well in The Half Marathon but did not have much of a chance of taking out the M70 Trophy. Arthur Leggett showed that he had a great day. Not many of us can say we were second when a world record was set.

Later in the year I ran The Albany Half Marathon and came home with the trophy for first in The Masters Category and 'The Masters' includes everyone over 60 years.

No; I don't know where John Gilmore was that day.

Running, in a man's senior years, can have its problems. The annual 'City to Surf Run' was coming up and I wanted to run well because No.1 Grandson, who now stood six inches taller than me, had implied this was the year when the old soldier was going to be run into the bitumen.

I was feeling in good shape on the Friday evening before the event when the phone rang. It was my old army mate, Owen, who has a voice sounding somewhat like a vehicle being driven slowly along a gravel driveway.

"Heh, Art!" it announced, "Alan Knee is over 'ere from Melbourne and what's left of The Sig Platoon 'as got to 'ave a few drinks with 'im. The Grosvenor Hotel. 11am termorrer. You be there, eh?"

As I replaced the phone I had a funny feeling this clarion call somehow sounded like the tolling of a distant bell.

Next day, complete with a Leave Pass which read: "Go on and have a couple of beers with your old mates". I assembled with the group from No1 (Signals) Platoon in a cosy corner of this hotel in town.

There was Alan Knee, Andy Mulgrave, Owen Kenrick, Vic Powell, myself and, just to make sure nobody told any lies, Arthur Robinson joined us as well.

It was one of those spontaneous assemblies where oft told episodes are recalled to mind and made to shine like precious gems polished with the magic of comradeship.

Mine Host of the hotel was intrigued with this bunch of bulldusting old blokes whose noisy yarn-spinning increased in volume as "the few drinks" expanded into "another round"; especially when two R.S.L. Members, visiting from Queensland, passed their table on journeys from the front bar to the back room.

Indeed, it was noticed that a nude female form reclining on a bed in a wall picture, at one stage, put her fingers in her ears and turned away.

Approximately 5 hours after assembling for "a few beers with your old mates" this group, which had obviously won the war on its own, rolled out on to the footpath leaving behind a bar full of wrecked and smoking Heinkel Bombers, Stukas, Benelli Motor Bikes, Italian Tanks and Junkers Troop Carriers liberally interspersed with barbed wire and Red Cross Food Parcels.

The T.V. News announced, on the Sunday evening, "3500 fit and healthy people lined up for The Annual City to Surf Fun Run" but I knew damn well there was only 3499 fit and healthy people there.

Oh; I ran the distance all right! 6 Divvy and all that sort of stuff. Besides, I had probably mentioned the event many times during the previous day's session, but during the 12km run there were several occasions when I had to peel off from the field to engage in a life and death struggle with a bad bout of "Brewer's Asthma".

After the event an indignant No1 Grandson loomed up. "I was trotting along slowly waiting for you to catch up and I didn't see you go past in the crowd. By Cripes! That's the last time! You wait until next year!"

Next year, I reckoned, if that telephone rings ...

Running, like all sports, is something you can get "hooked" on.

Mary Robinson and I were training for some event, which I have long since forgotten, and part of the routine was early morning jogs commencing just before sunrise three times a week. I wasn't wrapped in this idea but Mary said she felt safer when running in the early morning if she had someone with her. So, I got out my white horse and shining armour and galloped over to her place for escort duties.

That is how people get hooked on running:- A 'personal best' as a target, a running companion (preferably female), the mist slowly rising off the river, the sun gradually painting the treetops, the cycle path free of traffic, the air unpolluted and crisp. Shangri-la!

Mary mentioned, during one of these jogs, she had sent in her application to be in a hike down The Bibbulmun Track.

The Bibbulmun Track, in those days, was a 680 kilometre bush track stretching from the outer suburb of Kalamunda to Walpole. It had originally been laid out by The Department of Conservation and Land Management and the Department was organising this hike to commemorate the tenth anniversary of the track's formation.

Somehow I forgot all about the 780 kilometre march across Europe back in 1945. My application was mailed the next day.

The walk was still two months away thereby allowing time for preparation. I purchased a pair of work boots for $50 and proceeded to break them in by the simple process of getting out of bed early, putting on clothing, including boots, and walking for an hour instead of jogging. I was amazed at the difference in muscular action. I could run for miles in a pair of running shoes but to walk for an hour wearing heavy boots was physically demanding. I also purchased a two-man tent, a sleeping bag and a small backpack. My other personal gear was in a small suitcase.

The Department Of Conservation and Land Management had been working on this hike for some time. A contract had been let to a firm specialising in outdoor activities to supply transport and catering. The idea was for a bus to set up a cookhouse several days ahead. The bus was to pick us up at the end of a day, transport us to the campsite then, next morning, take us back to the spot where we had finished on the previous day. The contractor also had to provide a hot evening meal as well as breakfast and a cut lunch. When the campsite was eventually passed the bus struck camp and set up another site further ahead.

A splendid arrangement except for a few unexpected hitches. The contractor let the contract out to a sub-contractor equipped with a sub-standard bus and a sub-standard cook. Indeed, we never worked out if the cook got the job because he had some idea of how to drive a bus or whether some character got the job of bus driver because he had an elementary knowledge of how to cook. It was on this hike that I had my first meal of cold, burnt porridge for breakfast and I still don't know how he did it!

However, the arrangement itself was a good one. Our tents and personal gear were transported on the bus and all we had to carry was our cut lunch, water and wet gear.

Fred Hagger wasn't going on the hike so he volunteered to drive Mary and I to the starting point at Kalamunda where quite a crowd had assembled. A core of 35 hikers was going all the way but the total number would vary as the walk progressed.

Hikers could join or leave, depending upon the time they had available. Mary had taken her annual holidays in order to participate whereas I, being retired, don't get annual holidays but I went along anyway.

John Maddison appeared from amidst the crowd to wish us good hiking and we milled around amongst the walkers and well-wishers before the formal part of the farewell began. The bus arrived and was loaded with our kit bags, duffel bags, tents etc. and cut lunches were distributed.

The Minister for Sport and Recreation was there to make a short speech and to send us off. I admire this man. He lost both legs in Vietnam and returned to become a Member of Parliament and is very active in his job. He conveyed, in his address, a message from Ken Colbung, one of The Elders of The Bibbulmun Aboriginals who had asked The Minister to hand the hikers an Aboriginal Message Stick to present to The Shire of Manjimup when the hike ended at Walpole.

`I understand that Aboriginals, when travelling "inter-tribe" in the early days, carried a similar stick as a passport from one tribal leader to the others and ensured the safety of the traveller. The title "stick" is perhaps incorrect because the passport was about 4 inches long and notched with the appropriate carvings. It was entrusted to the care of Jim Freeman, an experienced bush-walker who, for reasons unknown to me at the time, bore the horrendous nickname of "The Mad Axeman".

So, 35 strangers commenced a venture that was to keep them in close contact with each other for a month.

The first few kilometres were hard going. The track was single file and scrambled over some rocks and rather steep climbs. We paused at 5kms to allow the back people to catch up before proceeding on to lunch at Mt Gungin. The weather was overcast and very humid whilst the hilly terrain showed that some of us are not in top physical condition but I know, from army experience, they will get tougher and improve as the hike progresses.

We only covered 19kms on the first day. The bus picked us up and took us to Pickering Brook Community Hall. This was a good spot to be at the end of our first day. The hall was a large, well-lit building with a kitchen, hot showers and heaters. Conditions were not too bad and the place soon resembled an army barracks as people began to spread bedding and arrange themselves to settle down for the night. I'm not very happy with this arrangement because I know some people stay up late and keep others awake whilst others get up exceptionally early and wake everyone else. No matter how shrewdly I survey the layout prior to grabbing a position, my sleeping spot is usually close to the door and people going to the toilet during the night stamp to and fro. I prefer to pitch my tent but the important thing, at this stage, was to get to know people so I laid my gear out with everyone else.

We had only been on the track one day but personalities were already becoming apparent. Jim and Mavis Freeman, who were obviously experienced hikers, had moved to the far side of the hall and made themselves comfortable; Brian Smith was attaching plaster to Don Champion's blistered feet and they were becoming known as Father Brian and Brother Don. Rod Brooks, a brickie by trade, is big, round and beginning to have trouble where his legs rub together high on the inner thigh and the skin is beginning to wear away; Geoff White, built as solid as a brick wall and British to the core, is obviously no mug when it comes to hiking; Walter Reeve beds down early and isolates himself from all that is going on around him; another chap named Peter whistles the opening bars of "Sir Joseph's Barge" from Gilbert and Sullivan's "H.M.S. Pinafore" over and over again; several women are in their sixties and appear to be quite strong walkers; and I wonder how I appear to the rest. Both Don Champion and I are in our seventies so I assume someone has already dubbed us as "the old blokes".

The hall was very noisy until around 9:30pm when everyone settled down.

So ended our first day.

The second day was a tough 30kms containing many steep, energy-sapping inclines beneath an overcast sky. Drew Griffiths, one of CALM's organisers, had preceded us to Mt Dale and had the billy boiling when we arrived. The hot drink was welcome because, whilst having lunch, rain commenced to fall heavily. Multi-coloured plastic blossomed forth from backpacks to drape itself over now upright human frames to create a colourful scene within the drabness of the green bush and drumming rain.

Umbrellas of many hues also appeared. I had never thought of bringing an umbrella yet they are commonsense equipment when bush-walking in winter. I wore a plastic ex-army poncho that covered the upper part of my body, including my pack, whilst a pair of waterproof pants protected my legs. This regalia proved quite efficient as heavy rain fell all the afternoon yet I remained quite dry.

We crowded into the bus at the end of the day's hike to be transported back to Pickering Brook Hall. The place soon resembled an Advanced Dressing Station adjacent to a battlefield.

Rod Brooks was in a bad way. The skin had completely worn away leaving big areas of raw flesh on his inner thighs; yet he was determined to continue. His situation didn't look too good until someone had a brilliant idea. He was transported back to Armadale where he purchased two pairs of black cycling pants and the friction problem was eliminated.

"She'll be right," maintained Rod, "only got the holes in my feet to worry about now." – a common problem, judging by the number of Band Aid wrappings in the rubbish bin.

Continuous mention of the wet weather could generate into monotonous reading so allow me to mention that the walk took thirty days and rain fell, oft times heavily, on twenty five of those days. This, coupled with a cold September wind, tended to make the open-air life a little less glamorous than the brochure.

However, the rain, and its attendant inconveniences, helped us to coalesce into groups of firm friends and, twelve years later, a group of us meet every fortnight for an early morning hike around the environs of Perth, followed by a communal breakfast in a convenient café.

The end of Day 2 found us pitching tents in the rain at Manjadel Boy Scouts Camp thanks to the courtesy of Brian Court, The State Secretary, who pulled a few strings on our behalf. Hot showers were available in a mobile shower unit. The womenfolk took possession of the showers first, leaving mere males standing in a queue outside in the rain. When the feminine numbers dwindled the males barged in and took possession until ousted by more ladies waiting outside in the rain.

The cook-bus-driver-stew-burner was having a bad time, too, in a makeshift canvas cookhouse that flapped and billowed in the squalls of rain-bearing wind.

Furthermore, the tents were hard to peg down efficiently in the rain-soaked earth. They squelched when we dived into them to make ourselves as comfortable as possible for the night.

Not exactly a happy day.

We hiked 16kms the next day and, upon returning to the campsite, we packed everything into the bus and set off for Dwellingup.

Rain fell heavily during the drive and problems were developing in the over-loaded bus which obviously wasn't developing full power. A following VW Kombi, at one stage, roared up beside the driver and signalled him to stop. A fan belt had snapped and hurled itself across the road. The Diesel engine had several fan belts so this wasn't a serious problem and we kept going. Later the oil and fuel gauges showed zero; a loose wire this time. But the engine wasn't running well at all and we limped into Dwellingup rather late in the day.

The engine was diagnosed as having a burnt valve. The head would have to come off and a new valve ground to fit. This was done during the next three days which brings me back to my original query concerning the cook's real trade.

The bus, too, presented more than just one problem – it was antiquated and licensed to carry 42 passengers; when carrying this number it also carried their kitbags and tents equal to another 30 people in weight plus the cooking gear and tables. The suspension wasn't too good either, and the bus leant outwards when going around bends and, during today's ride, there were quite a few of them on a very wet, winding road.

I hoped it would gradually sink into the wet gravel where it was parked and eventually disappear.

Dwellingup is a small town with a long established timber milling history. We were based here for several days and made ourselves as comfortable as hikers can hope to be. The discomfort of the ceaseless rain was offset by the locality of our campsite on the local football field where a cookhouse, hot showers and brick toilets were available. Immediately adjacent to the football field is a big circular gazebo made with big timber by people who think big – timber-wise that is. The uprights are tree-trunks, the high-pitched roof is supported by massive wooden beams and, in the centre, a large round fireplace burned continuously for three days. Clothes lines were soon strung between posts and washing was hung all over the place; the variety in garments of different hues, shapes and quality making a most intriguing and colourful scene.

There is no Laundromat in the town but The Mad Axeman had friends living nearby who lent us a couple of washing machines as well as a spin drier, thereby considerably speeding up the washing routine.

I was amazed for the remainder of the trek at the amount of washing the womenfolk found to do whenever we stopped at a campsite for more than one night. It was endless. However, I must acknowledge, most of them were experienced bushwalkers and this was one way of ensuring clean clothes were always available even if they were slightly wet. But clothes lines were strung wherever there was a sheltered spot and the possibility of being decapitated when moving around at night was a real danger.

We returned to the camp at the end of one day to find Jim Freeman's friends had cooked us a massive batch of scones, as well as a damper, which we promptly scoffed with jam and hot mugs of tea whilst drying ourselves around the fire.

My tent, sleeping bag and washed clothing had dried so Life was beginning to look brighter despite the inclement weather. My leg muscles ache and I am not sure if it is rheumatics or tiredness. Anyway, it will eventually clear up one way or another.

We usually arrived back at the campsite, purely by coincidence, just as the local hotel commences its "Happy Hour" and, after a while, I find I don't feel pain anymore.

On Saturday 23rd September, 1989, we moved on to our next base camp at Harvey Primary School. This was during school holidays and we occupied the big, newly-completed assembly hall. Once again we were billeted in "barrack-room" conditions but, somehow, this time they were welcome. The building was spacious with a new kitchen, electric light, central heating, carpeted floor, hot showers and, immediately adjacent, was a large sheltered area where, after seven days of continuous rain, we could dry our tents.

The hikers were becoming better acquainted and small groups were gradually forming into friendly, co-operative colleagues as the trek progressed.

Eileen was holidaying with our daughter, Susan, in Albany so I phoned her just to let her know I was still alive. I also phoned our other daughter, Maureen, in Perth with more or less the same message.

We hiked for two days using Harvey School as a base camp. This meant being ready to go and on the bus by 7am followed by a fifty-minute drive to yesterday's finishing point. We had agreed to walk the first hour in silence in order to hear any birdcalls or other sounds of forest life. I appreciated the silence but the birds obviously sensed our intrusion and refused to entertain us with songs of joy.

However, the wind pushing its way through the treetops thirty metres above our heads created its own peculiar type of music.

Next day was hustle and bustle. Out of bed by 5:30am to strike our tents and load our personal gear on to the bus.

Breakfast was ready by the time this routine was completed. Breakfast usually consisted of porridge (Where would the cook be without porridge?) or cornflakes followed by a fried egg and bread. My stomach had long ago made it clear that any fatty food first thing in the morning was not to be classified as "food" so I had a plate of cornflakes followed by another plate of cornflakes on the assumption that the flakes were untouched by human hand.

The cookhouse was dismantled and loaded on to the bus.

We clambered into the vehicle and this overloaded piece of antiquated machinery lurched, rolled and roared its way to our "debussing" point before disappearing through the bush on its way to our next base camp near Collie.

Today's walk commenced as a pleasant one with beautiful scenery. We skirted around the edge of Stirling Dam with the sun glistening on the water and the wind blowing through the treetops but, because of the volume of water flowing, we were unable to cross over the spillway. We clambered down a track beside the roaring water and considerable forward scouting was required before a log was discovered laying across the spillway where it commences to become The Harvey River.

Crossing this slippery, moss-covered log spanning the turbulent spillway required a sense of balance and courage. Brian Smith commented that several of the ladies were over sixty and the manner in which they accepted the dangers of the situation was most commendable.

I don't know about the ladies but I was scared stiff all the way!

Our problems were not yet over. Once across the log we had to climb an exceedingly steep and very long, grass-covered slope in order to regain the correct track. This slope was no walk; it was climbing all the way up and required numerous rests on the way. This was our first really exhausting and physically demanding situation; the co-operation and teamwork that blossomed augered good for the remainder of the walk.

We hiked 26kms that day before being picked up and taken to Wallsend Trotting Ground on the outskirts of Collie. We pitched our tents in pouring rain. Although facilities were installed in the adjacent buildings there were no hot showers, nor electric lights in the toilets. The food, which always seemed to vary from crook to bloody awful, was served around 8pm and generally classified as being in the latter category.

Next day we were taken back down the track and walked into Collie. Someone had had a yarn with the cook/bus driver. The food was better. Hot showers were available and electric lights were shining in the toilets.

Next day was a 'rest day' and I awoke in due course.

Collie was our base camp for several days and things just happened. Rain fell copiously all through the rest day. I was woken by the sounds of two trotters being exercised on the track adjacent to my tent. Mary Robinson and I gathered our washing and made our way to the town's Laundromat where fifty percent of the hikers were gathered. We also did shopping to purchase some of the essentials for hiking; such as chocolates, biscuits and plasters.

The proprietor of a sports store, where we called for plasters, presented us with a Lions Christmas Cake as a gesture of goodwill; Brian Smith, who lost a filling in a tooth several days ago, had the filling replaced free of charge by the local dentist as a gesture of goodwill and I met up with my old army mate, Chris Blackford, who invited Mary and I to his place for dinner as a gesture of friendship.

Rain fell heavily all day. I dug a trench around my tent – pitched on slightly sloping ground below an embankment – a shrewd move because the trench filled with water and drained it away for the rest of the stay in Collie.

Chris picked us up at around 5:30pm and took us to his place. What a delightful evening it turned out to be after all the rough conditions we had been experiencing!

His wife, Mavis, had cooked a mouth-watering meal of roast mutton, baked potatoes and peas with apple pie and cream to follow, all laid out on a linen cloth with red wine in sparkling glasses. Afterwards, sitting in the warm lounge-room, we listened to the rain pelting on the tin roof and rekindled mateship extending back over fifty years.

"Didn't get it like this in the prisoner of war camps, mate."

Chris drove us back to the campsite where we threw open the car doors and splashed across the sodden ground to dive into wet tents as he swished off down the puddled road.

Next day we left Collie and continued our walk south to Noggerup Hall. A night at the hall was followed by the standard mad scramble to pack gear and load the bus prior to moving off.

The overloaded bus didn't sound too good. It gave the impression it was trying to tell us something. While climbing up a steep hill it made a positive statement as a conrod punched a hole in the crankcase allowing sump oil to pour over the hot exhaust. The driver didn't really have to tell us to get out quick when the cloud of black smoke billowed into the vehicle.

Wardens from The Dept. Of Conservation and Land Management ferried us to our starting point. Rain fell heavily during our walk into Balingup although we finished the day in bright sunshine. The campsite was the local showground. It also happens to be the town's caravan park, and provided hot showers and a shed for the cook.

October dawned bright and sunny as we set out for Lewana Camp but, when we arrived, rain simply poured down. The climb through the hills should have been the most picturesque to date but all we could do was try to protect ourselves from the ice-cold wind and watch endless sheets of rain drift down into the valleys below.

We returned to camp and, after a hot shower and a more presentable meal, the group's high spirits took over. There was much laughter in recalling 'the most miserable moment in our most miserable day'. My socks were wet, my jeans were wet, my shirt, pullover and underclothes were also wet. I endeavoured to dry my gear by hanging it on a hook in the shower room as there are no fires. My waterproof pants and plastic poncho are showing signs of wear so I patched them with Elastoplast. I had often wondered why we were told to include a spool of Elastoplast in our kit. When I eventually scrambled into bed I shivered for about an hour before slipping off into an exhausted sleep. It had been quite a day.

Several days later we set up camp at The Scout Hall on the outskirts of Manjimup. Huts were available for the cookhouse and mess hut but selecting a tent site became a bit tricky. The surrounding area was a little undulating, only thirty centimetres or so, but the constant, heavy rain could fill a hollow with water so the slightest piece of 'high' ground suddenly became valuable.

Mary and I pitched our tents on a high spot and dug a trench around both tents. They were under a gum tree. This caused me some worry because sudden gusts of wind whipped through the area and rain-soaked gum trees have been known to shed a limb or two in sudden gusts of wind. But there was nowhere else to go. A raging storm on our last day at Manjimup made hiking so tough that we ran out of time.

We lunched in a delightful picnic spot but the rain, and our soaked condition, plus the shortage of time, made further progress for the day impossible.

This meant we were a half-day behind schedule and, during the next three days, we covered thirty kilometres a day.

We arrived at Pemberton to camp by The Pemberton School Camp where big sumptuous meals were prepared for us and eaten in the large dining hall.

We arrived at 'The Boorara Tree' around 2pm on Wednesday 11th October, 1989. Although the track has been extended beyond the tree this was the starting point of the first Bibbulmun Walk 10 years ago and it was from here that the surveying of the current track commenced.

Some of the group trekked up a side road to have a look at Larse Pool Falls, an eighty minute walk but most of us waited for the bus and, when it arrived, waited for the others to return. Life gets that way when you are hiking with a group.

Our next day's hike into our final campsite at the old Shannon Mill site was not a difficult one but rain fell heavily as we hiked across several kilometers of low-lying sand plain country and the going became very wet underfoot; from here we walked in stages to Walpole over the next four days.

We arrived at the campsite to find the cook had a big urn of hot soup waiting for our consumption. Just our luck to have him responding to training when the hike was in its final stages.

Shannon Mill was not a good campsite but it was better than most. An earthen wall allowed the cook to set up his cookhouse at one end. Adjacent was a small building containing two toilets. Admission to the toilets was gained by banging on the door and shouting: "Anybody in there?"

Three showers were available at the caravan park about a kilometre away but, first, the boiler had to be heated up so 'someone' had to go up there earlier and light the fire. Fortunately a few caravanners kept the fire going during the day. Admission to the showers was gained in a manner similar to entrance to the toilets. We were thirty-six in number so patience and tolerance were required as the capacity of the boiler was minimal and the hot water supply was soon gone.

Some elected to bed down in the building but Mary and I pitched our tents about 150 metres away because the area around the hut was much too noisy. The generator ran far into the night and recommenced at 5am.

This was our final campsite. Conditions in Walpole were said to be unsuitable. Anyway, I didn't care very much as I lay in my sleeping bag at night listening to the rain pelting on to the tent fly.

Our arrival at Walpole was a quiet affair. We were met by a small group of interested people and the Deputy Mayor made a short speech of congratulations and a very welcome afternoon tea was provided by The Country Women's Association.

So, it was all over.

We wandered around the town for a while buying edibles for the evening's 'break-up party' for which Brian Smith and I had purchased a bottle of port each before returning to the camp.

The break up party was not a rip-roaring affair. We had been through some very trying times together and had become a solid group of friends so we sat around yarning before eventually creeping off to bed.

Next day we loaded the bus and returned to Perth.

I often wonder, when looking back, why I joined that group of people who walked The Bibbulmun Track in 1989 because I am sure, when I completed The Long March across Europe back in 1945, I vowed and declared I would never walk another unnecessary step for the rest of my life; but the challenge was there and here was the chance to have a go.

Also, the organising was done by The Dept of Conservation and Land Management so all a man had to do was put one foot in front of the other and, providing he didn't mind being wet, cold and, at times hungry, it was piece of cake.

Besides – this is my country!

All of this was over 12 years ago yet, as I stated earlier, out of that assembly of hikers a small group formed which still regularly gathers to go hiking and camping.

Other people of similar attitudes have joined us and we have had some wonderful camps in country ranging from The Pilbara in the north to Denmark in the south.

Life, at times, had been very kind to me.

Chapter Twenty-Nine

My nephew, Bill, and his family were now living in The Atherton Tableland District of North Queensland. He had managed a large property down Esperance way in Western Australia for several years when his employers, who were based overseas and grew tea, decided to create a tea plantation in North Queensland and had nominated him to set it up and develop it.

Bill maintained he knew nothing about growing tea, particularly in Australia.

"Neither does anyone else," replied the Directors.

So they bought up some adjoining dairy properties a few miles out from Malanda, patted Bill on the back, and suggested he go ahead with the project. It's nice to accept a challenge in Life so Bill and Marsha got out the family atlas and found the location of some town named "Cairns". Inland from Cairns was a township named Malanda.

Well, that's how the story appeared to his Uncle Arthur and if ever you are out Glen Allyn way in North Queensland cast your eyes over The Nerada Tea Plantation and you will feel as proud of him as I am.

Occasionally he flies to the Esperance property to attend to some business down there and stays overnight with Eileen and I. I mention these points explaining why Bill now lives in North Queensland as a curtain-raiser for the rest of this yarn.

The Bi-Centenary Year of 1988 was celebrated as "the first two hundred years of a young nation" by the white population and as "two hundred years of degradation within the sixty thousand years they had occupied the country" by the Aboriginal community.

Numerous civil and civic organisations set about the business of celebrating The Bi-Centenary Year by organising events relative to the development of the country.

Bill, during one of his visits, casually mentioned the North Queensland Horse Trail Riders Association – of which he was the secretary – were planning a trail ride to follow the original trail from the early Maytown Goldfields back over the mountains then tracking north-east to Cooktown. He, Tex Costa and Clarrie Stonehouse had been out there quite a bit lately and it was shaping up rather well. They anticipated about 200 riders to cover the 250 kilometres in 10 days.

Now, this seemed like a pretty good sort of a venture to me – 200 horses following the original trail over The North Queensland Mountains. Should be a lot of fun.

"I'll see what I can do," said Bill. "I'll get back to you."

He 'got back' with a letter stating a horse, complete with a saddle and bridle, was available and I would require a tent, a sleeping bag, eating utensils, etc. etc. etc. I already owned all the necessary camping gear but considerable additional expenses were involved. Things like the return airfare to Cairns, the nomination fee, the cost of getting the horse shod and a few extra dollars for petty cash. The first item put quite a dent in Eileen's savings whilst the remainder gave my meagre bank account a bit of a nudge.

I flew direct to Cairns with a stopover at Alice Springs.

A simple statement but I am one of the diminishing generation born in the past and engaged in a constant mental effort to grasp changes taking place all around me.

I was one of the crowd at Maylands Aerodrome when Kingsford-Smith flew across Australia, from Sydney to Perth in a single day; now I was sitting in a luxurious, air-conditioned, jet-propelled plane flying right across my country where so many of the early explorers had perished and so many of the early settlers had slogged their guts out to retire beaten in the latter years of their lives.

I didn't see anything of Alice Springs. The plane landed, refuelled and took off again but landing at Cairns was quite an experience. The airstrip is on the coast and the plane, coming in from inland, flies down a valley and is at the same height as the railway climbing up to The Atherton Tablelands. The plane, emerging from the valley, banks steeply and lands. Nothing to it, really, but I thought it was terrific!

Marsha was there to meet me; another point worthy of mention. I fly across Australia and someone is there to meet me, but that is one of the advantages of being a mature-age uncle – eventually nephews and nieces become spread all over the country and they are such obliging people!

The horse was a skewbald named Patches. He stood about fourteen hands high and seemed in fairly good condition. We spent the next few days getting to know each other. This is a standard phrase used when, theoretically, man and beast are determining who is going to be the boss. Patches wasn't going to argue this point. He simply demonstrated tolerance while I went through a refresher course on 'How To Ride A Horse'. It wasn't easy for either of us; especially when following Bill down the steep, internal banks of an extinct volcano named Lynch Crater then slugging our way out again.

The marshalling took place at Malanda Showgrounds, the number of horses and people gradually increasing with the progress of the day. Riders came from all over Queensland as well as from other states and overseas although, it seemed, I had come furthest from within Australia.

An event of this magnitude brings a whole variety of people together; men who are bushmen and ladies who attend weekend pony clubs, teen-agers in harmony with their mounts and mature-age people who had been riding all their lives.

All was activity before sunrise next morning. Horses to be led to the water-trough then returned to their stalls, or trees, for a feed and a rub down before being loaded into carriers for transport to The Palmer River. The vehicles couldn't get into Maytown.

A great deal of planning had gone into this venture, big planning by big men who thought in a big way because they live in a big country. Big vehicles suddenly appeared in the showgrounds. Special types of vehicles to transport the horses, a truck to carry the feed and the equipment necessary for its distribution at the end of a day, another truck to carry the camping and personal gear and buses to carry the human animals.

All this unfamiliar activity tended to bewilder me but the organising was in the hands of experienced men and it all went well in a boisterous manner.

"Here, give him to me," said Bill, taking the halter out of my hands and bounding up the ramp into the horse float with Patches in tow.

The riders, when on the trail, were to carry a day's water and some lunch. All camping gear would be available at predetermined sites at the end of each day.

The journey to The Palmer River was long, hot, and terminated late in the afternoon when all was hustle and bustle again as horses were unloaded and tethered to nightlines.

The transporters and buses, when empty, drove away into the distance and I had an unusual feeling of loneliness amongst all the activity around me. I was amidst 200 horses and riders on the banks of a river somewhere in far north Queensland; the vehicles were moving away and I was left with a horse and a saddle as a means of transport for the next ten days.

Horses had to be watered at the river before being fed. I untied two.

"Take four!" yells Bill. "I'll follow you down!"

I set off for the river with four thirsty, haltered horses that were in a bit of a hurry and moved faster than I could walk down the slope. I slowed the two inside mounts by pulling on the halters but the two outside horses kept moving and, because of the restraint in the centre, swung around until they were facing me. I stood surrounded by horses showing their annoyance at my incompetence by blowing snot all over me.

"You'll get the hang of it after a while," laughed Bill as he passed.

The riverbank was lined with horses. The polite thing to do was to walk past them and take a place at the far end. My four spotted a space that would take half a horse. They bunched together and barged in, their size and strength pushing me forward and nearly depositing me in the river.

The walk back up the slope was slower and more dignified. They were fed and settled down.

I went looking for my gear. Night had fallen some time ago and, after stumbling around in the dark, I found the truck with the gear spread on the ground around it. These chaps had an unloading technique of their own. They threw every thing out of the truck as soon as it arrived at the campsite.

"Yours is there somewhere, mate. You've just got to sort it out a bit."

I carried my gear back nearer to the night lines, pulled out my eating utensils and made my way to the cookhouse wagons on the other side of the river. The water level was low and, at an appropriate crossing, rocks had been laid as stepping-stones and crossing a river by stepping on unstable stones on a dark night with plates and a mug in my hands is not my favourite past-time.

The mobile cookhouse, and the cooks, was supplied by the army and it seemed natural that they should set up the cookhouse on the other side of the river. A long queue wound its way towards the floodlit kitchen. That much, at least hadn't changed. I joined the queue and patiently shuffled my way towards my first taste of army cooking in over forty years. If the chops and vegetables tasted as good as they smelled then they were going to be delicious. I made my way past the hotplates until I came to the Sergeant Cook ladling out peaches and custard.

"By cripes, Sergeant," says I, "it's not just bully beef and biscuits these days."

"No," he replied, "We do pretty well."

"What's that yellow stuff you're trying to shake off the spoon?"

"Custard, of course! What do you think it is?"

I diplomatically refrained from answering that question.

All the adjacent rocks seemed to be occupied so I thumped down on the soft earth to eat a meal in the dark and compare the situation to the night before The Battle of Bardia.

The horses had to be watered and fed again before settling down for the night. The walk to the river this time was controlled better. I was tired, becoming bad-tempered, starting to swear and throw my weight around. The horses seemed to appreciate this change of attitude – or maybe they were tired, too.

After the horses had finished feeding, and the nosebags stashed for the night, I unrolled my sleeping bag, pulled off my boots then pulled my tent over me to keep the dew off.

I lay there quite some time listening to the horses snuffling, gazing at the brightly shining stars visible through the waving gum leaves and thinking, "It doesn't get much better than this, mate" before falling asleep.

People and horses were moving around before daylight.

"Come on, Uncle Arthur," called Bill. "Horses waiting to be fed and watered!"

The second generation has always acknowledged status within our family hierarchy and Bill, who is a mature man with children of his own, always addresses me in this manner, but the title "Uncle Arthur" was soon latched on to by his mates and I came in for quite a bit of good-natured rubbishing during the course of the ride.

But, irrespective of my family status, I had to pull on boots and take four horses down to the river for a drink then bring them back to the nightlines. This was easy. I simply held the halters and the horses showed me the way. After this successful manoeuvre I wandered around in the dark with their nosebags over my shoulder looking for the feed bin then, having filled the nosebags, stood in the pre-dawn darkness trying to work out the location of the nightlines.

Once this was accomplished I rolled up my sleeping bag and tent and carried them to the men loading the truck while the treetops were being painted with morning sunlight. My gear consisted of two ex army kit bags; in one was my sleeping bag and tent and the other contained a change of clothing and personal gear. I grabbed my eating utensils from the saddle-bag and, once again, took my place in the long queue leading to the cookhouse.

The horses were saddled and, by 8am, we were ready to commence the day's ride. Maytown, like so many other towns created by gold strikes, had vanished with the gold to leave behind a few small ruins and stone-bordered areas placed by modern historians to mark the sites of former buildings.

The first few days found muscles that I never knew I had. Patches was a good walker and quite docile but he kept trying me out by engaging in a high-stepping jog which caused me to bounce and pulverise my posterior even though I had a sheepskin cover over the saddle.

The pantyhose, too, were proving to be a hot garment to wear. (By 'hot' I mean heat-generating). Acting on Marsha's advice I had bought a pair of pantyhose to wear as they eliminated the manner in which stirrup straps tend to tear the hair out of legs and chafe calf muscles but I found them so hot I was in danger of becoming dehydrated and, quite frankly, I've never worn them since then.

The end of a day's ride was not the end of a day: horses had to be watered and fed; tents had to be found in the heap, carried to an area adjacent to our horses, and erected; a meal had to be obtained from the well set-up cookhouse which seemed to be always at a location furthest away from where we were camped then, before turning in for the night, the horses had to be fed and watered again.

Bill, another rider and I teamed up as trio. We may not see each other all day but we met again at the campsites. Setting up camp for 200 horses can take over a fair piece of country and our selected site could be a long way from where our gear had been dumped. Bill, before dismounting at the end of a day, would pick up our gear and carry it with us before becoming engaged in administrative commitments. We erected our own nightlines, attended to the horses and pitched our tents before wandering off, usually in the dark, towards the cookhouse.

There were incidents along the way.

An unwell horse had a heart attack and died on the night before the ride even started. Its body was dragged away on a rope pulled by a 4 wheel-drive truck. A horse is a beautiful creature but, once it is dead, it becomes nothing but a carcass to be disposed of as soon as possible and the sight of this one slithering along a gravel track behind a roaring truck to disappear into the night-enshrouded scrub caused me considerable distress.

A halt was called for lunch each day and I wasn't the only one to fall asleep during these breaks. I can fall asleep at any time, with no trouble at all. I put this down to my army experiences when, on route marches, we marched for 50 minutes and rested for 10 minutes in every hour. I could fall asleep in the 10 minutes. That was many years ago and, since then, I have managed to reverse the technique and I can now stay awake for 10 minutes in every hour.

Some people need quietness to snatch 10 minutes sleep but this requirement, amongst 200 horses and riders, is not always available. We halted one day at a dam site where one of the ladies led her horse well into the trees away from sight and sound.

Bill was riding as Drag Boss at the end of the column and, upon arriving at the evening campsite, made the usual check on numbers then rode around the entire spread-out camp before raising the alarm.

This was a very serious situation. A person lost in this type of country could perish. An unsuccessful search was organised during what was left of the day before night closed in.

The local station homestead was contacted by the R.F.D. radio carried in one of the trucks and a search party found her next morning. She had fallen asleep and, upon awakening, found we had all gone.

She had wandered around a bit but had enough sense to stay overnight at a water-trough where she was found. Phew!

A couple of 'North Queensland Type' characters had the important, morale-sustaining task of supplying a cold beer at the end of each day. They had a utility equipped with a large icebox containing numerous brands of 'tinnies' as well as a selection of wines in coolabahs.

I preferred an icy cold moselle at the end of a day and this was usually supplied with a great deal of showmanship and finesse for the benefit of "Uncle Arthur". However, after the first few days, all the cardboard containers had self-destructed in the ice leaving numerous, unmarked, aluminium sacks floating around.

After my evening request for a Moselle had received its usual acknowledgement an aluminium sack would be lifted out of the icebox and some its contents poured into a plastic cup.

"Dear me, it's a red!" stated the man, "Ah well; you had better drink this while I find a Moselle. My mistake. It's on the house."

There were several kinds of 'reds' and very few 'whites' so quite a few "My mistake, it's on the house" reds were drunk before my Moselle came to light. A delightful past-time which, somehow, made my return walk to the tent much longer than my original walk across the paddock to the utility.

The column, when travelling through scrub on hot days, stirred up a cloud of dust which, assisted by a slight following breeze, covered everyone with a dust that combined with perspiration to create a film of dirt overall.

"Serves you right!" said Bill, riding at the rear of the column, "Sitting amongst that lot. Why don't come back here where the air is clearer?"

A man is never too old to learn, I suppose.

The ride over the mountain range was picturesque but hard going and, on several occasions when resting, I gazed around and wondered how the early gold seekers ever survived.

Many of them didn't!

Western Australians are inclined to think of goldfields as scrub-covered, red dirt deserts but this was mountainous, well-watered, jungle country.

Numerous books have been written about the North Queensland gold rushes. They are horrendous tales of hardship. Supply wagons were winched down mountain slopes; robbery and murder were commonplace; Chinese immigrants poured into the diggings in the wake of the white man; the bush Aboriginals were cannibals and preferred Chinese to European and carried them off several at a time.

We wound our way down the mountains and trailed into the outskirts of Cooktown where we camped overnight on the racecourse.

Next morning we were issued with yellow and green tee shirts; a most welcome gift because everything else we owned was a bit on the nose.

We donned the shirts, formed up into a column four abreast and rode into Cooktown on the day our nation was celebrating its 200th Anniversary, but the population of Cooktown was celebrating its 218th Birthday on the premise that Captain Cook had beached 'The Endeavour" for careening at the mouth of the local river 18 years before Governor Philip landed at Sydney Cove.

The decorated town was full of revelry with many dressed in period costumes to mark the occasion.

Our ride down the main street was impressive and enjoyable. The crowd cheered and clapped our progress; costumed ladies hung over the balconies of the two-storied hotels and invited us back once we had been paid while enthusiastic drinkers dashed out of the pubs to hand us a beer.

There was a civic welcome before we dispersed.

I made my way to the local R.S.L. Hall where I was made welcome in the manner that is always extended to visitors; especially "this silly old bastard from Western Australia who had just ridden in from Maytown!"

Horses, men, women and material were loaded into the appropriate vehicles next morning and we made our seven-hour journey back to Malanda to unload at the showgrounds.

Ventures like this one don't come a man's way very often these days.

Chapter Thirty

Perth has several long streets running directly northwards from the city centre to the outer suburbs. One of them is Beaufort Street. It wiggles out of the city and snakes its way through Mt Lawley to Inglewood and beyond. For some inexplicable reason it has a dogleg at Dundas Road in Inglewood and, at the bend created by this dog-leg, stands a single-storey building with a clock-tower.

This building, during the halcyon days of my teenage years, was The Civic Picture Theatre. Saturday afternoons would find it packed with kids who screamed, shouted and stamped their feet just the same as I did when I was a child a whole eight or nine years ago but Saturday nights, pre-war, were different.

I took my girlfriend to the pictures on Saturday nights. The princely sum of four shillings and sixpence per person entitled us sit in the dress circle upstairs and I could also afford a sixpenny ice cream each. This was double the price for an ice cream from when I used to take Joan Mildwater to the matinees in Manly and I'm not sure if the cost of living had spiraled or whether I was more flamboyant; in either case, I was broke for the rest of the week.

The night's entertainment consisted of newsreels preceding two feature films with an interval between films. Sometimes the interval became a bit lengthy owing to circumstances beyond the management's control.

Further down Beaufort Street towards the city, at the corner of Walcott Street in Mt Lawley, was The State Theatre. Both these theatres were under the same management and the first film shown at

The State Theatre would be the second feature at The Civic Theatre and vice versa.

The method of transporting film from one theatre to the other was carried out in a rather spectacular manner. A motor-bike and sidecar, complete with a hair-brained, death-defying rider, would be parked outside The State Theatre. When the first film was finished the reels were packed in the sidecar and the bike disappeared into the distance with a roar that echoed between the buildings all the way to The Civic Theatre where it was unloaded and reloaded for the speed-limit defying return journey.

The films were usually delivered on time in the summer but winter had its problems as the unhelmeted rider sped up Beaufort Street with pouring rain in his eyes and battling with the occasional slide along the wet tramlines.

The impact of television caused The Civic Theatre to close down and eventually the building was taken over by Ron Dawson's Motor Cycles.

I had been to the bank on the other side of the road and, being in a sentimental mood, I wandered into the theatre for old time's sake.

Yes, the dress circle, screened off, was up there as in days gone by. At the other end of the building, on a wall now plastered with motor-cycle advertisements, once stood the curtain-enshrouded silver screen whilst the floor space, once covered by rows and rows of seats, was now covered by dozens and dozens of motor bikes.

I had been through "the motor bike phase" many years ago. When I was only fifty years of age I had purchased a Honda 350 twin and rode it across to Newcastle to visit Nancy and Peggy's families. It had been quite an adventure but I was no longer really interested in motorbikes.

I prowled through the stock noting how motor bikes had changed during the past twenty years and was making my way to the door when – there it was!

A Honda CX500C! It had a V twin water-cooled motor, shaft

drive, upswept handlebars, shining chrome and a headlight that winked and said, "Hoi! Over here!"

I nonchalantly meandered over just to look.

"Nice bike," said Ron who had mysteriously appeared in the manner peculiar to salesmen on a showroom floor.

"Yeah. But I'm just indulging in an old man's fantasy."

"Well, sit on it and get the feel."

I climbed aboard, making sure I didn't pull it over off the stand, put my hands on the handgrips, looked out past the upswept handlebars and through the walls of the old Civic Theatre to the miles and miles of highway stretching away into the distance beyond – beyond – beyond!

Reluctantly I came back to reality and stepped off.

"How much does a bike like this one cost these days?"

"Aw; you could get this one for two thousand dollars. It's a second-hand one that I'm selling for a mate of mine."

"Yeah, it's a nice bike."

That night, after a nervous cough at the evening meal, I commented, "I walked into the old Civic Theatre this arvo. The place is packed with motorbikes. There's one of them I liked the look of."

"You going to buy it?"

"Eh?"

"I said are you going to buy it?

"Aw; I dunno. Getting a bit too old for that sort of thing, now."

"How much will it cost?"

I whispered the price.

"How much have you got?"

"I could find a thousand."

"Then I'll lend you a thousand. Go and buy it."

How did I find a woman like this? (Just asked her for a dance, I suppose.)

Whenever some fantasy seems beyond my reach she just smiles, waves a magic wand and – Hey Presto! It happens!

My knowledge of motorbikes, over the next few months, increased in an alarming manner.

I was stooging along, during the first week, when the motor stopped for no reason at all. I couldn't see anything wrong with it. (My motor bike mechanical knowledge is limited to "looking".)

I phoned Ron Dawson's nearby shop and he sent a chap out to see what was wrong.

"Have you got petrol in the tank?"

"Yes. Filled it up yesterday."

"Well, why are you running on the reserve tank?"

"Eh?"

"You've got the petrol cock turned on to 'Reserve' which only holds a small quantity. Turn it on to the main tank and she'll go."

There were other problems.

When I originally sat on the bike in the showroom it was on a stand that lifted the rear wheel off the floor. Now that both wheels were on the ground I found I could just touch the roadway with my toes. This gave me no leverage when I pulled to a halt and if the bike was leaning slightly it leaned against my leg in a most belligerent manner. My leg strained to push it upright, the bike pushed harder, my leg began to tremble with the strain, the bike would win and I finished up laying down with the bike on top of me. Fortunately it had crash bars and I could wriggle out from underneath but the whole procedure was most embarrassing; especially when I was at the front of a line of traffic and put on this performance when the lights turned red. Car doors slammed, people came running, the lights turned green, the traffic banked up. Fortunately people came to my assistance because lifting the bike upright was a Herculean effort that I could barely manage on my own. I eventually overcame the problem with experience by making sure I was dead perpendicular when pulling up.

Sometimes, though, I reckoned Fate was crooked on me. Like the first time I rode it to The Veteran Athletes Sunday Meeting. I had owned the bike for a couple of months and reckoned it was time to make an appearance in my new role. I donned my leather gear as well as my all-encompassing helmet then rode to the meeting. I rode slowly past the gathering, did a Uee, came back and parked on the grass by the roadside. By now the crowd was interested. I kicked the stand down and leant the bike on it. The single stand penetrated the thin layer of grass and slowly disappeared into the soft sand; the bike leaned, I pushed, the bike won and I was lying on the ground again.

The mob rushed over to help and instead of such expressions as "Good old Arthur!" I heard several comments implying that I was not only mentally deficient and senile but my parents had also neglected to get married.

I joined The Ulysses Motor Cycle Club and set about the business of "Growing Old Disgracefully". I had several outings with them and, under some guidance from its members, gradually became a little more proficient although I was still a long way from "good". One of the club's membership conditions is that you have to be aged 50 years to be a full member or you can be a "junior" member at 45 years. I easily qualified as a full member and, much to my surprise, my nephew Garry and Marie, in Melbourne, were also members.

The club printed a monthly newsletter titled "Riding On" and the May 1992 edition contained this small paragraph: "A group of Melbourne members is planning to ride to Darwin and across to Cairns departing Melbourne on July 18th, 1992. Any member wishing to join the group or meet up with them on the way etc. etc. etc. –"

"By Cripes," I thought, "I've got to be in this!"

Quite a bit of planning is necessary for an activity of this nature. I phoned Melbourne, on several occasions, to talk to the chaps planning the show; purchased a considerable amount of camping gear and generally went into a bit of a flat spin.

I also phoned Garry but he was a non-starter due to a neck injury. No, he's not sure when he actually hurt his neck but it could have been any time during the past years when he was water ski-ing, cross-country beach-buggy safari-ing, motor-cycle scrambling:- "It's hard to tell, really."

That boy really packs his spare time with action -and it was also uplifting to hear a 53 year old grandfather still calling me "Uncle Arthur".

I took the bike to Ron Dawson's shop and asked them to give her a tune-up, fit a new front tyre and generally check her over. Ron phoned me later in the day to say they had considered it advisable to replace a few other things.

I guess that's all in order because when you explain what you are going to do and ask them to "check her over" you can't complain if they do the job properly. The trouble is I'm a stingy old coot and I don't like spending money – especially my own.

I had planned to have a few "dummy runs" just to get the feel of a loaded bike but the weather had changed dramatically. The colourful, sunny, mid-winter days had been chased away by big, ominous rain-bearing clouds that romped boisterously overhead, blanking out the blue sky, and pouring rain over all for days on end.

I phoned one of the chaps in Melbourne to make a few final arrangements. It seemed strange to be discussing such a long, and probably arduous, motor cycle venture with men whom I had never met and didn't even know what they looked like. This thought, coupled with the prolonged period of inactivity due to the wet weather, tended to become a little depressing so, desiring to rid myself of the mood, I lent hand as a marshal at The Veteran Athletes run the following Sunday.

It was an easy 10 kilometre run around the bridges spanning The Swan River. My job was to stand at the corner of Mill Point Road and Coode Street, South Perth, and ensure the runners didn't damage any cars or vice versa.

It sounds simple, and it was, except for those big, black clouds rollicking around overhead. They loomed over from Kings Park then chased the icy cold wind up the river until they were directly above me. Here the wind dropped, the clouds paused long enough to gain an accurate sighting then poured rain copiously over the surrounding suburb by using me as a centre point. Fortunately I had anticipated this circumstance and wore my wet gear so, except for my saturated feet, I was dry and warm.

Runners appeared at the crest of the hill up near the zoo and commenced running down the slope and past where I was standing. They were saturated with rain and red or blue with cold – but they were running!

Oh; to be able to run again right now!

My holiday, with its attendant worries, was fast approaching. It is going to be exciting and challenging but it won't be easy. Getting prepared has already created quite a few problems. Eileen, being the unpredictable female, and backed up by my family, strongly objected to me riding across The Nullabor Plain on my own so she chipped in with $285 to cover the bike's freight. Bikes, incidentally, are classified as "passenger's luggage" and travel in the guards van but extra expenses became involved. Naturally, I expected expenses but consider these:- Train fare to Port Augusta $275, motor bike freight $285, preparing the bike $275, purchasing extra clothing and equipment $200. That mounts up to over $1000 – and I haven't left home yet!

Ten days of steady rain hasn't helped. I know there is the possibility of eventually riding in wet weather but I can't see the sense in riding around in the rain for no demanding purpose so I read, wrote and became bored.

But, worst of all, I can't go running or jogging because of my crook ankle. Hitherto, when tensions built up, or I was emotionally at variance with myself, I could put on my running gear and – rain or sunshine – just go! Extend myself to the maximum! Make my body work, my heart pound, my lungs gasp for air and feel it was great to be alive and be capable of pushing myself to these perimeters – but I'm not doing it!

I'm standing at a junction in the road and watching my club mates go splashing past at 9am on a cold, wet, wintry, Sunday morning.

Long distance running is a very personal thing. I doubt if any of us are really enjoying ourselves when we are laying out a maximum effort but there is so much internal satisfaction when you have just run a personal best and there is always that peculiar sense of "one-ness" with the earth and the elements when leisurely jogging whilst training and I always felt I was privileged to be conducting myself in this manner at my age.

I am not unique. There are dozens of men and women, in any veteran athletes club, over 60 and approaching 70, who regularly run marathons and half-marathons. I'm nothing special in physical ability – I'm simply trying to express my emotional feelings at this moment.

The Olympic Games will commence in Barcelona within a few weeks. The greatest athletes in the world will be striving their utmost to demonstrate perfection and, because we strive to produce our best, we share in this mystique and we aren't just 'ordinary' people. We strive to extend our capabilities beyond the limits of our accepted horizons. Life has got to be a challenge – or it is nothing!

That's why I am going on this motorcycle holiday!

But this morning I am standing in the rain, with an aching ankle, watching my mates splash past – and I feel very much alone and miserable.

The weather cleared a few days later and I decided it was time for that dummy run out to York, across to Northam then back home.

Once I wheel the bike off the train at Port Augusta, and commence heading north, it will be too late to make adjustments so I spent an afternoon packing, unloading, rearranging, lifting everything on and off, but I eventually got it looking pretty good.

The next day was fine so I phoned Bill Barrett and he

enthusiastically agreed to come along for a day's outing.

I wheeled the bike along the driveway beside the house, loaded all my gear, dressed myself in the motor bike clothing I had recently purchased, said good-bye to Eileen, put on my helmet, straddled the bike, switched on the ignition, pressed the starter button – and the bloody battery was flat!

I couldn't believe it! The battery is a brand new one!

One of the principals of safe motorcycling is you mustn't get 'steamed up' or angry; try to remain calm under adverse conditions otherwise you could do a hasty or angry manoeuvre and cause an accident.

I calmly swore long and luridly before taking off my helmet and slowly climbing off the bike. I backed the Corolla to the bike and fired the motor by using jumper-leads from the car, re-parked the car, donned all my gear and roared off to meet Bill at a pre-arranged spot.

I reckoned, by the time I travelled to the meeting place, the battery would have charged sufficiently to restart the motor. Arriving at this destination I switched her off to have a yarn with Bill; a yarn which terminated with the statement: "O.K. Follow me to York."

Alas; it didn't work out that way.

The battery was as flat as a board! Bill rode over to my place and picked up the jumper leads. We fired the motor and came back to home. Something was definitely wrong. Bill couldn't help any more so he went home. I unloaded my gear, started the motor with the old jumper-lead routine, rode the bike up to the bike shop, told them the symptoms and left it there.

Ron Dawson phoned me later in the day: "I won't tell you what's wrong now. Drop in here tomorrow morning and I'll explain it all to you."

Somehow, this didn't sound too good.

"Well, it's this way," he explained as he opened the shop's doors next morning, "The wiring in the stator has burnt out. To get to the stator we have to take the motor out of the bike, detach the stator, have it rewired then re-assemble the bike again. If you say to go ahead you could have the bike back by Tuesday evening."

"Ron, how much will it cost?"

"Well: if we supply and fit a water-pump gasket, which I strongly recommend, it will cost you $560. I hate to tell you this but that is how it is."

"Better let me have a little thought about it."

"Sure, but if you are still planning to be on the train next Thursday night I suggest you let me know as soon as possible, preferably today."

On the way home I started to seriously think about this situation. I could go to the railway bookings and try to cancel my ticket. I could put my Toyota Corolla on the train but motoring wasn't the original intention.

I could say "Go ahead" and thereby considerably reduce the amount of budgeted spending money.

I felt miserable and sick inside. I could have gone on a plane and had two months holiday.

"What the hell!"

I could sense him grinning into the phone. "Knew you would say that," he said.

The following week-end was miserable emotionally and weather-wise. However there were two bright spots. Eileen and I sat in our lounge watching The Eagles thrash The Sydney Swans and, in the evening, Garry phoned to say he was trying to get his annual holidays and join us on the ride.

"I'll phone you back on Wensdee and let you know what happens, Uncle Arthur!"

Love that boy! Yes; I know he's a grandfather but everything is relative.

By Tuesday afternoon I was becoming a bit anxious so I phoned the bike shop.

"It's nearly ready. We'll phone when you can pick it up."

I picked up the bike at 4:30pm on Wednesday. Apparently a thrust washer had become mislaid in the water-pump area and a few extra man-hours were required.

Thursday morning I once again loaded the gear and went for that elusive dummy run through the hills; this time up to Kalamunda, across to Mundaring then home. Magic! Everything worked.

This evening, at 7pm, I'm going to load the bike on the train and, at 9pm, I'm going to get on that train and, for two days at least, nothing should go wrong.

Garry phoned. "I've arranged to meet Pat Bruce and Jim Maisie on Saturday. We'll be in Mildura on Saturday night and we'll see you in Port Augusta on Sunday. Should be fun."

The darkness of a stormy, blustery night had fallen long before 7pm. I phoned the railway station to ensure the train was leaving on time but it was leaving an hour and a half late. This was annoying because numerous friends planned to see me on my way. I phoned around to tell them not to bother as I didn't want them driving on such a night and the train was already late.

Nevertheless, I still had to get to the station an hour earlier in order to load the bike. Eileen was bringing my main pack to the station later so I strapped the remainder of my gear to the bike and set off. Riding a motorcycle at night is, to me, a nerve-wracking experience but to be riding one in pouring rain at night is simply horrendous!

The rain hits the Perspex visor and sits there. It forms into big globules that catch the lights of oncoming cars and makes forward vision very difficult. Invariably, whilst sorting it out, I run through a long puddle that sprays water all over the bike. My wet gear keeps me dry but my feet are soon soaking. I arrived in one piece and finalised loading arrangements. After that there was nothing to do but to get out of my wet gear and wait until Eileen arrived with some dry footwear. Hanging around a big railway station waiting to leave on a train, which is now leaving two hours late, is a frustrating business.

Some of my friends appeared but, because of the lateness of the train's departure, drifted off again.

Eileen. Maureen, Jeff and Stacey stayed until the train left at 11pm.

I hate modern departures!

Overseas travellers once went by ship. Crowds of well-wishers lined the wharf side, bands would play, streamers were thrown and people shouted farewells and 'Bon Voyage'. Nowadays, at the airport, travellers disappear through a door and you stand looking at a blank wall and wondering how much the car parking organisation is going to slug you for parking your car on the bitumen-covered piece of your country which they have managed to get a grip on.

The same circumstance develops at a railway station. When I was young (this, alas, was many years ago) train passengers simply dropped the window and leant out of the carriage to yarn with their mates, and as the train moved off, lean further out to vigorously wave until the crowded platform disappeared from sight. These days a passenger steps into a carriage, sits by a sealed window, and endeavours to communicate by sign language while inwardly praying the train will promptly depart so he won't have to sit any longer grinning like an incarcerated baboon in a glass cage.

I travelled 'Economy Class' (which is a modern, public relation's title meaning '3rd Class') and shared a two-bunk cabin with a pleasant chap who worked for Telecom and was on his annual holidays.

The train had left Perth so late in the night there was nothing to do but to go to bed and wake up in Kalgoorlie at 7:30am the next day. Soon after leaving Kalgoorlie the train moves out on to flat, featureless country prior to commencing its long haul across The Nullabor Plain which it traverses all day and into the night to arrive at Port Augusta around 8am the next morning.

The bike was unloaded and the train was on its way to Adelaide by 8:30am. I stood for a while with my gear beside the bike on an empty, wind-swept platform feeling rather lonely and a long way from home.

The porter and a truck driver ambled along the platform to have a yarn with me. They turned out to be a couple of bike enthusiasts and openly expressed their envy of my plans.

I began to feel better.

I found a caravan park in Cole Street on the other side of the bridge, pitched my tent, hired an overnight caravan for the following night and spent the remainder of the day walking around the locality in order to get some exercise but, after a couple of hours, my ankle became tired and further walking was ruled out. Sometimes it is convenient to have a bad ankle.

I had a chicken hamburger and coffee for my evening meal. Gawd! I hate hamburgers. Eating them is an exercise devoid of dignity.

I moved my gear into the overnight caravan next morning and went for a bit of a ride around the district. Garry, Pat and Jim had camped the night at Mildura, about 550kms away, so I didn't expect them until late in the afternoon.

They arrived at 4:30pm after a very bad day riding in such fierce cold, sleet, rain and hail that Garry reckoned it was "Bloody near snowing at one stage."

They are all riding BMWs; a K100S, a K100LT and a K100RT if you please, which kind of makes my Honda CX500C seem somewhat small; and I thought it was a massive bike!

The boys dumped their gear in the caravan and had a prolonged hot shower to thaw out before we wandered off to have a hot meal in a diner.

Monday was a slack day. Pat had strained his back and had to visit a chiropractor to get straightened out and we also had to buy some stores. One of the purchases was a 10 litre jerry can. The distance between petrol stations going north is beyond the range of my bike and extra fuel had to be carried. The jerry can was strapped on top of my gear and there it sat looking so incongruous that the silhouette looked more like a hay-carrying camel than a beauty, bonza Honda!

So the venture commenced. We set off northward and straight away I came up against factors that, for a day or so, made things rather hectic. BMWs glide along the road at 120kph which is not the sort of riding an old bloke like me usually indulges in; but I hung in there and, after a couple of days, became accustomed to the feel of this speed. The good quality bitumen road went straight ahead as far as the eye could see and there were no crossroads so it wasn't a bad place to learn.

The day was fine but a freezing cold gusty wind was blowing. My hands gradually became numb and devoid of feeling despite my leather gloves. My face, too, became quite cold and such was the force of the wind against my helmet that my cheeks were pushed between my teeth and the inside of my mouth became quite sore by the end of the day.

These were elementary problems at the beginning and they gradually sorted themselves out as the journey progressed.

The early afternoon found us at Woomera and we spent a couple of hours in the museum and the surrounding area. I had no idea so much had been going on out here but that was one of the characteristics of Woomera back in the 1950-1960s. It was all top secret stuff and nobody knew what was going on anyway.

We moved on a few kilometers and camped in the scrub in the vicinity of Glendambo. I had the same tent I had used on The Bibbulmun Track just on three years ago. A simple 'A' type, two-man tent but very efficient and cosy. Pat and Jim had the latest model 'Igloo' type and Garry had a flimsy, red arrangement which he poked up and disappeared into its cramped interior when retiring for the night. He claimed it kept the dew off and that is about the limit of its sheltering potential but Garry has spent more nights in the open than most people and seemed quite content with the arrangement.

Our meal consisted of heated tinned food. The lurk is to cut the top off a tin of Heinz Sausages and Vegetables and stand it beside the camp fire; then, when it is hot enough, grab it with a pair of multi-grip pliers and eat it out of the tin with a spoon. This eliminates washing up after a meal although I did notice the tips of the multi-grips grew a peculiar type of green fungus after a week or so. Consequently, the pliers were washed at least twice a week although we all agreed the fungus could have been penicillin.

Our first night's camp was typical of many to follow. We sat around yarning or just looking into the fire until 10pm. Life on the road gets you that way. It doesn't matter how hard the day has been – there is always time to sit around a camp fire at night.

We were out of the sleeping bags at first light next morning but it took two hours to roll up tents, have breakfast and pack the bikes before moving off to ride all morning into a freezing cold wind and arriving at Cooper Pedy around noon.

Cooper Pedy was a bit of a surprise to me. Tourist brochures and magazine articles tend to give the impression that it is all underground but most of it is on the surface. The town is scattered around a hollow and I could well imagine the heat of a summer's day supported by a gusty wind which, even on this winter's day, was picking up dust and whirling it around the street. The hotel gives the impression of being underground but I wasn't sure if the walls were Cooper Pedy rock or fibre-glass. I'm afraid I have become a little cynical of tourists developments in my old age. However, the beer was cold and we spent a few dollars in the establishment before riding on to camp the night near Marla.

Camping out reduces the cost of a holiday but it does have its problems. After several days we needed a wash although Garry maintained we needn't worry about that sort of thing until we pulled up at the end of a day and all the birds flew away but we arrived at Uluru before this condition prevailed. I agree, it could have already been prevailing but we weren't conscious of it.

Uluru is the tourist complex stuck out in the middle of nowhere about 25kms from Ayers Rock. I had, in my ignorance, hitherto regarded this complex as somewhat akin to a vulture watching Ayers Rock but, now that I was there, I realised how wrong I was and how necessary it is. Tourists were there in hundreds! Some came in buses that disgorged them like soldier ants to disappear through a hotel door and into the luxury beyond; others came in camper-vans, or cars towing caravans, or just cars, or riding motorbikes. Hundreds of people arriving in the centre of Australia for one thing – to climb, or just to see, Ayers Rock!

And it is out there – massive and magnificent – just as it has been for millions of years!

Although it was as far away as the horizon I could sense its brooding timelessness and, once again, I became conscious of that peculiar feeling which this vastness of Time and Space imparts.

We 'booked in' and were allocated three tent sites in the red dust that swirls and penetrates everything. The ground was solid and several pegs were bent before my tent seemed capable of standing in the wind. A hot shower was followed by some toil in the laundry.

Around sundown some more campers arrived and commenced pitching a tent on the space next to mine.

"Hullo," they said in cultivated correct English. "How are you?"

"Stone the crows!" I thought. "Fifty years ago nobody could have convinced me that someday I would be in the centre of Australia with a bunch of friendly Germans pitching a tent beside me!"

We bought our evening meal at a 'cook your own' barbeque at the Red Centre Hotel, walked several kilometres around the complex and crawled into our tents around 10pm.

We rode out of Ullaroo after breakfast, paid our admission fee to The Aboriginal Community who own the rock, and journeyed on to the rock itself. If Ayers Rock had previously affected me it now overwhelmed me with its awe-inspiring magnificence. I was a complete victim of its influence.

So much for romantic-minded old me. Garry, Jim and Pat looked at it differently.

"If we are going to climb the thing there is only one way and that is 'up'. Come on!"

I like to think I am reasonably fit but climbing Ayers Rock has to be experienced to be believed. A row of steel poles, with a chain running through them, is set in the rock to assist climbers but numerous stops for recovery are required as the task progresses. Indeed, prominent warning notices advised people with any kind of medical problem not to attempt the climb. I didn't have a medical problem when I started but I reckoned there was every chance I would have one by the time I arrived back!

The climb to the end of the first slope is not the end of the climb. We scrambled for over a kilometre to reach the centre, or highest point, in an hour and a half. The four of us, standing by the cairn at the summit, had our photo taken by another climber.

The view was limitless! Hundreds of square miles of saltbush, a cloudless blue sky and an icy cold wind – but we had climbed Ayers Rock and I felt elated.

We scrambled down in just 35 minutes.

We rode out to The Olgas and walked into the ravines between those mighty rocks before returning to camp for a clean-up and an evening meal. After tea I went to the lookout site to watch a spectacular sunset.

I arose at 6am on a cold morning and, still under the influence of The Rock, walked to the lookout site to watch the sunrise. Several people were already there. I love the way people with a common purpose talk to each other and share a moment in their lives with perfect strangers. The darkness gradually became grey as "Morning in The Bowl of Night flung The Stone that puts The Stars to flight". The sun slowly peeked over the horizon as though surveying the sparseness of the scene and determining if The Rock was still there. Having satisfied itself on that point it sent a ray of golden sunlight across the desert to wash the purple of night off the monolith and paint it pink followed by a reddish-brown hue. This sequence was so apparent even though The Rock was 25 kilometres away.

It reminded me of Banjo Patterson's words:

"Where the air's so clear, so clean, so bright,

Refracts the sun with wond'rous light"

And I could hear The Wogul whispering, "You're only passing through."

I returned to camp to find the others already up and having breakfast. This enabled us to make an early start and we travelled 450 kms to Alice Springs.

A friend of mine had informed me before I left Perth that her parents were caravanning around Australia and I might see them on my way.

"Oh, yes," I thought, "Australia is such a small place. I'm sure to see them along the track."

We rode into Alice Springs and parked our bikes in a car park in the centre of the town – and there they were standing on the footpath right beside our bikes! Like I said, "Australia is such a tiny place."

We took a room at a motel 4kms out of town. It worked out to $17.50 a night which wasn't too bad seeing as the temperature was 2 degrees Centigrade; besides, we had hot showers and could make a cup of coffee whenever we felt like it. We did just that. After coffee and a shower we rode back into town looking for somewhere to have meal and found a delightful pub by the bridge. Garry had been here before and told us a dramatic tale of how, as he sat here, the town's police appeared in force to usher the local inhabitants off the river's banks minutes before a massive wall of water, the product of some inland cloudburst, came roaring down the creek bed.

Next day was a Saturday and another surprise came my way. Kevin Dickinson was The Seven Day Adventist Pastor of Alice Springs. His wife, Jeannette, is my niece and I planned to pay them a surprise visit at the church on the outskirts of the town. A small group from the congregation was standing, talking, in the parking lot when I arrived.

I rode in to pull up beside this little gathering and revved my motor just to be a bit annoying before turning it off and slowly removed my skid lid.

"Jeannette!" I called.

She looked surprised as she walked to where this bikie-type had called her name.

"Yes?"

"I'm you're Uncle Arthur."

"Of course! So it is!" A grin spread over her face. "Then you probably know this lady over here."

There was my sister, Ida, and my brother-in-law, Frank, who were also visiting Alice Springs!

We had a pleasant "family chatting hour" before I left to go to the caravan park to have a yarn with Thelma and John before returning to the motel.

We left Alice Springs, under a cloudless blue sky, on a cool morning that gradually became warmer as we travelled north. Pushing on we passed Tennants Creek and The Devils Marbles before arriving at Three Ways where we took a cabin for the night; a most acceptable decision as we had covered 532kms into a head wind at an average speed of 110 to 120kph and, at the end of such a day, this old soldier tends to become a little weary.

Three Ways doesn't get its name for nothing. From here you can go north, south or east. The next day, 26th July, we packed our gear and assembled at The John Flynn Memorial for photographs.

Garry, being on annual holidays, had to return to Melbourne work and make money to pay taxes in order to pay my pension so I could ride on up to Malanda to stay a while with my other nephew, Bill Benson.

I have previously mentioned the advantages of an old uncle having nephews and nieces spread throughout the Commonwealth.

Pat and John were going north to Darwin with the intention of phoning me when they were leaving there and we were to meet again at either Cairns or Townsville to ride south together.

So, we went our several ways. Pat and John to Darwin, Garry and

I to Townsville about 1500kms east.

The road was straight and the countryside uninteresting. Riding became simply a matter of sitting on the bike and being buffeted by a strong headwind all day. I had, by now, seen enough of Aussie's wide, open spaces and was looking forward to a few hills, some trees and an occasional bend in the road.

The road is unfenced and frequent road signs warn of wildlife such as kangaroos and emus. They don't attack but they can certainly buckle a vehicle and, in the case of a motorbike, they could cause you to have an unexpected close-up look at the bitumen. Road trains, travelling at night, clobber kangaroos and emus in considerable numbers and the stench of rotting carcasses becomes very strong.

We passed a flock of twelve emus grazing by the roadside at one stage. We slowed down in case they decided to cross the road but they completely ignored us even though we were only 30 metres away.

We rode into Townsville three days later, booked a tent site in a caravan park, showered, changed into some clean clothes and had an hour's walk before our evening meal which, on this auspicious occasion, was hot fish and chips!

I phoned Bill to tell him I would be in Malanda the next day.

We arose early, packed our gear, and said "See you later, eh?"

I made my way out of Townsville on a clear, sunny day which gradually became cold and threatening as I rode north. I turned inland at Innisfail and climbed up to Ravenshoe. The road, fortunately, has been upgraded since I last saw it some five years ago. It twists and turns through very hilly and picturesque scenery which would have been enjoyable on a fine day but this day was black with clouds arguing amongst themselves on the surrounding mountain peaks. Cold, penetrating sleet at Milla Milla compelled me to pull up and don my wet gear.

I turned off the main road before entering Malanda and headed out towards the plantation and, for a while, I thought I wasn't going to make it!

Apparently this day was the first 'fine' day after a month of solid rain and the final kilometre of the dirt road was a quagmire of potholes, mud and churned-up slop along which I skidded, slipped, splashed and bounced my way to the house where I arrived covered in mud after riding all the way from Port Augusta on a clean bike!

Marsha, as always, made me welcome and, within a short space of time I had settled comfortably into their absent son's room complete with an en-suite containing a hot shower and heating lamps set in the ceiling to keep the room warm after a shower. That boy had been living well. The whole place seemed like a palace after two weeks on the road and travelling under fairly tough conditions.

Bill arrived home around 4pm. Alice, their daughter, arrived home from school full of energy and hungry.

We had a pleasant evening watching The Olympic Games in Barcelona on T.V.

This wasn't my first visit to Malanda and, during the next 12 days, I renewed acquaintances from the Bi-Centenary Horse Trail Ride; rode across to Atherton on several occasions; stayed a couple of nights at Henry Tranter's place: and, on one never-to-be-forgotten day, went down to Cairns with Marsha.

Marsha had a time-consuming medical appointment at a clinic on the edge of the town so I had the car. I drove it into town and parked it in a parking lot near the pier and strolled around for a couple of hours. I returned to find I had been fined $20 for parking in an area reserved for cars c/w boat trailers.

This was bad enough but, worse still, I couldn't find my way back to the clinic! I spent an hour trying to backtrack but all to no avail and I was getting desperate because it was long past the time when I was supposed to be there. Finally, I went to The Cairns Police Station seeking help. My answers to their questions weren't conducive to creating a good impression.

"I'm holidaying with my nephew in Malanda. I bought his wife into town for a clinical appointment three hours ago and I should have picked her up by now but I can't find the place."

"No, I don't know the name of the street."

"No, I don't know the name of the clinic but it's over that way – somewhere."

A few more probing questions convinced them that I was quite sane but had a problem. Furthermore, they decided which clinic I was seeking and sent me on my way. It was the wrong clinic but I eventually found the correct one by telling my tale of woe to a most obliging lady in an estate agents office.

Bloody Hell! But I was worried!

Marsha thought it was funny.

I am reading *Saigon* by Anthony Grey. One of the lasting impressions I gain when staying at other people's houses is by digging into their books. My store of books has been garnished in a haphazard manner without any real positive direction. Quite a few of them are Readers Digest abridged volumes that originally belonged to Bill's father. He commenced subscribing for them when he and Pat first went to New Guinea and I acquired them whenever Geoff returned to New Guinea after long service leave. I haven't a library or formal bookshelves. Most of my books are poked into cupboards or stashed in a box in the garage. I find, when visiting other people, I commence reading a book that truly opens up new horizons and sets me thinking along paths that are completely new to me. *Saigon* is one of those books. As a reader I accept the presented facts or background and I now find myself looking at the history of France's expulsion from Vietnam in a new light. Obviously, I won't have time to finish the book during my stay so I shall have to get a copy from a public library when I get home and I must, in all fairness, say that an impressive domestic library isn't necessary in the city because a suburban public library can supply all that is required in the field of literature.

Bill's holidaying niece, Leanne, arrived one evening with two girl friends.

I was courteously introduced to the girl friends as, "My Great-Uncle Arthur."

She was quite correct. I am her Great-Uncle but polite statements of family status from the third generation, these days, are unexpected and it shook me a bit.

The phone rang as we were dining one night. It was Jim Maisie phoning from Barclay Roadhouse. "We're on our way back. We've decided not to come to Cairns and we're going straight home from here. Have a safe ride home and we'll catch you some other time, eh?"

"Sure. Look after yourselves."

I replaced the phone and sat thinking for a while. I was inland from Cairns, I lived in Perth, I was riding a motorbike and I fervently wished I was forty – or maybe even fifty – years younger.

I stayed a further week but when you've got to go you've got to go. I packed my gear, said 'farewells' all around the town and headed down to Townsville. It was a long haul and I booked in to the caravan park where Garry and I had previously camped. The bike's rear tyre was looking worn so I had a new one fitted.

I wasn't heading straight for home. I was leisurely making my way down to Newcastle to visit my friends. Bundaberg was on the way so I called in to The Bert Hinkler Museum to visit my photograph. There it was hanging on a wall in 'The Canberra Room' with a very nice card stating:-

ORIGINAL.

Bert Hinkler's plane at Canberra.

Donated by Mr Arthur Leggett

of Bayswater. Western Australia.

I reckon my Mum, after seeing it hanging on my bedroom wall for 65 years, would be pleased to see it in this museum.

I felt good. It will be there long after I have ceased to exist.

I put in some long days riding south but the journey was without incident although it got a bit hairy at Toowoomba. I arrived there on a Monday evening just in time to become involved in all the traffic returning inland after a long weekend at the coast.

Next day I covered over 500kms and arrived at Tamworth where I phoned Peggy and Reg to tell them I would be in Newcastle the next day. The week at Newcastle was full of friendship and the old 'do-you-remember' routine. I stayed a few days with Reg and Peggy before being transferred to the care of Nancy and Doug then back to Peggy and Reg again but, eventually, I had to face up to the remainder of the journey home.

Parting wasn't easy. These people had been friends of mine for over 52 years. We are all at the twilight of our lives and there was no guarantee that this "Good-bye" would ever be repeated.

So, it was with a heavy heart that I rode out through Maitland and Singleton to Denham where I took a tent site with an en-suite. Can you beat that? A tent site with an en-suite! The temperature fell to zero that night and I awoke inside a tent crackling with a frost that covered the surrounding lawn.

I was packed and ready to go when an old timer invited me over to his caravan for a cup of tea. It was a permanent caravan with enclosed metal annex. He was aged 83 and he lived here with his wife.

"It's a bit rough," he said, "but it will do until we can get a place of our own."

I was in Dubbo by early mid-day and pitched my tent in a caravan park. I didn't fancy camping on my own where there are no rest areas or provisions for campers. Although it was fairly early in the day I didn't go past Dubbo. I was travelling westward and a look at a map will show long distances between towns on this route. Besides, I had left Newcastle allowing two extra days in my schedule.

I had lunch in a McDonalds food house where I met three members of The Ulysses Club; big rugged men dressed in black, riding

Harley Davidsons and heading south after a holiday in Queensland. But we all belonged to the same motorcycle club so we were mates. It was a most enjoyable meal.

The weather was fine but the wind was icy cold on the day I left Dubbo. I was determined to stay warm by donning woolen socks, long underpants, singlet, corduroy pants, a pullover, wind-proof, flannel-lined overalls and a scarf as well as gloves.

I still became cold!

I pulled into a roadside pub somewhere between Dubbo and Cobar. It wasn't a town. Just a pub by the roadside. I was damn cold and, after fuelling at the pump outside the pub door, I stepped inside to find a pot-bellied stove in a corner with a coffee dispenser right beside it.

It took a lot of will-power to leave that place!

The ride to Cobar was very monotonous. The road was good and stretched straight ahead to the distant horizon – hour after hour of it. The country was dry, feed was short and the local graziers were grazing their stock along the roadside. Hundreds of steers on the bitumen verge munching at whatever they could find. I slowed right down when passing through these herds and I had to stop on several occasions because, as I approached, a bunch of them would decide to cross the road in front of me. Invariably they propped and there we were standing about ten metres apart and having an eye to eye confrontation, in the middle of the road, a hundred kilometres from anywhere.

I don't know what they were thinking but I was thinking, "If those bastards decide to have a go at me, I'm gone!"

The longer I looked at them the longer their horns seemed to grow as they stood there, with their heads lowered, looking at me in a most unfriendly manner. After a while they would give a contemptuous snort, shake their heads and, much to my relief, disdainfully wander off. But they were BIG!

I found, at Cobar, a caravan park which is a credit to the city. Cement slabs for caravans and well kept grass throughout the whole area.

I was told, "Park your bike on any slab and put your tent up beside it." This I did.

The park gradually became full during the course of the afternoon and I became the centre of a group of caravanners who were charmed with my venture.

The more I told them of the miles and miles on my own, the cold nights, the freezing rides, the pitiless, boisterous headwinds, the problems of pitching a tent in a gale and trying to warm food, the more enchanted and envious the men folk became.

That is one thing I had come to realise in this venture. Motor cycling holidays are a romantic challenge – especially if someone else is doing it!

The next day dawned sunny but windy and my destination was Broken Hill.

"It's going to rain," informed one of my companions of the previous evening. "Rain with strong winds. It's blowing up from St Vincents Gulf."

I didn't think it would rain because the wind was too strong. Of course it was a head wind or a side wind. Buffeting and cold! Massive black clouds built up around 1pm and the scenery ahead was blotted out by grey rain falling in torrents all over the countryside. I pulled up, took my wet gear out of the panniers, put it on and rode into the weather. There was no alternative. The country was flat and featureless. Broken Hill was still hundreds of kilometers away and I didn't want to stay in Wilcania where I arrived quite early in the day.

I rode on into the storm and wind. I suppose I've been colder and more miserable in my day but I don't remember it. The road snaking straight ahead, hour after hour, across flat mundane country only added to the misery that was penetrating my mind and body.

A lone building, right by the roadside, took shape through the all-enveloping rain. Nothing else. Just this lone building with a few cars parked outside it. I stopped by the petrol pump and noticed the name "Little Topar Hotel." A young chap, wearing a cattleman's oilskin, came out to fill my tank.

"Can I get a coffee in there?"

"It's on all the time."

I wheeled the bike on to the hotel verandah and went inside.

"Coffee," said the Irish publican, "It's over there. Help yourself. $1 a cup."

I helped myself and crossed the room to the big, open fireplace where two railway sleepers were burning. I have no doubt, now, that I was suffering from hypothermia. I was chilled to the bone and couldn't stop my hands from shaking. I put the coffee down, took off my wet gear to allow the fire's warmth to penetrate my frozen body and had another go at drinking while the wind blew and the rain thundered down on the tin roof.

"Have another one on the house," said the Irish publican.

Any publican who says that has got to be Irish.

I drank that one slowly but there was no abatement in the storm.

I reluctantly donned my wet gear, left the warmth of the fire and the conviviality of the pub, walked out to the bike, pressed the starter button and rode off into the unhappiest hours of this whole venture.

Broken Hill appeared through the murk at around 3pm. Considering the weather, this wasn't bad going.

The first caravan park to appear was The Lake View. I parked under the canopy outside the reception office and walked inside to create a fair sized puddle in the middle of the tiled floor.

A fifteen-minute break in the rain enabled me to erect the tent in a sheltered spot. I unloaded everything and threw it inside the tent, covered the bike and dashed for the hot showers where I stood for half an hour thawing out before putting on my tracksuit, dashing back to the tent and crawling into the sleeping bag to keep warm. The plan was to make a cup of tea but I fell asleep and woke again, in the dark, five hours later.

I lit my little Gaz stove, made a cup of tea, heated a tin of sausages and vegetables and, after eating, fell asleep again until 7am next morning.

I was on the road again by 9am. The country between Broken Hill and Peterborough is very similar to the W.A. goldfields between Kalgoorlie and Leonora. Flat, featureless and bare, it had the same fierce, cold, blustery wind which created its problems. I could only travel at 80kph because I was, at times, leaning well over and, when the gust passed, hasty correction was required to prevent careering off the road. It blew all day and combating it was truly mentally and physically demanding.

Conditions changed as I approached Peterborough. The grey clouds turned black and poured rain all over me!

I never thought I would ever again be as cold as I was on the march across Europe in 1945 but here I was, in my own country, nearly frozen stiff. My neck ached, my shoulders hurt, my legs ached from cold and inaction and I couldn't feel my hands through the saturated gloves.

I rode into rain-sodden Wilmington, parked the bike under the overhanging verandah of a food shop and went inside for a cup of coffee and a pie.

The chap in the food shop was encouraging in his comments on the weather. "Once you get through the pass you'll find a change in the weather. We always get it worse this side of the hills."

I couldn't see how he came to this conclusion because the weather was coming from that direction and it was heavy.

The ride down through Wilmington Pass was horrendous!

The wind blew up the pass, rain poured down and water flowed across a road that twisted, turned, U-turned and wound its way downhill in a most demanding manner.

Finally it poured me on to the flat, coastal plain where,

miraculously, it wasn't raining and periodically, on the run up to Port Augusta, the sun came shining through patchy holes in the clouds.

I booked into the caravan park and pitched my tent on the same spot where I had pitched it six weeks ago.

Six weeks! It seemed like a thousand years!

I had a strange feeling of having accomplished something without being able to clearly define what it was. I had started here but I'm not going around again.

I had a take-away meal of Hawaiian Chicken. I phoned Garry. I phoned Eileen. I went early to bed.

A couple of days waiting for the train were spent walking and relaxing in the town, a past-time that had its tricky moments. The caravan park is separated from the town by a stretch of the gulf spanned by a long traffic bridge. The weather continued wet and squally and a calculated risk had to be taken in order to get across this bridge between showers. I found the public library and, for two days, only came out of its warm interior for meals.

Port Augusta also has an excellent Pioneer Museum which I recommend to people who are not passing through in a hurry.

I was over at the railway station by 7:30pm at the end of the second day. The train eventually arrived and the bike was loaded with the help of a couple of porters. I helped them tie it securely in the luggage van then wandered into the 'tourist coach' to find my seat. A young bloke was curled up fast asleep and laying across both seats. I woke him and explained the situation like, "Hey! You've got your feet on my seat!" He twisted around into a normal sitting position in his own seat but I honestly doubt if he woke during the whole manoeuvre.

Sitting up all night, even if it is in a lollabout seat, is not the most comfortable way to sleep but I was warm under a traveling rug and I slept until daylight. The inside of the 'Tourist Coach', at first light, once again reminded me of a front line casualty clearing station during a pitched battle. Bodies were everywhere. Arms, legs, torsos and heads lay around in the most grotesque manner. Eventually they start to move and attach themselves to bodies that had lain under blankets or sleeping bags all night and gradually the place took on some semblance of order. I found an unoccupied seat at the end of the carriage and moved down there for the day.

We were well out into the desert country, by now, which is O.K. if you want to look at desert country. The ground out here had become very muddy after heavy rain; long pools of water and mud were frequent. I mention this because Garry had, at one stage, contemplated crossing The Nullabor by driving along the service road running beside the railway line.

I read Emile Zola's book 'The Beast In Man'. I like his style. Short, concise sentences which take you along with them. Other than that – it was just another monotonous train journey.

We pulled into Kalgoorlie at 8:30pm on a wet night. I unloaded the bike, stood by it on a dark platform, looked at the streets lights of Kalgoorlie and thought, "What the hell do I do now?"

Standing there wasn't going to achieve much so I started the motor, rode out of the railway yard and commenced prowling the streets looking for a caravan park.

I found one but, as the hour was late, nobody was in attendance at the reception office. I found a grass patch, pitched my tent, threw everything inside in the routine manner, covered the bike and went to sleep.

The night was very windy with heavy rain. I crawled out in the morning to find two other motorcyclists had arrived during the night. Their bikes were completely plastered with mud. They had crossed The Nullabor by the service road that had simply ceased to exist in places and they had to do a bit of cross-country work over sodden plains which, at times, turned into quagmires. Arriving around 10pm they had pitched their tents then gone to a nearby hotel to see if they could get a meal. This apparently was a mistake as the goldfields people are noted for their hospitality and the riders never returned to their tents until 1am and, this morning, they were a little worse for wear.

I didn't hurry with my packing as I planned to camp overnight at Merredin and take two days to get to Perth. I had originally planned to visit Bob and Chris at Leonora but heavy rain had been falling all through the goldfields for days and the country was all mud and water.

I reached Coolgardie before rain commenced again. It poured down heavily and tossed in an occasional burst of hailstones for good measure. The road was lost to vision 100 metres ahead. All I could do was drive into it.

Cold! Cripes, I was cold!

I pushed on through Southern Cross and on to Merredin. The surrounding countryside was waterlogged and the caravan park was under centimetres of water.

After re-fuelling the bike I re-fuelled myself at a roadside restaurant and decided this was no place to stay overnight.

I headed for Perth in the rain-soaked distance.

I arrived home at 6pm on Thursday, 3rd September, 1992; which was exactly 53 years since the outbreak of the war.

On the 8th September, 1992, I celebrated my 74th birthday.

DON'T CRY FOR ME

Chapter Thirty-One

Kayaking, or canoeing, on The Swan River is a delightful way to spend a few leisurely hours on a summer's morning. The upper reaches near Guildford and Bassendean are placid, the trees grow right down to the water's edge, bird life is in abundance, the sun glints on the water and Life seems a bit beaut. Further downstream there is a beautiful stretch going past the boat-building yard to bend around past the old Maylands Aerodrome at the end of the peninsular and, further still, you can paddle past Herrison Island to Perth Water.

I get a bit smug when kayaking on Perth Water. The high-rise office buildings of the city tower in the background and, in the foreground, running right along the river's bank, is a very busy roadway carrying constantly flowing traffic and every vehicle, it seems, carries someone trying to earn a living.

"Good on yer!" I cry. "Been there! Done that!"

Of course, no one hears me because the noise of the traffic is too loud so I paddle across to South Perth to have a coffee in a riverside café.

Several years ago I belonged to The Ascot Kayak Club but I had gradually withdrawn from its activities. Actually, I didn't withdraw. I became hopelessly unfinancial and the club had, no doubt, come to regard me as a bad debt and scrubbed me from its books. I was too scared to approach the club to renew my membership in case it brought up the embarrassing topic of outstanding dues. The fault was mine because the club's members are a good mob and, whenever I met them, would always assist with constructive advice on how to paddle a kayak.

Back in Chapter 28 I mentioned the group that had formed from within the participants of The Bibbulmun Walk and several of them have also become interested in kayaking.

We had completed our regular Saturday morning hike and were sitting in a café having breakfast when two of the ladies sitting opposite me reached across the table and asked, "You'll be in it, won't you Arthur?"

I had no idea what they were talking about, and I could possibly have jumped to a hasty conclusion, but I promptly replied, "My oath! I'll be in it!"

"There," says Pat to Maggie. "That makes three of us."

I cautiously requested more details.

"Er – what is it that we are in?"

"The Avon Descent."

"You're joking?"

"No. It's eleven months away and that gives us time to get ready. You said you would be in it."

Sometimes, when reviewing a day's activities before dropping off to sleep at night, I come to the conclusion I have a big mouth.

The Avon Descent, one of the world's classic white-water challenges, is an annual winter two-day event down The Avon River from Northam to Bayswater. It is rough, tough and, to put it mildly, somewhat frightening and dangerous.

And I had committed myself to be in it!

"Getting ready" for The Avon Descent is similar to getting ready for a marathon. You must put in the man-hours training or you are not going to be capable of finishing because, after a day and a half of rapids, rocks and ti-trees, there is 18kms of flat-water paddling to the finish.

Maggie Cashman-Bailes was away on a holiday 'up north' somewhere but Pat Whittleston and I began serious training. Pat commenced by going into a kayak showroom, looking around, yarning with the proprietor and saying: "Yes, I'll have that one."

Training for a marathon simply meant putting on my running gear and going out the front door but training for a kayaking event meant putting the kayak on top of the car, driving to the river, unloading, pulling on warm gear and paddling. Sometimes, in winter, it could be rather miserable in the middle of the river with rain pouring down in sheets across the line of vision, and it can get cold – very cold!

Other times, in summer, the sun beats down on my sweat-soaked back and tries to penetrate the layers of sun block covering my legs, arms and face.

Gear had to be purchased. The kayak had to be packed with air-filled bags to assist in flotation if the craft overturns, special rubber boots, a flotation vest, a spray deck and a light helmet.

I always thought a flotation vest was a life jacket but one has to use the correct titles when mixing with the younger generation, otherwise they look at you in a peculiar manner; the spray deck fits around the body and also seals off the cockpit to prevent water splashing in; the light helmet is to stop your head from being damaged by rocks as you bounce down rapids in an inverted pose.

I thought most of this was unnecessary as I had no intention of being tipped upside down.

Pat and I met at Ascot Kayak Club and commenced our training under somewhat adverse circumstances. Rain was pouring down so heavily that I was reluctant to get out of the car.

"Come on!" yelled Pat, tapping on the window. "It could be as bad as this on The Day. Come on! Get out! We've got to go!"

We paddled 6 kilometres upstream then turned around and paddled back while the rain bounced globules of water and bubbles of air on the river's surface and drummed on the kayak's decking.

If this was how it could be on The Day then I couldn't see myself paddling along and reciting "I Love A Sunburnt Country" during the event.

We persisted and gradually improved whilst our enthusiasm expanded in proportion to our improving capabilities.

Near the end of June we drove to Bells Rapids, north of Perth, to see how they were looking that year. Water was roaring under the footbridge and cascading onwards in a turbulent mass of bouncing liquid!

Pat was rather perturbed.

"Good Lord!" she exclaimed, "Do we have to go down that?"

"Of course we do," said I, full of confidence and ignoring the sinking feeling inside me because I hadn't done much 'white water' work.

A group of kayakers came winding through the scrub growing across the river, beached their crafts and walked on to the footbridge. We knew them from the kayak club and discussed the rapids and the best way to go through them. They launched their crafts, shot under the bridge and made their way through the rapids to disappear around a bend downstream.

"There you are! Nothing to it!" said I standing there looking at the water as it roared under the bridge to twist and turn over the downstream rocks – and I wondered!

Pat enrolled in a white-water course under the guidance of skilled instructors; an advisable procedure which I couldn't afford.

She phoned me the following weekend.

"I shot Bells Rapids three times!" she yelled into the phone.

"I told you it was piece of cake."

"No it wasn't! It was frightening."

She did it all again the following weekend and progressed from that point on.

Maggie was back in town. She and I decided to have a go through the ti-trees growing downstream from The Upper Swan Bridge. This section is on The Swan River where there is always water but ti-trees are a real problem on The Avon River.

Maggie and I felt we needed some experience in this sort of canoeing. We successfully made our way through the rather sparse timber, without tipping over, and paddled a further 12km downstream.

Our trio's planned intention to enter The Avon Descent was, at first, viewed with considerable doubt by the more experienced canoeists. We were a 'mature-age' group of Senior Citizens. Owing to circumstances beyond my control, I was 76 years of age and that caused people to shake their heads.

Despite this encumbrance I passed a few 'white-water' tests and, in addition to this, I knew quite a few of the kayaking fraternity and I suspect this helped a bit.

Pat and Maggie are younger than me and as our training improved so did our determination and gradually it was generally accepted that we "might be alright".

The unexpected happened!

The Publicity Officer phoned to ask if I would help them with the publicity. This request was not based on my kayaking ability but it just so happened that I was the oldest person to ever enter the event and, from the organiser's point of view, it could be used to advantage. Being a sporting-minded person I readily agreed. Of course, it was just possible that vanity also played a part.

Radio interviews and press interviews cropped up during the following months and one suburban newspaper even had photos of Terry Boland and me on the same page; a bit flamboyant considering I had paddled up and down The Swan River whereas Terry had walked, cycled and kayaked 24,000kms right around Australia only 5 years previously.

Pat, too, was getting her share of publicity and appearing in the press as The Paddling Grandmother. She phoned, full of excitement, to advise that Channel Nine were coming to her house and the result was a nicely presented interview showing Pat on the river in her kayak followed by a constructive conversation with the reporter.

Life has many aspects and, while all this was going on, other facets were becoming prominent.

June 27th is an important date in our family traditions. Our granddaughter, Julie-Ann, and Eileen both have birthdays on the same day. Julie-Ann lived in Kalgoorlie but she was determined to be in Perth for her grandmother's 70th birthday.

Julie-Ann's parents insisted they take us to a Chinese Restaurant for a meal and, when Eileen entered, 43 guests stood and sang "Happy Birthday". Such moments are to be treasured. So many friends and relatives present and, alas, so many absent who have passed away over the years.

We arrived home around 10:30pm just as the phone commenced ringing. Marjorie was phoning from England to wish her sister "Happy Day".

It was truly a heart-warming night.

Pat, Maggie and I sent in our entry forms for the Avon Descent. This meant we now had to assemble a support crew. This wasn't too difficult as we were surrounded by friends and relatives whose doubts had changed to enthusiasm over the past few months.

Pat had contacted a caravan park at Toodyay and arranged to have use of a shed for her crew. My crew consisted of my two grandsons, Darin and Marc with Kylie and Vickie plus a crowd from The Bibbulmun Walkers who always support any outdoor activity in which members of the group are engaged. Involving my grandsons was a good move because Darin is a chef and good, sustaining food is essential.

The organisation was looking good. Our entry had been accepted and the compulsory scrutinising of kayaks and equipment, for all entrants, was due in a fortnight's time. Maggie had shot through on another safari 'up north' somewhere but Pat and I wanted to go to Northam and follow the river down as far as possible in order to determine points to meet our crew during the event and we also planned to do some more white-water work as the recent rain had raised the river considerably.

Then the phone rang!

It was Bob Bowring phoning from The Bronzewing Gold Mine out in the never-never beyond Leonora.

Hey! You doing anything at present?"

"Oh no!" I thought. "Not now!"

I decided to be firm. "I have to be in Perth on the 5th and 6th of August."

"O.K. I'll phone you back."

He phoned next day to announce, "I've booked you on Tuesday's flight. My offsider will show you what to do. You can live in my quarters and be back in Perth on the 26th July."

"You won't be there?"

"No."

"Where will you be?"

"Chris, Natalie, Michael and me are going to Bali for 10 days but you will be back in Perth in plenty of time."

"Gee, thanks! Will I see you at all?"

"Yeah. I step off the plane that you are leaving on. We can shake hands at the airstrip."

Bloody hell! But there is good money in these jobs and this one will cover my kayaking expenses.

More organising. I had to phone Darin and Marc and get them to take my kayak to the compulsory scrutinising as well as phone around all the support crew and arrange a meeting at Pat's house to discuss the planning of the event.

One of the peculiar aspects of worry is that once you have loaded it on to someone else you always feel more relaxed.

There was an additional 'spin-off'. A compulsory swim of 100 metres, complete with gear, was conducted on the same day as the scrutineering and it was done in the adjacent icy-cold river. Upon returning to Perth I did my swim in the heated public baths over at Rivervale. Tough, eh?

There was an additional worry. The Publicity Officer had arranged for me to be interviewed live by Michael Schultz on The ABC at 6:30 am. I don't know who listens to the radio at 6:30 in the morning but I had agreed to 'be in it' and I was now hundreds of miles away. I told The Plant Superintendent, during breakfast, of my dilemma.

"No problems," says he. "I'll pick you up at 6am and drive you over to the mine. You can use the phone in my office."

Michael Schultz battled with that interview. This was a new experience to me. I was dead scared of saying something stupid and I'm afraid some of my best answers were a bit that way.

'"Why do you want to do the Avon Descent?"

Prolonged pause. "Because it is there and I want to have a crack at it before I get too old." (Brilliant.)

"How do you plan to cope with rapids?"

I couldn't very well say, "I'm damned if I know! I haven't done nearly enough white water paddling!"

So I made some reply about 'dealing with whatever situation I'm in at the time as best I can."

Another brilliant reply because this is undoubtedly what I shall be doing.

The mine management had decided to modify the camp's reticulation. The current system, consisting of low-pressure sprinklers on 4mm diameter stems, had proved unsatisfactory. The new plan was to dispense with these and have a drip outlet on every plant, bush or tree. It sounds simple but 'the garden' is spread all the through the village and the village is spread over several hectares!

I 'tee-d' into numerous water outlets, laid out 200 metres of 4mm x 1.5mm reticulation tubing, and placed drip outlets to 800 plants!

The outlets are at ground level so I am bent over all day in a freezing cold wind and it takes a solid hour's workout in the gymnasium to get rid of all my aches and pains.

The gymnasium is splendidly equipped and the workouts keep me in good trim. I follow them with a hot shower and a good meal. Things seem to be under control.

I phoned Darin and Marc. My kayak and Pat's had passed the scrutineering. Rain had been falling heavily during the past fortnight and more was on the way according to those who know. The river is flowing boisterously and The Avon Descent should be quite an experience. I'll be out of here 10 days before the event and I certainly need some more white-water paddling.

But, Gee! A man's lucky to have grandsons like Darin and Marc. They make me feel good inside.

I ran out of reticulation material and spent the final two days changing hundreds of tap washers.

I was having a hurried meal around 5:30pm when Bob appeared. The plane had had a strong tail wind and arrived half an hour ahead of schedule. We had a bit of a yarn about the job, as well as his family trip to Bali, but I had to be on the plane at 6pm so there wasn't much time. Bob did manage to say, "Make out an invoice for $150 for Avon Descent Sponsorship and give it to Chris when you get to Perth."

He also implied I was a silly old bastard but, for $150 sponsorship, I readily accept such terms of endearment.

The Bibbulmun Walkers, after my return to Perth, gathered for their usual Saturday morning walk and, over the breakfast table, we made final arrangements.

I hired a caravan and towed it to the caravan park near Toodyay. I pulled on the caravan's hand brake and unhooked it from the car. The caravan slowly rolled down the slight gradient, hit a gravel bank, slewed around and wiped out a fence post. I attached the caravan to the car again, placed it back where I wanted it, jammed a couple of rocks against the wheels and reported the flattened fence post to the manager.

"Oh, that sort of thing often happens with hired caravans," he laughed. "You never know what's wrong with them. That's why we leave a few rocks laying around the place."

I took my kayak across to Northam where it was registered, placed on the crest of the river-bank and impounded under guard for the night.

Pat and Maggie took their craft direct to Northam before coming to the caravan park. The rest of the gang arrived by sundown.

We dined well, went to bed early and arose at sunrise next morning to drive across to Northam.

Over six hundred canoes lined the riverbank; each canoe had one or two paddlers and as well as a support crew and the event had thousands of spectators.

A joyous, colourful scene! Multi-coloured kayaks, garments of many hues, the water glistening in the early morning sunlight of a perfect day, the P.A. system counting down as power boats leapt away and the crowd swarming overall like bees at a honey spill. And among the bees were several members of The Veteran Athletes Association who wished me "Good Luck".

Pat, Maggie and I launched our kayaks and paddled out to the start line of The 1995 Avon Descent.

Our grid number was counted down: "5, 4, 3, 2, 1, GO!

We were on our way!

The first hazard, The Northam Weir, is only 500 metres from the start. Very little water was flowing at this point so the drill was to carry, or drag, the kayak along an unmade, slippery, muddy track around the weir; pushing and shoving through spectators standing on the track was no mean feat. They are amazing people – spectators!

I barged through to launch my kayak beside Pat and we paddled downstream into the unknown distance.

The first 15kms was mainly a matter of paddling as the river presented no threatening hazards; just an occasional small rapid or a bunch of ti-trees to test my untried skills.

Katrina Bridge presented no real problems even though the cement pylons are set at an angle to the river's flow. The water level allowed plenty of clearance; a few hefty strokes and I was through as our support crew yelled encouragement.

I didn't know if either Maggie or Pat were in my vicinity. I had lost sight of them in a wall of ti-trees some distance back and I didn't know if they were ahead or behind. So we were now travelling independent of each other and that was the situation for the remainder of The Descent as conditions up ahead made it impossible to maintain contact.

The Glen Avon Rapid made me sit up and take notice but I bounced through O.K. and paddled another 10kms to Extract Weir which I had been told was dangerous and competitors were advised to get out and drag their kayaks past this point.

But I had forgotten this along with hundreds of other pieces of information that had been poured over me during the past few weeks.

The weir, as I approached, appeared as a straight line across my vision. I moved over to the left bank where a spectator told me some kayaks were riding the spillway at the far end. Two canoes were preparing to go so I paddled over there to take a look. All I could see was the top of the spillway then nothing until the river reappeared about 200 metres downstream.

The first kayak took off and disappeared over the weir's lip.

"He's gone!" I thought, but he bobbed up in the waves further down the rapids.

The next chap disappeared to bob up again further down in the liquid turmoil.

"Well," I thought, "I need some white-water practice so here goes!"

I paddled forward and went over the rim.

Oh, My God!

The water was a maelstrom of white, roaring turbulence pouring down a 45 degree slope for 30 metres and, at the bottom, a 2 metre high wave was bouncing and shaking its crest in a most belligerent manner.

I careered down this slope at an amazing rate; just missing a big, black rock on the way.

"I'm gone! I'm gone!" I told myself, "But keep calm! You're going to need a level head here. Just keep the kayak straight and hope for the best!"

Fair dinkum. I told myself all this in about the space of two seconds as I hurtled towards this standing wave. I hit it fair in the middle and my kayak disappeared leaving only my waist, shoulders and head above the water. The kayak burst through to the other side, half its length in the air. The force of the water carried through the next wave and into a stretch of turbulence that gradually decreased as I progressed down the rapids.

I had made it! And above the roar of the water I could hear spectators cheering and car horns sounding! I felt terrific!

I learned a lot in that few minutes. The trick seemed to be to pick your line ahead, keep the kayak straight, allow the current to carry you and only use the paddle to guide you through.

Theoretically, if you don't hit an underwater rock, and stay upright, you should manage to come out at the other end – but things could pan out differently.

I applied this principle to several more minor rapids as I progressed downstream but, alas, ti-trees grew thickly across the river for the next 10 to 14 kilometres.

Ti-trees are a problem. The river dries up in summer and ti-trees grow thick and solid along its bed. Approaching them in a kayak on a flowing river is similar to charging a stockade on a bolting horse over which you have very little control. You have to thread your way through this woodland in a kayak that is riding on an unrelenting, forceful flow of water and if the craft gets up against a tree, and side on to the current, the force of the water pushes the craft up the tree and over you go; and there is always the danger of being trapped underwater amidst ti-trees.

Combating the current, towing a kayak and hanging on to a paddle as you fight your way through ti-trees, in icy-cold water, towards a muddy riverbank which you can't climb because the kayak is full of water is not recommended as being the way to spend a pleasant Saturday morning.

The water, rushing through the timber, creates froth and bubbles which seem to flow along the main stream so the lurk is to look ahead for froth trails and follow them. There isn't time for a quick change of direction. The line of travel has to be promptly decided and carried out; any hesitation allows the current to take control.

I had a couple of capsizes and went through the miserable procedure of getting the kayak to the bank to empty it. This requires considerable exertion and, in cold water, can result in dehydration and hypothermia.

I battled through to eventually go bouncing down Leatherhead Rapids near Western Quarries campsite, and completed Day One.

It had been a tough day! 57kms of rapids and ti-trees on a flowing river is not a bad day's work.

I felt terrific!

Pat and Maggie arrived soon afterwards and our wonderful companions took over. They gave us hot drinks and towels; placed our kayaks in the safety arena and generally further lifted our already high-flying morale.

The newspaper reporters and photographers were there, too. They asked me dozens of questions which I can't remember answering and took photos of the three of us in various poses.

Press photographers are a funny mob.

"Can you sit on your kayak for us?"

"Sure. Like this?"

"That's good. Can you lift one leg up and place it on the kayak?"

"Sure. How's this?"

"Good! But can you lift the other foot up as well?"

"No."

"Why not?"

"Because I'll fall off the bloody boat, that's why!"

I must have looked a sight with mud all over my canoe and clothing. I had, in addition, received a few cuts and bruises in my battle with the ti-trees. Some cuts were on my arms and a small one on the bridge of my nose proved most impressive as my face was wet and blood from this minute cut had spread all over my face.

A nice article, complete with photos, appeared in 'The Sunday Times' next day.

Our caravan was only 20 minutes away and, after a hot shower and a good feed, I slept well until 5:30am next morning when Maggie decided to withdraw from the event.

We had an early breakfast and drove back to the start line where the colourful scene was all hustle and bustle – the crowd moving to and fro like seaweed in a current, the early morning sunlight slanting down through the trees to alight on the green grass, the muddy banks, the multi-coloured kayaks laying along the bank or floating on the glistening water.

Pat and I launched our craft and paddled out on to the river to await the call for our grid number. Pat was in the grid ahead of me and left 30 seconds earlier.

A kilometre downstream and we were amongst the biggest and thickest stretch of ti-trees we had so far encountered. I had a few swims in the freezing water and went through the morale-destroying routine of emptying my kayak again.

The next few hours were packed with apprehension, tension, and excitement. I smashed, bashed or drifted my way through kilometres of ti-trees. Other times, when in the clear, I could hear rapids in the distance ahead and knew they would be draped with spectators on the banks or hanging on to adjacent rocks.

I had no idea of the names or the severity of any of the rapids. I simply yelled "Go for it" – and went!

'Super Chute' was a buzz! It is on a bend that I didn't see until I was on it. The banks were lined with spectators. My support crew and grandchildren were prominent on a rock close to the water.

"Down the centre, Pop!" they yelled. "Down the centre, Pop!"

The crowd took up the chant: "Down the centre, Pop! Down the centre, Pop!"

Pop swept around the bend, lined up the centre and rode into the turmoil. It was boisterous but I made it with the roar of the water and the chant of the crowd spurring me on.

Emu Falls Rapids are on a twisting down-gradient and, as I swept around the bend I was looking into a 2 metre deep whirlpool! Oh boy! I was glad to get past that one!

I was doing well. I had been pushing through ti-trees around the 24km mark when I came out of the clump and saw I was heading straight for a chap who was jammed right across my path. I back paddled as hard as I could and, in doing so, was forced up against a tree and emptied out into deep water at the head of some rapids.

I surfaced to see my kayak entering the rapids and I was close behind it. I was rolled, bowled, thumped and bumped until I didn't know which was up and which was down until I was whirled into a quieter pool where I hung on to a tree trunk to get my breath back. I swam to the bank and clambered ashore.

I didn't know where my kayak had gone and, at this stage, I didn't care if I never saw it again.

I had been in the cold water too long and become badly stricken with hypothermia.

I was chilled and shivering uncontrollably; I couldn't stand or walk; my vision was blurred and my co-ordination was gone. I felt physically exhausted and had no strength in my limbs.

I sat on a rock in the sunshine to try and steady down. Gradually my mind cleared and I began to think in a logical manner.

"Now, Arthur Old Chap," I thought, "if you were sitting over there, and looking at a chap who is in the mess you are in, you would say "You've had it, mate."

I decided, right then and there, to withdraw from The 1995 Avon Descent.

Besides, I didn't know where my bloody kayak was!

I commenced walking downstream along the river's edge. About 500 metres down I met a charming young lady who had found my kayak in a still pool and pushed it to the bank. We pulled it out and emptied it. I had hung on to my paddle and stood looking at the kayak and mentally debating.

"Don't think about it," smiled the lady, "you need medical attention."

"What makes you think that?"

"I'm a nurse. Just don't think about it."

"Are you going on?"

"No, I've had enough. I'm pulling out, too."

We walked for about a kilometre in the sunshine until an official in a four-wheel drive came along and asked how we were going.

"No good," I said through chattering teeth, "I'll have to pull out."

"O. K." he said. "Hop in and I'll take you to a check point."

"How about you?" he asked my companion, "You pulling out, too?"

"No," she replied, "I'm feeling much better now. I'll go back to my kayak and get going again."

She turned around and walked off to disappear around a bend in the road. I don't know who she was, and I have never seen her since, but I shall always remember her with gratitude. It is obvious, with hindsight, she had been willing to withdraw from The Descent because she had found an old bloke, sitting alone on the bank, suffering from hypothermia.

Unusual people – nurses.

The driver took me to a check point where, to my surprise, there was an ambulance manned by two enthusiastic female volunteers and if there is one thing enthusiastic female volunteers like it is a patient! In next to no time they had me stripped down to my underpants, wrapped in a blanket, and laying on a bed in the ambulance.

They gave me hot coffee, sat in the ambulance beside me, periodically took my pulse and occasionally slid their hands down my bare chest under the blanket and asked me if I was feeling warmer.

"Next year," I thought, "I'm going to bypass the kayaking bit and come direct to the ambulance!"

I was concerned about my kayak but a rescue crew had picked it up and brought it to the ambulance.

The section was closing down and the last vehicle through was The Race Director. He pulled up, got out of his vehicle and took a casual look in the ambulance.

"You!' he exclaimed, pulling his video camera out of its case, "I've just got to get this for T.V!"

And so, after all the newspaper articles and radio interviews, that was how I appeared on television that night – laying in an ambulance with a nurse holding my hand!

I stayed in the ambulance for over an hour until my clothes dried out and I was more or less back to normal. I dressed, thanked the ambulance crew for their assistance, climbed into another four-wheel drive and, in due course, the kayak and I were deposited at a centre point where wrecks, both plastic and human, were deposited.

Marc and Kylie found us there and took us to the finish at Bayswater where we milled around with the throng.

The Avon Descent finishes at 5pm and kayaks coming in after that time do not have a place recorded. So kayaks strung out for kilometres along the river are informed if they will not cover the remaining distance within the time allowed. The P.A. system announced that Pat had arrived at the Upper Swan Check Point but had run out of time. She could paddle for another hour and a half to finish if she wished but her effort would not be recognised, so she withdrew.

But what a magnificent effort!

Eight months ago this 63 year old woman couldn't paddle a kayak 100 metres in a straight line but she had hung in there and nearly conquered the longest and toughest white-water course in the world!

My support crew and the gang from The Bibbulmun Walkers came back to my place and filled it with noise.

My grandchildren presented me with a special trophy engraved: To Our Pop. To Us You Are Always A Winner. Love From The Grandkids.

A man can't ask for a better trophy than that!

The T.V. News that night showed a paddler separated from his kayak with a roaring torrent in between them. A helicopter picked him up and lifted him across the river to his craft. The news also showed me in the ambulance.

The T.V. News over in the eastern states showed 'the oldest competitor in the event being lifted out to an ambulance.'

The phone rang. It was Garry.

"Hey! Have we still got an Uncle Arthur?" Thus ended the challenge of The Avon Descent.

I didn't win but I doubt if I truly lost.

It has always been part of my philosophy in Life to reach out for goals but this one was obviously beyond my reach.

Marc had taken some scenes with his video camera and in them I see an old man moving around amongst the kayaks.

The old man is me yet it is not me.

I am the spirit encased in that human body but, no matter how fervently the spirit may wish to fly, the body is growing old and the spirit has to accept this circumstance.

I don't know what the next challenge may be but, instead of beating my chest and shouting "Go For It!" I shall be advised to first ask, "Can I Do It?"

It's a lousy situation and acceptance is not easy. But, by crikey, it had been a beaut weekend.

Chapter Thirty-Two

The Passage of Time is a relentless, inexorable process. It has allowed nations to flourish before fading into history; it has allowed the minds of men to develop to where they now have the means and the ability to destroy all the human life crawling around on the earth's surface; also, in the past, it plodded on to the point where I met Eileen and enticed her into marriage with a life in a new country, there to produce and raise a family.

And Time, on the 8th September, 1998, put its hand on my shoulder and said, "Today you are 80 years of age!"

This was a bit of a shock to me because I had come to regard birthdays as merely a little bit of fertiliser sprinkled on The Garden of Life to help it blossom more luxuriously.

The advent of this birthday was obviously due to circumstances beyond my control so, in modern terminology, I decided to 'go with the flow', a fortunate decision because the celebrations bounced along for a whole week!

Eileen had gone to bowls and, despite the hour of the morning, I was in the process of pulling the cork out of a bottle of port when the doorbell rang.

A hurried glance through the 'spy' window showed a massive 4-wheel-drive in the driveway. I opened the door to admit Brian and Sally accompanied by 80 inflated balloons which were gaily tossed all over the lounge room.

I surreptitiously slid the bottle of port out of sight and put the kettle on.

They left about an hour later because the phone kept ringing and conversation became rather disjointed and one-sided. I stayed home answering the phone and sipping port in between calls that became more vocal and boisterous as the day progressed.

Eileen came home in the early afternoon and was surprised to learn I had not been out, nor had I eaten any lunch.

I hadn't noticed lunch hour passing and, by mid-afternoon, I had no desire to venture forth into the great wide world beyond the confines of the balloon-filled lounge room.

Susan had arranged to take Eileen and I to see "The Phantom of The Opera" at The Entertainment Centre and, by sheer co-incidence, eight members of The Intrepid Walkers had arranged to see the show on the same night.

We assembled for a joyful, noisy, pre-show dinner at a nearby restaurant.

Friendship is a mysterious and wondrous emotion. You can't buy it. You have to wait until it is offered and, once it is offered, you have to prove yourself worthy of it; otherwise it is withdrawn and you have lost one of Life's most precious gifts.

I was thinking along these lines as I looked at my friends seated around the table when a woman nudged into the vacant chair beside me, gave me a dig in the ribs, and said, "How you going, Old Timer?"

Dee! Dee Chisholm! All the way from Batchelor in The Northern Territory! Over 2,000 miles away! Right here just for my birthday! Dee; the three-year-old niece who used to run down the footpath shouting "Arwee! Arwee!" when I came home from work away back in 1946!

Sometimes people do things that lift me up inside and I rejoice in the magic of the moment.

The gang wandered off to The Entertainment Centre after the meal and we all enjoyed a spectacular performance of "The Phantom Of The Opera".

The Veteran Athletes Association put on a 'special occasion' the following Sunday morning. I have been a member of the association for over 25 years and many members have had birthdays during that time but I had never seen a gathering like this before.

It was beautiful morning. The sun was shining and glistening amidst the black swans swimming sedately on the river, corellas argued overhead in the gum trees, and runners sat around in a big circle creating a colourful scene in their brightly-hued clothing.

Roma and Jacqueline produced a massive birthday cake featuring a wheelchair and the greeting, "Happy Birthday, Arthur." I cut the cake amidst applause from my running mates.

Roma announced the cake was in appreciation of the foot massaging I do for the ladies each year on the eve of The Bunbury Marathon; which just goes to show you never know what may eventuate when you massage feminine feet.

The 'official' birthday party began at twelve noon on the same day. Eileen had hired The North Perth Bowling Club Hall for the afternoon and that explains why my grand-daughter Julie-Ann, and her friend Janine, had been cooking for a week to produce a delightful meal for the guests.

Guests!

There were over eighty people there and they ranged from friends whom I had valued for over sixty years right through to my latest great-grandchild.

My eighty-five year old cousin with his son who had been a Boy Scout in my Scout Troop; the 'golden oldies' with whom Eileen and I had danced on Saturday nights during the early 60s: the retired C.E.O. of Hinco Engineering as well as several former workmates; members of my writing group; it goes on and on!

The bar was open and the afternoon slipped away.

My grandson, Marc, acted as Toastmaster and, during his official speech, stated my grandchildren had come to the conclusion that I had done enough running and it was time I gave it away so, to assist me with any 'withdrawal symptoms', they would like me to accept this little gift – and they wheeled out a mountain bike!

Not a bad sort of a present for an eighty-year-old bloke, I suppose.

All this was years ago but, inside me, I feel it is not a bad spot to sit down, take a bit of a breather, and say "Cheerio for now".

I don't regard this point as the end of Life's Story but this tale seems to have developed into a fairly lengthy sort of a yarn – probably because I didn't expect to live this long – and I don't know how much more Time I have left up my sleeve but, when it does run out:-

Don't Cry For Me.

Photo by courtesy of Vic Beaumont,
member of Master Athletics WA

About the Author

Arthur Leggett, at 87 years, is a member of the cycling club as well as a kayaking club, and still enjoys camping. He is a published poet and a member of the Western Australian Bush Poets and Yarns Spinners Association, and regularly attends Morley Senior High School, where he acts as a mentor to students.

In the year 2000, he received a "Senior Australian Achievers Award".

Arthur, who is the President of the Western Australian Ex-Prisoner of War Association, has been a Freemason for over 50 years and holds the rank of Past Grand Director of Ceremonies.

He was awarded the Order of Australia in 2004 for "Service to veterans and their families, through the Ex-Prisoners of War Association, Western Australia, and to the community".

Arthur and Eileen live in suburban Perth, Western Australia, where their house is regularly swamped by that horde of descendants, and they wouldn't have it otherwise because:–"Life is an ongoing event and there are no instant replays."

www.ingramcontent.com/pod-product-compliance
Lightning Source LLC
Chambersburg PA
CBHW071328080526
44587CB00017B/2763